Heinrich von Kleist, 1777–1811

Five Plays
Heinrich von Kleist

Also by Martin Greenberg

The Hamlet Vocation of Coleridge and Wordsworth
Kafka: The Terror of Art
Heinrich von Kleist, *The Marquise of O——— and Other Stories* (transl.)
Frank Kafka, *Diaries, 1914–23* (transl.)

Heinrich von Kleist
Five Plays

Translated from the German,
with an introduction,
by Martin Greenberg

Yale University Press
New Haven & London

Designed by Nancy Ovedovitz and set in Fournier type by Brevis Press. Printed in the United States of America by Vail-Ballou Press, Binghamton, N.Y.

Library of Congress Cataloging-in-Publication Data

Kleist, Heinrich von, 1777–1811.
[Plays. English Selections]
Five plays / Heinrich von Kleist ; translated from the German, with an introduction, by Martin Greenburg.
p. cm.
Contents: Amphitryon—The broken jug—Penthesilea—Prince Frederick of Homburg—The tragedy of Robert Guiscard, Duke of the Normans.
ISBN 0-300-04238-8
1. Kleist, Heinrich von, 1777–1811—Translations, English.
I. Greenberg, Martin, 1918 Feb. 3- II. Title.
PT2378.A2E5 1988
832'.6—dc19   88–63
                                              CIP

The paper in this book meets the guidelines for permanence and durability of the Committee on Production Guidelines for Book Longevity of the Council on Library Resources.

10   9   8   7   6   5   4   3   2   1

For David, Adam, and Gabriel
and to the memory of Sol Greenberg

Contents

Introduction

> *It is simply beyond one what it means for there to have been such a fellow*
> *at the turn of the 19th century.*
> —Rilke

There has never been anyone like Kleist, before or since. Kafka, who loved him dearly, is a little like him (in his understanding of things a *lot* like him)—but there has never been anyone like Kafka either. To read Kleist is to be constantly surprised, constantly taken aback. Sometimes the surprise has a questionable source; but it is always interesting. Kleist is interesting! Of course, all great art surprises, by its excellence; virtue in art as in life is always a surprise, no matter how familiar it may be. But Kleist is like somebody who jumps up behind you when you are looking ahead, ahead of you when you look behind. This is alarming, but also something of a joke. One doesn't get used to him, I find.

Here is a highly concentrated little piece of his in which the Kleistian surprise explodes like a bomb, one of the many "anecdotes" that he scribbled for the short-lived newspaper (*Berliner Abendblätter*) he edited in the calamitous last year of his life:

A Capuchin was accompanying a Swabian to the gallows on a day of pouring rain. The condemned man kept lamenting to God as they went along that he had to go so hard a way in such bad and disagreeable weather. The Capuchin, thinking to offer him some Christian consolation, said: Good-for-nothing, why do you complain so, all you have to do is go there, but I, I have to come back, in this awful weather, the same way again.—Whoever has felt, even on the best of days, how desolate the way back from the place of execution is, won't find the Capuchin's words so stupid.

The best consolation the monk can give the condemned man is no more than a coarse joke. But Kleist, entering the ancedote in the last sentence as commentator, tops the monk's joke with a joke of his own. But what a joke! A joke to end all jokes, an ultimate (and literal) gallows humor that drops the trap beneath our unsuspecting feet and leaves us swinging in the emptiness.

The wit here is strange, wit that is and isn't wit. Kleist's comment has the *form* of wit. By saying that the way back from the place of execution is desolate even on the best of days, that execution spares one not only the misery of coming back in the rain, but the misery of coming back at all, the misery of having to live, he brings about that lightning shift of understanding, that sudden expansion of meaning which is a characteristic movement of wit. And yet Kleist's sentence doesn't seem to have the intention of wit; it rings like wit because of its form, but it doesn't *feel* like wit. What we feel in it is his suffering and weariness with life, so nakedly expressed. If Kleist's comment had even a trace of sardonicism, the anecdote would be a straight witticism. But sardonicism defends one; his sentence is utterly defenseless. Nevertheless the anecdote is also a joke, a tragic joke. A peculiar humor, tending toward the grotesque, often haunts his most serious efforts. *Penthesilea,* so strange, so full of violence, so tending toward the grotesque in other respects as well, has it; but so does the perfectly controlled *Prince of Homburg.*

Is it morbid, his bitter repudiation of life in the anecdote? Kleist was famous for his suicide before he was famous for his literary works. All his life he startled one friend after another by proposing that they should kill themselves together; at last in 1811, at the age of thirty-four, such a companion turned up for him. Goethe thought him gifted but repellent, an example of modern confusion, feverishness, pathology. But I don't think the anecdote is an expression of his morbidity. The life that he repudiates is life in what he called the "infirm" (*gebrechlich*) world, an unsolid, flimsy, jerry-built world that rests on no foundation of unshakable truth. You find the phrase "the infirm world" being used in the story *The Marquise of O——,* a comedy (if that is the right word for it), and in the play *Penthesilea,* a tragedy (if that is the right word for *it*). In his own infirmity, as a soul-sick man, Kleist felt the need of a firmly based world more painfully, more urgently than happier constituted men. But in having the courage to feel it as he did, with the full force of his intellect and imagination, he exercised a poet's strength.

Behind all his works, Rilke said about him in a letter—what distress, what despair, what sacrifice. *Behind* all his works, Rilke said; because more than a few of these works, themselves, sparkle with gaiety, are marvelously light in their deep seriousness. Is there another play in the world like *Amphitryon* in its enchanting mixture of tenderness, confusion, and pain? I ask this about a work that is an *adaptation* of Molière's comedy, a work that takes for its story one which has been dramatized so often that Giraudoux called his own version of it *Amphitryon 38*. And *The Prince of Homburg*—how gay spirited it is, though its subject is the antique-Roman one of a soldier condemned to death for disobedience. And *The Marquise of O*——! And the essay *On the Puppet Theater!* Although he wrote his *Anecdotes*[1] in the shadow of his suicide, most of them sound a lively note. They breathe a born storyteller's pleasure in the stuff of life, in remarkable happenings and inexplicable occurrences, and in incidents that display the natural vigor of human beings acting with spontaneous élan. One, the "Anecdote of the Late Prussian War," a small masterpiece about a Prussian cavalryman, itself races along at a gallop to its exuberant conclusion. (I quote and paraphrase.)

> In a village near Jena [where Napoleon beat the Prussians in 1806], on my way to Frankfort, the innkeeper told me how a few hours after the battle, when the place had already been abandoned by the Prince von Hohenlohe's army and was being encircled by the French, who thought it still defended, a solitary Prussian cavalryman appeared on the scene; and if all the soldiers who fought that day, he assured me, had been as brave as that one, the French would have been beaten even if they had been three times the number that they were.

The sweating trooper pulls up in front of the inn door, covered with dust and bawling for a glass of brandy, he is dying of thirst. The French are very near, the innkeeper says excitedly, you must get away while you can, at once! "Is that so?" he says, sticking his sword in his scabbard and dropping the reins; "but I haven't had a thing to drink all day." The innkeeper is sure the devil's made off with his wits, but he calls Lizzie out with a bottle of Danziger, which he presses into his hands, hoping that will speed him on his way. The trooper pushes the bottle back. "What am I supposed to do with all this stuff—pour a glassful out for me, I'm pressed for time!" For sure he is a dead man, the innkeeper says, and pours him out a drink. Down it now, good health to you, and for God's sake, soldier, leave! "Another!" says the fellow, wiping his beard and leaning out of his saddle to blow his nose, even as musket fire starts to rattle down into the village, "and fill it to the top. I've got

---

1. See the valuable selection *An Abyss Deep Enough: Letters, Essays and Anecdotes of Heinrich von Kleist*, ed. Philip B. Miller (1982), for many of these anecdotes.

the cash right here!" So the innkeeper pours him a second, then a third. Is that enough for him? "That's real good schnapps!" he says. "And now what do I owe you?" Nothing, nothing, says the innkeeper, again imploring him to leave. The trooper says he hopes God will repay him, fetches a stub pipe out of his boot, and calls for a match. A match, a match, the innkeeper cries to heaven, now the fellow wants a match! While whole squadrons of the French—! "Yes, a match, so I can have a pipeful." And Lizzie having brought him a match—"Now let the Frenchmen have themselves the fits!" And he yanks his cap down, lifts the reins, wheels his horse and draws his sword. The innkeeper shrieks gallowsbird at him, vagabond whose end is near, won't he clear out, go off to where he belongs? Doesn't he see the three chasseurs already at the village gate?

> "Oh them," he says, and spits, taking the three in with a lightning look. "Ten of them don't scare me." And just then the three Frenchmen trot into the village. "Bassa Menelka!" he roars, spurs his horse and charges, charges right at them, so help me God, attacking just as if he had the entire Hohenlohe Corps at his back; with the result that the chasseurs, uncertain if there might not be more Germans in the village, hesitated for a moment, which is not a thing they often do, and he, upon my soul, like a flash cuts all three down from their saddles, catches up their horses careering around the square and as he gallops past me yells: "Bassa Teremtetem!"[2] and "How did you like that, Mr. Innkeeper?" and "Ta-ta!" and "So long!" and "Ha, ha ha!"—A fellow like that, said the innkeeper, I never saw the like of in all my born days.

What the anecdote celebrates is *nature,* an undivided nature in which the reflective mind does not intervene to cripple action. Notice that the chausseurs hesitate, think (which as hard-riding cavalrymen is "not a thing they often do")—that is what gives the unhesitating Prussian trooper his advantage. Kleist published essays, observations, and reflections as well as anecdotes in the *Berliner Abendblätter,* and one of these is a reflection on reflection, in which he writes: "The right time for reflection, beyond question, is *after* not *before* an action. If it comes into play before, or even in, the moment of decision, it only seems to confuse, obstruct and extinguish the power to act, whose glorious wellspring lies in feeling." One mustn't think he is an irrationalist or sentimentalist who is proclaiming that mind doesn't matter. Mind matters. But the right time

---

2. *Bassa Menelka! Bassa Teremtetem!* Cavalrymen's oaths of Hungarian (Hussar) origin.

for reflection is not in the midst of action; mind's purpose "is to make us conscious of what was faulty and infirm in our proceeding so that we may better regulate our feeling in future cases." The glorious well-spring of action is feeling; of right action, feeling *regulated* by the mind. Kleist writes *feeling (Gefühl)*, which is another word he uses over and over, not *feelings*; he means something which is psychological to be sure, but more than psychological: that harmony of the soul, or unity of being, in which our active side and our reflective side, our vitality and our spirituality move as one together. The trooper isn't a gross unthinking brute but a brave soldier in whom the naive inner unity of an earlier, unself-conscious time still vigorously lives.

A century and more after Kleist we find another great poet who suffered the pain of the disunited modern soul (one among many!) treating the same theme. Yeats wrestles with this theme in any number of poems, but the one I have in mind is "The Road at My Door," one of the *Meditations in Time of Civil War*:

An affable Irregular,
A heavily-built Falstaffian man,
Comes cracking jokes of civil war
As though to die by gunshot were
The finest play under the sun.

A brown Lieutenant and his men,
Half dressed in national uniform,
Stand at my door, and I complain
Of the foul weather, hail and rain,
A pear-tree broken by the storm.

I count these feathered balls of soot
The moor-hen guides upon the stream,
To silence the envy in my thought;
And turn towards my chamber, caught
In the cold snows of a dream.

Kleist's narrative is a burst of action, Yeats's poem a pang of self-disliking, yet the Prussian trooper and the affable Irregular are brothers: beings with the self-assured vitality of nature, of natures still not racked by Hamlet hesitations, cheerful fellows ready to kill or be killed on the spot. Kleist and Yeats are both modern poets seeking nature.[3] But when they find it, the German is able, as the narrator, to plunge enthusiastically

---

3. As Schiller says in his essay *On Naive and Sentimental Poetry*: the ancient poets *are* nature; the modern poets must seek it (though that is not the whole story).

into the experience of naive human force and courage and disappear from sight in it; the Irishman, separated from such experience by another century, looks at the joke-cracking soldier at his door and beats a dispirited retreat: back to the drab Lieutenant and to himself as householder whining about the weather, in the second stanza; to the envious poet returning to his cold and solitary tower of dreams in the last stanza. It is a wonderful poem and shows what a modern poet's courage consists in: not standing up to shot and shell but to the truth of his own feelings.

Kleist disappears into his experience of the unity of nature, but only for the moment of the anecdote. No more than to Yeats was the way back to such unity open to him. These moments of nature are only moments. Both poets know this very well. Yeats says that when

> ... a man is fighting mad,
> Something drops from eyes long blind,
> He completes his partial mind,
> For an instant stands at ease.   [*Under Ben Bulben*]

And Kleist writes a whole essay, *On the Puppet Theater*, to tell us that the way back to the paradise of an un-mindridden nature is barred shut and the Archangel behind us forever, since we ate of the Tree of Knowledge. What to do, then? We must "go a journey all around the world," through infinity, "to see if there is perhaps a way in for us again at the back." We must go *all* the way with mind, cram ourselves with the fruit of the Tree of Knowledge though we get the bellyache, till there is a second fall back into innocence again—but "that is the last chapter of the history of the world." History's last chapter ushers us into a knowing innocence[4] in which being-human is fully realized at last. This same philosophical imagination directly engaging modern existence is what moves the action in his poetic dramas.

Kleist was born in Frankfort on the Oder in 1777, into the great age of German literature that bridges the last quarter of the eighteenth century and the first quarter of the nineteenth. He is one of the great figures of that age, but a late accepted one whose work is nervous with modern feeling. Like Stendhal, Dostoyevsky, Melville, others, he speaks more strongly to succeeding times than he did to his own. His father, Captain (later Major) Friedrich von Kleist, belonged to an old noble family (orig-

---

4. About the same time Kleist wrote this, Blake was saying in England: "The Fool shall not enter into Heaven let him be ever so Holy" (*A Vision of the Last Judgment*).

inally Slavic, like so many) of Brandenburg-Prussia that was bred in the traditions of the Hohenzollern Fredericks to furnish officers to the Prussian army or officials to the state. In biographical accounts of their most famous son, one often reads that by the time the poet was born they had already produced eighteen (or twenty) generals and marshals. This is as much as to say: A Prussian and a poet! Major von Kleist died when his son was eleven, whereupon Heinrich was immediately parted from his mother, too, and sent to study with a pastor in Berlin. Many years after Kleist's death an anonymous woman friend testified that his early years, about which little is known, had been embittered by teachers who punished him for faults mostly provoked by their own unwillingness to try to understand the kind of child he was; with the result that he became timid and withdrawn on the one hand, and wildly defiant on the other. But it is likely such a disposition had already begun to form in him in what one surmises was a rigid parental milieu.

Following family tradition, he was enrolled in the King's Foot Guards at Potsdam as a cadet in 1792, at the age of fourteen, and the next year saw action at the Rhine against revolutionary France. He was a soldier seven years, during which time he read philosophy and mathematics on his own but showed no special literary interests. The wish to know something was unusual among young Prussian officers; hustled into the army as boys, they were insolent ignoramuses. In 1799, to his family's dismay, Kleist took the momentous step of resigning his commission as lieutenant. He had come to loathe military life. The officers were no better than drillmasters, he wrote in a letter (March 18, 1799), the soldiers slaves, "and when the whole regiment was put through its paces it seemed to me a living monument to tyranny." He himself suffered tortures: "always being in doubt whether to act as an officer or as a human being, for I consider it impossible to unite the duties of both under the conditions prevailing in the army today." The Prussian poet was no friend of Prussianism.

Outside the Guards, what would he do with himself? He was eager to study, to devote himself to learning, to the life of reason, he wrote in the same letter. Reason would show him the way to man's goal of virtue, whose reward is happiness, the only true happiness. These were standard Enlightenment ideas, worn thin by now but upheld by him with a passion. Still there was no hint of what would be his true vocation. He attended the local university in Frankfurt on the Oder for several semesters and soon became engaged to Wilhelmine von Zenge, a sweet-natured girl who was the daughter of a major general living next door.

In resigning his commission he turned away from his family; in engaging himself to a next door general's daughter he turned back to it. Writing in May 1799 to his half sister Ulrike, who was something of a misfit too and the only one of his family to whom he was closely attached all his life, he remarks about the two of them, Ulrike and himself, that they are no believers in "the rites of religion and rules of conventional well-being." But Wilhelmine was, as a matter of course. So in 1800 we find him entering, with some reluctance, the Berlin bureaucracy, with an eye to obtaining a salary to marry on.

He quit it very soon, objecting to an official's life on much the same grounds he objected to an officer's. He was expected to do the state's bidding, but he mustn't inquire if what it bade him do was good. He was to be a mere instrument employed by others for unknown ends, but he had his own ends which he must serve, and if the state's will was otherwise he *must* disobey the state. "My pride would compel me to follow the dictates of my reason against the will of my superiors—no, Wilhelmine, it's no use, I'm not cut out for any kind of post" (Nov. 13, 1800). What was he cut out for, then? Kleist had no idea; he suffered agonies of indecision about what to do. He goes on to tell Wilhelmine that it is only their birth and station which compel them to look for means to set up respectably—"away with noble birth, away with social station," they would live simply, perhaps go to France, where he might teach German philosophy, in such a life a future as an author would be open to him. (He doesn't mean author of imaginative works.) In his March 1799 letter renouncing a military career and electing knowledge and virtue as the goal of his life, he had said that "it was surely wise in changing times like these to attach oneself as little as possible to the existing order of things." Kleist was never able to attach himself to the existing order of things, not even in his last years when he tried hard to.

The engagement, which lasted some three years, was mostly conducted in letters because he soon began to wander and never stopped. In his letters to Wilhelmine one sees signs of passion, but not many of warm affection. Kleist is bent on making her a suitable wife by forming her mind and character to be serious and noble, and is oppressively, ridiculously tutorial—it isn't charming. The word *heart* and its equivalents occur often, but his heart is cold. What is hot is his head. The letters overflow with observations, asseverations, exclamations; they crackle with the writer's intensity of spirit. Here Wilhelmine seems mostly an occasion for reflections and self-reflections. More than once

Kleist says he wants from life only "a wife, my own house and *freedom.*" But what freedom meant to him, as it turned out, canceled wife and house. With him as with many another writer later in the century and the next one (from Flaubert to Kafka), it was a choice between the life and the work. Though in fact there was no choice for him; when he finally came to be a writer, he said he couldn't help himself, he *had* to write. It took him years to find this out. It was after all a long way from Prussian officer to poet.

A crucial step along that way had been his demission. A second step—blow, rather—was what is known as the "Kant crisis." This was preceded by a trip he took with an older friend, Ludwig von Brockes, to Würzburg with the medical purpose of removing an impediment to marriage, the exact nature of which he kept a secret. He returned triumphant, not to his fiancée in Frankfurt but to Berlin, writing her from there (Jan. 31, 1801) to sing Brockes' praises as one who understood him and his purposes at a level he could only hope Wilhelmine might be able to reach. Brockes' great principle was: "To do is better than to know. . . . He always called reason cold and only the heart potent and creative. . . . He always surrendered to his first impulse, what he called his heart-sight [*Gefühlsblick*], and I've never known it to deceive him. He always spoke disparagingly of reason, although in so doing showed he possessed more of it than those who boast of its possession." Brockes' "principle," which Kleist made his own and modified importantly (as we have seen), was a repudiation of the narrow rationality of the eighteenth century and, as Kleist reports it, has something of an angry, disabused tone to it. But it also aims ahead at the ever more intellectualized life of the nineteenth and twentieth centuries. It was for Kleist if not for Brockes a defense, not of irrationality, but of a rationality that searched more deeply.

Brockes' influence shook Kleist in his sense of purpose. He wrote Ulrike (Feb. 5, 1801) that what had been a pillar for him to cling to "in the vortex of life"—life for him was a vortex—was now swaying dangerously—"I mean my love of learning . . . oh, how sad it is to be a professor and nothing more." Not long after this we are told that he has been reading Kant, with shattering effect; his intellectual foundations, never really very solid but the basis of his ambition to become a man of learning, collapse. On March 22, 1801, he writes Wilhelmine, tragically (and the next day Ulrike), to say that truth is nowhere to be found on earth. "We can never be certain that what we call truth is really truth, or whether it only seems so. If the latter, the truth that we acquire here isn't truth after we die—and all our efforts to possess ourselves of something which might follow us to the grave are in vain. Oh Wilhelmine, if the point of this thought doesn't pierce you to the heart, don't smile at somebody who feels himself wounded by it in the innermost core of his being. My single, my supreme goal has sunk completely and I have no other—."

Kleist, it is said, misunderstood Kant. This is as it may be. He would have flunked a quiz in philosophy class. But he didn't misunderstand what he felt in himself when he read Kant, the text he read in himself when he read Kant's text; and what this text showed was the direction that the world was taking toward ever greater doubtfulness, uncertainty, infirmity, toward the "abyss" that he always feared for himself personally. As Professor Miller writes, "Kleist's shattering encounter with the Kantian philosophy ... is perhaps the most notorious emotional crisis in German literary history.... For here is a portent of radical problems for the new century and beyond, indeed for the entire post-Enlightenment world to the present." The violence of his response to Kant shows that more than philosophy was involved for him, or that he read philosophy with how much more than his head. When he read Kant, life was at stake for him, the whole meaning of life as *his* life. To feel such things so directly, personally, is "naive"; growing up (into the Wordsworthian prisonhouse) means not to feel them. Nietzsche wrote in his essay on Schopenhauer that "despair of truth is a danger menacing any thinker who starts out from the Kantian philosophy, assuming he is a vigorous, whole man and not merely a clattering electronic brain or adding machine." And he goes on to quote the passage from Kleist's letter quoted above, exclaiming at the end: "When will people again feel in this natural Kleistian way? When will they learn again to measure the meaning of philosophy by 'the innermost core of their being'?"

The consequence of Kleist's Kant crisis was that in losing his "supreme goal" the way was opened for him to his true one: to be a playwright and storyteller whose subject is just precisely uncertainty and doubtfulness, error and misunderstanding, confusion of the mind and confusion of the heart, under a heaven that has receded to an astronomical distance. Out of the ruins of his intellectual world, at long last, the poet emerged. This happened in the fall of the same year of 1801, during his stay in Paris, whither he had fled seeking relief in movement from his painful feelings of spiritual dismay, thwarted ambition, and ignominious purposelessness. But having found his purpose, he is never afforded relief in life and he never comes to rest anywhere, even (or especially) when he returns to his native Prussia three years later, and yet again to Prussia in the last two years of his life. Writing to Wilhelmine on April 9, 1801, just before running away to France, Switzerland, and elsewhere, he fears, with good reason, what life has in store for him because of his unstable nature: "Oh Wilhelmine, if Heaven would only grant me a green cottage I'd forget all this traveling forever, forget knowledge, forget ambition. For nothing but pain and suffering is what I have from this eternally agitated heart of mine that never stops lurching like a planet from right to left in its course, and I yearn with all my soul for what the whole creation strives for, and all the heavenly bodies spinning ever more slowly in their orbits—for rest!"

Kleist's first literary efforts were verse tragedies: *Robert Guiscard, Duke of the Normans,* and *The Family Schroffenstein.* It is likely these were conceived in Paris. His talent was not restricted to the dramatic. At some point he also began writing stories—tales—extraordinarily original and extraordinary for their narrative force. We hear later of a novel that apparently survived his death but then got lost. And there were other things he burned—for he was inclined when in despair to turn on his own work. In the French metropolis he haunted the museums and libraries. But Paris did not please him. The great numbers made him feel the insignificance of individual lives; and he thought the French frivolous and pleasure-seeking. After four months he removed to Switzerland to live and work in Rousseauist simplicity on the land. He asked Wilhelmine to join him there. She was not robust and the prospect of living as a peasant was too daunting for her. The shaky engagement collapsed.

In Switzerland Kleist didn't farm, he wrote, completing his first play, *The Family Schroffenstein,* starting the comedy *The Broken Jug,* and laboring away at the never completed *Robert Guiscard.* All of these are in blank verse. Dramatic blank verse, which provided the medium for the German classical drama of Lessing, Goethe, and Schiller, was a recent thing in Germany, going back only to the latter part of the eighteenth century. In England by that time it had been dead for nearly a century, having lost the power to express men and women acting in the world, and become, with the Romantic poets, a nondramatic medium of meditation. In England indeed the drama itself was dead (and nearly so, except for Germany, on the Continent); between Sheridan and Shaw all is a desert. German historical belatedness made a vigorous poetic drama possible at a time when it had disappeared or was disappearing elsewhere. At the same time belatedness, as is often the case, was the springboard to forwardness: the tardy German drama was the advance guard of the revived European drama of the twentieth century.[5] And that is where Kleist's place is, in the advance guard.

His first plays, indeed all his plays as well as his stories, differ widely from one another in subject matter, although their themes are closely related (*Robert Guiscard* excepted). *The Family Schroffenstein*[6] has, right off, the energy of feeling and language which Kleist brought to the drama, but also a Romeo-and-Juliet plot preposterously melodramatic. The comedy *The Broken Jug* has a Sophoclean plot, on the other hand, about a village magistrate sitting on a case in which he himself is the culprit; in its tight grip a homely anecdote, treated in a style of vigorous domestic realism, becomes something more than a smiling genre piece. Meanwhile Kleist continued to work in Switzerland on his epic tragedy about the eleventh-century Norman conqueror of southern Italy, Duke Guiscard. The ambition in this play, the overweening ambition, was to unite the first (Greek) age of tragedy with the second (Shakespearean) age, so as to bring to birth a third and ideal age of tragedy. It starts with fine dramatic verve, but that is all we have, a start. Kleist found that he was unable to bring the play off, though he labored at it with hysterical intensity. Back again in Paris in 1803 after further wanderings, forced to admit defeat, he pitched it into the fire in despair. The surviving fragment, consisting of the first ten scenes, was published in 1808 in a magazine, *Phoebus,* that he coedited for a year, presumably after he reconstructed these scenes.

The attempt to synthesize Greek and Shakespearean tragedy was bound to be a vain one. It looked backward to old literature rather than to his own sense of things. Kleist's desperate efforts with the play were vain, too, in the sense of being an expression of his vanity, of his bad ambition to stand above all others by raising himself up on the two highest pillars of the drama. He said later, about Goethe, "I'll tear the laurel wreath off his brow!" (And still later, in his last months, the man humbled by defeat after defeat remarked that he wouldn't "dare to compare" himself with Goethe.) All his life he was driven by his need, as an aberrant, delinquent son, to justify himself before his family and himself. He had worked five hundred days on end, and most nights as

5. "German drama from Lessing to Nietzsche, and on at least to Brecht . . . may be seen as the nucleus of the development of modern European drama as a whole" (Benjamin Bennett, *Modern Drama and German Classicism* [1979], p. 19).

6. Omitted from this selection, as are *Kätchen von Heilbronn* and *The Battle of the Teutoburger Wald* (*Die Hermannsschlacht*).

well, he wrote his sister (Oct. 5, 1803), "so as to win a victory which would add still another wreath to our family's many wreaths; but now our holy protector goddess cries enough. And tenderly kissing the sweat off my brow, she whispers consolingly that 'if every one of her dear sons had done as much, our name shouldn't lack for a place among the stars.'"

But he was not in fact consoled by the goddess. Defeated, he thought of suicide, a thought never very far from him at any time. He turned up in Boulogne in a distraught state with the mad intention of taking part in the French invasion of England so as to perish on the field of battle. Brought back to Paris, he was ordered to return to Germany by the Prussian ambassador, and when he reached Mainz suffered a nervous collapse. Kleist was received back, not too unkindly as it seems, into his family and into the Prussian administrative service on condition he should give up scribbling verses. For a year and half during 1804–06, in Berlin and then in Königsberg, he worked quietly in the offices of the state administration. But he didn't give up scribbling, instead wrote continuously, having begun work on the plays *Amphitryon* and *Penthesilea*. Through the unlikely figure of the Queen of the Amazons he tried to take account of himself and especially of the grip of bad ambition on him.

It wasn't to be expected that he should remain in an official position for long. Allowed six month's leave, he departed officialdom forever. Meanwhile Prussia was overwhelmed at Jena. Kleist, in Berlin on his way to Dresden, was arrested by the French, who had occupied the Prussian capital, on suspicion of being a spy and was imprisoned in France. He made good use of his time in captivity and continued to write. Ulrike, who was a standby in all his troubles (though they quarreled continually too), was able to persuade the French commandant of Berlin to have him released after six months, in July 1807.

Now Kleist was a writer and nothing but a writer, with important works finished and more in progress. *Amphitryon* had been published while he was in confinement. More than a few recognized his genius. He arrived in Saxon Dresden from France with the reputation of a man of talent. There he found friends and a flattering reception in the literary and diplomatic milieux. At a dinner given for him on his thirtieth birthday by the Austrian minister in Dresden, he was crowned with a laurel wreath. (Perhaps he came to think that premature—as premature as the wreath the dreaming Prince of Homburg twines for himself in the first scene of that play.) With a friend he started the literary magazine *Phoebus,* soliciting Germany's best known writers, Goethe among them, to contribute to it. At last he seemed to have joined "the existing order of things"—as a writer.

It wasn't so. Writers as a class didn't belong to "the existing order" in any case; they were a loose element in the feudal-absolutist system of the German princes, an intelligentsia a little like the Russian.[7] But Kleist was unable to attach himself even to the unattached literary world. The big literary names sent him nothing for the *Phoebus*. His own contributions got a mixed reception; a sentimental public found many of them indecent. When Goethe read the first number containing an extract from *Penthesilea*, he didn't care for the play one bit; his opinion of the very different long story *Michael Kohlhaas*, when it appeared, was only a little better. In a conversation in 1810 he kept calling Kleist "hypochondriacal," meaning sick. Goethe had not been unforthcoming in 1807, however, when he had been sent *The Broken Jug*; he thought he might be able to stage the comedy in Weimar, he said, although he criticized the author's inclination toward "the dialectical" on the grounds that debate and discussion were not action and therefore not dramatic. The dialectical, apparently—usually—uncongenial matter for imaginative literature, is one of the glories of Kleist's art, theatrical and narrative. Jupiter's interrogation of Alcmene in *Amphitryon*; Kohlhaas' interview with Luther, the debates among the Elector of Saxony's councillors; Princess Natalie's pleading with the Elector of Brandenburg for mercy for Homburg, the Elector's debate with his officers; as well as *The Broken Jug* with its whole plot based on a trial—these are purely dramatic. (Kafka is his great heir here, in the debates and discussions about the nature of the court and the castle in *The Trial* and *The Castle*.)

Goethe was as good as his word and *The Broken Jug* was put on in Weimar on March 2, 1808. The production—which Kleist didn't see, he never saw any professional productions of his plays—was a fiasco, for various reasons it appears, one of which was Goethe's breaking up the quick succession of scenes into three lumpish parts. Kleist was furious, insulting, there was a rupture; and long after his death his reputation was still struggling to make its way past the roadblock represented by

---

7. "The difference between German and English literature of this period can hardly be understood without considering that the German writers as such had simply no status in society; this is one reason why many of them strike us as so curiously modern" (Michael Hamburger, "Heinrich von Kleist," in *Contraries: Studies in German Literature* [1970]).

Goethe's distaste for him and all his works. The existence of a new (sixth) play, *Kätchen of Heilbronn*—a fairy tale about knights and maidens, angels and witches, absurdly extravagant but charged and overcharged with a sense of unconscious forces and remarkable for the figure of Kätchen, that astonishing flower of indomitable, smiling, naive love—was signaled by the publication of an excerpt from it in *Phoebus*. But the magazine was not proving a success and it ceased publication early in 1809.

Kleist's last effort to find a place for himself in the existing order was political, as a poet and a publicist drumming up German nationalist hatred against the French. He had been indifferent to politics in his youth. In Königsberg in 1805–06 his meeting Prussian reformers in the bureaucracy whose goal was a modern liberal state, first awakened his interest in public affairs. Professor Richard Samuel writes (in the excellent introduction to his fine edition of *Prinz Friedrich von Homburg*[8]) that "Kleist's ultimate political ideal [was] a unified constitutional German state enjoying individual and civic freedom within its own borders and being a part of a 'world republic' of free nations." But when his hostility toward Napoleon turned into a frenzy of hatred, with an abruptness that Professor Samuel speculates was linked to his quarrel with Goethe, who admired the French emperor extravagantly, his immediate ideal became barbaric nationalism—represented in his play *The Battle of the Teutoburger Wald* in the person of Arminius, the barbarian chief of the Cheruskian tribe that defeated the Romans in A.D. 9. Kleist exalts Arminius as a cunning German hero triumphing by lies, treachery, and horrifying brutality over the contemptuous foreign intruder and his damned (so the poet seems to be saying) Roman nobility of mind. German nationalism was basically antiliberal from the first, for, as A. J. P. Taylor observed in *The Course of German History*, it was "in defence of Prussia and Austria, the two despotic and half-Slav states to whose existence Germany owed in fact her lack both of unity and freedom," whereas French rule, alien though it was, "was synonymous with liberal reform." Kleist's play glorified the retrograde character of German nationalism. The work has dramatic power (dissipated as it passes over into open political exhortation), but it is repellent in itself and as a prophecy of the course of German nationalism culminating in Hitler's barbaric rage. Kleist betrayed

8. London, 1962. Prof. Samuel's edition of *Der zerbrochene Krug* (London, 1950) is also superior.

his own spirit of liberal humanity when he offered his unmastered fury as an expression of German patriotism.

In his final play and masterpiece, *Prince Frederick of Homburg,* he recovered himself and held up a self-critical and humane ideal to Prussia. But Prussia would have none of it, nor Austria either. Kleist thought *The Prince of Homburg* was a "patriotic drama"—so he describes it in a letter offering the work to his publisher (who did not publish it; it was first published after his death). He dedicated it to King Frederick William III's sister-in-law, who had the historical Homburg for an ancestor. The princess's response to the offered dignity (after Kleist's death, as reported by Heine) was to forbid the play's production, scandalized to see a Prussian prince and officer depicted as collapsing in fear of death. When the play was staged in Vienna in 1821, the police were called in to close the theater lest the morale of the Austrian army should be undermined.

Not by way of German patriotism or any other way was he destined to become attached to the existing order. His final publicistic effort, in Berlin in 1810–11, had Prussian sponsorship. This was the daily newspaper already mentioned, the *Berliner Abendblätter,* in which political articles shared place with a variety of literary and journalistic pieces, among them his essay *On the Puppet Theater* and his *Anecdotes.* The newspaper did well at first, then poorly after the fearful Prussian government imposed a political censorship on it following warnings by the French ambassador. It died in the spring of 1811, leaving Kleist beggared and once again without attachment anywhere.

The course is all downward now. In a letter (Sept. 17, 1811) to Marie von Kleist, a relative by marriage with influence at the Prussian court who was his faithful friend and defender, he writes that "it is extraordinary how everything I undertake these days goes to smash; how the ground always slides away from underneath my feet whenever I am able to make up my mind to take a positive step." He asks her dispiritedly if it wouldn't be best for him to leave Berlin and go to Vienna, though he feels about going there as he would about going out into the pitch darkness of a night of sleeting rain. It's not Vienna, in and of itself, that is so distasteful to him; "but what seems so desolate to me as not to be described is always to be looking elsewhere for what I've never yet found anywhere, because of this strange nature of mine.... Still, it's possible my love of art might reawaken there." This is ominous; his love of art, his only possession after all, needs reawakening.

His advance toward death became a quick march after a humiliating episode at the family table in Frankfurt on the Oder, where he had gone on September 18, 1811, to borrow money from Ulrike once again. At lunch with her and another sister, he was turned on in exasperation and berated for betraying the traditions of the Kleists, for leading a vagabond life, for squandering his own small inheritance and Ulrike's ampler one. He tells Marie von Kleist about it in his letter of November 10, 1811, prefacing the account by saying that it is impossible for him to go on living, his soul is so sore if he so much as sticks his nose out of the window the daylight falling on it hurts. "By having kept up, from my earliest youth, a constant intercourse in my thoughts and writings with beautiful objects and courteous conduct, I have at last grown so sensitive that the slightest offense, to which everybody here on earth is after all exposed as a matter of course, wounds me doubly and triply. So I assure you I would suffer death ten times over rather than endure again what I had to endure at the lunch table from my two sisters the last time in Frankfurt.... I have always loved my sisters with all my heart ... it has always been one of my dearest, most fervent wishes that they should have great joy and honor of me from my works and labors ... but the thought that merits, be they great or small, which I may after all lay claim to, should go entirely unacknowledged, and I should find myself regarded as an entirely useless member of society no longer deserving of any sympathy, is extremely painful to me, really it robs me not only of my hope of future joy, but poisons all the past for me as well."

Meanwhile he had met a woman, Henriette Vogel, an official's wife, who was ill with cancer and shrank from the painful death awaiting her. Love of music drew them together, the wish to die drew them into a compact. On November 21, 1811, in an inn garden overlooking the Wannsee, near Potsdam, he shot Henriette Vogel and himself, both in a state of high exaltation—his soul, as he wrote Marie von Kleist two days before, singing "a song of triumph." Kleist was given to fits of hysteria in his life, but perhaps his suicide was not one of these. His melancholy, he had written in the same letter, was "deep-rooted," "incurable," extending all the way back to his youth. It had always been a burden, but one he was able to set down. Now he couldn't. "The truth is," he wrote Ulrike on the morning of his death, "there was no help for me on earth"—echoing what Prothoe says about the Queen, also a suicide, at the end of *Penthesilea*: "There was no more going on here for her any more."

The death he embraced with joy and relief had the double aspect for him of a defeat and a triumph. The metaphors he applies to it express this. On the one hand his suicide aimed downward, into an abyss, "an abyss deep enough" for him to be swallowed up in forever, he wrote Marie von Kleist in his letter of November 19. As part of this defeat he burned all his manuscripts and papers. On the other hand it aimed upward, toward a heaven into which he and Henrietta feel themselves ascending "like two happy balloonists," so he writes another woman friend on November 20. "The joys of this world lack all interest for us and we dream only of heavenly pastures and suns in whose warm glow, with long wings on our shoulders, we will stray about. Adieu!" When the Prince of Homburg, having triumphed over the fear of death, is awaiting execution, he too speaks about wings unfolding on his shoulders and his soul ascending upward. Down into an abyss, up into the heavens—so Kleist felt his death; and apparently he saw no conflict between the two feelings.

We do. We think we understand his despair, but are appalled that he should go to this death with loud cries of joy and exultation and triumph which seem to express much more than relief. Was it Northern morbidity, "Romanticism," what? A close friend, Ernst von Pfuel, didn't deplore the suicide because he felt that "dear, good Heinrich's" soul had been shattered beyond repair, but he did deplore the "exaltation": "As far as I know Kleist, his exaltation here was spurious, forced, and that is what I regret." That is a friend's judgment on the letters, but it isn't an obvious one by any means. I find it difficult to read the exaltation as spurious. Kleist was a man of exaltations. The letters aside, the suicide couple's conduct in their last hours, as reported by the inn people, seems simple, genuine, not forced (in Pfuel's sense) at all. A letter Kleist wrote Wilhelmine ten years before (July 21, 1801), in which he speaks with vehement conviction about death and the fear of death, perhaps makes this "triumphant" side of the suicide more comprehensible.

He is describing a trip by boat down the Rhine during which a violent storm suddenly blew up and the vessel pitched and rolled out of control. "Each person clung to a beam with no thought for anybody else, holding on for dear life, *myself* not excepted.—Oh, there is nothing more repulsive than the fear of death. Life is the one possession that is worth something only if you are indifferent to it. How abject it is not to be able to relinquish it without a struggle—only a man who is able to cast it aside easily and joyfully can make it serve great ends. A man who has too much care of it is, morally speaking, already dead, for the highest power of his life, which is his ability to lay it down, decays in the degree that he is solicitous of it. And yet, and yet—oh, how incomprehensible the will that rules us is!—This mysterious thing we have, from whom we've no idea, that leads us on, we've no idea where, that we possess, but don't know with what rights, a possession without value if we value it, a contradictory thing, shallow and deep, barren and rich, noble and abject, full of meanings and absolutely unfathomable, a thing everybody would be inclined to throw aside like a book impossible to understand if a law of nature didn't compel us to cherish it. We must tremble before annihilation, which surely can't be the torture that life often is, and at the same time that many a man weeps over the unhappy gift of life, he must struggle to sustain it with food and drink and guard from going out a flame that affords him neither light nor heat."

Kleist finds himself hanging on for dear life and is humiliated by the law of nature which compels him to preserve himself from death. Psychologically, it would seem, he wishes to overcome his fear of death—his extreme fear of death, as *The Prince of Homburg* suggests—by embracing it. And yet there is more than psychology here, powerful as he allows psychology to be. A law of nature robs him of his freedom, and he reclaims it for himself—wishes to reclaim it—by being ready at any moment to throw his life away. Kleist asserts his freedom by rebelling against nature, his abject submission to nature, just as he rebelled against military and bureaucratic submission. However, his freedom is only a freedom of attitude, not the freedom of knowing ends. When it comes to ends, he has no idea what ultimate ends our "mysterious" human life and freedom are supposed to serve—except that he knows that a human being *must* be free, if only in striking the attitude of freedom. This is aristocratic. I am reminded, again, of Yeats, whose gravestone in Drumcliffe churchyard tells us to

> Cast a cold eye
> On life, on death,
> Horseman, pass by!

Yeats's freedom, his "cold eye," is only a freedom of attitude too (the last line has rather too much attitude!), for as a man of the modern world he has no more idea than Kleist what ultimate ends human freedom is supposed to serve. Of course Yeats didn't kill himself, with his freedom. Kleist, whose eye was feverish and bloodshot, not cold, did. His suicide was a terrible defeat; but something of his lifelong struggle to be free was in it too.

Although placed last in this selection as a fragment, *Robert Guiscard, Duke of the Normans,* is among the earliest if not the earliest of Kleist's works. It shows one what he thought of first, in his ambition, when he sat down to write: poetry in the grand style, in the heroic style. Like his own Prince of Homburg he was in a rush to win laurel wreaths, and like him he went astray by being in a rush. For it was no longer possible, in the nineteenth century, to write heroic tragedy; the social and spiritual conditions for such drama had passed away. Fame in the nineteenth century was no longer won by following in the beaten path of the traditional; the laurel was a withered symbol capable only of ironical employment now. And that is how it is on its way to being used at the end of his last play, *The Prince of Homburg*—ironically. For when at last he is crowned by love and honor with the classical symbol of victory, what does Homburg do? He *faints,* this dashing hero with his very unheroic dimension of a problematic interior life.

But if Kleist failed in his first effort because anxious ambition stopped his ears to the true preoccupations of his soul, which were not with the heroical, he failed bravely. One has no right to expect anything but bombast and unreality from latter-day attempts to write heroic drama, yet the ten scenes of *Robert Guiscard* are vigorous and strong. And especially the blank verse (dating from the later time of the fragment's reconstruction) is strong—long, rolling periods which translation into modern English, with its small sounds (apart from one's own limitations as translator), can give only an imperfect idea of, I am afraid. The play opens with a declamation by the people, very splendid, whose theme is Guiscard the rock: the rock of their salvation, but also the rock of their destruction if he won't confess himself defeated by the plague and bring his army home from before the gates of Constantinople. The complicated situation, in which the blind fatality of a plague comes between Guiscard and his towering ambition (the classical plot of fate joined to the Shakespearean plot of character), is unfolded swiftly. But how Kleist hoped to resolve the situation, before he lost all hope, isn't clear.

In anticipation of the Norman Duke's appearance, which is delayed with fine theatrical effect till the tenth scene, we are given two important descriptions of him. These present him as a monumental figure. The first, Abelard's, shows us the sick captain in his tent as a prostrate colossus who employs a gigantesque diction (Titans, Etna, the Dardanelles) to answer the question of how he feels. The second, by the boy on the hillside peering up into the tent, shows Guiscard, who has pulled himself together, donning his armor and preparing to appear before his people: statuelike he stands "erect upon his own two legs," with "swelling chest," "bulky shoulders," and "a great helmet" on his high-domed head. And Guiscard's own description of himself in the last scene is also of a monument, an architectural rather than a sculptural one: he says, dismissing any suspicion that he should be ill, that his

> clear-ringing voice peals freely from his breast
> and fills, like steeple bells, the air around.

He is a great bell tower.

These passages are impressive. But monuments aren't living heroes; the monumentality rather suggests that Kleist was only able to see Guiscard from the outside, conventionally. The bluff and canny great commander who knows his men and knows how to win their love and bend them to his tiger's will—isn't this a platitude? Did it really interest Kleist, interest his imagination? What always interests him is the soul's uncertainty, its stumbles and mistakes on the terra infirma of the world. With Guiscard's appearance, although the energy of the verse is kept up, a certain hollowness enters in. Of course this hollowness belongs to the dramatic scheme (as far as one is able to discern a scheme): Guiscard assuring his people with false heartiness he isn't sick with plague because the hero means to conquer Byzantium, plague or no plague. But the hollowness also seems a hollowness in the tragic hero, Guiscard's monumentality a shell. Perhaps the figure seized by weakness at the end of the fragment and letting itself down on the drum with a sigh also expressed its author's feeling of defeat with his own conception. If so, the fragment becomes the story of that defeat. As such, it ceases to be a fragment.

Robert Guiscard owes its animation to its strikingly declared epic situation, which is then unfolded in the powerful exchanges between the Old Man, Abelard, and the Duke's son. The ambiguous intriguer Abelard, heir by right of inheritance to the crown that Guiscard has usurped, but who tells Guiscard's heir that it is an "unawed" people's love which awards the crown, not heirdom, whose young force, maneuvering this way and that, his young author really feels—he is the one, I judge, who might have enlisted Kleist's imagination. But with Abelard at the center it would have been a different kind of play entirely from the heroic tragedy upon which his first ambition had fixed.

Kleist's *Amphitryon* starts out in the beaten path too, of translation of a classic. Perhaps that is all he meant it to be at first, a translation of Molière, but then it turned—twisted—under his hand to become this unexampled work, quite in keeping with the principle of spontaneity he learned to recognize as being at the heart of the imagination. For as he says in his essay *On the Gradual Formation of Thoughts While Speaking* (*Über die allmähliche Verfertigung der Gedanken beim Reden*): "*We* don't know; it is rather a certain condition we happen to be in that knows." What his imagination knows, and writes, in his *Amphitryon* is a comedy that is very serious, very grave, without ceasing to be a comedy, without turning into a tragedy, and without being a tragicomedy either—for in tragicomedy the comic and the serious elements alternate with one another, or a menacing situation unexpectedly finds a benign conclusion, whereas in Kleist's play what is most grave is just what is most comic, and vice versa, and for Alcmene there is no clear conclusion. Or as Thomas Mann puts it in his *Amphitryon* essay, the play has an "intrinsic double essence . . . at once social comedy and metaphysical exercise."

But the consequence of this is a loss of unity. Molière's *Amphitryon* is all of a piece, modulating effortlessly from high (Amphitryon-Jupiter) to low (Sosia-Mercury) along a single register of brilliant comic effects. The elephantine waggishness of the old humor of cuckoldry has been refined and sublimated into the purest kind of courtly wit. This wit, which has its basis in farce, embraces both the masters and the servants in its comic unity. In Kleist, the Sosia-Mercury story remains what it is in Molière, the type of the old traditional servant-farce; but the Amphitryon-Jupiter story, enlarged so that Alcmene now occupies its center with her tender sexual charm and anguished innocence, is utterly transformed, and transformed in its wit, into something new and strange. This new kind of comedy, whose content is a bold-minded exploration of the nature of love, cohabits more or less uneasily with the humor of the Sosia side of the play.

This is not to say that Kleist's Sosia is not well done. He is. The same as Molière's Sosia in his comic substance, he is very different in his style, as Kleist's play differs in general from Molière's elegant and worldly style. The French Sosia, who possesses a certain refinement, is capable of flashes of wit; he is part of the courtly world. Kleist coarsens him, turning the gentleman's valet into a clownish servant. Both are gluttons, but the German Sosia much more so, with his bratwurst, cabbage, and horseradish. Sosia is funnier in German, wittier in French—this is only partly due to the difference between the two languages. Never could the German servant utter those wonderful lines

Le véritable Amphitryon
Est l'Amphitryon où l'on dîne

—with their delicate suggestion of a materialist first principle for determining who the true Amphitryon is.[9] On the other hand, you don't find Molière's Charis uttering these lines with which Kleist's Charis is trying to reassure the frightened Alcmene:

> ... Dresses, pots and pans, you snatch
> the wrong one up, but not your husband, in the dark.

Molière is courtly; with Kleist we leave courts behind and pass into a much more human, much more realistic emotional world, one that is deadly serious and at the same time deliciously witty.

Jupiter and Alcmene make their appearance in the first act still glowing from the warmth of their bed of love. This sensual glow suffuses the entire play. Mercury's words have prepared us for the notorious Olympian seducer, the irrepressible satyr god. However, this Jove discovers an unusual interest in examining analytically into the pleasure Alcmene has enjoyed with him; he presses her to distinguish between the lover and the husband, between the divine (free) love they have savored and the obligatory (official) embraces of matrimony. At first this seems clever joking, a part of the adultery joke that the play never stops being to the very end, and nothing more. But we learn later, in the great fifth scene of act II, that Jupiter's use of the word "divine" to describe their night of love had not been only an amusing allusion to himself, nor was it conventionally hyperbolical; we learn he meant it literally. We learn what is the subject of the play: Alcmene's instruction in the divine element of love, in transcendence[10]—a painful lesson.

Alcmene is an extraordinarily charming, extraordinarily touching woman in her ardent innocence. But the play is an attack on innocence, her innocence, by a radical moralist and psychologist. Her innocence is based on feeling. Feelings don't mislead; thanks to feeling she is confident she knows infallibly what is true and what is false. How could it not have been Amphitryon who made love to her?

---

9. Kleist's version of the line is:

Der is der wirkliche Amphitryon,
Bei dem zu Mittag jetzt gegessen wird.

10. Richard March well says: "Kleist touches on a mystical element in erotic experience on which in fact the whole love relationship in its profounder aspects turns [which is] that sensuality is rooted in the soul, or conversely, that there is *soul*, a spiritual overtone, in the most diverse and abandoned sensual transports" (*Heinrich von Kleist* [1954], p. 28).

Oh Charis! As soon mistake myself
I would! As soon imagine I'm a Persian
or a Parthian, in spite of that profoundest feeling
sucked in with my mother's milk, which tells
me I am I, Alcmene. . . .
       He would have had
to be more strange to me than my own self!
Put out my eye, still I would hear him; stop
my ear and I would feel him; take touch away
I'd breathe his presence in; take all my senses,
every one, but only leave my heart,
that bell—its note is all I need to find
him out, wherever, in the world.

Did her heart, that bell of truth, mislead her? No.

You mustn't put a wrong construction on the fact
that I have never felt he was so handsome
as last night. I might have thought he was
a portrait of himself, a painting by a master's
hand showing him exactly as
he is, and yet transfigured, like a god!
Standing there he seemed, I don't know what,
a dream; unspeakable the bliss I felt,
whose like I'd never known before, when he,
Pharissa's conqueror, radiant
as if with Heaven's glory, appeared to me.
Amphitryon it was, the son of the gods!

This is a true report of her feelings, and her feelings gave a true report:
it was Amphitryon who appeared to her, an Amphitryon "transfigured,
like a god!" But although Alcmene *felt* the presence of the god in Jupiter's
embrace, she puts a "wrong construction" on this feeling, in her innocence—for if she were to acknowledge a stranger's presence in her bliss
she would convict herself of having made love to a stranger. Her feeling
heart recognizes a truth that her thinking mind starts back from in fear
and disbelief.

 The truth she feels but will not recognize is that in her love for her
husband there is something that exceeds her husband, something *not* her
husband. Her loving sensuality reaches the anonymous supersensuality
of the divine in the arms of Amphitryon-Jupiter. What is Alcmene guilty
of, in failing to understand this? Of something which, in a man, is called,
familiarly enough, uxoriousness, but which in a woman goes by the very
unfamiliar term of "maritality." Uxoriousness is a familiar term because

men have never had any difficulty in recognizing the limitations, the spiritual parochialness of a too doting fondness for one's wife; but "maritality" is so unfamiliar because men have wished their wives to dote on them.

Jupiter's long interrogation of Alcmene in the second act, so incomparably witty and so wounding to her innocence, is an attempt to make her understand her "maritality," to enlarge her understanding of love beyond its cozy cottage limits so that she learns how to distinguish "me from him," the god from the husband (the god in the husband). But first he must reassure her, for, seeing a *J* on the diadem where she thought there had been an *A*, confused and suffering, in her ingenuous uprightness and nobility of heart she is ready to condemn herself as an unfaithful wife. The argument he uses is that "nothing not Amphitryon is ever able to come near you." This does not satisfy her—he is being sophistical only to be kind. But a revision of that argument does satisfy her. He tells her it was Zeus who visited her, but a Zeus who must steal her husband's features to insinuate himself into her affections. No one else could have deceived the finely poised gold-balance of her feeling, eluded the antennae of her woman's soul, failed to jar the bells the whisper of a breath sets ringing in her bosom.

With some persuasion, on the grounds of reverence, she accepts that she has been honored by great Jove. Her innocent reliance on the infallibility of her feelings is reestablished, allowance being made for the exceptional case of divine deception—an exception which, in her innocence, it never occurs to her is taking place again, at the very moment. She accepts "all the pain that Jupiter has caused" her, "if only everything is nice again between" her husband and herself. This is so amusing. Alcmene is incorrigible in her maritality. The "miracle," as Jupiter calls it, of the blissful intervention of the divine in what would otherwise have been commonplace domestic pleasure, in her *understanding* is something "painful" which she is content to have endured if only everything is nice again between Amphitryon and herself. Alcmene's only reverence is for her husband; it is her husband the dear idolatress adores. So Jupiter reads her a pantheistic homily on religion, thundering a little (thundering in late eighteenth-century style) from the pulpit, as befits the Thunder God. Alcmene, admonished by Amphitryon (as she deems the deity) to think less about him and more about Jupiter, becomes contrite and promises amendment. But no sooner has she promised than she backslides:

> Fine, good—you'll see how satisfied
> you'll be with me. My first waking hour,

from now on, I swear it, I'll not give
a thought to you. But after that I shall
forget Lord Jupiter.

Delicious!

Jupiter must relentlessly cross-examine Alcmene because her mind stubbornly rejects transcendence and clings to her husband's clay. ("Am I supposed to pray to marble walls? Well, I need features I can see.") Her narrow wife's devotion stops her from seeing that the individual soul needs the featureless (universal) divine to realize itself, as the featureless divine needs the features of the individual soul for its realization. ("Olympus, too, Alcmene, without love, is desolate!" [*Öde*—"desolate," but also "empty," "void"]). Jupiter finally gets her to admit that she would choose him, the blissful divine presence her arms are presently wound around, over Amphitryon by leading her down a dazzling dialectical path of apparently hypothetical questions to that conclusion. He is triumphant. But he is able to obtain the admission from her only because she thinks he is Amphitryon and the questions hypothetical. With her arms around the god, she *feels* the divine presence, but her *thinking* mind knows and honors only Amphitryon's husbandship. The intrusion from above has split her innocent soul.

That is what she is made to know in the last scene of the play, division of the soul. And knowing that, her bright-winged innocence flies out the window never to return. Confronted with the two Amphitryons, the dear, the gentle Alcmene chooses Jove and denounces her own husband with a violence that rages like Penthesilea's. Hers is the voice of outraged innocence: although she has suffered outrage and has been demeaned, her soul is innocent of having consented to a stranger's love. But it is also the voice of complete and utter delusion. For then Jupiter reveals himself, and Alcmene's head must finally acknowledge her heart's adultery with the stranger god that lives in love.

Where is all this happening? For stories have to happen somewhere, the thin air isn't good enough. If we ask this question of Molière's courtly farce, with its Jupiter who is so much the royal sovereign, we must say, the court of Louis XIV. About Kleist's play and its dialectical Jupiter it is harder to say. It is, I think, a story of the soul; the place where all this is happening is in the modern soul, "the haunt and the main region" of his verse (to quote Wordsworth) as it is of the greatest works of the twentieth century. And as a story of the soul, Alcmene's infidelity to her husband (a bawdy joke) is fidelity to the god in her husband (an epiphanic wonder). Amphitryon affirms this at the end of the play, as he has affirmed his wife's integrity twice before with powerful conviction— all ends triumphantly for him. But how does it end for Alcmene? Her famous "Ah!" which is the comedy's last, ambiguous word, expresses painful confusion and discomfiture, surely. But she is back safely in the arms of her husband, who caught her as she fainted, an innocent and doting wife (thank god) no longer. For innocent means ignorant.

As always with Kleist, we find a shaky world in *The Broken Jug,* one that is stuffed with error and misunderstanding, not to speak of worse—but still, the millennial air of villages blows through it, and in spite of the cupidity and bureaucratism of officials the air is fresh, fresh with the innocence of natural life. Ruprecht, describing how he broke into Eve's room and the great outcry which followed, says:

> Well, Frau Martha came
> spitting fire like a dragon, and neighbor Ralph
> and neighbor Hans, and Tante Liese came
> and Tante Anna, servants came and maids,
> and dogs and cats, oh what a sight it was.... (scene 7)

This is much in the same way as Chaucer writes, centuries before, in the Nun's Priest's Tale, when the fox makes off with Chanticleer:

> Ran Colle oure dogge, and Talbot, and Gerland,
> And Malkyn, with a dystaf in hir hand;
> Ran cow and calf, and eek the verray hogges,
> So fered for the berkyng of the dogges,
> And shoutyng of the men and wommen eeke....

Kleist in his comedy can reach as far back as this, to Chaucer and the Middle Ages. And he can reach as far forward, at the same time, as Brecht, to this (Ruprecht recounting in court how he wooed Eve):

> Oh she's a strapping miss, she is, at harvest
> time she made the hay fly with her fork
> as thick as rain. So I asked her: Eve dear, will you?
> And she answered: How you talk! But later she
> said: Yes! (scene 7)

In the last three lines of the above I hear "Der Song vom Nein und Ja" ("The Song of No and Yes") of *The Three-Penny Opera.* And I can hear Brecht in the following, in which Frau Martha is saying what she would have done to Eve if she were convinced it wasn't her daughter's fiancé who had been in her room:

> I wouldn't have wasted another minute here
> in court. I would have stood a chair outside
> the door for her dowry, so she could start housekeeping
> under the sky, and said: Go, my child,
> the world is wide, and for the open spaces
> no one charges rent, and long hair,
> too, you have inherited, to hang yourself
> with when the time arrives!   (scene 9)

This has the same note of unsentimental delight in life lived below the level of refinement and social pretension, life which for that reason isn't mealy-mouthed, that Brecht sounds so vigorously. The chronicle of the jug's heirs, in Frau Martha's wonderful speech describing the pitcher's decoration and history, is Brechtian. But of course it is Brecht who is Kleistian. Ruprecht "cashing in his chips" in Batavia in the East Indies is a little anticipation of the Brecht of *Mahagonny* and his world of freebooting and imperialism.

The life that Kleist shows us in his comedy is small, concerned with jugs, but it is not treated as contemptible. Adam derives from Falstaff; but Kleist has derived nothing of Shakespeare's good-natured contempt for Bottom and Flute and Quince and Snout. There is nothing in the play of the Renaissance sneer or guffaw at the ignobility of common people. Instead we find it pointing in the direction of Brecht.

The plot is the Oedipus one of "justice judged," to quote Clerk Licht (scene 3), but turned, most unusually, to comic purpose. (Kleist alludes to Oedipus in his preface.) The theme of justice is a very serious one indeed for him (one need mention only *Michael Kohlhaas* and *The Prince of Homburg*), and a certain seriousness lurks within the play which erupts into the open when Eve bursts out against Adam's wicked efforts to intimidate her into silence, and against Ruprecht for his lack of trust—trust being, for Kleist, part and parcel of the question of justice, since Justice is so blind in a sense not figured by her blindfold. But Adam is treated indulgently, a sinner like us all, human, all too human. In spite of his limp, and allusion after allusion, he is no devil, no Tartuffe. The Kleistian Court of Justice, as Judge Walter observes, does not admit denunciations of the devil. Evil is the result of ignorance and error and misunderstanding. Men are wicked, but hardly ever devilish. Adam's impudently exhibiting his left (bad) foot and not his good one when he is asked to show he doesn't have a cloven hoof, is perhaps devilish. But it is the only touch of that kind. Like Falstaff, Adam is a great liar, never shamed and never at a loss. But unlike Falstaff, he is not a supreme poet of effrontery and lying, though Falstaff speaks in prose and Adam in verse; he does not command that kind of language.

Adam is different from Falstaff in another essential way: in his feeling of self, for he is burdened with a sense of guilt. Self-consciousness is more advanced in him. Falstaff says he is a rascal, but doesn't feel it. Adam feels it and, like Joseph K. in *The Trial,* has bad dreams:

> I dreamt I was
> accused and dragged before the bar, and yet I
> was the judge and hounded, skinned and bullied my
> own self, and at last condemned myself
> to put my neck inside an iron collar.   (scene 3)

Really, in this way he is more human than Falstaff, more likable. We *like* to see and hear Falstaff, but he is not, himself, likable. In fact he's something of a monster, like Tartuffe. Comedy reaches one of its peaks in monstrousness, of which Falstaff and Tartuffe are supreme examples. But Adam is likable. The character in the play who is *not* likable is Licht: a clever, calculating worm, a treacherous, ignoble clerk, his name is legion.

The comedy in *The Broken Jug* is one of cross-purposes. The principals in the case are all in hot pursuit of their own ends, one group wanting to conceal the truth, the other wanting it to be discovered, each for his or her own reasons.[11] Even Judge Walter discovers some bureaucratic heat in himself when it is a question of protecting the "honor" of the court. With each one's mind fixed on his own purposes, what another person says acts as an intrusion into his self-absorption, and so we have the many what?-what?'s of the text and the many broken and half-finished utterances. This, as Robert Helbling says, "reflects the isolation of men into islands of pure subjectivity, one of the central themes of Kleist's works." But this is perhaps less a theme than a part of the fundamental (metaphysical) structure of Kleist's world. From all this "subjective" criss-crossing, a picture of the truth does gradually emerge in the courtroom. And that is the action of the play.

Judge Walter, overseeing the conduct of the trial, sees to it that the

---

11. See Robert E. Helbling's chapter on *The Broken Jug* in his excellent study of *The Major Works of Heinrich von Kleist* (1975).

course of justice should not be obstructed and the truth should emerge. But when it does, an official after all, he is concerned most of all to end the case and protect officialdom. Ruprecht can go to Utrecht and appeal in the Superior Court the verdict that Judge Adam has pronounced on him. At which Eve exclaims to Judge Walter: "And you, too, call yourself / a judge?" With these words not only Adam but the judicial system, covering up the crimes of its officials, is indicted, and Eve becomes a revolutionary. Like *Liberty Guiding the People* in the Delacroix painting, crying "Ruprecht, arise!" she starts an uprising in court and Adam is chased from the bench. It is fine comedy. But revolutions are abortive in Kleist, and the matter of the verdict is glossed over as the playwright winds up the play as swiftly as Judge Walter wants Adam to wind up the case. It is left to the Superior Court in Utrecht to take care of justice (including the justice that needs to be done Frau Martha and the broken jug, as the amusing finale tells us).

After demonstrating the unreliability of all the courts of this world whether superior or otherwise, Kleist always asks us to trust in a Superior Court—whose name is usually the Elector of Brandenburg (as in *Kohlhaas* and *Homburg*). For the writer and the work he has written, this is really a nominal conclusion, denied by all that has gone before. But for the man and the Prussian, perhaps it wasn't. As an heir of Kleist, Brecht completes the Prussian's work by showing us how (at the end of *The Three-Penny Opera*) the superior authorities administer justice: that champion murderer and thief, Mac the Knife, is let off, so that it may be seen how justice in this world is tempered with mercy. And Kafka, another heir, has the condemned man Joseph K., as he is being executed, cry out: "Where was the Judge whom he had never seen? Where was the Superior Court which he had never been able to reach?"

It is a shocking transition to pass from *The Broken Jug* to *Penthesilea*, from a Northern realism crammed with domestic detail to a Hellas that is states of violent feeling, from Breughel to—I don't know what. The Greek setting of *Penthesilea* is not as nominal as *Amphitryon*'s, but still— there is not a trace of Hellenophilic reverence in this astonishing play, not for Greece's bright gods, certainly, but neither for its dark. If the play is "Dionysian," it is so in a general sense that has no particular connection with classical tradition. Indeed there is a kind of modern mockery, or burlesque, of the classical that runs through the work. I don't know whether Kleist *intended* this; but it is there. Sometimes the mockery is just a slight suggestion, as in scene 2 when the Greek captain describes how Achilles' charioteer manages finally to straighten out the overturned chariot's confusion of horses and harness: "in that same time Hephaestus could / have forged a whole new car of bronze, almost." But sometimes the mockery is blatant. When Diomedes is shocked, in scene 21, by Achilles' telling him he is going to let Penthesilea take him prisoner, Achilles says he only means to suit her wishes for a month or so, no more—"surely that won't cause / your old peninsula the sea's been gnawing / at since time began, to founder / on the spot!" Hellas is "your old peninsula"!

The whole scene is a mockery of the classical. Odysseus is an "old puritan" who clenches his jaws disapprovingly in a way Achilles can't abide. Diomedes, a blue-eyed, blank-faced hero, understands nothing he can't see in front of his nose. (Yet both are right and Achilles is grossly deluded—Penthesilea is coming to destroy him. Yet both are thick-skinned practical types and Achilles is right—Penthesilea loves him madly.) When Odysseus asks if Achilles is a madman, does he think he can drop the Trojan War just like that, "like a child a toy / because another bright thing's caught its eye," Achilles' answer is:

> If Dardanusburg, Laertides,
> sank from sight, in its place the waters,
> blue-hued, of a lake; if in the night
> moon-gray fishermen tied their skiffs up
> to the weathercocks of Troy; if a pikefish ruled
> in Priam's palace, rats or otters hugged
> in Helen's bed,

he wouldn't give a damn. *This* Achilles doesn't give a damn about the Trojan War, after he has been charmed by Penthesilea ("half Grace, half Fury") and says so, but in a language of enchantment that turns Troy into a fairy tale. And yet the play isn't a burlesque or a fairy tale but a tragedy, though a very strange one.

In the long fifteenth scene, in which Penthesilea instructs Achilles in Amazonianism, he responds with civilized horror to its mastectomical rite ("this monstrous myth") with ill-concealed amusement to its progenitive. His attitude toward Penthesilea's beliefs is one of sophisticated irony; he is no mythic figure encountering another. Nor is she—the last word I would apply to the play is barbaric or primitive. In the opening scenes each is mad to conquer the other. But her needing to conquer him in battle before she can embrace him as a lover, which, he says in scene 21, "for her is a religious / thing," for him is some "freakish notion that she's got." All this mocks the classical. The mockery sometimes borders on the grotesque, as in the case of Achilles' calling Greece your old peninsula. Goethe said, very hostilely, that "the tragedy verges on the highly comical in some places," citing as an example the passage in scene 15 in which Penthesilea assures Achilles that though she has only one breast, he won't find that she is deficient in feelings of love, for they "all escaped from right to left and there / they live the nearer to my heart." This is more grotesque than comical. It is grotesque, I think, because the mythic is being treated unmythically, with a modernizing literalness. The *whole* play is touched with grotesquerie because a classical myth, wrenched around so that Penthesilea kills Achilles, is being treated unclassically—anticlassically—yet still tragically. Kleist modernizes. But this is poles apart from the kind of clever modernizing of a classical story which is usually so much shallower than the original.

The theme of *Penthesilea* is war and love, war as love and love as war. There is no plot; Greeks and Amazons attack and counterattack from beginning to end. The play drives breathlessly, with few respites, whipped on by its furious verse. The dominant mood, or voice, is a tempestuous-blazing one (thunder and lightning) interrupted by a tender, melting one. There is about as much war in this play, I suppose, as the theater has ever seen—or rather heard, for most of the fighting is reported from a hilltop (the Homeric teichoscopy: "looking from the walls" of Troy). Amazons, the Trojan War, Achilles and Odysseus, teichoscopy, even a fair number of traditional epic similes (as distinguished from Kleist's own long-drawn-out, often tortuous and tortured metaphors)— and yet *Penthesilea* isn't at all epical, either in style or substance. Kleist didn't make that mistake again. In place of the epical there is the hyperbolical, whose excessiveness and extravagance lead the attention away from the bounded external scene of action inward into a world of unbounded feeling. Penthesilea galloping hard to catch Achilles in scene 3 is described as follows:

> See how between her thighs she hotly hugs
> her tiger horse's trunk! How, leaning forward
> all along his mane, she drinks the opposing
> wind with thirsty gulps! She flies as if
> a bowstring shot her, Numidian arrows don't
> fly quicker! In the rear her panting army
> trails along like winded mongrels when the
> mastiff goes all out! Her helmet plume
> has trouble keeping up with her!

xl

This isn't so much action as feeling, the love and violence, tenderness and aggression, submissiveness and domineeringness which are tragically confused inside the breast of the Amazonian queen. And the hyperbole in the last sentence, dropping all pretense of describing actual movement, is a kind of joke.

Kleist's gigantism in this work is the gigantism of feelings, of dreams, of nightmares. For where is all this taking place? Not in Greece (Homeric or Euripidean or whatever), not in Prussia (though there is a Prussian touch to Odysseus and Diomedes), and surely not just on the printed page—but in the soul. Coleridge has a scintillating sentence in the *Biographia Literaria* about "the madness prepense of Pseudo-poesy, or the startling *hysteric* of weakness over-exerting itself." Is the "madness" of *Penthesilea,* the fury and the exaltation—the furious exaltation—prepensive, forced, false? Only a complete lack of sympathy with the play, with Kleist, would find it so. No, the poetry is not pseudo. There is overexertion of language, to be sure, but not because of weakness straining for effect. The verse makes inordinate efforts to reach an inordinate expressiveness of emotion, the strain is sometimes too much for it, and it becomes entangled in itself—for example, the passage in the last scene comparing Penthesilea's tear to a firebell, or the speech in which she commits suicide by heartbreak. But in general the inordinancy, the hyperbolicalness, is proper to the poetry, for it is a means for defining Penthesilea and her tragedy. As Prothoe says to her in scene 14 when she sings her wild aria of triumph under the delusion she has beaten Achilles:

> Joy's just as bad as grief for you, I see,
> you're driven raving mad by both of them.

Like Alcmene, like all Kleist's splendid women, Penthesilea possesses sexual charm. But unlike Alcmene's innocent love for her husband, Penthesilea's passion for Achilles isn't innocent. Her ambition to conquer him as a soldier is mixed up with her passion to conquer him as a woman, until the confusion culminates in grotesque tragedy. Achilles, using a metaphor Kleist already used in *Duke Guiscard,* calls war with the Amazons the "bed of battle." Used thus about a war with women, the metaphor of war as love is more pointed, and he elaborates it at length in a brilliant passage (scene 4). For Achilles the metaphor is a metaphor and not a confusion of emotions. He means to "marry" her and conduct her in a "bridal" procession "through the streets of Troy—feet first." But when Achilles comes to recognize that he is in love with Penthesilea, he makes up his mind at once to surrender to her and let himself be carried to Themiscyra as her prisoner (scene 21). Love-passion expels the war-passion.

For an orthodox Amazon (if I may be permitted the adjective), of course there can be no question of the lover displacing the warrior; that would spell the end of Amazonianism. The Amazons select prisoners to bring home as studs, then send them away when they have served their purpose—though "many a heart heaves dismally" and there is even some murmuring against the great Foundress of their race, Tanaïs. Penthesilea, however, is a heretic, a rebel. For her, too, war is love, but not only metaphorically:

> This steel I have here,
> comrades, with the softest hug (since our
> hugging must be done with steel), this
> steel shall draw him down onto my bosom, with
> no pain.   (scene 5)

She must hug Achilles, as an Amazon, with steel, but it will be the softest kind of hug and he shan't suffer any pain. Lover and warrior are confused. Penthesilea is tormented by heretical tendencies she can't understand, can't reconcile with her being an Amazon. In the same fifth scene she had said:

> I'll see him dust
> I kick through, high and mighty Greek, who on
> this glorious battle day confuses and
> distracts, as never was the case with me
> before, the martial exultation of my blood.
> Is that the conqueror, the all-feared
> she, the proud Queen of the Amazons,
> whom I see mirrored there in his bronze breast-
> plate when we meet face to face? Oh,
> how the gods all hate me! Don't I feel—
> even as the Greek troops break and run
> on every side before me—*crippled* at the sight
> of this one hero, pierced within
> my inmost being, I myself the beaten
> and defeated one?

By arousing a distracting emotion in her, Achilles lames her martial strength. This is before Achilles defeats her in battle. When he does, she cries feebly but furiously to set the dogs and elephants on him, and she also complains pathetically that he should have smashed her in the breast the way he did: if a bear came toward her feeling as she feels for Achilles, she would kneel down at its feet, she would stroke a panther's fur. At the end, when he does indeed come toward her feeling for her as she feels for him, her confusion of feelings has become too great, passing over into frenzy, and she slaughters him.

Penthesilea is a heretic because she feels personal, elective love for Achilles instead of obeying the impersonal biological drive which the Amazons satisfy in their ritual orgies. But her personal love is adulterated with the lust for conquering him and for the fame of such a conquest. Although she inveighs against her people for rescuing her from Achilles, she is never ready to surrender completely and go with him to Phthia, as in the end he is ready to go with her to Themiscyra. Like *Amphitryon, Penthesilea* is a play that swims in sexual feeling—in lust, it is sometimes said, because of the raging love-as-war encounters between the Greek hero and the Amazon heroine, ending in anthropophagy. But Penthesilea's true sexual note is the nightingale's pipe, not the eagle's scream:

> You thought
> the nightingale that haunts Diana's temple
> bore her in her nest. The oak tree
> rocked her in its top, she piped and sang
> and sang and piped through the silent night
> so that the traveler, arrested, felt,
> far off, his heart swell with emotion.   (scene 23)

In scene 15, thinking Achilles her prisoner, she is not all the greedy amorist but a businesslike commander who cautions him that all love must be postponed and he must remain with the other prisoners until she has led her army home to Themiscyra. The real lust in the play is the lust for conquest, for victorious possession. The deluded Penthesilea, reveling in her supposed victory over Achilles, asks rhetorically if it is really Achilles she has beaten, and when Prothoe assures her that is so, she exclaims:

> Very well—
> then with this kiss I greet you, the most
> *unbridled* of all men, now mine! Young
> god of war, it's me whom you belong
> to; and when people ask you, say *my* name.   (scene 15)

She has put a bridle on the most untamed man of all.

It is Penthesilea's baffled confusion of desires—warrior's with woman's—which leads to the murdering act of love by which she destroys the Greek. The old rationalistic psychology placed love and gentleness, hatred and violence, quite logically, at opposite ends of the moral-emotional scale; but love and hate jostle side by side, are mixed in confusion in Kleist. Michael Kohlhaas is "one of the most upright, and at the same time one of the most terrible, men of his day." The Marquise of O——'s family have no fear the Count F—— would do anything not "in keeping with all those superior qualities he had demonstrated on the night the Russians stormed the fortress." Well, on that night Count F—— had also raped the Marquise, who lay helpless in a swoon. One of the greatest modern psychologists, later in the century, said: "Alas, whoever knows the heart will guess how poor, stupid, helpless, arrogant, blundering, more apt to destroy than to save is even the best and profoundest love" (Nietzsche, in *Beyond Good and Evil*). In Dostoyevsky's comic (comic?) short novel *The Eternal Husband,* of an unsurpassed moral-psychological acuteness, the eternal cuckold Pavel Pavlovitch Trusotsky, who so much admires and loves and hates the man who betrayed him with his wife, nurses the charming, intelligent man-of-the-world Velchaninov through a crisis in his illness and tries to murder him, all in the same night; Trusotsky—that underground creature, that worm (as Velchaninov thought him)—is the moral hero of the story.

Penthesilea's being awakened to what she had done leads from horror to pity and death. Does she reach any kind of tragic self-understanding? When she "abjures the law of our women" at the end of the play, the law of the Amazon state, she abjures love as conquest, as ambition, as impersonal sexual drive. In favor of what does she abjure it? A tender kiss "and nothing more," bestowed on Achilles' corpse. In a most extraordinary fashion, grotesquely joking and not joking, she calls her tearing his white flesh with her teeth an error.

> A kiss, a bite—how cheek by jowl
> they are, and when you love straight from the heart
> the greedy mouth so easily mistakes
> one for the other[12]. . . .
> > It was a slip—
> I swear it by Diana—of the tongue, no more,
> because I am remiss and fail to stand

---

12.   Küsse, Bisse,
  Das reimt sich, und wer recht von Herzen liebt,
  Kann schon das eine für das andre greifen.

guard over my rash mouth the way
I should. But now I say it to you as
I meant it, unmistakably.

And then she kisses the mangled body chastely.

Penthesilea is driven from within. She delivers her long speeches as if with half-closed eyes; the words, fired off from inside her, hardly engage with an interlocutor. There is a chill in the play, in spite of the hot language, in spite of Penthesilea's charm—the chill of isolation. Kleist said about the play that it had in it "all the grubbiness and all the brightness of my soul, both." Penthesilea's tragedy is his: the tragedy of an ingenuous and ardent spirit, at odds with itself and its world, straining desperately, bewildered, angry, violent. She is not noble, classical. A beautiful woman, she is clumsy, even grotesque, as she lurches this way and that in her confusion of soul—but so touching, so tragic.

> *His sword's still at his side: in pieces.*
> *Not dead but flattened, on his back he lies*
> *With all the enemies of Brandenburg, down in*
> *the dust.*
> Brecht, *On Kleist's "Prince of Homburg."*

With Kleist's last play, *The Prince of Homburg,* we seem to leave behind the interior worlds of *Amphitryon* and *Penthesilea* to tread the ground of his own Prussia. We are indeed in Prussia—not the historical Prussia, however, but a legendary one. For though the play concerns an actual battle which was crucial to the growth of Prussian power—the Great Elector's victory over the Swedish invader at Fehrbellin, to the northwest of Berlin, in 1675—the story of the Landgrave of Hesse-Homburg's disobedience to orders during the battle was a patriotic legend which the poet altered drastically to suit his own purposes. "The Prussia of this play," writes Walter Silz, "is not a reality of 1675, nor of 1810, but a poetic legend of the past and a brave dream of the future; there was no basis in fact at either date for Natalie's picture of Prussia's coming splendor [V.1]; this is genuine prophecy, a *credo quia impossible.*"[13] Homburg is as much of a troubled spirit as Alcmene and Penthesilea. His self-contention is played out in a story world of the soul, too, but also in response to the problems and demands of political-social circumstances,

13. *Heinrich von Kleist: Studies in His Works and Literary Characters,* 1961.

and especially in response to the problem of authority. Kleist is a modern writer and authority in his work is always problematic.

Kleist's imagination is a "psychoanalytic" one—an imagination concerned with the play between surface and depth, conscious and unconscious, the deliberative-rational and the spontaneous-intuitive, but perhaps nowhere is it more so than in *The Prince of Homburg*. The drama opens brilliantly, on a castle garden glittering in the moonlight and in its midst a dreaming Prince. The note sounded at once is one of gaiety, amused wonder tinged with mockery of the sonambulist weaving a victor's crown for himself before there has been a victory. Like Penthesilea (and like his author), Homburg is ardent and ingenuous, and therefore vulnerable and a little clumsy. A more adept man would have more self-knowledge; he would never make a spectacle of himself by unconsciously exposing before the whole court how much he thirsts for fame. When the Elector indulges in a bit of court frivolity and allows himself his "little joke" with Homburg, it not only exposes further the latter's burning desire for personal glory, but something else which the Prince is not aware of, that he has fallen in love with Princess Natalie. Now gaiety and amusement turn into embarrassment before this public exhibition of hidden desires, the Elector hurriedly retreats into the castle, and as he does so he admonishes Homburg: "Such things are never won in dreams!"

The Elector admonishes him again the next morning, before the battle: he must behave himself and take care not to cost him a third, absolutely essential victory, after having cost him two already by his irresponsible conduct at the Rhine. The victory is gained at Fehrbellin, but Homburg's attacking before he is ordered to, impulsively, in a fever of excitement and ambition, makes it a less complete one than the Elector's strategy had aimed at. However, because the poet's exposition of the tactical situation is very clear it is possible to judge it for oneself, and one may just as well conclude that there might have been no victory at all if Homburg had not violated orders and charged. The Elector denies this possibility in his debate with Kottwitz in the last act: but then why does he have Homburg proclaimed the victor of the day from the pulpit of the church at the victory service? However this may be, there is no doubt that Homburg is guilty of reckless insubordination, and the Elector has him court-martialed and sentenced to death. Homburg, we see, is a man under correction, and the series of his admonishments by the highest authority concludes with nothing less than a death sentence.

When the Elector orders Homburg locked up and his head forfeit, in a scene of brilliant drama (II.10), Homburg's dream of glory, which he thinks has just been fulfilled, explodes in his face. Now it is a different kind of dream he finds himself in. "Am I dreaming?" he asks, on his sword's being demanded from him. To the very engaging, but rash and self-indulgent dreamer, the harsh reality of judgment seems a dream. Petulantly he turns to the Elector:

> My cousin
> Frederick has in mind to play the Brutus
> with me, as it seems, and sees the scene
> already sketched on canvas: himself erect
> on the curule seat, before him on
> the table the Articles of War of Brandenburg,
> and in the foreground all the Swedish flags.

Homburg doesn't deny he is at fault, but his fault is trivial, a flaw, he calls it later, in the jewel of victory he presented the Elector which it would need a magnifying glass to detect. The issue of law, of justice, for him, is trivial. So should it be for the Elector; but the latter is "playing" Brutus. Well, he won't play along with him, he is not the kind of "son who looks up in awed wonder" at the father-god "from underneath the ax," subserviently consenting to his own death.

> My heart is German, the old stamp of German,
> and what it understands is magnanimity
> and love; and if he acts the antique Roman
> toward me now, inflexible as marble,
> well, I pity him, I do indeed!

But the last line, which makes so weak a conclusion to his big declaration, betrays the subservient son. He is a plant, he tells Hohenzollern, which the Elector nursed with his own hands: it isn't possible he should destroy his own nursling "because it bloomed / a little hastily, a little too exuberantly." What counts first for Homburg is "magnanimity and love," the readiness to take circumstances into account, to understand, to sympathize—German heart rather than Roman marble. That is an issue, too, in the drama; but as Homburg raises it, it is not a real one. What *he* wants, and expects, is to be let off, excused his high-handed, irresponsible conduct by a paternal Elector. As Professor Samuel writes: "He does not ask of the Elector justice ... but *Gnade,* clemency and mercy in the religious sense, emanating naturally from someone who is Father, the ultimate authority and God at the same time."

It costs Hohenzollern some trouble to disabuse his friend of his naive understanding of the Elector's intentions. And when he succeeds, Homburg breaks down completely. In his interview with the Electress, he grovels in dreadful terror of death before her and Princess Natalie. Thinking his claim on Natalie's love (by interfering with the Elector's plan to marry her to the Swedish king) is the reason why the Brandenburg ruler will not pardon him, he surrenders it in shameless haste. At this point we are confronted with a hero who is positively vile. The Dostoyevskian man is making his appearance. Homburg suffers a complete collapse when his trust in the benevolence of ultimate authority fails him. That has its psychological side: he is a spoiled Prince who has never been called to account before. The officer who tried to do that—to prevent the unauthorized charge by demanding Homburg's sword from him—was stripped of his sword and arrested on the spot by a not especially magnanimous commander. But when it is done to him it is an outrage, to be explained by heartless machinations on the part of an Elector who has suddenly turned ignoble and vicious.

There is another side to Homburg's collapse, however, a metaphysical side: he is devastated by the realization that he is a man under judgment, that men are judged for what they do. He not only shivers in the cold of imminent death, but in the universal air of judgment. And that unmans him. But then the new man is born, slowly, out of the Elector's giving over to him, after Natalie's intercession, the decision as to whether he has been treated unjustly or not. The heart, the heart, is what Homburg pleads; but when he is finally confronted with the reality of law by being asked to judge himself, there is no doubt of the outcome, which is why Natalie blanches on hearing the contents of the Elector's letter. Homburg must judge himself; *he* is the ultimate authority, not Electors of Brandenburg. And he finds against himself. There *is* a highest authority, a Superior Court, higher than electors and kings, it lies in each man's bosom.

Is the Elector who is thus able to bring the inglorious Prince into the path of manhood and glory a great and wise monarch? He may be a great one, he is not a wise one. "My son," said Gustav Adolphus' wise chancellor Axel Oxenstierna, "with how little wisdom the world is governed." This is no less true of the Elector's government. The Frederick William of Kleist's play isn't an unkind man, and certainly he is no tyrant. He conducts himself with dignity, usually. The playwright treats him respectfully at all times. But he shows himself to be no wiser than the next man. The smile with which the play begins becomes a giggle when the Elector allows himself his fun with Homburg. His joke feeds Homburg's dream, his preoccupation with himself and his own feelings and ambitions. Homburg is a dreamer by nature. But the Elector must bear a large share of the responsibility for the fact that the Prince doesn't really awaken from this dream until his arrest. And this responsibility carries with it a share in the responsibility for Homburg's disobedience—as Hohenzollern dares to tell the Elector (V.5). In the remarkable briefing scene, with its shuttling back and forth of perspective between the Field Marshal dictating orders to his officers and the Electress and the Princess having breakfast just before departing, between the army and the court, the public realm and a more private realm, external world and interior self (II.5),[14] Homburg's attention is jerked this way and that way until he understands little more of what he is supposed to do than that at some point he must sound the trumpets and attack. (Of course, this is what the heedless Prince is most inclined to understand! Is it ever possible to disentangle the intricate knot which the responsible subjective will makes with the circumstances imposed on it from the outside?) What really claims his attention is the discovery that the glove tucked in his doublet is Princess Natalie's; it is Fortune's "pledge" to him that his dream of love and glory is moving toward fulfillment. Just before the battle starts he asks Hohenzollern to remind him of his orders, which the Count does. But a stage direction tells us that Homburg "stares down dreamily" while Hohenzollern is speaking (II.2). The dream goes on.

So there are questions surrounding Homburg's insubordination, when its circumstances are looked into, circumstances in which the Elector himself figures importantly. Questionable, too, is the way in which the Elector angrily passes a sentence of death on "whichever officer it was who led the cavalry" in the attack. Evidently he has heard the rumor that the Prince's fall from his horse took him out of the action, though he must still reassure himself it wasn't "Cousin Homburg" who was in command. When the latter enters loaded down with captured Swedish flags and the Elector finds out his mistake, it is too late to retreat—too late, that is, for a monarch too embarrassed and afraid to confess his justice is not impartial: which is to say, the usual, the ordinary kind of monarch (and man).

Subsequently, however, the Elector is appalled to learn from Natalie

---

14. To be compared with the ironical mingling of voices and perspectives in the scene of the agricultural show in *Madame Bovary*. It is a modern sensibility, of course, which is so conscious of perspective.

about Homburg's collapse. In tears, she accuses his justice of having broken a brave man's spirit. She makes sublimity a charge against him:

> To crown his head because he conquered, then
> cut off his head— . . . Dear uncle,
> that would be an action *so* sublime
> one would almost have to call it cruel, inhuman. (IV.1)

This is not without its humor, in the strange Kleistian way. Sublimity is a fault; it is too lofty, reaching up to the heavens in its claim, too inhuman, too classical. We are in the nineteenth century; to be classical is to be cruel, presumptuous. And indeed it is. How dare the Elector condemn another man to death, seeing that it would need a god to weigh properly all the circumstances leading up to and surrounding a human act? Hohenzollern shows that the Elector's joke was responsible for Homburg's crime, the Elector retorts that Hohenzollern was responsible for the joke by having called him down into the garden in the first place (V.5)—we glimpse an infinity here. But this Elector makes no claim to being a god able to survey infinity: hastily he gives over the responsibility for judging Homburg to Homburg himself. And Homburg, accepting it, judges himself guilty in spite of all the circumstances. For to be human, to be free, is to be responsible in spite of circumstances.

Homburg's accepting the responsibility for his insubordinate action doesn't settle the issue of law versus impulse. In his debate with the Elector, Kottwitz defends "quick-acting instinct" and "spontaneous impulse" against mechanical obedience; he makes a strong case, despite some bad arguments. But the "heart," or vital impulse, must never be an excuse for contempt of the law, contempt of reason. The drama's truth is double. Hailed at the end of the play as the one who conquered gloriously at Fehrbellin, Homburg is also a commander guilty of gross insubordination. The drama holds another double truth as well, related but different: Homburg is a brave man and a wretch. With this truth he gives the lie to Prussia. As Brecht's poem puts it, so wittily: his sword's still at the hero's side, only in pieces; victorious yet flattened, he isn't prancing in heartless glory high up on a marble monument but has crossed the lines to join the enemies of Brandenburg and Prussianism "down in the dust."

There is one false note at the end. It isn't, as it is often said, the Elector's "cruelty" in going through the motions of executing the Prince after he has decided to pardon him. To read the ending so is to read the play as a novel. As a masterpiece of theatricality as well as dramaturgy,

1

the end scene is necessary to bring the play around to its starting point. As a dramatic spectacle, we don't see cruelty but a crescendo of light and glory. No, the false note is Homburg's *wanting* (as Hohenzollern says) to die so as "to glorify, / before the eyes of the whole army, the sacred / rule of war against which [he] offended." This is the subservient son of Prussia speaking obsequiously—speaking in defense of just what the young Kleist denounced when he quit the army. The rule of obedience, and the Elector's authority, aren't absolute but conditional. That is just what the play dramatizes. And indeed what armies prize in soldiers, in the great confusion of war, isn't blind obedience but initiative and judgment (as Kottwitz argues). The sacred obligation laid on all those aspiring to be human, free, is to judge themselves and to judge for themselves. In the twentieth century, the "sacred rule" of obedience has helped to promote massacres and exterminations, and afterward to exonerate the criminals.

The play closes as it opens, on the inward-turned man, who meanwhile has traversed the world of war and history, crime and punishment. In his soliloquy he turns inward to the dream of death and immortal life, not glory and love. He is awakened from this dream, too, into a reality which is the fulfillment of his first dream. But not really. For meanwhile he has traversed death and *all* is a dream:

HOMBURG: No, it's a dream! Do say—
   is it a dream?
KOTTWITZ: A dream, what else? (V.11)

How light the play is, how serious, how swift! It is one of the most original works of the modern theater, as Kleist is one of the most original writers of the modern world.

A Note about the Translation

I have tried in these translations to put Kleist's plays into living English—into "the real language of men," in Wordsworth's words, meaning by real language, as Wordsworth's own example testifies, not only the spoken language of spontaneous feeling but also the literary language of thought and consideration. Kleist's German is vigorous and, in spite of an idiosyncratic syntax, generally clear. I have tried to render it in English that is vigorous and clear, an English that keeps to Kleist and at the same time keeps faith with English. From a certain point of view, it is impossible to be true to the words of a foreign language and the words of one's own language, at the same time. But that can never be the point of view of a translator, who must always be on the side of man as man and not of German man or French man or American man.

My aim being to render Kleist's plays in living English, I have allowed myself a certain latitude of diction and syntax—all the more readily as Kleist himself is no stickler for decorum and ranges freely from colloquial to formal, low to lofty in his pursuit of expressiveness. But I don't believe this latitude makes the translations free—my object was to be neither free nor literal but, as far as I was able, true.

But I have not tried to keep to Kleist's blank verse. On the contrary. The old dramatic blank verse is no longer able to speak with the accents of living English; its effect is to make language unreal. My struggle has been to break out of the dead man's grip of blank verse. I have counted stressed syllables but not unstressed ones, allowing myself as many or as few of the latter as sounded right. Five seemed a convenient number of stresses, but there are any number of four-stress and six-stress lines. The line is no longer the essential, integral line of blank verse, so the number of stresses is only a convenience and the first letter of the line isn't capitalized. The sentence is what is essential, not the line. The movement aimed at is a rhythmical not a metrical one. The effect of all this is to shift the verse over in the direction of prose.

I have had the assistance of earlier translations of Kleist's plays. As all translators know, that is a very valuable assistance, even though one aims at different or better work.

More than two decades ago I translated Kleist's tales under the title of *The Marquise of O—— & Other Stories.* I always had in mind to follow this up by translating a selection of his plays. I am glad to have been able to do so.

I should like to thank Paula Fox and Gunther Stuhlmann for the generous interest they took in this work and the help they gave, and Ellen Graham of the Yale University Press for her strong encouragement and support.

Amphitryon
A Comedy after Molière

Cast of Characters

Jupiter (in the shape of Amphitryon)
Mercury (in the shape of Sosia)
Amphitryon, Commander-in-Chief of the Thebans
Sosia, his servant
Alcmene, wife to Amphitryon
Charis, wife to Sosia
Generals
Colonels

Scene: Before the Palace of Amphitryon in Thebes

ACT I

Night

SCENE I

Enter Sosia, with a lantern.

SOSIA. Hello there, who's that sneaking through the dark?
Hello!—If day would only break I'd like
it better, the night is—What was that! A friend,
I'm a friend, good sirs, a fellow traveler on
this road! You've run into the most honest
man the sun did ever shine on—
or rather I should say the moon. Scoundrels
they must be, I'm sure, but craven ones,
without the stomach to attack me openly—
or else it was the night wind in the leaves.
In these mountains every sound's a shriek.
Careful, now, don't rush! But if I don't
soon bump my head against Thebes' walls, I'll bump
my way straight down to Hell. Damnation take it!
My master could have found some other way
to test my mettle, see how brave I am.
The whole world says he is a famous man,
with honors heaped on him, but still, to send
me out into the black of night was not
much better than a dirty trick. Some charity
on his part, a show of some consideration,
would please me quite as much as all those armored
virtues with which he splits the foeman's ranks.
Sosia, he said, my servant, I
have work for you—off to Thebes at once
and there proclaim the victory I've won
and tell my tender mistress the good news:
she may expect me soon.—And if the morning
wasn't time enough for that, let me
be changed into a horse, a saddled one!
But look, that's our house there, isn't it?
You've made it home, dear Sosia, hurrah,

3

may your enemies be pardoned, every one!
And now it's time, my friend, to give some thought
to your commission. You will be conducted,
very ceremoniously, into
the presence of Princess Alcmene, where
you are expected to deliver, with oratorical
finesse, a full account of the victory
Amphitryon has won the Fatherland.—But how
the devil can I do that if I never saw
the battle? Damn. I wish now I had dared
to sneak a look, now and then, out
of the tent when the two armies were going at each other
hand to hand. Oh well! I'll talk of cut
and thrust and bowshot and carry the whole thing
off as confidently as many another one
who never heard an arrow whistle.—Wait,
though: if you practiced up your part beforehand,
what do you think? Right, Sosia, what a good idea!
We'll do it now. The audience chamber, let
it be right here, and let this lantern be
Alcmene, seated on her throne.
                    (*Sets the lantern on the ground.*)
                    "Serenest
Majesty, I come to you from my
great Lord Amphitryon and your most noble
spouse, bearing the glad news that victory
over the Athenians is his."—A good
beginning, that!—"*My dearest Sosia,
how truly overjoyed I am to see
you once again.*"—"Your graciousness, good Lady,
makes me blush for modesty, not puffs me up
with pride, as I am sure would be the case
with any other man."—Not bad,
either, that, though I'm the one to say it!
—"*And how is he, the treasure of my soul,
Amphitryon?*"—"In one word, gracious Lady:
as any brave man is, upon the field
of honor!"—What a fellow I am, hear
my silver tongue!—"*And when may I expect
him home?*"—"No later, surely, than his duties

4

give him leave, though not so soon perhaps
as he might wish."—Did you hear that, by god!—
*"And was there nothing else he said to tell
me, my good Sosia?"*—"He speaks in deeds,
not words, and the whole world trembles at
his name."—A plague on me if I know where
I get my wit!—*You say the Athenians are
retreating, do you?"*—"Yes, they are. Labdacus,
their commander, has been killed. Pharissa's
stormed and you can hear our victory cry
wherever there are mountains to echo it."
—*"Oh dearest Sosia, I entreat you, tell
me the whole story, do, omitting nothing!"*
—"I'm more than willing, my dear Lady, to oblige
you. For indeed I flatter myself that I
am able to tell you everything there is
to tell about our victory. Be
so good, then, to imagine here (*pointing the places out upon his palm*)
    Pharissa—
which is a city, as I'm sure you know,
not to exaggerate, as big around
as, *praeter propter,*[1] Thebes, unless it's bigger.
Here the river is. Our men in battle
order on a hilltop here, and in the valley
there the enemy, great crowds of him—
who, after sending up a vow to Heaven
that shakes the skies and issuing the needful
orders, came roaring like a torrent at us! We,
however, no less brave, point out his way
back home again to him, as in a moment
you will hear. First he met our vanguard,
here—it fled. Then drove against our archers
there—they ran. Bold as he can be
now, he turned against our slingers drawn up
in a body—they decamped, and when
he came on recklessly against our main
corps, they all made a rush"—no, wait! The part

---

1. *Praetor propter:* more or less.

about the main corps, it's not right.—I thought
I heard a noise from over there.

SCENE 2

*Enter Mercury (in the shape of Sosia), coming out of
Amphitryon's house.*

MERCURY (*aside*).

        If I
don't get that intruding jackass out of here
right now, then by the Styx the joy that Zeus
Olympian came down today to have
a taste of in Alcmene's arms by putting on
the shape of her Amphitryon is looking
very chancy.

SOSIA (*failing to notice Mercury*).

      It was nothing, no
cause for alarm. But no adventures, please—
I'll go indoors at once and discharge my
commission.

MERCURY (*aside*).

      I will stop you doing that,
my friend, or else you've found the way to best
me, Mercury.

SOSIA.   But this night has no end!
If I've not been five hours on the road,
and the Theban dial don't prove it, I'll shoot
the damn thing off its tower piece by piece.
I do believe my master, drunk on victory,
mistook the evening for the dawn, or else
high living Phoebus hugs his pillow still
after staring too deep into bottles the whole
night.

MERCURY. Just hear how disrespectfully
that rascal talks about us gods! But wait—
this arm of mine will soon teach him respect.

SOSIA. (*catching sight of Mercury*).

You spirits of the night, I'm lost! A robber's
prowling around the house who's sure to end

6

up on the gallows when the time comes.—I
must play it bold and brave and confident.
(*Whistles.*)
MERCURY (*aloud*).
What clown is that who takes the liberty,
as if this was his home, to whistle me
an earful of such noise? I wonder if
my stick should also dance to it—on him?
SOSIA. That one's no friend of music, it appears.
MERCURY. A whole week now I've not found anybody
to break the bones of. Stiff, my arm feels, from
disuse, and a hump as big as yours is just
what I've been looking for to practice on.
SOSIA. Devil, who's responsible for him!
I'm gripped by such a deathly fear it stops
my breath. If Hell itself had vomited
him out in front of me, I'd not be so
dumbfounded. Maybe, though, that bumpkin feels
the way I do and plays the fire-eater
just to scare me off. Then just a moment,
fellow, I can do the same. And if
I'm here alone, so's he; if I've just got
two fists, I don't think he's got more;
and if luck goes against me, well,
I have a safe line of retreat behind
me there. So forward march!
MERCURY (*blocking his way*).
                  Halt! Who goes there?
SOSIA. Me.
MERCURY. Me? What me, man?
SOSIA.   Me myself,
sir, if you please, who's got as much right as another
to walk this road toll free.—Courage, Sosia!
MERCURY. Halt! You don't get off so easily.
What's your position?
SOSIA.   My position? Standing
here in front of you, on two feet,
as you see.
MERCURY.   Master, are you, or a menial,
is what I want to know.

SOSIA.   I'm a master or a menial,
    either, it all depends on how you look at it.
MERCURY. Oh good, oh very good!—*I* don't think
    I care for you.
SOSIA.   That desolates me, I
    am sure.
MERCURY. Now traitor, listen here: I want
    to know, you good-for-nothing corner loafer,
    street dust stirrer, who you are, where
    you are coming from and going to, and what
    you think you're doing skulking around this gate?
SOSIA. The only answer I can give to all
    that is, I am a man, I came
    from over there, I'm going this way
    here, and I foresee my being drawn
    into a long drawn out affair.
MERCURY. Such a clever fellow I perceive
    you are, already looking how to get
    around me. Yet I'm inclined to pursue the acquaintance
    we've struck up a little further, and by way
    of introduction to our nearer interest
    in each other, I have in mind to smack
    you in the ear with this hand here.
SOSIA.   Smack me?
MERCURY. Smack you. [*Smacks him.*] There—now you've been spared
        the tortures
    of uncertainty. So what do you conclude
    from all of this?
SOSIA.   My goodness, what a heavy
    hand you hit with, friend!
MERCURY.   Just middle weight,
    that one. Sometimes I hit lots harder.
SOSIA.   If I
    were so inclined as you, we'd have a little
    set-to.
MERCURY. That would suit me fine. I do
    love the exertion.
SOSIA.   Urgent business
    elsewhere compels me to excuse myself, however.
                        (*Starts forward.*)

8

MERCURY (*blocking his way*).
  Where to?
SOSIA.   Now what the devil's that to you?
MERCURY. Let me repeat myself: I'd like to know
  just where you think you're going.
SOSIA.   Through that gate
  right there, which I expect to open when
  I knock. Now let me pass.
MERCURY.   If you have got
  the impudence to go and knock at that gate
  there, expect a hailstorm of hard blows
  around your head.
SOSIA.   What—I'm not allowed
  to enter my own house?
MERCURY.   Your own house?
  Repeat that, please.
SOSIA.   Yes, my own house.
MERCURY.   You claim
  you are a member of this house?
SOSIA.   And what
  is wrong with that? It's Lord Amphitryon's palace,
  isn't it?
MERCURY. It's Lord Amphitryon's palace?
  Yes, of course, you scoundrel, it's the palace
  of the General-in-Chief of Thebes. But what
  do you conclude from that?
SOSIA.   Conclude from that?
  Why, I conclude that I'm going straight
  into that palace—I'm his servant.
MERCURY.   Servant?
SOSIA.   Yes,
  his servant.
MERCURY.   You?
SOSIA.   Yes, me.
MERCURY.   The servant
  of Amphitryon?
SOSIA.   The servant of the General-
  in-Chief of Thebes, Amphitryon.
MERCURY.   And the name
  you bear is—?

SOSIA.   Sosia.

MERCURY.   Sosia?

SOSIA.   Yes.

MERCURY.   I'll break
every bone you've got, you hear?

SOSIA.   Have you
gone mad?

MERCURY.   Who gave you any right, you brazen
rogue, to take the name of Sosia for
yourself?

SOSIA.   I never took it, it was given
me. My father is the one must answer
for it.

MERCURY. Whoever heard of such effrontery?
You dare to tell me to my face, without
a blush, that you are Sosia?

SOSIA.   Yes, I do.
And for the best of reasons, too: because
the gods would have it so; because it's quite
beyond my power to quarrel with them over
who I am and try to be somebody
else; because it is my fate to be
myself, the servant of Amphitryon,
though I would like it ten times better if
I could have been Amphitryon himself,
his brother-in-law or cousin.

MERCURY.   Patience, and I'll see
what I can do to metamorphose you.

SOSIA. Help, citizens! Help, Thebans! There are murderers
and thieves!

MERCURY.   How dare you scream like that, you good-
for-nothing fellow!

SOSIA.   What the devil! Beat
me up, you do, and I am not allowed
to cry for help?

MERCURY.   But don't you know it's nighttime,
people are in bed and the wife of Lord
Amphitryon, Alcmene, is fast asleep
inside the palace here?

SOSIA.   If I don't hope
  to see you hanged! I'll knuckle under, yes,
  because you have a club—I don't. All
  the same, it's not a brave heroic deed
  to deal out blows and never have to worry
  any will be dealt you back. I'll tell
  you my opinion: showing off your courage
  against those whom fate compels to keep theirs
  under wraps, is wrong.
MERCURY.   Don't wander
  from the point, please. Once again I ask: Who are
  you?
SOSIA *(aside)*.
    If I'm ever able to get shut of him,
  I'll spill the gods out half a bottle of red
  wine upon the ground.
MERCURY.   Are you still Sosia?
SOSIA. Let me go, I beg you. Your stick can make
  it so that I'm no more, but not that I'm
  not I, because I am. The only difference
  is that now I feel I'm Sosia-Who's-
  Been-Beaten.
MERCURY *(raising his stick)*
    Careful, cur, or I will stretch
  you out.
SOSIA.   No, don't! O won't you please stop hounding
  me?
MERCURY. Not until you stop—
SOSIA.   I'll stop, I'll stop!
  I'll not deny what you say any more,
  you're right, you're always right, whichever way
  you want it, that's the way it is.
MERCURY.   Are you
  still Sosia, then, you sneaking spy?
SOSIA.   Alas
  for me, now I am what you please. Order
  me to be whoever, and I am, your stick
  makes you the master of my life.
MERCURY.   You said your name
  was Sosia once?

SOSIA.   It's true that till today
  I had supposed there were some grounds for thinking
  so. But now the force of your close
  reasoning has quite persuaded me—
  I see I erred.
MERCURY.   *I* am the one whose name
  is Sosia.
SOSIA.   Sosia—you?
MERCURY.   Yes, me. And any
  one who thinks it calls for comment on his part
  had better watch his step—and this stick here.
SOSIA (*aside*).
  Eternal gods above! Do I now have
  to give up all claim to myself and let
  an imposter steal my name?
MERCURY.   You're muttering
  between your teeth, are you?
SOSIA.   Oh, nothing that
  might cause you to take umbrage, it's only
  that I beg you, in the name of Greece's gods
  who have dominion over both of us,
  to let me speak to you quite candidly
  for just a moment.
MERCURY.   Speak.
SOSIA.   But promise me
  your stick won't have a talking part in our
  dialogue, that it is truce between
  us.
MERCURY. I agree. We have a truce.
SOSIA.   Now tell
  me, please: your wild idea that you should do
  me out of my own name, without
  a blush—wherever did you get it from?
  I'd understand it if it was my cloak
  or supper—but my name! Can you put it on
  and wear it? Eat it? Drink it? Turn it into
  ready cash? So what good is your theft
  to you?
MERCURY. What's that! You have the impudence—?
SOSIA. Please, please, we have a truce!

MERCURY.   Unblushing scoundrel!
  Good-for-nothing wretch!
SOSIA.   I bear your curses
  meekly—violent *language* doesn't put
  a stop to conversation.
MERCURY.   Sosia,
  you say you're called?
SOSIA.   I do confess it, yes.
  A rumor that I heard—
MERCURY.   That's it! The truce
  is over. *I* will do the talking from now on again.
SOSIA. Oh, go to hell, why don't you? I can't simply
  wipe myself out of existence just to suit
  your whim, become another person—slough
  my own skin off and drape it around your shoulders.
  Since the world began, did you ever hear
  of such a thing? I wonder if I'm dreaming?
  If I overdid it with my regular
  refresher dose this morning? If I'm not
  in full possession of my wits? Didn't Lord
  Amphitryon dispatch me here to tell
  the Princess he's returning? Describe to her
  the battle that he fought and won and how
  Pharissa yielded? Isn't it the case
  I've just arrived? Don't I hold this lantern
  in my hand? And who was hanging around the palace
  gate but you—you who took your stick,
  when I went up to knock on the door,
  and beat me black and blue upon the shoulders,
  without mercy, saying to my face that you,
  not I, was servant to Amphitryon?
  All this, I feel, is too true, all
  too true—if only the great gods vouchsafed
  it was a fit of madness, nothing more!
MERCURY. Careful, cur, my anger's ready to rain
  down on you again like hailstones! Every
  thing you've just now said is true of me,
  exactly—except of course the part about
  the beating.

SOSIA.　　　　True of you? This lantern here,
　I swear by all the gods, is evidence—
MERCURY. You lie, you sneaking traitor, in your teeth.
　I am the one Amphitryon sent here.
　For yesterday the General-in-Chief
　of Thebes, still covered with the dust of deadly battle,
　while leaving Mars's temple after sacrificing
　to the god, charged me formally to make
　it known to all the city how his arms
　had won the day and how Labdacus,
　captain of the foe, had fallen by
　his hand. For I am Sosia, I will have
　you know, his servant, son of Davus, valiant
　shepherd of this country, Harpagon's my bother,
　he who died in foreign parts, and Charis
　is my wife, who drives me crazy with
　her freaks and fancies—Sosia, who sat
　in jail and had some fifty hard ones counted
　off on his backside not long ago
　for carrying honesty too far.
SOSIA (*aside*).
　He's right! Unless he's Sosia himself,
　he couldn't know the things he seems to know
　so well. A little bit of credit, oh
　dear me, he has to be allowed. Now that
　I look at him, moreover, I can see
　he has my shape and size and manner, and my
　own knavish look as well. By quizzing him
　I'll try to search this mystery out. (*Aloud.*) About
　the booty we collected from the Athenian
　camp—I'd like to hear from you how Lord
　Amphitryon thought to share it out and what
　he took for his own share.
MERCURY.　　　　　　His own share
　was the diadem of Lord Labdacus,
　discovered in that general's tent.
SOSIA.　　　　　　　The diadem—
　what did they do with it?

14

MERCURY.   Engraved Amphitryon's
  initial on its golden front in glittering
  strokes.

SOSIA.   And he is wearing it himself
  now, I suppose?

MERCURY.   It's for Alcmene. She
  shall wear it as an ornament around
  her breast, souvenir of victory.

SOSIA. And the present's being sent her from the camp?

MERCURY.   Inside
  a casket, all of gold, on which the coat
  of arms of Lord Amphitryon is stamped.

SOSIA (*aside*).
  There's not a thing he doesn't know, the devil
  take him! I'm beginning to have doubts about
  myself. Already he was Sosia thanks
  to his bold face and stick, but now he's got
  good reasons, too, for being him, which makes
  his case complete. Yet when I pinch myself
  I'd swear this flesh here is pure Sosia.
  —Oh what a fix to be in! Wait: the things
  I did when not a soul was by, which no
  one saw—those things no one can know unless
  he's really me the way that I am me.
  Good, I've got a question for him that'll throw a beam
  into this labyrinth. I'll catch him out, I will!
  Now we shall see. (*Aloud.*) When the Theban army battled
  the Athenians hand to hand, I'd like to know
  what you were up to, back among the tents,
  where you knew how to slink away to
  slyly?

MERCURY. From a ham—

SOSIA.   The devil
  must have—!

MERCURY.   —I discovered in the corner of a tent,
  I carved myself a juicy slice of meat,
  expertly drew the cork of two or three
  good bottles, and made things comfortable and cozy

for myself by way of antidote
to all the fighting going on outside.

SOSIA (*aside*).

That's it! I give up now! The earth can swallow
me here on this spot, I'll never mind.
Because, without the key that fits the locker
where the wine is kept, nobody drinks,
unless he's stumbled on it quite by accident,
inside a sack, as I did. (*Aloud.*) I can see
now, my old friend, that you make up the full
amount of Sosia that is needed on
this earth. Any more of him, I think,
would be an excess quantity. The last
thing I should wish to do is to obtrude myself
on anyone, gladly I give up
my place to you. Be so good, however,
as to tell me, since I am not the man
I thought I was, *who* I am, for surely,
you'll allow, some one or other I
must be?

MERCURY.   When I am finished being Sosia,
you may be him, it's quite all right with me,
I give you my consent. But while I'm him,
your neck's in danger if you have the impudence
to think you are.

SOSIA.   All right, all right!
My brain's all in a whirl. I see the shape
of things, even though I can't make head
or tail of them. However—this business has
to have an end some time, and the best way
I can see to end it is—to leave.
And so good-bye. (*Starts toward the house.*)

MERCURY (*pushing him back*).

            How's that, you gallows-bird!
I have to break your bones, do I? (*Beats him.*)

SOSIA.   Oh, you
just gods! Where is the care you should take
of innocence? My back won't heal for weeks,
not even if Amphitryon doesn't touch
his stick. O dear, oh dear! I'll shun this devil

16

and go back to camp, let the night gape black
as Hell itself!—Well, I have made a famous
embassy of it! I wonder how
your master's going to receive you, Sosia!
                    (*Exit.*)

SCENE 3

MERCURY. At last, thank God! Why didn't you go trotting
off lots sooner, you'd have saved yourself
a thumping. The scamp cares nothing for the honor
of being beaten by a god's good arm. I gave
it to him like a jailor, too, I did.
Well, that's the way it is. He's sinned enough,
god knows, and well deserved his punishment,
if not perhaps today. Then let it be
deducted from the bill he owes. If only
all the howling that he did, which sounded like
I was about to spit and roast him, has
not waked the lovers!—As I live, here's Zeus
already, leaving. He comes, the Father of the Gods!
And at his side Alcmene the adoring, to see
him off, as if he were her darling spouse Amphitryon.

SCENE 4
*Enter Jupiter (in the shape of Amphitryon), Alcmene,
Charis, with torchbearers.*

JUPITER. Dear Alcmene, command those torches there
to be withdrawn. I know their blaze illuminates
the most bewitching flower that ever blossomed
on this earth, and even the Olympians
have never seen a finer. But still,
how shall I say? They give away him whom
your loveliness has tempted here, my sweet.
Much better it should stay a secret your
Amphitryon has been in Thebes, these
moments I have offered up on love's
altar have all been stolen from the battlefield.
The world might misinterpret it, my theft,
and I am glad to have no other witness
but the one whose thanks I have for it.

17

ALCMENE. Amphitryon! You must be going, dear?
Oh, what a burden so much fame is, love!
How gladly I'd give up the diadem
you won for me, for a bunch of violets picked
outside a cottage door. What do we need,
we two, except ourselves? Why should so
much which is really alien to you,
royal crowns and marshal's maces, be imposed
upon you still? It's true that when the people
cheer you to the skies and give expression
to their rapturous feelings by heaping every
glorious title on your head they can
invent, the thought that you belong to me
is sweet—but how can that ephemeral
delight make up to me for what I feel
when in the hot affray the enemy aims
his arrow straight at this beloved breast?
Desolate, this house is, oh, without
you! When you are far from me, how sluggishly
the wheel of hours turns upon the axle
of the day, not merrily as it should. Oh dear,
today for the first time, after having you
entirely to myself for two short hours,
I feel how much, Amphitryon my lord,
our country has robbed me of.

JUPITER.   My love,
the fascination that you have for me!
But I confess that you inspire me
with a misgiving I must voice, as whimsical
as it may sound to you. You know that love
is matrimony's law, and duty too,
and he who is denied it can go to law
and claim it from the court. This law is spoiling
the perfection of my bliss! I would like
to know I owe the favors I've received
to *you,* my dearest, to your heart, and not
to a legality, to what perhaps you deem
your bounden duty. Surely it's not hard
for you to dissipate this nagging doubt
I have? So open up your heart to me

18

and tell: Was it your lawful husband, or
your lover, whom you received into your arms this night?
ALCMENE. My husband *and* my lover! What a thing
　　to say! It's only our holy state
　　of lawful matrimony, isn't it,
　　that justifies me in receiving you? Pray, why
　　should it torment you so—a law of all
　　the world which far from being a restriction on
　　us rather sweeps away, for our delight,
　　every bar between us and our boldest wishes?
JUPITER. What I feel for you, my dear Alcmene,
　　goes as far beyond the duty owed
　　you by a husband as the sun the earth. From
　　the husband wean yourself away, love,
　　and learn how to distinguish me from him.
　　This ignominious mixing of us up,
　　it pains me, and I find it more than I can bear
　　to think it is the coxcomb you have welcomed
　　to your arms, him merely, he who only
　　knows how, coldly, to presume on his connubial
　　rights. But I should like, my angel light,
　　to have seemed to you a being of a nature all
　　his own, your conqueror because the gods themselves
　　instructed him in that fine art, the way
　　to conquer you. The smug Commander-in-Chief
　　of Thebes who wooed and won, just recently,
　　a rich Princess for his great house, whyever
　　should we bring him into our affair? What
　　do you think, then? Don't you see? I'd like to leave
　　your virtue all to him, that imposing ninny
　　of a public man, and keep your love for me,
　　no one but me.
ALCMENE. 　　　　Amphitryon, you must
　　be joking! If people here should hear you going
　　on so in that way against Amphitryon,
　　they couldn't help but think you were somebody
　　else, I don't know who. You don't hear me,
　　in our night of joy, blurting out
　　remarks about distinctions which
　　it's possible to make between the husband

19

and the lover. But as the gods made both one,
for my sake, in you, gladly I
forgive the latter all the offenses the former
may be guilty of.

JUPITER.   Promise me, then, that
this festive night which our reunion's been
for us, shall never wither in your memory;
that this divine time we have passed together,
dearest heart, you never will confound
it in your mind with the banal course of onward
plodding married love. Oh promise me,
I beg you, you will think of me long after
your Amphitryon's come back—!

ALCMENE.   Yes,
all right—I don't know what to say!

JUPITER.   Oh thank
you! All of this has more significance
than you imagine. Good-bye, then, my duties
press.

ALCMENE. You're going, are you—will not spend
the rest of this short night, which passes
in a moment on ten thousand wingbeats, here
beside me?

JUPITER.   Did this night seem shorter than
all others?

ALCMENE.   Ah!

JUPITER.   You darling child! But I'm
afraid Aurora could not do more than she
has done already to promote our bliss. Good-bye.
I'll see to it the other nights don't last
a second longer than Earth finds absolutely
necessary.

ALCMENE.   He is drunk—as I am!

                         (*Exeunt.*)

SCENE 5
Mercury and Charis remaining.

CHARIS (*aside*).
That's what I call true affection, true
fidelity! When man and wife are re-

20

united after a long separation,
that's how they ought to celebrate! But that
gross peasant there to whom I'm tied—a block
of wood has got more tender feelings.

MERCURY (*aside*).
I must hurry now and give Night
a nudge, or otherwise the universe
will find itself turned upside-down, completely.
Our good goddess-bawd of darkness has lingered
out her stay above Thebes's roofs some seventeen
hours—now let her move along and draw
her curtain around still other love affairs.

CHARIS (*aloud*).
There's that indifferent man of mine, departing!

MERCURY. I'm not supposed to follow Lord Amphitryon,
am I? When he returns to camp, I'm not
supposed to lie down on my bearskin too?

CHARIS. You might tell me something.

MERCURY.   Nonsense, time
enough for talking later. What you know
is, I must go, and that is quite enough.
In this present business I am a Laconian.

CHARIS. A graceless oaf you are. The thing to say
is, Darling wife, be comforted, don't ever
fail to love me dearly—things like that.

MERCURY. What the devil are you dreaming of? Do
you think I ought to spend my time grimacing
and sighing over you? Eleven years
of marriage dry up the springs of conversation,
in the long ago already every
thing I had to say I said.

CHARIS.   Betrayer,
look how lovingly Amphitryon
behaves, just like the commonest people do,
and feel ashamed to see a lord of the great
world excelling you in devotion to his wife,
in husbandly affection.

MERCURY.   It's still
his honeymoon. There is a time when nothing
that we do is unbecoming.

What suits a couple young as they, if we
should do the same, I'd want to see it only
from as far away as possible. A spectacle
we'd be, old donkeys as we are,
if we began to dear-and-darling one
another back and forth.
CHARIS.   Coarse brute! To say
such things! Am I no longer able—?
MERCURY.   No,
I never said that. Yes, it's possible
to overlook the ravages time's made;
when the light's dim, so are they. But what
a to-do it would cause if the devil ever
put it in my head to play the gallant
with you here in public on this square.
CHARIS. The minute you arrived, betrayer, didn't
I take all pains possible, comb
my hair as you can see, and put a freshly
laundered dress on? And for what? To have
you bark and bellow at me.
MERCURY.   Never mind
your laundered dresses! The trouble is the dress
that Nature gave you—take that off and greasy
aprons wouldn't matter.
CHARIS.   It was to your taste
when you were wooing me, I recollect,
my natural dress. Then I might have worn
it in the kitchen doing washing,
or haying in the fields. I can't help
it, can I, the wear and tear the years have caused?
MERCURY. No, dear wife, you can't. But neither can
I mend your dress for you.
CHARIS.   What a dreadful
man you are! You don't deserve the wife
you have, with the reputation she has earned
for spotless virtue.
MERCURY.   I might wish you had
a little bit less virtue, wife, and didn't
wear my ears out with your everlasting squabbling
and scolding.

CHARIS. What! It displeases you to know
that I have always kept my virtue and good
reputation?
MERCURY. Heaven help us, no.
Preserve your virtue, by all means,
only don't drive it, like a sled horse, jingling
through the streets and marketplace.
CHARIS. You deserve
the kind of wife that Thebes is full of, slyboots
busy with intrigues, a wife who'd have you swallow,
as she pours you out a flood of loving compliments,
your own cuckolding.
MERCURY. Well, my dear,
as far as that's concerned, I'll tell you what
I think: scandal only thought about,
only upsets fools. Indeed I rather
envy him who has a friend to pay
his marriage tax for him: growing old, he keeps
the life he would have lost by giving children life.
CHARIS. Oh, but you are shameless, aren't you,
to drive me to it? You actually would urge
me, would you, never blushing, to find
myself a friend, perhaps that grinning fellow
who comes hanging around me after dark?
MERCURY. Devil
take me, yes! Only spare me hearing the details.
In my opinion, sinning comfortably
is quite as good as sweating under virtue's
pack; what I always say is, Thebes
would be much better off with a little
less morality and a lot more
peace and quiet. Farewell now, dear Charis,
sweetheart mine, I have to go. I'm sure
Amphitryon's reached camp already.
(*Exit.*)
CHARIS. Why
don't I possess the courage to punish that disgusting
man with actions, not with words? My god,
how I regret it now, my reputation
for respectability!

ACT II

Day

SCENE I

Enter Amphitryon and Sosia.

AMPHITRYON. The truth, you beggar, you damned rascal! Don't
you know that talking gibberish like that
will land your neck inside a noose? That if
I dealt with you as you deserve, the only
thing I'd need is a stout stick?

SOSIA. If that's the tone you mean to take with me,
I'll never speak a word. Order me
and I will say I dreamt it all, or drank
too much.

AMPHITRYON. To try and foist off fairy tales
on me, with a straight face! The kind of bedtime
stories nannies tell the children! Do
you think I'm going to believe such stuff?

SOSIA.   No, no,
never! You're the master, I'm the servant
only, you do and don't do what you please.

AMPHITRYON. All right. I'll try to hold my anger back
and hear the whole thing over patiently
again.—I won't set foot in that house there
till I've unraveled this damned mystery.—
Now collect your wits and answer all my questions
point by point.

SOSIA.   But Sire, please forgive
me—lest I give offense I'd like to know,
before we settle down to business, how
I am to speak. Shall I speak from conviction—
like an honest man, you understand—
or speak as people do at court? Do I speak
the truth straight out to you, or do as wellbred
people do?

AMPHITRYON. Don't be smart. What
I want from you is a full and frank account
of everything that happened.

24

SOSIA.   Fine. Here goes,
  then. As you wish. Just ask away.
AMPHITRYON.   According
  to my order—?
SOSIA.   Off I went into
  pitch darkness so ungodly you'd have thought
  the day was sunk ten thousand fathoms deep,
  damning you to hell, Sir, all your orders,
  the long way to Thebes, and the royal palace
  too.
AMPHITRYON. Your tongue, you villain!
SOSIA.   Sire, it's
  the truth.
AMPHITRYON. All right. Go on. And as you went
  along—?
SOSIA.   I put my left foot down and then
  my right, first one and then the other, and left
  my tracks behind me.
AMPHITRYON.   What! I want to know
  what happened, damn you!
SOSIA.   Nothing, Sir, except
  to say that, *salva venia,*[2] I became
  so frightened—terrified!
AMPHITRYON.   And then when you
  arrived here—?
SOSIA.   I practiced up a little on the speech
  that I was going to deliver, pretending,
  with my clever head, the lantern was your wife
  the Princess.
AMPHITRYON.   And having done that, then you—?
SOSIA.   I
  was interrupted. Here we go now.
AMPHITRYON.   Interrupted?
  Who? Who interrupted you?
SOSIA.   Sosia.
AMPHITRYON. Please explain that, I don't understand.

---

2. *Salva venia:* by your leave.

SOSIA. Explain that? On my soul, that's asking me
  too much! Sosia interrupted me
  when I was practicing.
AMPHITRYON.   Sosia? What Sosia?
  What rascal of a Sosia was that, what gallows bird
  of Thebes who goes by the same name you
  do, interrupted you when you were practicing?
SOSIA. Sosia! The one who is your servant,
  whom you sent off last night to Thebes from camp
  to announce your imminent arrival home.
AMPHITRYON. You, you mean?
SOSIA.   Yes, me. A me that knows
  our secrets, every one, knows all about
  the diamonds in the casket, a me who is a perfect
  likeness of the one who's talking to you now.
AMPHITRYON. What kind of story's that!
SOSIA.   A true one, on
  my soul. And if it isn't, strike me dead.
  The me I'm telling you about got here
  ahead of me, so that means I got here,
  oh dear, before myself.
AMPHITRYON.   I'd like to know
  where these absurdities, these insane things
  you're babbling, come from? Dreams? Or drunkenness? Or your
  disordered brain? Or it's supposed to be
  a joke, perhaps?
SOSIA.   No joke, Sir, I am speaking
  in dead earnest, so do be good enough
  to credit what I say. I swear to you
  I left the camp a single soul, and arrived
  in Thebes a double; that I stared with popping eyes
  when I encountered my own self right here;
  that this here I who's standing right in front
  of you was dropping with fatigue and hunger when
  the other one I'm telling you about
  came out the palace door as fresh as he
  could be, a bully boy if ever I
  did see one; that these two rascals, emulous
  each one to execute your orders, got
  into an argument right off and I found

myself compelled to beat it back to camp
again, for being such a brainless brute.
AMPHITRYON. You have to have a temper mild as mine
is, uncontentious, perfectly forbearing,
to let a servant go on talking so.
SOSIA. Sir, if this exasperates you I
will say no more, we'll find some other subject
for discussion.
AMPHITRYON.   Just go on, go on.
You see how I restrain myself. Patiently
I'll hear you out. But tell me right now, on
your conscience, please, if you believe what you
put forward as the truth can claim a shred
of plausibility? Can anybody
understand it, fathom it, make any
sense of it at all?
SOSIA.   No, never! But who
is asking that of you? I'd show him where
the madhouse is, any man who claimed
he understood a thing about what happened
here. It's such a crazy business, hobgoblin
stuff straight out of fairy tales, yet there
it *is,* a fact, unarguable as sunlight.
AMPHITRYON. But how can anyone with all his wits
about him possibly believe it?
SOSIA.   Goodness,
but the pain it cost me, just like you,
before I managed that! I was sure
I was possessed when I found my own self planted
here on the square and making a great
racket; I cursed myself a good long while
for playing knavish tricks on me. But I
was forced to recognize at last that he
was me with just as good a right as I.
As if the air had been a looking glass,
face to face with me he stood, a being
who resembled me in all respects, his manners
mine, his build—two drops of water aren't
more alike. And if he'd only been
the least bit friendly, instead of such

an ugly-tempered brute, I do believe
I would have liked him, honestly.

AMPHITRYON.   The self-control
that I'm condemned to exercise!—But finally
you went inside the palace, didn't you?

SOSIA. Inside the palace? That's a good one! How?
Would I allow it? Listen the least bit
to reason? Didn't I refuse myself
permission to go in, over and over, stubbornly?

AMPHITRYON. What the devil are you saying? How—?

SOSIA. How? With a thick stick is how, the marks
of which I've still got on my back.

AMPHITRYON.   So someone
beat you.

SOSIA.   Did he ever!

AMPHITRYON.   Who? Who beat
you? Dared do that?

SOSIA.   Me.

AMPHITRYON.   You beat yourself?

SOSIA. I did, for sure I did! Oh, not the one
who's talking to you now, but that one, curse
him, from the palace there, who stroked away
on me like a whole rowing crew.

AMPHITRYON.   Bad
luck dog you always, for talking such
a lot of drivel to me!

SOSIA.   If you like,
Sir, I can prove it to you soon enough.
As my trustworthy witness: my comrade in adversity,
my back! The Sosia who chased me out
of here had lots of fighting spirit
and a boxer's educated fists—that
was the edge he had on me.

AMPHITRYON.   Well, finish with
your story. You gave my wife the message, yes?

SOSIA. No.

AMPHITRYON. You didn't! Why not?

SOSIA.   For compelling
reasons, Jupiter!

AMPHITRYON. Who, you traitor,
stopped you in your duty? Villain! Good-
for-nothing wretch!

SOSIA. How often do I have
to say it? For the tenth time: it was me,
that demon-me who took possession of the gate,
the me who wants to be the one and only
me, who came out of the palace there,
who beat me half to death.

AMPHITRYON. The beast is drunk,
he's lost what little wits he had.

SOSIA. Devil
take me if I've drunk a drop more
than my usual. I swear that it's the truth,
you must believe me.

AMPHITRYON. Then you must have slept
too much, is that it? Dreamt a bad dream
full of these absurdities and got
them mixed up with reality, in your
account?

SOSIA. No, not at all. I haven't slept
since yesterday, nor did I have the least
wish to, going through the woods; when I
arrived here I was wide awake, as he
was too, the other Sosia, awake
and on his toes when he handed me out such
a thumping.

AMPHITRYON. Silence! That's enough! Why
should I tire out my brain? I'm mad myself
to listen to such stuff—useless, senseless,
childish gabble, devoid of any trace
of reason or intelligence. Now come along.

SOSIA (*aside*).
—That's the way it is. If it's my mouth
it comes out of, it's childish nonsense, pay
it no attention. But if it'd been a great
one flogged himself himself, you'd hear the whole world
crying miracle.

AMPHITRYON. Inside with you
and have them open up the gates to me.

—But look there, that's Alcmene, isn't it?
My coming's a surprise, I know—I'm not expected.

SCENE 2

Enter Alcmene and Charis.

ALCMENE. Come, Charis dear, and we will lay an offering
    to the gods on the altar, gratefully;
    beseech them to continue to protect, with their holy
    mantle, the best of husbands. (*Sees Amphitryon.*)
                                     Heavens, it's
Amphitryon!

AMPHITRYON.   God grant my darling wife
    won't start back in dismay to see me here.
    I have no fear that after the brief time
    of our separation, she'll receive
    me any less adoringly than I
    return to her.

ALCMENE.   Come back so soon—?

AMPHITRYON.   Well!
    That exclamation really makes me think
    it's most unlikely that the gods have heard
    my prayer. "Come back so soon!" are not the accents
    ardent love employs. What a fool
    I've been! Deluded, I believed the war
    had separated me from you too long;
    the way it seemed to *me,* I come back home
    to you too late. But now you teach me how
    much I have erred; astonished, I perceive
    I've fallen on you from the blue, a presence
    inconvenient and intrusive.

ALCMENE.   I cannot—

AMPHITRYON. Alcmene, no!—I'm sorry. But your exclamation
    poured cold water on my flames of love.
    In all the time that I have been away,
    you never condescended even once
    to vouchsafe the dial a passing glance. The
    wings of time beat here unperceived, and five
    months by the calendar flew by for you,

30

amid this castle's loud uproarious pleasures,
like so many minutes.

ALCMENE.   I find it hard,
dear friend, to understand why you should think
you have some reason for reproaching me.
If it's coldness that you blame me for,
then I am mystified what I must do
to satisfy you. Yesterday when you
appeared to me at nightfall, I paid off,
out of my warm bosom and in full, the debt
that I am being dunned for now—or so
I thought. But if you're able still to wish
for more, require more, you force me to confess
my bankruptcy—all I had to give
I gave you, truly.

AMPHITRYON.   What? What's that?

ALCMENE.   That you
should ask me what! Last night when I was spinning
in my room, entirely lost in my own thoughts,
and you slipped in and stole a kiss
on the neck from me—I flew into your arms
and hugged you, didn't I? Can one delight
more in a lover than I did?

AMPHITRYON.   What is
it you are saying?

ALCMENE.   The questions that you ask! And you
on your side felt a joy beyond all bounds
to find yourself so passionately loved;
and as I laughed and wept by turns you swore
to me, in a voice unusually solemn,
that Jupiter himself had never had
such joy of Here.

AMPHITRYON.   You immortal gods!

ALCMENE. But with the day's first glow no pleading
on my part can keep you longer by my side,
off you have to go before the rising
of the sun. You go, I fling myself
on the couch, toss sleeplessly because the morning
is too warm, am moved to make an offering
to the gods, and in the forecourt I encounter

31

you! If I was taken by surprise,
was flabbergasted, even, if you will,
I think I am the one, I do, who's owed
an explanation here. But in any case
there is no reason for berating me so angrily.
AMPHITRYON. Was my homecoming heralded to you,
Alcmene, in a dream, is that it? In
your sleep, perhaps, you welcomed me home
and so you think your debt of love's already
satisfied?
ALCMENE.   Has an evil spirit robbed
you of all recollection, is that it,
Amphitryon? Or has a god perhaps
been able to undermine the happy disposition
of your mind so that you wish, insultingly,
to strip your wife's chaste love of all
its purity?
AMPHITRYON. You dare to stand there telling
me I slipped into your room at nightfall
yesterday? That playfully, on your neck,
I pressed—the devil, oh!
ALCMENE.   You dare
to stand there and deny you slipped in here
at nightfall yesterday? Took every liberty
with me a husband is permitted?
AMPHITRYON.   No,
you're joking, let's be serious. A joke
like that is really out of place.
ALCMENE.   *You*
are joking. Yes, speak seriously, I find
the joke a coarse and painful one.
AMPHITRYON.   Took
every liberty with you, you say, a husband
is permitted? Am I quoting you
correctly?
ALCMENE.   What a low mind you have, go!
AMPHITRYON. Good god, the blow this is to me! Oh Sosia,
my friend!
SOSIA.   Five grains of hellebore is what
she needs; she's not quite right upstairs.

AMPHITRYON.   Alcmene!
  You're not thinking what the consequences
  of such talk can be. Collect your wits, consider
  what you say. From now on I'll believe
  your every word.
ALCMENE.   Whatever consequences
  it may have, Amphitryon, I pray
  you to believe me always: never for an instant
  think I'm capable of such gross jokes.
  How calm I am about the outcome, you
  can see. If you are able, without flinching,
  to look me in the eye and say you didn't
  visit me here in the palace yesterday—
  and the gods don't strike you dead! Why, I don't care
  a straw for any shabby reasons
  you think you have, you'll never shake the calm
  assurance I have here inside me, nor,
  as is my trust, the good opinion of the world.
  But that my love should wish to wound me cruelly—
  that cut only makes my bosom bleed.
AMPHITRYON. You wretched girl! What kind of speech is that?—
  And I suppose that you have got the proof
  to show for what you say?
ALCMENE.   The proof, my god!
  Every servant in this castle is my witness.
  Why, the pavement that you walked on, all
  the trees, the dogs that crowded around your knees,
  tails wagging, would swear to it that you were here,
  if they were able.
AMPHITRYON.   All the servants? That's
  impossible!
ALCMENE.   Incomprehensible,
  you are. Proof positive, is that what you
  would like to have? Then look: from whom did I
  receive this girdle here?
AMPHITRYON.   A girdle? You?
  From me? Already wearing it!
ALCMENE.   The diadem,
  you told me, of Labdacus, struck down by you in your
  last battle.

33

AMPHITRYON (*to Sosia*).
>Traitor, you! Now what am I
to think?

SOSIA. Please, one moment. These are feeble
efforts to deceive; I have the diadem in my
possession.

AMPHITRYON. Where?

SOSIA. Right here.
>(*Takes a casket out of his pocket.*)

AMPHITRYON. The seal is still
unbroken! (*Looks hard at the band around Alcmene's breast.*)
>And yet I'd swear—unless my senses
all deceive me—(*To Sosia.*) Open it at once!

SOSIA. Good god, there's nothing here! The devil's gone
and flown away with it, there is no diadem
of King Labdacus to be seen.

AMPHITRYON. O you almighty
gods who rule this nether world, what fate
have you in store for me!

SOSIA. In store for you?
They've doubled you, that's what, Amphitryon's
been here, the one who swings a stick, and *my*
opinion is, you are a lucky man—

AMPHITRYON. Keep quiet, fool!

ALCMENE (*to Charis*).
>Whatever is it that's
affected him so violently? Why such
dismay, such consternation at the sight of something
not unknown to him, this ornament?

AMPHITRYON. How many tales of wonder I have listened
to, about unnatural phenomena,
appearances in this world from another—
but now it's me, my honor, that a thread spun
from the skies has wound itself around and chokes to death.

ALCMENE (*to Amphitryon*).
Strange friend of mine, confronted with this evidence,
will you continue to deny that last night
you appeared to me and that I already have
redeemed my obligation to you as a wife?

AMPHITRYON. I won't. But you must tell me the whole
   story, all of it.
ALCMENE.   Amphitryon!
AMPHITRYON. It's not because I doubt you, understand.
   The diadem is not to be gainsaid.
   It's just that I have certain reasons, don't
   you know, for wanting you to tell me in detail
   what happened on my visit.
ALCMENE.   You're not ill,
   my friend, are you?
AMPHITRYON.   No, I'm not ill.
ALCMENE.   Perhaps
   one of your urgent cares as general-in-chief
   weighs upon your mind, engrossing all
   its cheerful vigor—?
AMPHITRYON.   Yes, I do feel rather
   dull, now.
ALCMENE.   Come inside and rest awhile.
AMPHITRYON. No, later on will do. As I just said,
   I'd like to hear, before I go indoors,
   your account of my homecoming yesterday.
ALCMENE. It's quickly told. The dark had come, I sat
   inside my closet at the wheel, the humming
   of the spindle lulled me off into the field,
   among armed warriors, when I heard a loud
   exulting shout from the direction of the farther gate.
AMPHITRYON. Who was shouting?
ALCMENE.   Our people.
AMPHITRYON.   And?
ALCMENE. And promptly I forgot it, for even in
   my dreams it never crossed my mind what pure
   joy the gods in all their graciousness
   had destined for me. But just as I took up
   the thread again, a tremor ran through all
   my limbs—
AMPHITRYON. I know.
ALCMENE.   That part you know.
AMPHITRYON.   And then?
ALCMENE. And then there was, my goodness, so much talk,
   so much merriment, and how the questions

which we had for one another flew back
and forth! We both sat down. You told me, in
your soldier's style, the story of Pharissa's fall
and how Labdacus had gone down into the eternal
night—and every gory detail of the battle.
And then—I received a gift, the gorgeous diadem,
paid for with a kiss; we studied it a long time
in the candlelight. And when I put it around
me like a girdle, your hand fastened it
beneath my breast.

AMPHITRYON (*aside*).
                    Is a dagger's cut, I wonder,
any sharper?

ALCMENE.   Supper soon was served
us, but neither you nor I showed any interest
in the ortolan on the serving plate,
and very little in the wine—very drolly,
you said you lived upon the nectar of my love,
you said you were a god, all sorts of things:
my heavens, what your fancy, wantoning,
put into your mouth!

AMPHITRYON.   My fancy, wantoning,
put into my mouth!

ALCMENE.   Yes, into your mouth. Well, after
that—you look so grim. What is it?

AMPHITRYON.   After
that—?

ALCMENE. We stood up from the table—then—

AMPHITRYON. Yes—then?

ALCMENE.   Having stood up from the table—

AMPHITRYON.   Having
stood up from the table—

ALCMENE.   We went—

AMPHITRYON.   You went—

ALCMENE. We went—but good lord, look how red your face
is! Why?

AMPHITRYON. It strikes right to my heart, this dagger
does! No, no, betrayer, it was never
me! It was a scoundrel, the greatest villain

ever—that Amphitryon who slipped in here
at nightfall yesterday!

ALCMENE.   Nasty fellow!

AMPHITRYON. Faithless woman! Thankless girl!—Restraint,
farewell! And that which only injured me
in what regards my honor, love, farewell
to you! Farewell to memories, and hope,
and happiness—and welcome bitter hatred
and revenge!

ALCMENE.   Farewell to you as well, ignoble-minded
man, I snatch my heart back, bleeding, out
of your breast. The deception you are practicing
on me is detestable, revolting.
If all your longing now looks elsewhere, to another,
if love has smitten you resistlessly,
by honestly avowing it to me
the goal of your desire would have been
attained as fast as by your coward's trick.
My mind is quite made up, I do assure
you, to cut the tie which now oppresses your
inconstant soul. Never fear: before
this day is over you will know you're free
of all connection that exists between us.

AMPHITRYON. Seeing what a shameful injury's
been done me, that's the least my wounded honor
may demand. It's clear there is a plot
afoot against me, even though I still
can't trace out all the strands that go to make
the insidious web. But I will call in witnesses
to tear it into shreds. I'll call your brother
in, the generals, the whole Theban
army I'll call in, from the midst of whom
I never ventured even for a second till dawn's
first light today. Then we'll see
to the bottom of this mystery—and woe to him
by whom I've been deceived!

SOSIA.   Perhaps, Sir, I
should—?

AMPHITRYON. Silence, not a word. Stay here till I
return. (*Exit*).

37

CHARIS.   Your wishes, Princess?

ALCMENE.   Silence, not
  a word. Don't follow me, I wish to be alone. (*Exit*).

SCENE 3

Charis. Sosia.

CHARIS. What a scene that was! He's crazy if
  he claims he spent last night in camp. Well, when
  her brother comes we'll see what's what.

SOSIA. That was a hard knock for my master, I'm
  afraid.—But suppose I've had the same hand
  dealt me too? I think I better sniff
  around a bit.

CHARIS (*aside*).
                    What now? The shameless fellow,
  to turn his back on me so sulkily!

SOSIA. I tremble at the thought of touching on
  so ticklish a business. I'm half-inclined
  to give up trying to find out; it's all
  one in the end so long as you don't look
  too closely into things. But Sosia, come,
  stake all, I've got to know!—Heaven help
  you and reward you, Charis!

CHARIS.   What? Come near me, do
  you, you betrayer? Dare, when I'm incensed,
  to speak to me as airily as that?

SOSIA. Now what's got into you, I'd like to know?
  When people meet again they say hello.
  How you ruffle up your feathers for no reason,
  over nothing!

CHARIS.   Tell me what you call
  no reason, nothing, do, you wretch!

SOSIA.   I'll tell
  you truthfully: I mean by nothing what
  it means in prose and verse, which is,
  approximately speaking, nothing whatsoever,
  if you follow me, or anyhow
  a very small amount.

38

CHARIS.　　　　　I wish I knew
　what keeps my hands from flying out at you.
　Oh, I can hardly hold them back from scratching
　out your eyes and teaching you to know
　an angry woman when you see one.
SOSIA.　　　　　　　　What
　an onslaught! Do protect me, Heaven!
CHARIS.　　　　　　　　Nothing,
　do you call it, the shameless conduct you allowed
　yourself with me?
SOSIA.　　　　What was it I allowed
　myself? What happened?
CHARIS.　　　　　Happened? Look at him,
　so innocent! The next thing he
　will tell me, like his lord, he's not set foot
　in Thebes till just this minute.
SOSIA.　　　　　　　As for that,
　well, let me say that I don't go around
　concocting mysteries. We drank a devil's
　brew, I think, that purged our brains
　of all our sense.
CHARIS.　　　　Do you imagine you'll
　escape from me with such an explanation?
SOSIA.　　　　　　　　Charis,
　no, I swear. I arrived here yesterday—
　I would be a villain if I told
　you differently. But I know absolutely
　nothing about the things that happened here.
　The whole world was a bedlam yesterday.
CHARIS. You don't remember how you treated me
　when you walked into the house last night?
SOSIA.　　　　　　　　I remember
　next to nothing, hang me if it isn't
　so! Come on, then, tell me the whole story,
　you know what a good soul I am, if I've
　behaved offensively I am the first
　to say so.
CHARIS.　　Good-for-nothing! Twelve o'clock
　had come and gone, the royal pair had been
　abed for hours, and still you lingered on

in Amphitryon's apartment, looking in
not once on your own place. So finally
your wife it was who had to pad off
in the dark, in stocking feet, to look for you.
And tell me where I found you, your duties all
forgotten? Stretched out on a cushion, at
your ease, ensconced as if at home. In my
concern, I remonstrated with you tenderly—
Master's orders, you growled out,
so that you shouldn't oversleep your starting
time, he means to ride off early—that
and other reasons which smelt no better. Never
once a kindly uttered word. And when
I stooped down lovingly to press
a kiss on your lips, you rolled face
to the wall, you lout, and Let me sleep! I heard.

SOSIA. Good for you, old Sosia!

CHARIS.   What? You praise
yourself for that, do you?

SOSIA.   Good grief, I'd think
you'd be a little grateful to me there;
I'd eaten horseradish, my dear, and did
the proper thing, which was to turn my breath
away.

CHARIS. Get out with you! I didn't catch
a whiff. Besides, we'd had horseradish,
too, at dinner.

SOSIA.   Goodness me, I didn't
know. Well, then you couldn't smell it.

CHARIS.   No,
you don't get off like that. The scorn with which
I see how I am used, you'll pay for it,
I promise you. It rankles in me so,
I can't get over it, the things I had
to listen to this morning. Just you wait,
I'll use the liberty you gave me, gladly,
as I'm an honest woman.

SOSIA.   Liberty
I gave you—what was that?

40

CHARIS. You said to me,
and knew exactly what you said: you wouldn't
mind a pair of horns to decorate
your brow. Indeed, you'd like it very well
if I chose to while away the time with that Theban
fellow who, as you well know, is always
trailing after me. All right, my friend,
agreed, you'll have your way.
SOSIA. A donkey told
you that, not me. No joking, now. That's nothing
that I ever said. You must be sensible.
CHARIS. Oh, I don't know if I am able to,
be sensible.
SOSIA. Hush now, the princess comes, Alcmene.

SCENE 4
Enter Alcmene.

ALCMENE. Charis dear, what's happened to me, tell
me, do, I'm overcome with misery.
You see this treasure I have here?
CHARIS. I do.
What is it, pray?
ALCMENE. The diadem of King
Labdacus, a princely gift to me from Lord
Amphitryon, with his own initial
engraved on it.
CHARIS. The diadem of Lord
Labdacus, that! But I don't see Amphitryon's
initial on it anywhere.
ALCMENE. Wretched
woman, have you taken leave of all
your senses? Can't you see it there—so clearly
cut, with a bold flourish, in the gold, one's finger
has no difficulty tracing it,
an *A.*
CHARIS. I can't, indeed I can't, dear Mistress.
What's come over you? The letter I
see there is quite another one. A *J.*
ALCMENE. A *J?*

41

CHARIS. A *J*. There's no mistaking it.

ALCMENE. Then pity me, oh pity me, for I
am lost!

CHARIS.   Your agitation's so extreme—
please explain, what is it?

ALCMENE.   Charis dear,
how find words to explain a thing
that's inexplicable? When I made my way
back to my room again, not knowing if
I was awake or dreaming, in a state
of shock to hear it charged against me, to
my face, that the man who came to visit me
last night was someone else—which was mad,
I know, but still, I couldn't banish from my mind
the anguish of Amphitryon and his last words,
that he would summon my own brother (think
of it!) to prove me wrong—when I asked myself
if I perhaps might be mistaken, for one
of us must be deceived since neither one
is capable of perfidy; when through
my mind it flashed how equivocal his wit
had seemed to me (I don't know if you heard
him) when Amphitryon the lover spoke
with such disdain about Amphitryon
the husband: I shuddered, seized with horror, my senses
all deserting me—but then I clutched
the diadem to me, this precious, priceless,
only pledge, only ungainsayable
assurance of my innocence. I clutch it to me,
am just about to press my lips in rapture
to the letter worth my life, my well-beloved
liar's own belier: and it is pointed
out to me it is an altogether
different letter—it's a *J*! I feel
as if a lightning bolt just struck me.

CHARIS.   Dreadful!
Is it possible you were mistaken, then?

ALCMENE. Mistaken!

CHARIS.   No, I mean about the letter.

ALCMENE. Oh—about the letter: so it seems,
  I fear.
CHARIS. And therefore—?
ALCMENE.   Therefore what!
CHARIS.   Oh, do
  please calm yourself. It all will end well, I
  am sure.
CHARIS.   Oh Charis! As soon mistake myself,
  I would! As soon imagine I'm a Persian
  or a Parthian, in spite of that profoundest feeling,
  sucked in with my mother's milk, which tells
  me I am I, Alcmene. Look, this hand,
  does it belong to me? This bosom? My
  reflection in the mirror? He would have had
  to be stranger to me than my own self!
  Put out my eye, still I would hear him; stop
  my ear and I would feel him; take touch away
  I'd breathe his presence in; take all my senses,
  every one, but only leave my heart,
  that bell—its note is all I need to find
  him out, wherever, in the world.
CHARIS.   Oh yes,
  oh yes, and would I ever doubt it, Princess?
  How could any woman err in such
  a matter? Dresses, pots, and pans, you snatch
  the wrong one up, but not your husband, in the dark.
  Besides, we saw him, all of us, as clear
  as clear, the servants waved their caps and cheered
  when he came through the gate. To blind so many
  eyes it needed to be midnight, but
  it still was light.
ALCMENE.   Yet notwithstanding here's
  this unaccountable initial! Why,
  I wonder, should this strange-appearing letter,
  which the weakest eye could not misread,
  fail to strike me at first glance? If I
  can't tell two such names apart,
  dear Charis, might they not, just possibly,
  belong to two commanders no easier
  to tell apart?

CHARIS.   But you are absolutely
  certain, are you?
ALCMENE.   Certain as I am
  my soul is pure, my soul is innocent!
  You mustn't put a wrong construction on the fact
  that I never felt he was so handsome
  as last night. I might have thought he was
  a portrait of himself, a painting by a master's
  hand showing him exactly as
  he is, and yet transfigured, like a god!
  Standing there he seemed, I don't know what,
  a dream; unspeakable the bliss I felt,
  whose like I'd never known before, when he,
  Pharissa's conqueror, radiant
  as if with Heaven's glory, appeared to me.
  Amphitryon it was, the son of the gods!
  I would have asked him if he had descended
  from the stars, except he seemed so in my eyes
  already—star born, from the skies.
CHARIS.   It was
  imagination, dear—love's way of seeing
  things.
ALCMENE. But oh, the way he kept on joking,
  so equivocally about the difference between
  himself and the Prince Amphitryon! If the man
  I gave myself to was the Prince, why
  is it that he called himself my lover,
  a stealer from my table only?
  A curse on me, if the joke I smiled at
  with a shallow grin was never uttered by
  my husband's lips!
CHARIS.   You mustn't rush ahead
  and torture yourself with doubts. When you showed
  Amphitryon the diadem today, he acknowledged
  its inscription, didn't he? Something
  is amiss here, to be sure. But if
  he didn't wonder at the marking, well,
  it follows it belongs there properly.
  Moreover, we were blinded yesterday,
  deluded; today we see things as they are.

ALCMENE. But suppose his eye passed over it too quickly
    and he returns with all his officers
    repeating his mad claim he never crossed
    the threshold of the palace yesterday! Not only
    do I lack all proof, this ornament's
    a proof *against* me. Utterly confounded,
    what should I answer then? Where should I flee
    from pain, destruction even, when those men
    with their hard eyes examine it? Confess,
    I'd have to, this inscription's not at all
    an *A;* that a gift so strangely marked
    could never have been given me by him.
    And even if I swore upon the altar
    that he himself had put it in my hands
    last night, can I be *sure,* I'd like to know,
    that I received this token I have here
    from him?

CHARIS.   Do calm yourself. I see
    him coming. Everything shall have its explanation.

SCENE 5

Enter Jupiter.

ALCMENE. My lord and husband! On my knees allow
    me, if I may, to give you back this diadem.
    Loyally my life's laid at your feet.
    Look close at your gift, and if you gave
    it to me bearing, as it does, the initial
    of a foreign name, I'll shower it with kisses
    and with tears, for joy. If not, if you deny
    the gift is yours, disavow it, let
    my lot be death and night eternal swallow
    up my shame.

JUPITER.   Loveliest of wives! Shall I
    receive this treasure here, and let *this* treasure
    still stoop in the dust? Stand up. What is
    it? Try to calm yourself.

ALCMENE.   I know I spoke
    too absolutely, that offended you;
    then I was feeling innocent and strong.

45

But since I've looked at this initial here,
I've come to doubt my inmost feelings. Yes—
it was—another man—I do believe
it, if you tell me so.

JUPITER.   Noblest of wives!
I'm put to shame by you! Whatever do
you think you're telling me? How should another
man appear to you, to you whose soul
has eyes for one face only, only one?
A saint you are, protected from the least
annoyance by a diamond girdle. Even he
who has the luck to be received into your presence,
leaves it pure and blameless still, for nothing
not Amphitryon is ever able
to come near you.

ALCMENE.   Oh my dear husband, please
do tell me, was it you or not? Speak, it
was you, it was!

JUPITER.   Yes, it was me. But it's
no matter who it was. I beg you: make
an effort to be calm, for everything you saw,
you thought, you touched, you felt was me—and who
else should it be? Whatever man it was
that stepped across your threshold, it was me
whom you received, and for every single favor
you allowed him I'm the one who's in
your debt, for which I thank you heartily.

ALCMENE. Amphitryon, oh no, that's wrong! Now I
must say good-bye to you forever, my
beloved. Oh, I steeled myself against
this possibility!

JUPITER.   Alcmene dear!

ALCMENE. Good-bye! Good-bye!

JUPITER.   You surely don't—

ALCMENE.   Go, will
you, go—

JUPITER.   The light of my existence!

ALCMENE.   Go!

JUPITER. But listen!

ALCMENE.　　　　I'll not listen, I don't want
　to live with a soul no longer irreproachable,
　with a spotted bosom.
JUPITER.　　　　　What! What kind of words are these
　from the wife I hold in reverence? How could
　a saint like you do wrong? If it had been
　a devil that appeared last night and vomited up,
　all over you, every filthy sin
　there is in Hell, he'd not mar
　by one spot the brightness of the bosom of my wife.
　Oh what insanity!
ALCMENE.　　　　How shamefully
　deceived I was!
JUPITER.　　　　*He* was deceived, my idol! His wicked
　swindle took *him* in, not you, not your
　unerring feeling! When he imagined it was you
　he wound his arms around, all the while
　you lay upon Amphitryon's beloved
　breast, and when he dreamt he kissed your lips,
　your lips were pressed tight to Amphitryon's.
　Oh, he has got a sting, let me assure
　you, planted in his fevered bosom all
　the skill the gods possess can't pull out.
ALCMENE. If only Zeus would strike him down, here
　at my feet! Now you and I must separate,
　oh god, forever!
JUPITER.　　　　The kiss you granted him
　unites me with you more, much more than all the love
　that ever made your heart burn bright
　for me. If I had the power
　from the spinning round of days to shoot
　down yesterday as easy as
　I do a blackbird from the sky, I'd never
　do it, not for all the joys of Mount
　Olympus, for Zeus's immortality.
ALCMENE. And if I had the power, I would kill
　myself ten times at least. Now go! You shan't
　see me again, or present me to another woman
　here in Greece.

JUPITER.   To all the gods who live
  on high Olympus! What a thing to say!
  I'll usher you into the shining company
  of all the gods, I will! If I were Zeus,
  when you approached the circle deathless Here
  would have to rise and Artemis the strict
  come forward smiling welcome.

ALCMENE.   Go, your goodness
  overwhelms me. Let me disappear.

JUPITER. Alcmene!

ALCMENE.   Let me.

JUPITER.   My soul's mate!

ALCMENE.   I want
  to go now, do you hear?

JUPITER.   You think you will
  break out of my embrace?

ALCMENE.   Amphitryon,
  I'm leaving, let me go.

JUPITER.   Why, if you ran
  away from me, as far away as to the horrid
  desert dwellers, as far as to the edge of Ocean,
  I'd race and overtake you, kiss you, cry,
  and lifting you in my arms, carry you in triumph
  to my bed.

ALCMENE.   If that is your idea, I swear—
  and hear me, you immortal gods, you
  dread punishers of all false swearing—
  sooner will I go down to my grave
  than come back, while there's breath still in
  my bosom, to your bed.

JUPITER.   The powers I
  possess are such, I'll break your oath and scatter
  all its pieces in the air.—It was no mortal man
  appeared to you but Zeus himself, the Thunder God!

ALCMENE. Who?

JUPITER.   Jupiter.

ALCMENE.   Who, madman, did you say?

JUPITER. Don't you hear me—Jupiter.

ALCMENE.   Jupiter!
  How dare you, wretch—?

JUPITER.   Jupiter, I said,
  and I repeat it. It was he, no other,
  who appeared to you last evening.
ALCMENE.   You
  ungodly man, you dare to charge Olympian
  Zeus with committing such a gross offense?
JUPITER. Such a gross offense? You rash woman,
  never say a thing like that again!
ALCMENE. Never say a thing like that—? It wasn't
  such a gross offense?
JUPITER.   Silence, I command
  you!
ALCMENE. Oh, lost soul!
JUPITER.   If mounting up into
  the ranks of the immortals is an honor you
  don't feel—well, I do: so pray, allow me to.
  If you don't envy glorious Callisto,
  Europa too, and Leda, well, all right—but I,
  how much I envy King Tyndareus
  and long for sons like the Tyndarides!
ALCMENE. Not envy glorious Callisto and Europa?
  Whom Zeus chose for his own? Hellas'
  exalted women? Dwellers in the eternal realms
  of light?
JUPITER.   Yes, them. Why should you envy them,
  since glory quite enough is yours from seeing
  one poor mortal at your feet?
ALCMENE.   Whatever are
  you saying? Do I dare even to think
  of such a thing? How would I fail to be
  submerged and drowned in such radiance?
  How could I feel, if it was he, life
  still pulsing warmly inside my bosom? I
  who am unworthy of such grace, a sinner I?
JUPITER. It's not for you to be the judge of your
  own worthiness. As he finds grace in you,
  so must you needs submit to him, without demur.
  Do you presume, blind girl, to overrule the god
  who reads all human hearts?

ALCMENE.   Amphitryon,
enough. I see what you are doing, I
am on the verge of tears because of your
great magnanimity; you've said these things,
I realize, to turn my mind away
from all its painful thoughts—but it returns
to them again. Go, darling, my whole life,
and find another mate, rejoice; while I
must weep away my days in thinking how
I may no longer gladden yours.
JUPITER.   Dear wife,
how much you touch me! Do look, won't you, at
the diadem you're holding in your hands.
ALCMENE. Oh save me, all you Powers above, from madness!
JUPITER. You see his name there, don't you? And last night
it was mine, not so? Isn't all
that we see happening around us here
a miracle? The diadem was under
lock and key, in my possession, wasn't
it, today? But when the box was opened,
I found the empty impress in the cotton, am
I right? And looked and saw it on your breast
already, glittering?
ALCMENE.   And that is how I am
to understand it? Jupiter? The Father
of the deathless gods and all ourselves?
JUPITER.   Who else,
I'd like to know, could ever have deceived
the finely poised gold-balance of your feeling,
eluded the antennae your woman's soul puts out
toward all around it, failed to jar the bells
the whisper of a breath sets ringing in your bosom?
ALCMENE. He himself!
JUPITER.   Only the All-powerful
dare to visit you as boldly as
that stranger did—and see how I defeat
such rivals! I am glad indeed to witness
how the All-knowing find their way into your heart,
witness how the Omnipresent creep
into your soul—dressed up in my stolen

features, dearest, forced to play, if they
expect to be received by you, me,
Amphitryon!

ALCMENE.   Oh yes, that's true! (*Kisses him.*)

JUPITER.   My angel!

ALCMENE. I'm so happy now! And oh how glad,
how very glad that I'm so happy. I'll
be glad to have suffered all the pain that Jupiter
has caused me, if only everything is nice
again between us.

JUPITER.   Let me tell you what
my thought is, shall I?

ALCMENE.   Yes, please do.

JUPITER.   And even
though no revelation should declare
it to us from on high, I'm nonetheless
inclined to think it's so.

ALCMENE.   Speak, do, you're making
me feel anxious—

JUPITER.   What—now don't be frightened—
what if you offended him?

ALCMENE.   I?
Offended him?

JUPITER.   Is he a being who exists
for you? His glorious handiwork, the world—
do you have eyes for it? Do you see him in the sunset
glow that lights up the hushed underwoods?
Do you hear him in the pleasant noise of waters
and the nightingale's voluptuous chorusing?
Don't the mountains towering up to Heaven
announce him to you all in vain, in vain
the cataract plunges from the steep to shatter
on the rocks below? When the sun aloft
in his great temple sends his beams abroad,
when through Creation beats a pulse of joy
and all things hymn his praise, don't you
descend into the mine shaft of your heart
to adore your idol?

ALCMENE.   What a shocking thing
to say! Can he be reverenced more piously,

more trustingly? Has there been a single day
I failed to go down on my knees before
his altar, giving thanks for life, for love,
for you? And didn't I, an hour or so
ago, beneath the stars, fling myself
face down before him, fervently, my ebullient
feelings sending up to Heaven, like steam
of sacrifice, adoring worship?

JUPITER.   Yes,
you flung yourself down on your face—but *why?*
I'll tell you why—in the lightning's bright electric
flourish you read a well-known letter.

ALCMENE. Oh, you're frightening! How did you find that out?

JUPITER. Who is it that you pray to at His altar? To Him,
perhaps, who sits above the clouds? Can a mind
that's so enslaved as yours is, comprehend
Him in the least? Can feelings, used to his
nest only, aspire to fly so high?
You grovel in the dust, but always to the man
you love, Amphitryon, am I correct?

ALCMENE. How you confuse me, poor unhappy woman that I am!
The involuntary movements of the soul, must they be censured
too? Am I supposed to pray to marble
walls? Well, I need features I can see
if I'm to think of him.

JUPITER.   You see? Just what
I said. And don't you think that such idolatry
offends him? Is he pleased to know
your lovely heart's not his? To feel himself
adored by you, that's his wish too, don't you
agree?

ALCMENE. Oh yes, I do, I do. Where should
there be a sinner whose pious homage isn't
pleasing to the gods?

JUPITER.   Of course! And if it's true
that he came down to you, the only reason
was, to *make* you think of him, to be
revenged, forgetful girl, on you.

ALCMENE.   Oh, dreadful!

JUPITER. Have no fear. You shan't be punished more
   than you deserve. But in the future, do
   you understand, it's he you have to think
   of at his altar, the one who appeared to you
   at night, not me.
ALCMENE.   Oh yes! I swear it, by
   the sacred gods! I recollect the way
   he looked, every feature of him, perfectly,
   and shan't mix up the two of you.
JUPITER.   Just so.
   For otherwise you risk his coming back.
   Every time you see his sacred *J*
   upon the diadem, concentrate
   your heart and soul in thinking how
   he appeared to you. Remember every detail
   of it, remember your quick start of fear,
   at the distaff, when the Immortal stood
   before you there, the treasure that he gave you
   and what you gave him in return, who helped
   you fasten it around yourself, and the never
   eaten ortolan—remember! And if
   your husband interrupts your meditation,
   beg him to be good enough to let you have
   an hour to yourself.
ALCMENE.   Fine, good—you'll see how satisfied
   you'll be with me. My first waking hour,
   from now on, I swear it, I'll not give
   a thought to you. But after that I shall
   forget Lord Jupiter.
JUPITER.   If great Cloud-shaking Zeus,
   touched to see the better woman you've
   become, should show himself to you in all
   his glory now, how, beloved, say,
   would you receive him?
ALCMENE.   Oh, I'd be so frightened!
   If only I had made a point of thinking
   of him at the altar always—after
   all, there is so little difference
   between you two.

JUPITER.   You've still not seen, Alcmene,
  his immortal countenance. In his presence,
  how it would dissolve with bliss unspeakable,
  your heart, your feeling for him seem like fire,
  like ice your feeling for Amphitryon.
  Why, if he were to touch your soul right now,
  then part from you and go back to Olympus,
  you would feel an unimaginable
  ravishment and weep to follow him.
ALCMENE. No, never think that, my Amphitryon.
  If I could turn back time one single day,
  I'd bolt my closet shut against all gods
  and heroes, yes, I would—
JUPITER.   You would? You really
  would?
ALCMENE. Indeed I would, oh gladly.
JUPITER (*aside*).
  Damn the deluded hope that tempted me
  down here!
ALCMENE.   What is it? Are you angry? Did I
  say something to annoy you, dear?
JUPITER.   My good child,
  you have no wish to solace his stupendous being?
  Won't allow his head, that superintends
  the worlds, the pillow of your breast when he seeks to rest
  it there? Olympus too, Alcmene, without love,
  is desolate! What good is it to see
  whole nations bowed down in the dust
  in adoration, to a bosom panting with desire?
  It's love he wants, not all those mad ideas
  they entertain about him. Veiled from sight
  forever as he is, what he longs
  for is to see himself reflected in a living
  soul, his own image mirrored in a tear
  of ecstasy. Beloved, think of how
  much joy, here between our Earth and Heaven,
  joy unending, he pours out; suppose,
  now, fate appointed you to render him
  the thanks of all the millions of Earth's beings,
  paying back the debt Creation owes

him with a single smile. Would you, I wonder—
no, I'll never think it, don't, please, let
me ever think—

ALCMENE.　　　　　Far be it from me ever
to strive against the gods' decree. If I've
been chosen for such sacred office, to him
who made me I submit my will. However—

JUPITER. Yes?

ALCMENE.　　If it were left to me to choose—?

JUPITER. Were left to you to choose?

ALCMENE.　　　　　　　　*He* would have
my deepest reverence, and *you* would have,
Amphitryon, my love.

JUPITER.　　　　　But now suppose
I were, for you, the god—?

ALCMENE.　　　　　　　　Suppose that you—
my head is spinning!—were, for me, the god?
Should I go down before you in the dust, or shouldn't
I? The god—it's you, it's you?

JUPITER.　　　　　　　For you
to say. Myself, I am Amphitryon.

ALCMENE. Amphitryon—

JUPITER.　　　　　　　For you, Amphitryon,
oh yes. But let me ask you: if I were,
for you, this god who came down to you from
Olympus out of love, what then, what then?

ALCMENE. If you, love, were, for me, this god—then I'd
not know where my Amphitryon might be
and I would follow you no matter where,
down to Orcus, if I had to, like
Eurydice.

JUPITER.　　Yes, if you didn't know
where your Amphitryon was—but if Lord
Amphitryon should now appear?

ALCMENE.　　　　　　　　If he
should now appear—ah, but you want to torture
me! How can Amphitryon *appear*
when my arms are wound around Amphitryon
this very moment?

JUPITER.   Yes—but it could be the god
  your arms are wound around, all the while believing
  it's Amphitryon. Then your feeling as you do
  is no surprise, is it? But now suppose
  I am the god embracing you, and lo,
  Amphitryon appears—your heart, what would
  it say to that?

ALCMENE.   You were the god embracing
  me, and lo, Amphitryon appeared?—
  I'd be so very sad, oh so dejected,
  and wish that he could be the god and you
  would go on being my Amphitryon
  forever, as you are.

JUPITER.   My creature whom
  I worship! In whom I am so blessed—in blessing,
  blessed! So perfectly concordant with
  the great original divine conception,
  in shape and substance, string and sound! Such a one
  as has not issued from my hand in eons!

ALCMENE. Amphitryon!

JUPITER.   Don't be alarmed, oh don't!
  The darkness will dissolve, revealing you
  triumphant. He longs, the god, to show himself
  to you, and well before the legions of the stars
  have trooped across the silent fields of night
  you'll know the one on whose account your bosom
  kindles.—Sosia!

SOSIA.   Sir!

JUPITER.   Up now, my faithful
  fellow, so we may celebrate this day!
  Alcmene's reconciled with me in dearest
  love, and you must hurry back to camp
  to find our guests and summon them to feast with us.
                (*Exeunt Jupiter and Alcmene.*)

SCENE 6
Charis. Sosia.

CHARIS (*aside*).
  Unlucky woman, what was that
  you heard? They may have been Olympians?

And this one here, who passes for my Sosia—
perhaps he is an Immortal too, Apollo,
Hermes or Ganymede?

SOSIA (*aside*).
                    The Lightning God,
great Zeus, it was perhaps!

CHARIS (*aside*).
                    Oh, shame on you
for treating him the way you did!

SOSIA (*aside*).
                    He wasn't
badly served—stood up to his man,
the fellow did, and hit out like a tiger
for his master.

CHARIS (*aside*).
              But I might be wrong.
Let me see. (*Aloud.*) Come, Sosia, we'll make peace
between us too.

SOSIA.   Some other time. I've got
a lot to do.

CHARIS.   You're going? Where?

SOSIA.   To summon
our officers.

CHARIS.   Can I have a word with you,
dear husband, first?

SOSIA.   Dear husband, is it? Very
well.

CHARIS. Perhaps you've heard how yesterday,
at nightfall, two great gods descended
from Olympus to my Princess here and to
her faithful servant—Zeus Cloud-gatherer,
and with him Shining Phoebus?

SOSIA.   Yes, but is
it true? I didn't hear it gladly, Charis.
I have always been against such marriages.

CHARIS. Against them? Why, I wonder?

SOSIA.   Well, to speak
quite frankly, it strikes me as a case of horse
and ass.

CHARIS.   Horse and ass! A god and princess!
(*Aside.*) He's not from Olympus, I don't think.
(*Aloud.*) You're pleased to joke with your unworthy servant.
Thebes never has enjoyed, in all its years,
an honor such as this is for us all.

SOSIA. For me it was no honor. Dishonor would
have made me ache no more than these damned
trophies honoring my shoulders. I
must hurry off.

CHARIS.   I know. As I was saying—
whoever dreamt such guests would come to us?
Who would have thought, wrapped up inside poor human
flesh, to find Immortals? We have got
our good side, I assure you, more than one,
but kept them turned away, I fear—they
might have been on view more than they were.

SOSIA. Yes indeed, that would have been a help!
For you were not much gentler than a wildcat
with me, wife. Learn nicer ways.

CHARIS.   I didn't
know that I offended you, not really.
Did more than—

SOSIA.   Not offended me! Damn
me for a Turk if you didn't deserve,
this morning, as good a beating as any woman's
ever had dealt out to her.

CHARIS.   What happened,
then?

SOSIA. What happened, booby girl, you'd like
to know? You told me, didn't you, you'd go
and have that Theban for yourself, a rascal
I kicked out the door no more than a few
days ago? Promised me a pair of horns,
you did. Called me a cuckold to my face.

CHARIS. Oh, that was just a joke, believe me!

SOSIA.   Joke
indeed! Joke with me again like that,
I promise you, and you will feel this hand!

CHARIS. Good heavens, what is happening to me?

SOSIA. That awful swine!

CHARIS. Don't look so fierce, my dear!
  My heart is breaking into little pieces!
SOSIA. Shame on you, blasphemer, to mock your marriage
  vows like that! Go, and sin no more,
  I counsel you—and when I come again
  I want bratwurst and cabbage for my supper.
CHARIS. Whatever you desire.—Why doubt him any
  longer, oh why hesitate? It's him,
  oh is it him?
SOSIA. It's who?
CHARIS. I grovel in the dust,
  oh see!
SOSIA. What's wrong with you?
CHARIS. In the dust
  before you, penitent!
SOSIA. Have you gone mad?
CHARIS. You're him, I know it.
SOSIA. *Who* am I?
CHARIS. Oh, why
  should you deny it?
SOSIA. Is everybody raving
  mad today?
CHARIS. I know I saw, in
  the flames of anger darting from your eyes,
  Apollo the Far-darter.
SOSIA. I, Apollo?
  You're possessed, I think. I'm cur to one,
  and to another god. But what I am's
  the old familiar donkey Sosia!
  (*Exit.*)
CHARIS. My old familiar donkey Sosia?
  How glad I am to know it, I must say—
  you'll find your bratwurst served you cold today.
  (*Exit.*)

ACT III

SCENE I
Enter Amphitryon.

AMPHITRYON. How I hate the sight of all these generals'
  faces! Each one comes to offer me

59

congratulations on our victory,
I receive each one with an embrace, and all
the while I'm thinking, Go to hell, each one!
Not one with heart enough for me to pour
out my own heart, that is so full, to him.
—A diadem kept under seal is stolen
from its casket, and the seal remains intact!
Well, it can happen: magicians at a distance can spirit
something we are holding right out
of our hands. But to steal a man's own form
and figure from him and do his office by his wife—
that is surely one of Satan's tricks!
In rooms ablaze with candles, no one with his
five senses still intact ever mistook his friends,
oh never—till today! Eyes unsocketed
and rolling on a table top—severed limbs,
ears, fingers, stuffed in boxes—these
used to be enough to tell a husband
by. But now—from now on we shall need
to brand the hides of married men, hang
bells around their necks the way we do
with sheep. She is as capable of base
deception as her turtle dove: I'll sooner
trust the honesty of rogues escaped the noose
than think her false. But she has lost her wits;
tomorrow when it dawns, the doctors must
be sent for, I am sure, if only there's
an opportunity for doing so.

SCENE 2

Enter Mercury on a balcony above.

MERCURY (*aside*).

It shows you what a true friend, Papa
Jupiter, I am, my coming with you
down to Earth upon your love-adventure.
For by the Styx, my part in all this is
so boring! Playing husband to that lady's-maid,
that Charis, any further than is needed,
all the way, does not excite my ardor.

I'll have a little fun here of my own
and drive him mad, that jealous ninny there.
AMPHITRYON. Why should this house's gate be barred by day?
MERCURY. Hello there! Patience! Who's that knocking?
AMPHITRYON.   Me.
MERCURY. Who's me?
AMPHITRYON.   Come, open up, will you?
MERCURY.   Will I?
You clumsy peasant, making all that noise
and speaking in that way to me! Who do
you think you are?
AMPHITRYON.   You don't know who I am,
do you?
MERCURY. Oh yes I do. There's not a one
who lifts the latch that I don't know.—Don't
know who he is!
AMPHITRYON.   Has every one in Thebes
chewed locoweed and lost their minds today?
Oh Sosia, Sosia!
MERCURY.   Yes, that's what I'm called.
The rascal shouts my name so loud you'd think
he was afraid I might forget it.
AMPHITRYON.   Good
god, don't you see me standing here?
MERCURY.   I see
you perfectly. What's on your mind?
AMPHITRYON.   What's on
my mind, you rogue!
MERCURY.   All right—then what's not on
your mind? Talk up, fellow, if you want
an answer.
AMPHITRYON. Scoundrel, wait and see! I'll come
up there and teach you with a stick to speak to me
like that.
MERCURY.   Oh my, oh my! Such a roughneck
down below. I hope I haven't given you
offense.
AMPHITRYON. You devil!
MERCURY.   Calmly, please.
AMPHITRYON.   Hello!
Is anybody home in there?

MERCURY [*falsetto*]. Oh Philip,
Charmion, where can you be hiding?
AMPHITRYON. Villain!
MERCURY. Somebody's bound to answer soon downstairs.
But if you are impatient and touch that knocker
one more time, I have an emissary
here I'm ready to send down to you—
upon your head.
AMPHITRYON. The insolence of him,
my god! A fellow I have booted I
don't know how many times! To crucify
whom all I need to do is nod!
MERCURY. Finished,
are you, done? You've looked me over thoroughly?
Measured me from head to foot with those
pop eyes? Oh, how he stares! If looks
could kill, I would have been a corpse by now.
AMPHITRYON. I tremble like a leaf, myself, to think
what you are getting ready for yourself
by talking so. The merciless beatings waiting
for you!—Now come down and open up
the door.
MERCURY. Oh, finally!
AMPHITRYON. Don't make me wait,
I'm in a hurry.
MERCURY. Then say what is it that
you want. The door unbolted down there?
AMPHITRYON. Yes.
MERCURY. All right. You could have spoken more politely,
don't you think? Now who is it you are looking
for?
AMPHITRYON. Who is it I am looking for?
MERCURY. Yes, yes. You're deaf, I think. You'd like to speak
with whom?
AMPHITRYON. Whom I'd like to speak with? Cur!
I'll break your every bone for you when I'm
let in!
MERCURY. You know what, friend? My advice to you
is, leave. You rub me the wrong way. Now leave.

AMPHITRYON. I'll teach you, villain, what a servant may
  expect who mocks his master.
MERCURY.   Master? Mock
  my master, me? You're supposed to be my master?
AMPHITRYON. And now all the denials start.
MERCURY.   I only
  have one master, and he's Amphitryon.
AMPHITRYON. And who except myself's Amphitryon,
  you blear-eyed rascal, you, who can't tell night
  from day.
MERCURY.   Amphitryon?
AMPHITRYON.   Amphitryon,
  you heard me.
MERCURY.   Ha, ha! Thebans, come here, do.
AMPHITRYON. I wish the earth would swallow me. Such shame!
MERCURY. My friend down there! I'd like to know the tavern's
  name you got so good and drunk in.
AMPHITRYON.   Heavens!
MERCURY. You drank new wine, did you, or old?
AMPHITRYON.   Oh gods!
MERCURY. And why not one more glass or so? You might
  have drunk your way along to being King
  of Egypt.
AMPHITRYON. It's the end of me, this!
MERCURY.   On
  your way, my boy. I'm sorry for you, really.
  Go and sleep it off. Amphitryon
  lives here, Commander-in-Chief of Thebes. I shouldn't
  like you to disturb his rest.
AMPHITRYON.   What's that? Amphitryon
  in there?
MERCURY.   That's right, inside the palace, he
  and his Alcmene. Go along now, I
  must ask you once again, and don't disturb
  the lovers' joy, unless you want him to appear
  himself and punish you for your impertinence.
(*Exit.*)

SCENE 3

AMPHITRYON. What a blow you've suffered, miserable
  man, an absolutely crushing one!

Oh, it's the end of me. Buried in the ground
I am, already, and my wife already married
to another man. I can't think what to do.
Make a public explanation of the shame
my house has suffered, or keep silent? There
is nothing here that calls for mercy, no,
no voice, when I take counsel with myself,
but that of burning vengeance! Let it be
my sole, my only care to see the traitor
shan't get off alive!

SCENE 4

Enter Sosia and Generals.

SOSIA.   All here,
  Sire, all the guests I could collect
  on such short notice. Whew! I don't sit
  at your table, to be sure, but I have earned
  a dinner.
AMPHITRYON. There you are, I see!
SOSIA.   Yes, Sir?
AMPHITRYON. You dog, prepare to die!
SOSIA.   To die?
AMPHITRYON.   I'll teach
  you who I am!
SOSIA.   Damn, don't I know it very
  well?
AMPHITRYON. You knew it, traitor, you?
              (*His hand goes to his sword.*)
SOSIA.   Oh sirs,
  I beg you, help me!
FIRST GENERAL.   Pardon, Sire! (*Stops his hand.*)
AMPHITRYON.   No,
  don't stop me.
SOSIA.   Only tell me what my crime
  is!
AMPHITRYON. You can ask me that? Out of my way,
  you hear, and let my vengeance have the satisfaction
  due it.

SOSIA.   When a man is hanged, they always
   tell him why.
FIRST GENERAL. If you would be so good, Sir?
SECOND GENERAL. Tell us what he's done.
SOSIA.   Oh yes, go on,
   sirs, if you would!
AMPHITRYON.   This lump of insolence,
   you hear, five minutes since refused to open
   up the door to me and poured down
   torrents of abuse on my head one drop
   of which is grounds enough to have him crucified.
   Dog, die!
SOSIA (*sinking to his knees*).
              I'm dead already.
FIRST GENERAL.   Steady now.
SOSIA. Please, generals!
SECOND GENERAL.   What is it?
SOSIA.   Does he mean
   to run me through?
AMPHITRYON.   For the second time, out
   of my way! He has to be paid back in full
   for all the indignities he made me suffer.
SOSIA. But what can I have done this time when every
   one of the nine hours past I spent
   in camp, as you commanded.
FIRST GENERAL.   It's the truth.
   He invited us to dine with you. The last
   two hours he was there in camp with us
   and never once out of our sight.
AMPHITRYON.   Who gave
   you such an order?
SOSIA.   Who did? You yourself!
AMPHITRYON. I did? When?
SOSIA.   It was right after you
   were reconciled with our Princess. Overjoyed, you instantly commanded a great
   feast for all the palace.
AMPHITRYON.   Every hour
   that passes, every step I take, draws
   me ever deeper into this labyrinth!

What shall I make of all this, friends?
You've heard what's happened here, have you?
FIRST GENERAL.   It's hopeless
   trying to make sense of what he says;
   right now your only care should be, to act
   with a bold spirit and tear to shreds the web
   of falsehoods spun by this intrigue.
AMPHITRYON.   Good, that's
   what I will do! But I shall need your help.
   My lucky star has led you here to me.
   I'll put it to the proof now, all my happiness
   of life. Oh, how I am on fire to know
   the truth, and how I fear to know it—equally.
                              (*Knocks.*)

                              SCENE 5
                          Enter Jupiter.

JUPITER. What noise is that compels me to descend below?
   Who is it knocking at my door? My generals,
   is it?
AMPHITRYON. Almighty gods! Who are you?
SECOND GENERAL.   Jupiter,
   I'm seeing double—two Amphitryons!
AMPHITRYON. I'm numb with shock, completely! Alas for me!
   The riddle has been answered now.
FIRST GENERAL.   Which one
   of you is Amphitryon?
SECOND GENERAL.   Yes, ask! No eye
   can tell apart two creatures so exactly
   like each other.
SOSIA (*placing himself beside Jupiter*).
                  Good sirs, here is the true
   Amphitryon, the other is a mountebank
   who should be given a good hiding.
THIRD GENERAL (*pointing to Amphitryon*).
                              Un-
   believable! An impostor, this one here?
AMPHITRYON. I've suffered quite enough humiliation
   from all this hocus-pocus! (*Gripping his sword.*) This key
   here will unlock the mystery.

FIRST GENERAL.   Stop, will
    you?

AMPHITRYON. No!

SECOND GENERAL. Why, what do you intend to do?

AMPHITRYON. Punish the most villainous deception
    ever practiced! Out of my way, I tell
    you!

JUPITER. Calmly, my good man. Such violence
    of feeling is not needed here. One
    so much concerned about his name must doubt
    his title to it.

SOSIA.   Exactly my opinion.
    The clever rascal's stuffed a pillow in his shirt,
    painted his face up and now presents
    himself as our master.

AMPHITRYON.   Traitor! That
    revolting nonsense which you keep on mouthing
    will have for its reward—three hundred lashes
    laid on you uninterruptedly
    by three arms taking turns.

SOSIA.   Ha, ha!
    My master is a man of spirit, he
    will teach you to mistreat his servants.

AMPHITRYON.   No, I'll not
    be stopped a minute longer from blotting out,
    with that pretender's blood, the rank dishonor
    I have suffered.

FIRST GENERAL.   Forgive us, Sir. We can't
    allow it, no—Amphitryon against
    Amphitryon!

AMPHITRYON.   *You* won't allow it!

FIRST GENERAL.   Calm yourself.

AMPHITRYON. Is this the kind of friendship, generals,
    you show me, the unwavering support you swore?
    Instead of you yourself avenging your commander's
    honor, you take this cheap dissembler's side
    and prevent the sword of justice from descending on
    his neck?

FIRST GENERAL. If you possessed an independent
    judgment here, as you do not, you would

approve our conduct. Who, of you two,
is Amphitryon? Why you, of course.
Now that's all very well, but so is he.
Where is god's finger pointing from on high
to show us in which bosom, one so like
the other, the traitor's heart's concealed? Once that's
discovered, our vengeance will know what
to do, oh never doubt it. But now when all
one could do would be to brandish his sheathed
sword angrily in the air, not knowing whom
to draw against, it is better off remaining
sheathed. The matter needs to be
investigated calmly, and if you're quite
convinced that you are Lord Amphitryon,
as we for our part hope you are, but have
to doubt it too, considering how strange
the circumstances are, you'll find it no
whit harder to prove your case to us than he.

AMPHITRYON. I—*I* must prove to you—?

FIRST GENERAL.   By arguments
compelling our assent, and till you do,
the matter rests.

JUPITER.   How right you are, Photidas,
I must say; and the likeness which we seem
to share, this man and I, excuses your
irresolution as concerns myself.
I will not take offense if you should wish
to make comparison between the two
of us. But no deciding things, as cowards
do, by violence. My intention is
to summon all of Thebes together in a body
here and prove what blood I am descended
from. My lineage is royal, I
am Lord in Thebes: he shall acknowledge it
himself. Before me in the dust he'll bow
his face. The fertile fields around us, the pastures
black with herds, this house here
and the dame who exercises quiet sway
within its rooms—all these he shall acknowledge
mine. The entire world shall know no shame

attaches to Amphitryon. All those
misgivings which that fool aroused: here stands
the one to prove them nought. All Thebes will be
here shortly. Come, meanwhile, and honor with your presence
the board to which my Sosia has invited you.

SOSIA.   I knew it, didn't I? These words
good sirs, like a fresh wind, blow
away all doubts that still remain. The real
Amphitryon is the Amphitryon where dinner's waiting
for you on the table.

AMPHITRYON.   You justice-dealing gods!
How can a man be humbled down so low?
To see my wife, my honor, rulership
and name stolen from me by a villainous
impostor! And my own friends to tie
my hands!

FIRST GENERAL. Whoever you may be, Sir, patience,
please. A few more hours only and we
shall know the truth, and then we'll have our vengeance
quick enough! And alas for him, say I,
on whom it falls.

AMPHITRYON.   All right, you craven creatures,
go and offer homage to the impostor! Other
friends than you are left me still in Thebes,
men who feel the hurt I feel, who'll rally
to my side and not refuse their arm
to help avenge it.

JUPITER.   By all means. D   call
them to you. I await them.

AMPHITRYON.   Loud-mouthed
mountebank! Pure fraud! And meanwhile you'll
sneak out the back gate to the fields. But you won't
escape my vengeance!

JUPITER.   Go on, please, and call
your friends, and after you have brought them here
to me, I'll say a word or two, but nothing now.

AMPHITRYON. You're right there, by the Lord of Clouds, great Zeus!
For if it's granted me to track you down,
you won't say more than two words, brute, before

69

my blade is planted in your throat, up
to the hilt.
JUPITER.   Your friends, man, call them here. I'll never
speak a word meanwhile, only look
my words, if that's your wish.
AMPHITRYON.   I'm off as fast
as legs can take me, before he vanishes!
Gods, let mine be the pleasure, oh you must,
of sending him down to your Orcus, straight
to Hell, today! I'll come back here with friends,
all armed, they'll post themselves around this house,
and like a wasp I'll sting him in the breast
and drawing out the sting, suck out
his last breath so that the wind
will blow his dry bones all around.
                    (*Exit.*)

SCENE 6

JUPITER. Do my house the honor, gentlemen,
of going in now, if you would.
FIRST GENERAL.   I swear
all this is too much for my wits to comprehend.
SOSIA. Well, call a truce to your astonishment.
Go in and eat and drink away till morning.
                    (*Exeunt Jupiter and Generals.*)

SCENE 7
Sosia alone.

SOSIA. Now I'll sit down to dinner, too! And when
the war is talked about, the stories I
will tell! I'm all afire to describe just how
we fought our way into Pharissa. And never
have I been so famished, like a wolf.

SCENE 8
Enter Mercury.

MERCURY. Where to, fellow? Poking around
here too, are you, unblushing noser-out
of kitchen scraps?

70

SOSIA.   Oh no, sir—please
   excuse me!
MERCURY.   Off with you, you hear? Clear out!
   Unless you'd like to have me put your cap
   on straight for you?
SOSIA.   Oh dear! My generous
   and noble self: control yourself! Spare Sosia
   a little, please! How can you always be
   so grimly bent on beating up yourself?
MERCURY. Oh, back to your old tricks again? Appropriating
   my name for yourself, you scamp?
SOSIA. Oh never! God forbid, brave self of mine,
   that I should be so grasping, so ungenerous.
   Take half my name, it's yours, take all of it,
   if that's your wish, it's rubbish after all.
   And even if the name were Castor, Pollux—
   is there anything I wouldn't share with you,
   O brother as you are to me? I meekly
   bear your presence in my master's house,
   then you bear mine, in a fraternal spirit,
   and while those two Amphitryons are trying
   hard to break each other's neck, why shouldn't
   the two Sosias sit down together full
   of peace and concord, clink glasses cheerfully
   and wish each other a long life?
MERCURY.   No, no,
   that's nonsense, man! Am I supposed to suck
   my thumb for hunger while you dine—the table's
   only set for one.
SOSIA.   It doesn't matter
   in the least. The same womb gave
   us birth, the same roof sheltered us,
   we slept in the same bed, we shared one shirt,
   one fate, then why not share one plate?
MERCURY. About such sharing I know nothing, neither
   bed, nor shirt, nor bite of bread I've shared
   with anyone. From childhood up I've been
   entirely on my own.
SOSIA.   Consider. We
   are twins. The elder, you; I know my place;

the precedence in everything is yours.
The first spoon in the pot is yours, the second,
mine, third yours, mine fourth, and so on.
MERCURY.   None
of that. I can't do without the entire
portion, me, and what's left over I
put by for later. Let a man's hand stray
too near my plate and I will teach him a good
lesson, by the gods!
SOSIA.   If nothing else,
then let me be the shadow cast behind
you as you sit and eat.
MERCURY.   No, not my footprint
in the sand! Clear off!
SOSIA.   Oh savage heart! A man
of iron hammered out on an anvil!
MERCURY. Am I supposed to stretch out, like a journey-
man, on the grass outside the gate and live
off the blue sky? No horse has earned
so good a feed, by god, as me today.
First was the trip from camp to here, by night;
then back to camp again this morning, early,
to hunt up guests to fill the palace table.
Don't you think my poor old busy legs
are worn almost to stumps from this damned running
back and forth? We're having wurst today,
and cabbage—just what is needed to recruit
my strength.
SOSIA.   How right you are! A fellow breaks
a leg, and his neck too, so easily
on those damned tree roots twisting every which
way all along the path.
MERCURY.   So there you are!
SOSIA. —Forsaken by the gods I am! She's fixed
some wurst, has Charis?
MERCURY.   Yes—fresh wurst. But not
for you. They killed a pig. We've made it up
between us, she and I.

SOSIA. Good, oh very good—
I'll go and lie down in my grave. And cabbage
too?

MERCURY. Yes, cabbage. And anyone whose mouth should water
too much hearing this, look out, I say,
for Charis and myself.

SOSIA. Charis and yourself may stuff
yourselves with cabbage till you choke. I
can do without your wurst, I can. The providence
that feeds the birds of heaven shall feed old Sosia
too, I think, that honest man.

MERCURY. You dare
to call yourself that still, you rascal?
Donkey, dog—

SOSIA. Oh no, oh no, I didn't
mean myself, I meant a relative
of mine called Sosia too who used to be
in service here—he always used to flog
the other servants, till one day a fellow
came along who seemed to fall straight from
the clouds and pitched him out the door, at dinner
time exactly.

MERCURY. Watch your tongue, you hear,
no more of that! Just watch your tongue is my
advice, if you want to go on being counted
in the census of the living.

SOSIA (*aside*).
How I'd throw
you out, I would, if only I were brave
enough—you misbegotten faker, cheat,
as swollen as a toad with arrogance.

MERCURY. What's that you said?

SOSIA. I said?

MERCURY. I thought I heard
you say—?

SOSIA. I say?

MERCURY. Yes, you.

SOSIA. I never uttered
a peep.

MERCURY. I'd swear I heard something about
   throw out, and misbegotten faker,
   cheat, unless I'm much mistaken.
SOSIA.   A parrot's
   what you heard, I'll bet. They chatter
   when the weather's good.
MERCURY.   All right—a parrot.
   Now good-bye. But if your back starts itching,
   knock here at this door and ask for me.
                              (*Exit.*)

SCENE 9

SOSIA. The arrogance of Satan! I hope the pig
   they killed kills you!—"He'll teach the man a lesson
   whose hand strays too near to his plate"!—I'd rather
   share my dinner with a sheepdog than eat
   out of the same plate with him. His own
   father, I am sure, might starve to death
   in front of him before he'd let him have
   as much as what his toothpick pokes out
   from between his teeth. But renegade I am,
   I've got my just deserts! If I had a wurst
   in both hands now, I'd not allow myself
   a single bite. To desert your master that's
   so good to you, poor man, when he was driven
   from his house by superior force! But there he comes
   already, with a band of stout friends at his back.
   And crowds of people streaming this way
   from the other side! What's happening, I wonder?

SCENE 10
Enter Amphitryon and Colonels from one side,
populace from the other.

AMPHITRYON. Greetings to you all! But friends, who called
   you here?
A CITIZEN.   Heralds cried in every street
   for us to rally at your palace.
AMPHITRYON.   Heralds! Why?

74

CITIZEN. To hear your lips pronounce the words, they said,
   that will dispel the mystery that has plunged
   the entire city into such confusion.
AMPHITRYON (*to the Colonels*).
                                   Oh,
   the insolence of him! Can impudence
   be carried any further?
SECOND COLONEL.   Then it seems
   he's going to appear.
AMPHITRYON.   What does it matter?
   Let him.
FIRST COLONEL. Never fear, Sir. At your side
   you have me, Argatiphontidas—and once
   I fix him with my eye, his life will dance for it
   upon this sword point.
AMPHITRYON (*to the populace*).
                    Hear me, citizens
   of Thebes! I'm not the one who called this great
   assembly together, although I welcome it
   with all my heart. That spirit out of Hell
   and spewing lies it was, the one who'd like
   to drive me out of Thebes, out of my own
   wife's heart, out of the world's remembrance—
   yes, if he could, out of the fortress of my own
   consciousness. And therefore concentrate
   your senses now, I beg you. And even if
   each one of you were Argus, thousand-eyed,
   expert to tell, in the midnight's dark, the presence
   of the cricket by its footprint in the sand, spare no
   exertion of your faculties—dilate your eyes
   like moles at midday looking for the sun;
   oh, focus all your glances in a mirror, which then
   as one united beam throw full on me,
   minutely searching up and down, from head
   to foot, my person here, and say, declare,
   reply: Who am I?
PEOPLE.   Who are you? Amphitryon!
AMPHITRYON. Good—so I am. Now when that son of darkness
   appears before us all, that miscreation
   on whose head not one hair doesn't

    curl like mine; when your tricked and baffled senses
    even lack the marks that mothers need to tell
    their babies by; when you must judge between us
    as between two drops of water, but one
    drop sweet and pure and silver in its truth, the other
    poison, fraud, and craft and murder, death;
    then, citizens of Thebes, remember who
    I am: Amphitryon, the one who bent [*crumpling his crest*]
    this helmet plume.
PEOPLE.   Oh no, oh no, don't do
    that, never break the feather off while you
    stand here before us in the bloom of life!
SECOND COLONEL.   Do you
    imagine we would also—?
AMPHITRYON.   Please, my friends.
    I am in full possession of my wits and know
    what I am doing.
FIRST COLONEL.   Do just as you wish.
    However, I must hope that bit of farce
    was not staged for my benefit. If all
    your generals proved vacillators when
    that ape performed his trick, it doesn't follow
    in the least that that will happen
    with Argatiphontidas. In an affair
    of honor, if your friend requires help, you jam
    your helmet down around your ears and drive
    straight at the foe. It's all right for old
    women to listen meekly while the enemy
    brags on; but as for me, I'm for the shortest
    way of doing things; in cases such
    as these, you run your man through with your sword
    right off and never mind formalities.
    In short, Argatiphontidas today
    will show the stuff he's made of—by the God
    of War, no other hand but mine, you'll see,
    will make this fellow chew the grass.
AMPHITRYON.   Then to
    it!
SOSIA. Let me kneel down at your feet, my true,
    my gentle, dreadfully abused, good master.

I repent me my offense entirely—
punish me as I deserve, with fist
and foot, with slaps and kicks and buffets. Kill
me, even, I'll not whimper once.
AMPHITRYON.   Stand up.
  What's happened?
SOSIA.   Not so much as one whiff
  of their dinner did they let me have! My other
  I, who serves your other you, was once
  again possessed completely by the devil—
  I, in short, am de-Sosialated,
  as you are de-Amphitryonitized.
AMPHITRYON. You hear him, citizens?
SOSIA.   Yes, citizens
  of Thebes, the one who's standing here's the true
  Amphitryon, and that one sitting
  down to dinner in the palace there
  deserves to be himself a dinner—for the crows.
  Up! Storm the palace, if you would, good sirs,
  the cabbage don't keep warm for ever.
AMPHITRYON.   Follow
  me!
SOSIA. Look, there he is now, he and she!

SCENE 11

Enter Jupiter, Alcmene, Mercury, Charis, Generals.

ALCMENE (*to Jupiter*).
  Oh, but you are dreadful! You say he is
  a mortal man, and would have me suffer the disgrace
  of being seen by him?
PEOPLE.   You deathless gods,
  what's this?
JUPITER.   Your husband, Lord Amphitryon,
  and *no one else* has ever been allowed
  within the precincts of your soul—
  and I wish the world to know it.
AMPHITRYON.   Lord of all
  my life! Unhappy woman!

77

ALCMENE.   No one else
  indeed! Can I undo what is already
  done?
COLONELS. O you Olympians! See there!
  Amphitryon!
JUPITER. You owe it to yourself, to me,
  my dearest one. I beg you, master your
  repugnance, oh you must. Come, muster all
  your courage, a triumph is prepared for you!
AMPHITRYON. Lightning, hell, the devil! Look on such
  a scene, must I?
JUPITER.   Good citizens, be welcome
  here.
AMPHITRYON. It's your death, brute, that they are here
  for—come to cut your throat! (*Draws his sword.*) Now forward!
SECOND GENERAL (*interposing himself*).

                                              Halt, you!

AMPHITRYON. Thebans, forward, forward!
FIRST GENERAL (*pointing to Amphitryon*).

                              Thebans, seize
  him, the impostor, do you hear!
AMPHITRYON.   Argatiphontidas!
FIRST COLONEL [*Argatiphontidas*].
  Am I bewitched?
PEOPLE.   How is a man's eye
  to decide between them?
AMPHITRYON.   Death! The devil! Rage
  unspeakable and no revenge! Oh, I
  am crushed! (*Collapses in Sosia's arms.*)
JUPITER.   Do listen to me for a moment, fool.
SOSIA. My goodness, he can't hear very well, he's dead.
FIRST COLONEL. What good was it to bend his helmet plume?
  —"Dilate your eyes like moles" indeed! The one
  his wife acknowledges, he is the one.
FIRST GENERAL (*pointing to Jupiter*).
  Here, colonels, here is your Amphitryon.
AMPHITRYON (*reviving*).
  Who does his own wife say it is?
FIRST COLONEL.   She recognizes
  him she came out of the house with, him.

Whoever would she cling to, vinelike, for support,
if not to her Amphitryon?

AMPHITRYON.   If only
I possessed enough strength still
to stamp the tongue that said that in the dust!
She doesn't recognize him—never, no! (*Gets to his feet again.*)

SECOND GENERAL. You lie! Do you imagine you can shake
the people's judgment when they can see
with their own eyes?

AMPHITRYON.   I repeat, she doesn't
recognize him! If she does—can think
he is her husband—I will never ask
who I am any more and hail him as
Amphitryon.

FIRST GENERAL. Agreed. Then let her speak.

SECOND GENERAL. My Princess, say.

AMPHITRYON.   Alcmene, bride, oh say!
Bestow the bright light of your eyes once more
on me! Acknowledge him the man, and quick
as that thought flashes to the brain, my sword relieves
you of all sight of me.

FIRST GENERAL.   Good, good! The sentence
shan't have long to wait for execution.

SECOND GENERAL. Do you know the man whom you see there?

FIRST GENERAL.   The stranger,
do you know him?

AMPHITRYON.   How could it be you shouldn't
know this bosom, bosom that you often
pressed your ear to, reporting how it beat
with oh so many strokes of love for you?
Nor recognize these accents which, so often,
before I gave them voice, your eyes had stolen
from my lips already?

ALCMENE.   Let me disappear
into the everlasting night!

AMPHITRYON.   I knew
it, didn't I? See, citizens of Thebes—
Peneus, that swift stream, would sooner
backwards roll, the Bosphorus carve out
a bed on Ida's top, dromedaries

79

crisscross Ocean, than she should recognize
that stranger there.
PEOPLE.   Is he Amphitryon then,
this one, I wonder? She still hesitates.
FIRST GENERAL. Speak, Lady!
SECOND GENERAL.   Speak!
THIRD GENERAL.   Oh tell us!—
SECOND GENERAL.   Princess, do!
FIRST GENERAL. If she continues silent, we are lost.
JUPITER. The truth, child, tell the truth.
ALCMENE.   Friends, *this* one is
Amphitryon.
AMPHITRYON.   He!—That one!—Gods almighty!
FIRST GENERAL. Good, that decides the matter. Now depart.
AMPHITRYON. Alcmene!
SECOND GENERAL.   Impostor, go—unless you'd like
ourselves to execute the sentence on you.
AMPHITRYON. My own love!
ALCMENE.   Vile creature! Odious man!
You dare to call me so? Before my husband's
awe-commanding countenance, I am
not shielded from your mania? You monster!
Far more hideous to me than bloated
shapes that squat in fens! What harm did I
do you that you should creep up on me under
cover of a night engendered out of Hell
and dribble your disgusting venom on my wings?
What more than that I caught your eye, corrupted
creature, like a glowworm, in the silence?
Oh, finally it's clear to me the mad
delusion under which I labored. What
I needed was the brightness of the sun by which to see
the difference between the cringing figure
of a vulgar peasant and the heroic architecture
of these royal limbs, between the ox and stag.
A curse on senses that surrendered to so gross
a hoax, a breast that rang so falsely to the touch,
a soul so little worth as not to know
its own true love! Without a sentry to mount guard
on my heart and keep it blameless,

I'll hide myself away, I swear,
where nothing lives, on a mountain peak not even
visited by owls. Your odious
deceit's succeeded, go! My peace of soul
is snapped and broken now.

AMPHITRYON.   Oh, you unhappy
creature! Do you believe that I'm
the one who appeared to you last night?

ALCMENE.   Enough!
(To Jupiter).
Allow me now, my husband, to depart. I ask
you to be good enough to curtail a little what is
the bitterest hour of my life. I must escape
these thousand stares which beat me down, like clubs,
from one side and the other.

JUPITER.   Oh heavenly
creature, you! Oh brighter than the sun!
A triumph is awaiting you the like
of which no daughter of a Prince of Thebes has ever
had. I beg you, stay a moment more.
(To Amphitryon.)
And now do you believe that I'm Amphitryon?

AMPHITRYON. Do I believe that you're Amphitryon?
A low fellow—more hideous to me
than words of mine are able to express!—

FIRST GENERAL.   Impostor!
What, you still refuse—?

SECOND GENERAL.   You still deny
the truth?

FIRST GENERAL. Is it your idea, perhaps, to prove
the Princess false?

AMPHITRYON.   Every word she utters
is the truth—not gold ten times refined
is truer. More than oracles—than what
the lightning writes upon the night, than what
the thunder says—I trust the strict integrity
of what her lips have just declared. I'll swear
an oath upon the altar here and now,
die ten times over if I'm not

unshakably persuaded: to her he is
Amphitryon.

JUPITER.   Just so! And you're Amphitryon.

AMPHITRYON. I am—Then, awful spirit, who are you?

JUPITER. Amphitryon. I thought you understood.

AMPHITRYON. Amphitryon! But that's too much for mortal
wits. Do make more sense.

ALCMENE.   What's going on
here, I would like to know.

JUPITER.   Amphitryon,
you fool! Uncertain still, are you?
Argatiphontidas, Photidas too,
the Cadmean citadel, the continent
of Greece, the light, the ether, water, all—
what was, what is, and what shall be.

AMPHITRYON.   Around
me, friends, and try to see how we may solve
this riddle.

ALCMENE.   Oh, how dreadful!

GENERALS.   What's a man
to think about all this?

JUPITER (*to Alcmene*).

                  Do you believe
it was Amphitryon appeared to you?

ALCMENE. Let me stay deceived forever, if your light
is going to plunge my soul into eternal night.

JUPITER. Why, I would curse the bliss you've brought me if I couldn't
be a living presence to you, dear, eternally.

AMPHITRYON. Speak up, you there, will you? Now, who are
you?

          (*Lightning and thunder. Clouds obscure the stage. An eagle
          clutching the thunderbolt of Zeus drops out of the clouds.*)

JUPITER. *Who* am I, you want to know?

          (*Seizes the thunderbolt. The eagle flies off.*)

PEOPLE.   O gods!

JUPITER. Who am I, then?

GENERALS AND COLONELS. The Dread One! He himself!
Great Jupiter!

ALCMENE.   Protect me, all you Heavenly
    Powers!

(Falls into Amphitryon's arms.)

AMPHITRYON. From the dust my adoration, Jove!
    Great Thunderer! And all I have is thine.

PEOPLE. The god! The god! Our faces in the dust!

(All prostrate themselves except Amphitryon.)

JUPITER. Zeus wishes you to know, Amphitryon,
    that he has been well pleased by his reception
    in your house, and his divine contentment shall
    be shown you by a sign. No longer feel
    chagrined; cast out resentment; welcome with
    an open heart the triumph which is yours.
    The injury that you, in me, inflicted
    on yourself, no injury is, in my
    eternal Allness. If you are able, in my fault,
    to find some compensation for yourself, why, well
    and good, we'll kiss and part as friends. The boundaries
    of your fame shall henceforth, like my universe,
    extend as far as to the stars. But if
    you find such gratitude is not enough,
    why, well and good again: your dearest wish
    shall be fulfilled, and I give the utterance
    of it before me here full leave.

AMPHITRYON.   No, Father
    Zeus, it's not enough! And by your leave,
    I'll give my heart's desire utterance.
    What you did for Tyndareus, do for
    Amphitryon too: bestow a son on him
    as great as are the two Tyndarides.

JUPITER. So be it, then. To you there shall be born
    a son, and Hercules his name. No hero
    of the times gone by shall rival him in fame,
    not even my immortal Dioscuri.
    Twelve gigantic labors he'll perform,
    which piled together, one on top of the other,
    in a heap, shall raise him up an everlasting
    monument. And when the pyramid
    is built at last, grazing with its top
    the Empyrean's cloudy fringe, heavenwards

83

he'll mount its steps and on Olympus I'll
receive him then, a god.

AMPHITRYON.   I thank you, Lord.
But her I'm holding here, your will is not
to take her from me, Sir? See, she hardly
breathes.

JUPITER.   She shall remain with you. But only
if you don't disturb the complete repose
she needs!—Come, Hermes!

> (*He disappears into the clouds, which meanwhile
> have opened overhead to disclose Olympus and the
> Olympians reclining at their ease upon its summit.*)

ALCMENE.   Oh, Amphitryon!

MERCURY. I'm coming in a minute, thou Divine One!
But first I have to tell that character
that I am sick to death of putting on
his ugly face; that I'm about to dip
a cloth into ambrosia and scrub
it off Olympian cheeks; that he has got
some knocks deserving to be sung in verse; and that
I am no more nor less a one than Hermes
the wing-footed!

> (*Exit.*)

SOSIA.   If only you had left
me obscure still, no theme for song! In all
my life I never have encountered one
like him for beating up on fellows.

FIRST GENERAL. My goodness, such a triumph!

SECOND GENERAL.   So much glory!

FIRST COLONEL. Wonderstruck we are!

AMPHITRYON.   Alcmene!

ALCMENE.   Ah!

The Broken Jug
A Comedy

PREFACE

The basis of my comedy in all likelihood is an actual case, but more than this I have not been able to discover. I was prompted to write it by a copper engraving which I saw in Switzerland several years ago. One saw depicted in it, first, a judge gravely seated in his chair; standing before him an old woman with a broken jug in her hand, who seemed to be pointing out the injurious treatment it had received; the accused, a young peasant whom the judge thundered at as one whose guilt was already proved, was still defending himself, but feebly; a girl who had probably testified in the case (who knows what the offense was and how it had occurred?) stood between her mother and her fiancé wringing her apron—she couldn't have stood there more shamefacedly if she had given false evidence; and the Clerk (who had probably been staring at the girl a moment before) was now looking sideways at the judge, suspiciously, much as Creon looked at Oedipus in similar circumstances. Below it read: The Broken Jug.—The original, if I am not mistaken, was by a Dutch master.

[H.v.K.]

Cast of Characters

Walter, District Magistrate
Adam, Village Judge
Licht, Clerk of the Court
Frau Martha Rull
Eve, her daughter
Veit Tümpel, a peasant
Ruprecht, his son
Frau Brigitta
A Servant, Bailiff, Two Maids, etc.

The action takes place in a village in the Netherlands near Utrecht
[in the courtroom of Judge Adam's house].

SCENE I

Adam seated bandaging his leg. Enter Licht.

LICHT. What the devil, Adam, sir! Something's
  happened, tell me—oh, you look a sight!
ADAM. A sight, you bet. To stumble, all you need
  are feet. On this smooth floor what's there
  to stumble over? All the same, I stumbled—
  for we've got, each one of us, a nasty stumbling block
  inside ourselves.
LICHT.   We do! Each one of us—?
ADAM. Inside himself!
LICHT.   A curse, damn it!
ADAM.   What, what?
LICHT.   You've got
  an ancestor, a ne'er-do-well he was, who fell
  when things began. His fall's notorious.
  Your case and his—
ADAM.   Well, what? Go on.
LICHT. —are not the same?
ADAM.   The same? Get out! I told
  you, here, right here, is where I fell.
LICHT.   Fell literally?
ADAM. Fell literally.
LICHT.   And when did this all happen?
ADAM. Just now, as I was getting out of bed. Lifting
  up my voice to welcome in the morning,
  I tripped and fell smack into it.
  Before the day has started, the Lord God
  makes me wrench my foot!
LICHT.   And I bet it was
  the left one.
ADAM.   Left one?
LICHT.   This one here, the one
  that isn't frolicsome?
ADAM.   Yes, that one.
LICHT.   God be praised!
  The one that found the way of sin too rough
  a road?

89

ADAM.   Too rough a road? My foot? Will you explain—
LICHT. Your clumping foot—your clubfoot.
ADAM.   Clubfoot! One foot
   clumps along just like the other.
LICHT.   Pardon me,
   but there you do your right foot an injustice.
   True, it cannot boast the other's ... gravity,
   but then it's not afraid to venture out
   on slippery slopes.
ADAM.   That's nonsense! Where one dares
   to go, the other follows.
LICHT.   What's happened to your face,
   it's all cut up.
ADAM.   My face? Cut up?
LICHT.   You mean
   to say you don't know it's cut up?
ADAM.   I'd be
   a liar if—how does it look?
LICHT. How does it look?
ADAM.   Yes, old friend.
LICHT.   Gruesome!
ADAM. More exactly, please.
LICHT.   All scraped and skinned,
   not very nice to see. Your cheek has got
   a piece gouged out of it. How big a piece?
   I'd need a scales to know.
ADAM.   The devil!
LICHT (*bringing him a mirror*).
                          Here,
   see for yourself. A sheep the dogs chase through
   the briars leaves no more wool behind than you've
   left skin somewhere.
ADAM.   Dear me, yes, I see! Lord, Lord,
   I look a fright. My nose is banged up too.
LICHT. Also an eye.
ADAM.   Oh no!
LICHT.   Oh yes! A cut
   across the brow, so help me God, as if
   you had a run-in with a surly peasant.

ADAM. I think
    I see the bone. And yet I didn't feel
    a thing.
LICHT.   Yes, that's what happens in the heat of battle.
ADAM. Battle! If that is what you call it when
    you bang your head against that damned goat
    on the stove.[1] It's coming back to me. I lost
    my balance, and grabbing at the air around me like
    a drunkard, I caught hold of my pants which I'd
    hung up last night, because they were wet through,
    by the belt, above the stove. But poor fool
    that I am, the belt it breaks and down we go,
    belt and pants and me, head first to the floor,
    and on the way I hit my head against
    the stove just where the goat has got its nose
    stuck out.
LICHT (*laughing*).
        Great, great!
ADAM.   Damnation!
LICHT.   Adam's fall!
    Your first time *out* of bed.
ADAM.   Lord, Lord!
    But what I meant to ask you was, What's new?
LICHT. What's new. Let's see. Oh yes, it almost slipped
    my mind.
ADAM.   What was that?
LICHT.   Get ready for a visit,
    unannounced, from Utrecht.
ADAM.   What?
LICHT.   The District Magistrate
    is coming.
ADAM.   Who?
LICHT.   Justice Walter's coming
    here from Utrecht. He's making an inspection tour
    of all the local courts, and today's the day
    he comes to us.
ADAM.   Today! You must be crazy.

---

1. Cast iron figure decorating a Dutch stove.

LICHT. No, I'm not. He was in Holla, at the border,
yesterday, and finished his inspection there.
A peasant saw the relays being hitched up
to his coach to bring him here to Huisum.
ADAM. The District Magistrate! From Utrecht! Coming
here today for an inspection! But he's the best
of fellows who shaves his own sheep close
and hates silly tricks. No, I don't believe it—
that he'd come here to Huisum just to annoy us!
LICHT. He came to Holla, he'll come here. On guard!
ADAM. Oh pooh!
LICHT.　　　　You heard me.
ADAM.　　　　　　　　　Fairy tales, I say.
LICHT. Damn it, man, the peasant saw him there
with his own eyes.
ADAM.　　　　　　God knows who the squinting
bumpkin saw. These yokels can't distinguish
front from back if the man's bald-headed.
Clap a cocked hat on my cane, wrap
a cloak around it, add two boots below
and the clod thinks it's whoever you may wish.
LICHT. Very well, then have it your own way—
till he walks in the door.
ADAM.　　　　　　　　Walks in the door!
Without a word of warning—never!
LICHT.　　　　　　　　　　You
don't understand! It's not the old inspector
any more, Justice Wachholder, it's
Justice Walter.
ADAM.　　　　So let it be Judge Walter,
I don't care! The fellow's sworn his oath
of office and must conduct himself, as we do,
in the time-honored way.
LICHT.　　　　　　　I swear to you
Judge Walter showed up yesterday in Holla
unexpectedly, went through all their accounts
and files, then sent the judge and clerk home,
both, suspended. Why? I've no idea—
not officially.

ADAM.   The devil! Did the peasant tell
  you that?
LICHT.   He did, and other things as well.
ADAM. And what were they?
LICHT.   You want to know, then, do you?
  All right. The judge, placed under house arrest
  last night, is looked for in the morning, and found,
  guess where: inside his barn, suspended—from a rafter.
ADAM. Oh no!
LICHT.   But help arrives, they cut him down,
  they chafe his neck and wrists, douse him with cold
  water, and bring him back to life, but only
  just.
ADAM. They do, do they? Back to life?
LICHT. And now his house is under seal, inventoried,
  locked, and bolted—they might have left him hanging,
  he's as good as dead. And a new man's
  in his place as judge, already.
ADAM. Oh well! The rascal did things in a slipshod
  way—but otherwise an honest beast,
  so help me, a fellow it was easy to get on
  with; but no administrator, if you make me say so:
  too slipshod. If the District Magistrate paid
  the poor old fellow a visit today, I fear
  for him, I do.
LICHT.   The peasant says this business
  is the only reason why the Justice hasn't
  shown up here already. But he'll arrive
  for sure by noon.
ADAM.   By noon! All right, my friend,
  what counts now, as I'm sure you understand,
  is friendship. One hand must wash the other. I know
  you'd like to be a judge some day; by God,
  if anyone deserves it, you do. However,
  it's not the right time now. Today you have
  to let the cup pass from you.
LICHT.   Me a judge!
  You've got the wrong idea about me!
ADAM.   You
  love eloquence, you know your Cicero

as well as anyone that went to school
in Amsterdam. But I'm asking you to bridle
your ambition for today. I'm sure there will
be opportunities in the future, lots
of them, for you to demonstrate your talents.

LICHT. Oh please! We're two old friends, old colleagues!

ADAM. In his day, too, the great Demosthenes
knew when to hold his tongue.[2] Follow his
example. I'm not the King of Macedonia,
I know, but I have ways to say my thanks.

LICHT. Enough, enough! You're so suspicious. Tell
me, have I ever—?

ADAM.   And I, on my side, too,
will do just as the great Greek did.
Consider: about payments on account and interest
charges it's also possible to speak
with eloquence. But who's got any interest
in delivering long orations?

LICHT.   For sure!

ADAM.   From any blame
for those aforementioned things I'm free, the devil
take it! All that stuff, why, I regard
it as a joke, a bit of nighttime foolery
that doesn't like the finger of the daylight
poking into it.

LICHT.   I quite agree.

ADAM. Bless me, is there any reason why
a judge, when he's not planted in his judge's
seat, should be as solemn as a bear?

LICHT. My view exactly.

ADAM.   Well then, dear colleague,
into the registry with us. We need to stack
the files up, for they are toppled on
the floor like the Tower of Babel, everywhere.

2. Plutarch tells the story that Demosthenes, having accepted a bribe from the Macedonians, excused himself from speaking the next day by saying he was hoarse with a sore throat.

SCENE 2

Enter a Servant to Adam and Licht.

SERVANT. Your Honor, sir, the Justice Walter sends
his greetings, he's on his way here now.
ADAM.   Good heavens,
done so fast with Holla, is he?
SERVANT.   Yes.
And now he's come to Huisum.
ADAM.   Lizzie!
Maggie!
LICHT.   Easy, easy, please.
ADAM.   But did
you hear—?
LICHT.   Just say you're honored to receive him.
SERVANT. And our next stop is Hussahe, that's tomorrow.
ADAM. Oh dear, what should I do? There is no time—
                    (*Lunges for his clothes.*)
FIRST MAID (*entering*).
Here I am, Your Honor.
LICHT.   Now your coat.
ADAM (*looking around*).
Is that the magistrate!
LICHT.   The maid. Calm down.
ADAM. My bands! My robe! My collar!
FIRST MAID.   You forgot the vest.
ADAM. The vest? Get the coat off—quick!
LICHT (*to the Servant*).
                          The District
Magistrate is very welcome. We
are ready to receive him. Please tell him so.
ADAM.   To receive
the devil! Adam asks to be excused.
LICHT. Excused!
ADAM.   Excused. He's on his way, is he?
SERVANT. He's at the inn. We had to have the smith called,
for our coach—it smashed.
ADAM.   Good, good. The smith's
a lazy dog. My respects to the Inspector

and I ask to be excused. I nearly broke
my neck, as you can see. Oh, I'm a sight,
I am. And every time I'm frightened, it's like
a laxative. I'm sick, please tell him.

LICHT.   Are you
in your right mind? The magistrate expects
to be received. Unless you want—?

ADAM.   Oh damn,
oh damn!

LICHT.   What is it?

ADAM.   It's just as if the doctor
dosed me double—may the devil take me!

LICHT. He will, he will, if you light the way for him.

ADAM. Hey, Margaret, you old scarecrow! Lizzie!

BOTH MAIDS.   Here
we are, what is it?

ADAM.   Go and clear the cheese,
the ham, the butter, wurst, and bottles out
of the registry—be quick! Not you, the other
one! You, stupid, you! Jesus,
Margaret, I mean Lizzie here, the dairy maid!
                    (*Exit First Maid.*)

SECOND MAID. Make some sense, for God's sake.

ADAM.   You shut up.
Go and get my wig! March, march, it's in the bookcase,
on the double!   (*Exit Second Maid.*)

LICHT (*to the Servant*).
                        I trust Judge Walter's journey
here was uneventful.

SERVANT.   Yes, if turning
over our coach was no event.

ADAM. Oh damn it, my poor foot's so bruised I
will never get these boots—!

LICHT.   My goodness, turned
it over! But nothing more than that, I hope?

SERVANT. Nothing much. My master sprained his wrist
a little. And we snapped the shaft.

ADAM. [*sotto voce*].
                                Snapped his neck,
I wish!

LICHT.   Sprained his wrist, how dreadful! And the blacksmith
  came?
SERVANT. About the shaft, yes.
LICHT.   What?
ADAM.   You mean
  the doctor.
LICHT.   What?
SERVANT.   About the shaft?
ADAM.   His wrist!
  About his wrist!
SERVANT.   Sirs, good day to you,
  I must be going.—Addled all these fellows
  are, I think! (*Exit.*)
LICHT.   I meant the smith.
ADAM.   You're much
  too nervous, colleague. Careful.
LICHT.   What?
ADAM.   Try not
  to show it.

Enter First Maid.

        Lizzie, what is that you've
  got there?
FIRST MAID. Braunschweiger wurst, good master.
ADAM. Wrong. Wardship files.
LICHT.   *He* says I
  am nervous!
ADAM.   They belong back in the registry.
FIRST MAID.   The wurst?
ADAM. No, not the wurst! The papers they are wrapped in.
LICHT. I misunderstood him, that was all.
SECOND MAID (*entering*).
                        No wig,
  Judge, I could see in the bookcase, anywhere.
ADAM. How come?
SECOND MAID.   Well—.
ADAM.   Well?
SECOND MAID.   Because, you see,
  last night—eleven, yes, it was—
ADAM.   I'm listening.
SECOND MAID. Well, you came home, remember, without your wig.

97

ADAM. Without my wig?

SECOND MAID.   It's true. Ask Lizzie, she
   will swear to it as well. And your other's at
   the wigmaker's.

ADAM.   Am I supposed—?

FIRST MAID.   It's true,
   Judge Adam, you came home bald-headed.
   You said you tripped and fell, remember? I had
   to bathe your head, it was so bloody.

ADAM.   Lying
   hussy!

FIRST MAID. Your Honor, sir, it's true, I swear!

ADAM. Keep quiet, do you hear? Not a word
   of truth in it.

LICHT.   So it was yesterday
   you got your wound?

ADAM.   Today, today. The wound
   today, and yesterday the wig. As I
   came in the house I pulled my hat off
   with a jerk, and with it, by mistake, my powdered wig—
   I swear. As for what she thinks she washed, I've no
   idea.—Clear out, report to Satan who's
   your master! Clean up the registry! (*Exit First Maid.*)
                              Margaret,
   go and tell the sexton I would like
   to borrow his. Say the cat used mine
   to have a litter in this morning, dirty
   beast! It's underneath my bed, a mess—
   now I remember.

LICHT.   The cat?

ADAM.   The cat. Five kittens,
   two are black and two are yellow. One
   is white. I'll have to drown the black ones
   in the Vecht. But tell me, what else
   can I do? Do you think you'd like to take one?

LICHT. In your wig?

ADAM.   So help me. Hung it on
   a chair, I did, before getting into bed.
   By accident I knocked it over in the night,
   the chair, the wig fell on the floor—.

98

LICHT. The cat then took it in her mouth—

ADAM. Right, right!

LICHT. Dragged it under the bed and had her litter
in it.

ADAM. In her mouth? No, that can't be.

LICHT. If not, how then?

ADAM. The cat?

LICHT. No—not the cat?
Then you perhaps?

ADAM. In her mouth! I do believe—. She got
a good kick for herself from me when I
discovered what she'd done.

LICHT. Good, good!

ADAM. What creatures!
Go at it anywhere, then drop
their babies in my wig!

SECOND MAID (*giggling*).
Should I go now?

ADAM. Yes, go. Convey my greetings to our sexton's faithful
wife, Frau Schwarzgewand.[3] I'll send her back
the wig, as good as new, before the day
is over—no need that he should know about
it. Do you understand me?

SECOND MAID. I'll do it right away.

(*Exit.*)

SCENE 3

Adam and Licht.

ADAM. Today, dear colleague, doesn't promise, I'm afraid,
auspiciously.

LICHT. And pray why not?

ADAM. Everything
is mixed up, in confusion. And don't I also
have to sit today?

LICHT. You do. People
are waiting at the door already.

ADAM. I dreamt I was
accused and dragged before the bar, and yet I

---

3. *Schwarzgewand*: "Dressed-in-black."

99

was the judge and hounded, skinned, and bullied my
own self and at last condemned myself
to put my neck inside an iron collar.

LICHT. Condemned yourself?

ADAM.   I did indeed. And then the two
of us were one and fled into the woods and cowered
there all night.

LICHT.   So your idea
is that the dream—

ADAM.   Dream or no dream,
what's the difference? Something is
afoot, I don't know what, that doesn't wish
me well!

LICHT.   That's foolish, Come, be brave! In the presence
of the magistrate deal evenhandedly with all,
exactly as the rules prescribe, lest
the dream of justice judged should come to pass.

SCENE 4
Enter the District Magistrate Walter.

WALTER. I wish you a good morning.

ADAM.   Oh welcome,
oh, Your Worship, welcome to Huisum!
Whoever would have thought that we should have
the pleasure of a visit from yourself,
that it's no dream we should be blessed with such
good fortune before the clock's struck eight!

WALTER. I come a little unexpectedly,
I know. However, my satisfaction is,
as I go about the district in my country's service,
that those whose guest I am, on my departure,
should mean it quite sincerely when they wish me a farewell.
Meanwhile on coming here, I on my side
wish *you* well, with all my heart. The Superior Court
in Utrecht aims to raise the standard of the administration
of justice in the countryside, which leaves much
to be desired in any number of respects. Expect
abuses to be severely reprimanded.
But my own object on this tour is a milder

one, to observe and not to punish, and if
I find everything is not just as it should be,
still, I'll be content to find it passable.
ADAM. A most praiseworthy way of viewing things.
I have no doubt Your Worship will come on things
here and there in our old ways of doing
justice deserving of your censure—even though
they have been the practice in the Netherlands
since the time of Charles the Fifth.
What won't people think of next? The world,
as it is often said, gets wiser by the day
and everybody knows his Pufendorf,
for sure. But Huisum is only a small
part of this great world and it enjoys
no more or less of the great wisdom than its
small part. Throw the bright light of your knowledge
on our justice here and rest assured,
before you have turned your back to leave, you will thrill
with satisfaction! But it would be a miracle,
I swear, if you found our courtroom as you like
courtrooms to be, since we have no inkling what
you like.
WALTER.   Quite right. We need regulations.
Or rather we've too many, they need sifting.
ADAM. With a giant sieve. The chaff, my God, the chaff!
WALTER. And he's your clerk, this gentleman?
LICHT.   Clerk Licht,
sir, at Your Worship's service, sir. Come Pentecost
I'm clerk nine years in Justice Adam's court.
ADAM (*bringing up a chair.*)
Do have a seat.
WALTER.   No need.
ADAM.   So you come from Holla, sir?
WALTER. A pair of miles, no more. But how do you
know that?
ADAM.   How do I know that?
Your Worship's man—
LICHT.   A peasant just arrived
from Holla reported it.

WALTER. A peasant? Yes.
Something most unpleasant happened there
which spoiled the cheerful disposition magistrates
endeavor to bring to their proceedings.
You know about it, do you?

ADAM. I heard, am I
correct, Judge Pfaul, the fool, placed under house
arrest, despaired and hanged himself?

WALTER. And that
way made a bad thing worse. What seemed no more
than muddled records and mismanagement now looks
like misappropriation of funds, which the law,
as you know very well, can scarcely tolerate.
—And what about your funds? You collect
how many levies?

ADAM. Five, Your Worship.

WALTER. What, five!
Five current levies? Four, was my impression.

ADAM. Excuse me, but—the Rhine River Special
Inundation Fund!

WALTER. The Rhine River
Inundation Fund! There's been no inundation
to collect for—. But never mind. Your court's in session,
isn't it, today?

ADAM. In session—?

LICHT. Yes,
the first one of the week.

WALTER. Those people I saw
outside in the passageway, are they—?

ADAM. Are they—?

LICHT. They are waiting to be heard, sir, they come early.

WALTER. Good,
gentlemen, that's good. Have them enter,
if you would. I'll witness the proceedings and see
how you do things in Huisum. Your files
and your accounts can wait till later when
the session's done.

ADAM. As you wish.—Bailiff! Hans!

SCENE 5

Enter Second Maid.

SECOND MAID. The Frau Sexton sends her greetings, Judge.
　She wishes she were able to oblige you—

ADAM. 　　　　　　　　　　　　　　　What!
　No wig?

SECOND MAID. This morning there's a service and the sexton
　needs it for himself. His other one's
　so bad it's going to the wigmaker's today.

ADAM. Oh damn!

SECOND MAID. 　When he comes home from church she'll let
　you have the one he's wearing.

ADAM. 　　　　　　　　　　Your Worship, please.
　I've had bad luck with both my wigs, and now
　I find a third one which I sent to borrow
　can't be had—I'll have to sit today
　without a wig.

WALTER. 　　　　Bald-headed!

ADAM. 　　　　　　　　　　Bald-headed—in spite
　of the acute embarrassment I'll feel in my
　judicial dignity to be without
　a wig. Maybe I should try the tenant
　of my farm?

WALTER. 　　Your farm? Can't someone here—?

ADAM. No, I'm afraid.

WALTER. 　　　　　　　The parson?

ADAM. 　　　　　　　　　　　Him?

WALTER. 　　　　　　　　　　　　　The schoolteacher,
　perhaps?

ADAM. 　　Well, you see—. Since their tithe rights
　were abolished, which I played some part in having
　done, I can't expect a helping hand from them.

WALTER. Well, Judge, Your Honor, well? And what about
　the court? Do you intend to wait until
　your hair grows back?

ADAM. 　　　　　　　Please, if I may, sir,
　I'll send out to the farm.

WALTER. 　　　　　　　How far is it?

ADAM. Oh—hardly a half hour.

WALTER.   A half hour!
We are late in starting now. Enough delays!
I have to be in Hussahe today.

ADAM.   Right—
enough delays!

WALTER.   For God's sake, sprinkle
powder on your head! Do something, anything!
I have no time to spare. Where the devil
have you stuck your wigs?

BAILIFF (*entering*).
                             I'm here!

ADAM. A little breakfast now, perhaps? It won't
take but a minute. Braunschweiger wurst, a glass
of Danziger—?

WALTER.   No, thanks.

ADAM.   No trouble, not at all.

WALTER. I've had my breakfast, thank you. Don't waste time,
begin. Meanwhile I have something to note down
in my book.

ADAM.   It's as you say.—Oh Margaret!

WALTER. You've hurt yourself, Judge Adam—did you fall?

ADAM. Nearly killed myself, I did, Your Worship,
when I got out of bed early this morning.
Took such a header into the room, I thought
it was good night.

WALTER.   Too bad. You are quite able
to carry on?

ADAM.   Oh quite! Nothing must interfere
with my duties as justice of the peace.
—With your permission, sir.

WALTER. Go on, go on!

ADAM (*to the Bailiff*).
                 Don't stand there—call the parties!

SCENE 6
Enter Frau Martha, Eve, Veit, and Ruprecht. In the rear,
Walter and Licht.

FRAU MARTHA. You like to smash jugs, do you, scoundrels,
but you'll pay for it!

VEIT.   Calmly, calmly,
good Frau Martha! We'll settle the whole business
before the judge.
FRAU MARTHA.   Settle it, oh yes!
King Solomon! I'll settle you! My jug
is broken, gone forever, and here it will
be settled that I have a broken jug. I wouldn't
give, for such a settlement, the bits and pieces
of my broken jug.
VEIT.   If you're proved right, I promise
to replace it.
FRAU MARTHA. Replace my jug? So I can stand
it on my mantelpiece again? Oh, I
would like to see that, yes, I would—my jug
that doesn't have a leg to stand on, a bottom,
even, it can sit on, such a lovely jug!
VEIT. That's what I will do. Why carry on?
What more can you ask? If one
of us broke your jug, we'll make amends for it.
FRAU MARTHA. Amends for it. Oh jackass! The law's a potter,
I suppose, Their Dignities will mend
my broken pot with your amends!
It's likelier they'll fill my pot for me,
Their Honors, with you know what, than they
should mend it. Mend my pot, he says!
RUPRECHT. Father, let her be. Oh, she's a dragon!
It's the wedding, not the pot, she's mad about.
That's what's got a hole in it, which she thinks
she'll patch up again by threatening us.
Well, she can think it till the cows come home—
I'll be damned if I will ever marry
that false slut!
FRAU MARTHA.   That conceited ox!
Patch the wedding up! A wedding which
I wouldn't waste an inch of thread on to patch up,
that isn't worth two smithereens of my lovely jug.
If his precious wedding stood in front
of me right now, without a mark on it,
a chip, as my jug stood on the shelf just
yesterday, I'd grab it by its handle

with both hands and bring it crashing down
on that one's head! Me want to patch things up
again!

EVE.   Ruprecht!

RUPRECHT.   Never!

EVE.   Dearest Ruprecht!

RUPRECHT. Get away from me!

EVE.   I beg you—please!

RUPRECHT. You damned—I won't say what.

EVE.   Just one
word, between us two.

RUPRECHT.   Never!

EVE. Oh Ruprecht, soon you'll join your regiment
and shoulder arms. And after that who knows
if I will ever see you alive again.
It's war you are going off to, war, remember—
do you want to part from me with angry feelings?

RUPRECHT. Angry feelings? No, I don't. May
you have as much good fortune as God
can find it in himself to let you have.
But if I come back from the wars
a hale man, strong as iron, and live in Huisum
for eighty years, I'll keep on saying it
to you: false bitch!

FRAU MARTHA (*to Eve*).
    Come away from him!
I told you so. Do you like to be abused?
The man for you is Corporal Holzgebein,[4]
who swung his baton in the army, not
that booby there whose back God made
for corporals to beat on with their batons.
Get yourself engaged today, get married,
perhaps we'll have a baptism as well, to be followed
by my funeral, it doesn't matter,
I don't care—if only I can knock
that lout who knocks down jugs at night
off his high horse.

4. *Holzgebein*: "Wooden-leg."

EVE.   Mother, please, enough
about the jug! I'll see in town if there's
a master craftsman who can put the pieces back
together to your satisfaction. If not,
I'll buy a new one for you with what I've saved.
Who would want, for a piece of earthenware,
even if it went back all the way
to Herod's time, to raise such a commotion,
cause all this dreadful trouble?

FRAU MARTHA.   Do you know what you
are saying? Is it the pillory you want,
do you want to go to church next Sunday to do penance?
What was in that pot, would you like to know?
Your reputation. Now both are wrecked, in people's
eyes if not the eyes of God and me and you.
Magistrate and thieftaker, they are
the master craftsmen that I want, their tools
the stocks and hard blows of the whip,
and at the stake, bound hand and foot, that riffraff—
if our honor is ever to blaze bright again
and this jug have its former glaze restored!

SCENE 7

Enter Adam gowned, without a wig.

ADAM *(aside)*.
It's Evie, look! And that hulking rascal Ruprecht!
What the devil, the whole clan! Have they come,
I wonder, to bring a suit against myself before
myself?

EVE.   Mother, please let's leave this place
where nothing good can happen!

ADAM.   Colleague, what's the story?

LICHT. How should I know? It's a great to-do about
a trifle. Someone broke a jug, I hear.

ADAM. A jug! Oh well—who broke the jug?

LICHT. Who broke it?

ADAM.   Yes.

LICHT.   Sit—and then inquire.

ADAM (*whispering*).
Evie!

EVE.   No!

ADAM.   Just one word.

EVE.   Don't
bother me.

ADAM.   Why are you in court?

EVE. I said don't bother me.

ADAM.   Evie, please—
tell me what this means.

EVE.   Stop pestering me,
and if you don't—!

ADAM (*to Licht*).
          I can't go on, Licht, do
you hear? My shinbone's killing me, I'm feeling
sick to my stomach. You conduct the court, I'm going
to bed.

LICHT.   You're going where? I think you've lost
your mind.

ADAM.   Oh Jesus, I think I'm going to throw up!

LICHT. You're raving, I'm convinced. No sooner are
you here—but please yourself. There's the magistrate,
ask him. Maybe he'll permit it. What's gotten
into you, I wonder?

ADAM (*again to Eve, whispering*).
          Evie, please, I'm begging
you! Tell me for sweet Jesus' sake
the reason why you've come to court.

EVE.   You'll soon
hear why.

ADAM.   Is it just because of that broken jug
your mother's holding, which I'm certain—

EVE. Yes, just because of the broken jug.

ADAM.   And nothing
else.

EVE.   No, nothing.

ADAM.   You wouldn't fool me, would you?

EVE. Don't bother me, I said.

ADAM.   Think twice and then
again, is my advice to you, unless—

EVE. You have no shame!

ADAM.   I've got a notice handy
in my pocket, with the name of Ruprecht Tümpel
on it in block letters. Hear the parchment
crackle? In one year's time I'll kindly give
you it to make yourself a neckerchief
to wear in mourning when the news arrives that Ruprecht
in Batavia cashed in his chips—from which fever
I don't know exactly, yellow, scarlet,
take your pick.

WALTER.   Judge Adam! No conversation
with the litigants before the hearing. Take
your seat, please, start your questioning.

ADAM. What, what? I think I missed Your Worship's words.

WALTER. My words were clear enough. I said: Don't carry
private conversations on with litigants
before the case is heard. Your place is on the bench;
I expect you to conduct your examinations publicly.

ADAM (*aside*).
Oh damn! I can't be sure—! I heard the sound
of something breaking just as I jumped out—

LICHT (*nudging him*).
Judge Adam, did you—

ADAM.   I? Oh no—I set
the wig down on it carefully, I'm not
so clumsy as to—

LICHT.   What?

ADAM.   What?

LICHT.   You are deaf,
is what. His Worship spoke to you.

ADAM. I thought—! Who spoke to me?

LICHT.   The magistrate!

ADAM (*aside*).
What the hell! It's one way or the other.
If things don't bend, they break, and that is that.
—Here I am, Your Worship, sir! Shall we
commence the proceedings?

WALTER.   Your mind seems elsewhere, Judge.
Is something wrong?

ADAM.   Oh pardon, sir! A guinea
  hen I bought from a fellow home from the East Indies
  has got the pip. It needs cramming, I
  am sure, but how should I know what to do,
  so I begged advice from this young woman here.
  My birds, you know, I dote on them as if
  they were my children.
WALTER.   Be seated, Judge! Call
  the plaintiff for examination. Clerk, record
  the depositions.
ADAM.   Does Your Worship wish the case conducted
  exactly as the law prescribes, or as
  is customary here in Huisum?
WALTER.   Exactly
  as the law prescribes, according to the procedure
  customarily observed in Huisum, not otherwise.
ADAM. Very well, I'll do my best to satisfy
  you, sir. Clerk, are you ready?
LICHT.   Ready, sir.
ADAM. Then Justice, take your course! Plaintiff, please
  step forward.
FRAU MARTHA.   Here I am.
ADAM.   State who you are.
FRAU MARTHA. State who—?
ADAM.   You are.
FRAU MARTHA.   Who I am?
ADAM.   Yes, who you are,
  your name, your station, place of residence,
  and so forth.
FRAU MARTHA.   You must be joking, Judge.
ADAM.   Joking,
  did you say! I sit here as the representative
  of Justice, and Justice has to be informed
  of who you are.
LICHT (*sotto voce*).
                  Oh, you can skip all that—
FRAU MARTHA. You squint at me each Sunday through my window,
  walking out to see your farm!
WALTER.   You know
  the woman?

110

ADAM.   She lives around the corner, sir,
  where the path goes through the hedge. The widow
  of a lodgekeeper, a midwife now. Oh, she's
  an honest soul, her reputation's of the best.
WALTER. Since the Judge is well acquainted with her, these
  questions are superfluous. Record the woman's
  name and make a note: well known to the court.
ADAM. As you say. Not such a stickler for formalities
  after all.
WALTER.   Now ask her what her complaint concerns.
ADAM. Now, you mean?
WALTER.   Yes! Why she is appearing here!
ADAM. Well, you see, a jug, I happen to know.
WALTER. You happen to know!
ADAM.   A jug, an ordinary
  jug. Record it is a jug and make
  a note: well known to the court.
LICHT.   Your Honor,
  on the basis of a casual remark of mine, surely
  you don't mean—
ADAM.   If I say something's so,
  then write it down. Isn't it a jug,
  Frau Martha?
FRAU MARTHA. Yes, a jug. And here it is.
ADAM. I told you so.
FRAU MARTHA.   It's broken.
ADAM.   Let's not get
  bogged down in petty details.
LICHT.   Your Honor!
ADAM.   So the jug
  is broken. And who's the one that broke it? That rascal
  there, for sure.
FRAU MARTHA.   Yes, him, that skulking rogue—.
ADAM (*aside*).
  Ha, that does it! End of case.
RUPRECHT.   It's not so,
  please Your Honor!
ADAM (*aside*).
                Oh, the old Adam's back
  to life again!

RUPRECHT.   She's lying in her teeth—

ADAM. Silence, scamp! You'll wear an iron collar
   soon enough. Clerk, write jug, as previously
   stated, and next to it the rascal's name
   who broke it. And that is that—case settled!

WALTER. Your Honor, please! You are bullying the defendant, it
   is quite improper.

LICHT. Try to observe the formalities—.

ADAM. Oh no! His Worship has no use for the formalities.

WALTER. If you are unaware, Judge Adam, of the right way
   to conduct a case, this is not the place
   to teach you it. If you can't administer justice
   better than this, step down and let your clerk
   preside.

ADAM.   Sorry, sorry! I did as we do things
   in Huisum, which is how I thought Your Worship
   instructed me to do.

WALTER.   How I instructed
   you!

ADAM. You did, sir!

WALTER.   I instructed you to conduct
   the proceedings exactly as the law prescribes—
   which it's my impression is no different
   in Huisum from elsewhere in the United Provinces.

ADAM. But sir, I beg to differ with you there, most
   respectfully! We have, sir, if you please,
   statutes of our own in Huisum,
   not *written* statutes, I'll admit, but tried
   and true traditions handed down to us
   from one generation to the next. And from
   our form of law, I may confidently say,
   I have not deviated one iota.
   But I am also quite at home in that other
   way of doing things that may be
   customary with you elsewhere in the realm.
   You have your doubts? Just say the word and I
   will show you! I can deal out justice in any style
   you please.

WALTER.   You put a wrong interpretation
  on my words, Judge Adam. However—. Start
  all over again.
ADAM.   I promise you will be completely
  satisfied with me. Now watch!—Frau Martha Rull!
  Declare your grievance to the court.
FRAU MARTHA.   My grievance, as you know,
  concerns this jug. But before I tell you how
  it was abused, I wish you to understand
  how much the jug has meant to me.
ADAM.   You have
  the floor.
FRAU MARTHA. You see it, do you, worthy sirs,
  this jug?
ADAM.   We do.
FRAU MARTHA.   You don't—begging your pardon.
  You see pieces—the loveliest jug that ever
  was now lies in pieces. Right where this hole
  is, all the Netherlands were handed over
  to the Spanish Philip. Here Emperor Charles
  stood in his royal robes. Those are his legs,
  that's all that's left of him. Here Philip knelt
  before his father to receive the crown—he's
  still there, down to his backside,
  but even it did not get off without a whack.
  There his two aunts, the Queens of France and Hungary,
  so touched, are dabbing at their eyes with handkerchiefs—
  but now one of them looks like she is weeping
  for herself. Here's Sir Philibert in the retinue,
  still leaning on his sword, spared destruction
  by the Emperor's catching it—but he'll
  fall on his face now, him and that damned Maximilian,
  because they haven't any swords to lean on.
  Here at the center with his miter on
  once stood the Archbishop of Arras—the devil
  came and carried him away. All
  that's left of him is his long shadow on the pavement.
  In the background, standing in a circle in close
  order, were the Royal Guards with halberds
  and spears. And just look here and you can see

the houses lining the great marketplace of Brussels,
and from a window someone peering curiously.
But what there is for him to see now, I don't know.

ADAM. Frau Martha! They broke the treaty,[5] yes, but spare
us that. The hole your jug got, that's our business
here, and not the provinces surrendered on it.

FRAU MARTHA. I beg to differ, Judge! The beauty of the jug
is our business!—Childeric the tinker
captured it when the Prince of Orange and his fighting
tars took Briel. A Spaniard was about to put
it to his lips and drink it dry when Childeric
came up on him from behind and cut him down
and drank up all the wine himself and went his way.

ADAM. A true Dutchman, that one was!

FRAU MARTHA.   Fürchtegott[6]
the gravedigger inherited it next. A sobersided
man, no rioter: three times he drank
from it, all told, and even so he mixed
his wine with water. The first time was,
when he reached sixty and married a young thing;
three years later, when she rejoiced
his heart by presenting him with an heir; and after
she had borne him fifteen children, he drank
from it a third time, when she died.

ADAM. Oh, that's good, that's good!

FRAU MARTHA.   The next hands
it came into were Zacharias',
a tailor out of Tirlemont, who told
my husband, him of blessed memory,
with his own mouth, what I'm about to tell
to you. When the Frenchmen came a-plundering
he pitched the jug and with it everything
he owned straight out the window, then jumped out of it
himself and broke his neck, the oaf, but the jug,
an earthenware one, made of clay, it landed
on its feet and never broke.

ADAM. Get to the point, Frau Martha Rull, the point!

---

5. The Treaty of Brussels, 1555, whose inauguration is depicted on the jug.
6. *Fürchtegott*: "Fear-God."

FRAU MARTHA. Then in sixty-six in the great fire, by
    which time it had come into the possession of my husband, bless
    his soul—
ADAM.   The devil, woman, is there any
    end in sight?
FRAU MARTHA. If I am not to speak,
    Judge Adam, I see no purpose in my coming here.
    I'll say good-bye and find a court where I
    am listened to.
WALTER.   My good woman, you are free to speak:
    but not about what has no bearing on your
    matter. If you tell us that the jug
    was treasured by you, as judges that is all
    we need to know.
FRAU MARTHA.   What Your Judgeships need
    to know I've no idea, it's none of my
    affair. One thing I know, however:
    if I'm to state my case I must be free
    to utter more than a few monosyllables.
WALTER. Yes ma'am. So how does it all end? What happened
    to the jug in Anno Domini sixty-six,
    in the great fire? The court is most concerned
    to learn what happened to the jug.
FRAU MARTHA.   What happened
    to it? Nothing. Nothing happened to it
    in Anno Domini sixty-six. Intact
    it stood amid the flames, and when I drew
    it from the ashes of the house next morning, it glittered
    newly glazed as if fresh from the kiln.
WALTER. Excellent. So now we are well acquainted
    with the jug. All the vicissitudes that it has
    survived, we are informed about. What more, then?
FRAU MARTHA. This jug, which even in its broken state
    is worthy of a lady's drinking from it, which would
    not sully even the Frau Stadtholder's lips,
    this jug, I must inform Your Judgeships,
    that scoundrel there smashed to bits.
ADAM.   Who?
FRAU MARTHA. That one there, that Ruprecht.

RUPRECHT. It's a lie,
Your Honor.
ADAM. Hold your tongue until you're asked.
You've got it all down, Clerk?
LICHT. I have.
ADAM. My dear Frau Martha, please relate the circumstances.
FRAU MARTHA. Yesterday, eleven o'clock it was—
ADAM. Was when?
FRAU MARTHA. Eleven.
ADAM. In the morning?
FRAU MARTHA. No, the night—
excuse me. I was just about to blow my bed lamp
out when an uproar of men's voices, coming
from my daughter's bedroom on the ground floor,
scared me half to death. Down the stairs
I rush and find her door forced open,
someone's screaming accusations like a madman,
and what do you think I see in the candlelight,
Your Honor, what do you think I find? The jug,
smashed all to bits, to smithereens, in every
corner there's a piece, my poor child
wringing her hands, and *him,* that lout there,
storming like a madman in the middle of the floor.
ADAM. My goodness!
FRAU MARTHA. Outraged, and with good reason, feeling
as if I have grown ten arms and each one tipped
with vulture's talons, I demand to know what he
is doing in my house so late at night and what
he means by trying to destroy every vase
and pitcher I possess. Can you imagine
what his answer is? The rogue has no shame,
none! I won't rest easy till I see
him broken on the wheel. He says somebody else,
can you believe it, knocked my jug down from
the mantelpiece, somebody else that took
to his heels just as he arrived. And then
he showers my poor child with his abuse.
ADAM. Very fishy, oh indeed!
FRAU MARTHA. When I
hear this, I look at Eve. She's like a ghost.

Eve! I say, and she collapses in a chair. Was it
somebody else, I ask. By Joseph and the Virgin Mary,
Mother, she exclaims, surely you
don't think—? Then tell me who it was.—Who else
could it have been? And then she swears to me he
was the one.

EVE.   But that's not so! I didn't
swear! I swore nothing!

FRAU MARTHA.   Eve!

EVE.   No, it's
a lie—.

RUPRECHT. There you are.

ADAM.   Silence, you damned brute,
unless you want my fist to shut your mouth!
Your time's later, not before.

FRAU MARTHA.   You didn't
swear—?

EVE.   No, Mother. It makes me miserable
to have to say it publicly, but I
swore nothing, nothing whatsoever.

ADAM. Children, you're not being sensible.

LICHT. How very strange.

FRAU MARTHA.   Eve, you didn't swear
an oath by Joseph and the Virgin Mary—?

EVE.   No oath!
It wasn't swearing—that I'll swear an oath to,
by Joseph and the Virgin Mary!

ADAM.   Good people, please!
Frau Martha, think of what you're doing, you
don't want to frighten the dear child. Give
her time to think things over quietly
and remember everything that happened
—I say *happened,* and if she doesn't say
what is required of her, *can* happen. Believe
me, she will say as much today as she
said yesterday, no matter if she swears
to it or not. We don't need to drag
Joseph and the Virgin Mary into this.

WALTER. No, no, Your Honor, no! We mustn't seek
to counsel witnesses by suggestion.

FRAU MARTHA. If the shameless thing has the effrontery to tell
me to my face it wasn't Ruprecht, then as far
as I'm concerned, she can—no, I won't
say what. Nevertheless, I assure Your Honor, even
if I'm unable positively to declare she *swore*
he was the one, I will swear to it she *said*
he was the one, by Joseph and the Virgin Mary.

ADAM. I'm sure now she won't want—

WALTER. Judge Adam!

ADAM. What's wrong,
Your Honor? Isn't it so, Eve dear?

FRAU MARTHA. Out
with it. Did you tell me so last night or not?

EVE. Well, I don't deny that's what I said—.

ADAM. There you are.

RUPRECHT. The false bitch!

ADAM. Record it, Clerk.

VEIT. For shame!

WALTER. Judge Adam, I'm baffled by your conduct of this case. If you
yourself had been the one to break the jug,
you couldn't exert yourself more eagerly
to shift suspicion from yourself onto the youth.
Clerk, record the girl admits to what
she said last night, but nothing as to what
in fact occurred. Is it her turn next to testify?

ADAM. If it's not her turn, Your Worship,
I don't know whose turn it is. Who do you think
should be interrogated now, sir? The accused?
Believe me, I am always pleased to be instructed.

WALTER. Ingenuous, you are!—Yes, question the accused,
question and let's have an end to it, by God!
This is the last case you will ever try.

ADAM. The last case! Really? Oh well. Call the accused!
Where were your thoughts at this time, old friend Adam?
Confound that guinea hen that's got the pip!
I wish the Indies plague had done it in!
The noodle cram it needs is always on my mind.

WALTER. What is on your mind?

ADAM. The cram, sir, if
you please, I meant to give my bird. If

the beast won't swallow it, God only knows what
will happen to it.

WALTER. The devil, do what it's
your job to do.

ADAM. Accused, step forward!

RUPRECHT. Here
I am, Your Honor, Ruprecht, son of Veit
the cottager, from Huisum.

ADAM. Have you heard the charge
Frau Martha has made against you here?

RUPRECHT. I have,
Your Honor.

ADAM. Dare you say anything in your defense?
Do you confess its truth, or are you bold
enough to defy God and deny it?

RUPRECHT. Say anything in my defense, Your Honor?
Yes, with your permission—there's not a word of truth
in what she said.

ADAM. Oh so. And you can prove
that to the court?

RUPRECHT. Yes, I can.

ADAM. Good Frau Martha,
rest assured, there's no cause for concern.
The truth will out.

WALTER. Why the devil do
you worry so about Frau Martha, sir?

ADAM. Why, you ask! As a Christian, sir—

WALTER. Accused, state what you have to say in your
defense.—Clerk Licht, do you think you're able to conduct
this trial?

ADAM. Of course not!

LICHT. Am I able—? Well,
you see, Your Worship—.

ADAM (*to Ruprecht*).
What are you gawking at, you?
Speak your piece, now out with it! The donkey
stands there like an ox, I think. What
have you got to say for yourself?

RUPRECHT. Got to say?

ADAM. Yes, stop shilly-shallying. Tell your story.

RUPRECHT. Oh sir, if only you will let me!

WALTER. Judge Adam, really, this is not
  to be endured.

RUPRECHT.   Ten by the clock I think it was,
  the January evening mild as May,
  when I tell my father: Pa, I would like to visit
  with that Eve! For you see, I meant to marry her.
  Oh, she's a strapping miss, she is, at harvest
  time she made the hay fly with her fork
  as thick as rain. So I asked: Eve dear, will you?
  And she answered! How you talk! But later she
  said: Yes!

ADAM.   Don't wander from the subject with your "how you talk"
  and "she said yes"!

RUPRECHT.   She did, sir.

ADAM.   Never mind!

RUPRECHT. Well, let's see. So I said: Pa, please let me
  as we sat awhile together, and he said: Oh well,
  run along—but you'll not set foot inside,
  I hope? Oh no, I swear, I said. All right,
  he said, but back here by eleven.

ADAM.   Is there
  any end in sight to all this—this dialogue!
  So how many more "saids" are there?

RUPRECHT.   So I say:
  Yes, for sure, put on my cap and go—
  by the path that goes back to the village,
  since the brook has overflowed its banks.
  Thunder, Ruprecht, suddenly I think, I'll find
  the garden gate at Martha's locked, I'm sure,
  Eve closes it at ten, if I'm not there
  by ten I've come out for no reason.

ADAM. Humph! What a way to run a house!

WALTER.   And then?

RUPRECHT. And then—as I'm passing through the linden alley
  just before you come to Martha's, where
  the trees arch overhead and it's as dark
  as under Utrecht's dome, I hear the gate creak
  and I say: Hear that? That's Eve, and try to make out
  in the darkness with my eyes what my ears report—

but they are blind. I strain my eyes a second
time. Not blind this time, but false: lying troublemakers,
nasty scandalmongers. So I try
again. And what I think the third time is,
they've done their duty faithfully, they have,
and now my eyes are popping out of my head:
with indignation—for there is Eve, I know
her by her dress, and someone's with her, too,
a man!

ADAM.　　Who? Who was it, Know-it-all?
So tell us who it was.

RUPRECHT.　　　　Who was it, are you asking?

ADAM. Oh well, it hardly matters—to hang a thief,
you have to catch him first.

WALTER.　　　　　Go on! Continue!
Let him speak! Why do you interrupt him, Judge?

RUPRECHT. I couldn't swear an oath about it on the sacrament.
You see, it was pitch dark, when every cat is gray.
But I think you should know this: the shoemaker Lebrecht,
who's just out of his apprenticeship, has been trailing
after Evie a good long time. Last fall
I said: Listen, Evie, I don't care
for it one bit, the way that good-for-nothing
hangs around your house; tell him you're
no dish for him, or else I'll let him have
what-for. She tells him something, I believe—
Your attentions are annoying—it's neither here nor there,
not fish, not fowl. So I go in and pitch
him out the door.

ADAM.　　　　So the fellow's name is Lebrecht?

RUPRECHT. Yes, sir.

ADAM.　　　　Good. So now we've got a name.
We'll have the whole truth soon. Is it recorded,
Clerk?

LICHT.　Yes, Your Honor, and all the rest.

ADAM. And now continue, my dear boy.

RUPRECHT.　　　　　My blood
boils when I see that pair there at eleven—
I always left at ten. I think: Hold
your horses, Ruprecht, there's still time,

you've not grown horns yet: feel your forehead carefully
to see if something's starting there. And quietly
I slip into the garden through the gate
and hide behind a clump of yews. The sound
of whispering, of teasing and of fooling, pushing,
pulling, can be heard—good Lord, I think,
how I would like—!

EVE.   You wicked man, it's shameful
what you're saying.

FRAU MARTHA.   Gallows bird, when we're
alone, you'll learn what kind of stuff I'm made of!

RUPRECHT. It all goes on about a quarter of an hour.
What next, I wonder, there's been no wedding here
today, I'm sure, and before that thought is finished,
flash, they're in her house without first calling
on the pastor.

EVE.   Leave, Mother, it doesn't matter
any more.

ADAM.   Stop jabbering over there,
is my advice to you, with your unasked-
for comments! Wait till you are called on.

WALTER. Very curious, by God!

RUPRECHT.   I feel, Your Honor, as if
an artery is about to burst. I gasp
for air so hard a button pops off
from my doublet. Air, air, I cry and yank
the doublet open, I need air! And go and beat
and kick and thunder on her door when I
discover that the slut has locked it, till
with a tremendous kick I kick it in.

ADAM. Oh, what a fellow that is!

RUPRECHT.   The instant it
swings open, with a bang, down the jug falls
from the mantelpiece inside the room
and someone jumps out of the window with his coattails
flying.

ADAM.   And it was Lebrecht, wasn't it?

RUPRECHT. Sir, who else? I push aside the girl,
who's standing there, hurry to the window and find
the scoundrel entangled in the trellis on which the grapevine

climbs up to the roof; he's hanging from a post. My fist
still held the door latch from when I broke
into the room, so I lean out and with the poundsweight
of steel I pound his headpiece hard,
which, Your Honor, is just within my reach.
ADAM. Was it a door latch?
RUPRECHT.   What?
ADAM.   I asked—
RUPRECHT. A latch, oh yes.
ADAM.   So that was what it was.
LICHT. Perhaps you thought it was a sword?
ADAM.   A sword?
     Why a sword?
RUPRECHT.   A sword!
LICHT.   Well, you see, it's easy
     to mistake things. A door latch and a sword
     have a lot in common.
ADAM.   You're talking nonsense!
LICHT. The shank and blade, Your Honor!
ADAM. Shank and blade!
RUPRECHT.   The shank! That wasn't it.
     It was the handle end.
ADAM.   Handle end!
LICHT.   Well, well!
RUPRECHT. It's true the handle had a knob of lead
     on it just like the hilt of a sword.
ADAM.   It did!
LICHT. In any case a nasty sort of weapon—
     as I thought.
WALTER.   Gentlemen, we are forgetting
     our business!
ADAM.   Just a bit of banter on the side!
     Don't record it, Clerk. Resume!
RUPRECHT.   The fellow
     crashes down and I'm about to make
     for the door when I see him staggering up. Still alive,
     are you, I think, and I climb up on the sill so as
     to jump and put a stop to his going anywhere.
     And it's just then that a handful of thick sand
     flying in my face like hail puts out my eyes—

like a collapsing tent, so help me God,
darkness falls on me, on that villain, the whole world.
ADAM. Damnation, who did that?
RUPRECHT.   Lebrecht.
ADAM. The rogue!
RUPRECHT.   I think so anyhow.
ADAM.   Who else?
RUPRECHT. As if a hailstorm hurled me down ten fathoms
    from a cliff top, I tumble backwards to the floor
    and think I'm going through the boards. Nothing's
    broken, back or sides or otherwise,
    but the bird is flown, and I sit up and rub
    my eyes. You've hurt yourself, dear Ruprecht, oh
    my God, she cries, kneeling down to me.
    My foot drew back, I thank the Lord I couldn't
    see to aim my kick.
ADAM.   Because of the sand,
    was that?
RUPRECHT. Oh yes.
ADAM.   A good shot, damn me,
    if it wasn't!
RUPRECHT.   I struggle to my feet and think:
    I won't insult my fists, so I call her dirty slut
    and other things and leave it go at that.
    But my voice gets choked with tears. For when Frau Martha
    comes into the room holding up a lamp,
    and I can see how Eve is trembling violently,
    the poor girl, who used to look the whole world
    in the face so bravely, I tell myself: it isn't
    the worst thing there is, being blind. Gladly
    at that moment I'd have given my two eyes
    to anyone who wanted them, to play marbles with.
EVE. The wretch does not deserve—
ADAM.   Silence!
RUPRECHT.   The rest
    you know about.
ADAM.   We do?
RUPRECHT.   Well, Frau Martha came
    spitting fire like a dragon, and neighbor Ralph
    and neighbor Hans, and Tante Liese came

and Tante Anna, servants came and maids,
and dogs and cats, oh what a sight it was,
and Frau Martha asked who broke the jug, and she,
as you already know, said I had done it.
She wasn't off the mark by much, by God!—
for the shoemaker got a hole in the head from me:
that pitcher went to the well with her just once
too often.

ADAM.　　　Frau Martha, how do you respond
　　to this?

FRAU MARTHA. Respond, Your Honor? I respond
　　that like a marten he breaks into the coop
　　and strangles shrieking truth. Whoever values
　　justice, seize a stick and beat that prowling
　　creature of the night to death!

ADAM.　　　　　　　　But proof—we need
　　some proof.

FRAU MARTHA. I'll give it to you. Here's my witness.
　　Speak!

ADAM.　　Your daughter? That won't do, Frau Martha.

FRAU MARTHA. And why not, I would like to know?

ADAM. Is her testimony admissible, Your Worship?
　　Doesn't the Statute Book declare, in Section
　　quarto or I think it's quinto,
　　that whenas jugs are broken, or who knows what
　　(I don't), by country clowns, a daughter
　　may not testify in favor of her mother?

WALTER. Knowledge and nonsense are an inextricable
　　hodgepodge in your head; everything
　　you say has got a bit of each in it.
　　The young woman isn't testifying yet,
　　it's simply a statement which she makes. Whether
　　she can testify, and for whom, will be
　　determined by her statement.

ADAM.　　　　　　　　Oh yes, her statement. Good.
　　Section sexto, then. But as for what
　　she's got to say—who can believe it?

WALTER. Come forward, child.

ADAM. Hey, Lizzie!—Oh, I'm sorry! But my throat is parched.
　　—Oh Margaret!

SCENE 8
Enter a Maid.

ADAM. A glass of water.

MAID. Yes, Your Honor. (*Exit Maid.*)

ADAM. And you,
  sir, will you take—.

WALTER. No, nothing, thank you.

ADAM. A French Red,
  or a Moselle, whatever your heart desires.
  (*Walter declines with a bow. The Maid brings water and exits.*)

SCENE 9

ADAM. If you'll allow me, sir, I think the case
  calls for a compromise.

WALTER. A compromise?
  What makes you think so, Judge? Reasonable
  people find it possible to compromise;
  but how you imagine you can arrange one here,
  when so much in the case is still obscure,
  I should be delighted to discover. Do tell me how
  you think it can be done. Your mind's made up
  already about the verdict, is it?

ADAM. Upon
  my soul, sir, since the law has shown itself
  a weak reed here, I'll try philosophy and say:
  the guilty party's—Lebrecht!

WALTER. Who?

ADAM. Or Ruprecht—?

WALTER. Who?

ADAM. Maybe Lebrecht, after all.

WALTER. Well, which one is it, Ruprecht or the other?
  You grope around uncertainly, like a hand
  inside a sack of peas.

ADAM. Sorry, sorry!

WALTER. I wish you wouldn't go on so.

ADAM. As you say, sir.
  Let them both be guilty, I don't care.

WALTER. Keep up the questioning, I promise you,
   and the truth is certain to come out.
ADAM.   Gladly. But I'm a villain
   if it ever does. Are you ready, Licht?
LICHT. I am, sir.
ADAM.   Good.
LICHT.   With a new page broken
   out, and all on edge to see what will
   be written on it.
ADAM.   A new page, very good.
WALTER. And now, child, speak.
ADAM.   Yes, Evie, speak, my little Evie!
   Tell God and all the world whatever you
   may know. In standing here, remember, you stand
   before God's judgment seat—don't distress
   your judge with lies, or babble endlessly
   to no point. After all, you are a reasonable
   girl. Judges are in the business of judging,
   you know that. Today it's this one needs
   him, tomorrow it's another. If you say it
   was Lebrecht, fine; if you say Ruprecht, that's
   fine, too! Whichever one you say, it doesn't
   matter, everything will turn out
   just the way you wish. But if you like
   to wag your tongue and bring in someone else
   entirely, some third person, naming
   stupid names, then, my child, take care,
   I'll say no more. There's not a soul in Huisum
   who will believe you, no, nor in all the Netherlands.
   Whitewashed walls are dumb in court, and he'll
   know how to give as good as he gets—then our Ruprecht's
   case will be a sorry one.
WALTER.   Goodness, Judge,
   you go on endlessly—and arrive nowhere.
ADAM. Your Worship doesn't understand me?
WALTER.   Please!
   You have spoken too long from the bench.
ADAM.   I never
   studied at the University, Your Worship,
   so maybe gentlemen from Utrecht miss my drift.

But not the people of this village, nor this
young woman, I will lay a bet.

FRAU MARTHA. What's going
on here? Say what you have to say, girl, out
with it!

EVE. Mother dear!

FRAU MARTHA. Now do as you've
been told—come on!

RUPRECHT. Speaking up is hard,
Frau Martha, when your conscience has you by the throat.

ADAM. Shut up, Sir Impudence, we've had enough
from you!

FRAU MARTHA. Who was it, speak!

EVE. O Jesus!

FRAU MARTHA. No, not Jesus, but that booby there,
that dolt, that good-for-nothing! Letting herself
look like a whore!

ADAM. Frau Martha, please control
yourself! What a way to carry on!
Look at her, the poor thing's scared to death.
Calling her a whore! We'll get nowhere
that way. Give her time to think things
over.

RUPRECHT. Think indeed.

ADAM. Quiet, peasant.

RUPRECHT. It will come to her it was the shoemaker, finally.

ADAM. The devil! Call the bailiff! Hans!

RUPRECHT. All right,
all right, I'll hold my tongue. But the first name
on the list is mine, I'll bet.

FRAU MARTHA. Come on, come on,
don't put a play on, please. I've reached the age
of forty-nine respectably, my eye
is fixed on fifty. February 3rd's
my birthday and today's the 1st. So get
a move on. Name him.

ADAM. Excellent, Frau Martha,
excellent!

FRAU MARTHA. When her father went, he said:
Martha, listen, find her an honest man

to marry her; if she's a slut, put
a penny in the gravedigger's fist and have
him roll me on my back again—for I'll
have turned over in my grave for sure.

ADAM.   Not bad,
either, that.

FRAU MARTHA [*sarcastically*].
            Evie dear, so as to honor
your father and your mother as the Fourth Commandment
bids us, do tell the court you let the shoemaker
in your room, or let in somebody or other—
but not the man you are engaged to.

RUPRECHT.   I pity her,
I do. Never mind the jug; I'll go
to Utrecht with it. Oh, that jug—I wish
I'd broken it indeed.

EVE.   Shame, shame
on you! You haven't a spark of generous feeling
in you! You couldn't say: *I* broke the jug,
could you? Ruprecht, shame on you
because you have so little trust in me!
When you asked me, Will you have me? I took your hand
and answered, Yes. Do you think that you mean less
to me than the shoemaker? Even if
you had stooped and seen me through the keyhole drinking
from the jug with Lebrecht, you should have thought: Eve's
an honest girl and I am confident there is
an explanation for all this which honors her,
if not in this life, then the next one,
for with Resurrection there's another day.

RUPRECHT. Evie, that's too long a wait for me
and I believe what I can lay my hands on.

EVE. Let's suppose for argument's sake that Lebrecht
was the one, why shouldn't I (or let me
die!) confide in you at once, uniquely you?
And suppose there were reasons why I should want
to hide it from the neighbors and the servants, why, Ruprecht,
tell me, shouldn't I, relying on
your trust, have said you were the one?
Why shouldn't I? Why shouldn't I?

RUPRECHT. Well, say
it, damn it, it's all right with me, if it
will save you from the stocks.

EVE. You odious, ungrateful man!
Yes, I should spare myself the stocks, for you
deserve it—deserve that by one word
I should preserve my honor and give *you* over to destruction!

WALTER. Yes? Go on. The one word is—? Don't keep
us in suspense. But it wasn't Ruprecht,
is how I understand you, was it?

EVE. No,
it wasn't. That's what he wants to hear. But I
kept silent only for his sake. Ruprecht
didn't break the jug. When he denies
he did, you can believe him.

FRAU MARTHA. Eve, it wasn't
Ruprecht?

EVE. No, Mother, no! When I said he was
the one last night, I lied.

FRAU MARTHA. Every bone
she has, I'll break! (*Sets down the jug.*)

EVE. I don't care.

WALTER (*in a threatening tone*).
Frau Martha!

ADAM. Bailiff, bailiff! Throw the old hag out!
Ruprecht doesn't have to be the man.
I bet she held the candle in the business.
But the young woman is the one to know.
Hang me for a liar if it wasn't Lebrecht.

FRAU MARTHA. Then was it Lebrecht? Speak!

ADAM. Speak, Evie, it was Lebrecht, sweetheart, wasn't it?

EVE. You're shameless, vile! To say that it was Lebrecht!
Oh, how can you?

WALTER. Miss! What way is that
to talk? Where is the respect you owe a judge?

EVE. Respect indeed! A judge! A miserable sinner
who should be standing in the dock himself!
He's the one who knows best who it was!
(*Turning to Adam.*)

Lebrecht was sent by you to the Military Commission
in Utrecht, wasn't he, to turn over to them
the list of recruits? How can you say that it
was Lebrecht when you know very well he was in Utrecht?
ADAM. Well, who was it then, if it wasn't Lebrecht?
    It wasn't Ruprecht, and neither was it Lebrecht—
    what's going on here?
RUPRECHT.   Your Honor, listen,
    what the girl is saying now is true,
    for I myself met Lebrecht yesterday
    at eight in the morning on his way to Utrecht.
    Unless a wagon picked him up
    the fellow couldn't have got back home
    before ten at night at the earliest, with his bowlegs.
    So it must have been somebody else.
ADAM. His bowlegs! What a nincompoop
    you are! The fellow shakes a leg as well
    as anyone. Curse me for a crawling worm,
    if a sheepdog wouldn't have to break
    into a trot to keep up with him.
WALTER [*to Eve.*]   Say
    what happened.
ADAM.   Excuse me, sir, but the girl can't help
    us here.
WALTER.   Can't help us, do you say? And pray,
    why not?
ADAM.   She's just a simple thing. Good,
    but very simple. Young, just recently
    confirmed; when a beard appears above the horizon, she blushes.
    Such people suffer in the dark, but when the day
    dawns, they deny that anything has happened.
WALTER. How very thoughtful, Judge, you are, how mild
    and merciful in what concerns the girl.
ADAM. The truth is, sir, her father was a friend
    of mine. If Your Worship chose to be benevolent
    today, it would be doing no more than our duty
    to let his daughter go.
WALTER.   Judge Adam, I feel
    a great desire in myself to get to the bottom
    of this case.—Don't be timid, child;

say who broke the jug. No one in
whose presence you stand now, would refuse to pardon
a misstep.

EVE.   Honorable and worthy Sir,
I beg to be excused from answering
your question. Don't take it amiss that I refuse
to speak. An extraordinary act of Providence seals
my lips. I'll confirm by oath, on the altar
steps, if that's your wish, that Ruprecht didn't break
the jug. But what happened yesterday and everything
else about it, is my affair, and just
because a thread of the yarn is my mother's it doesn't
give her a claim on the whole ball. I can't
say who broke the jug; doing so
would be a betrayal of secrets not my own
in which the jug is not concerned. I'll tell
her what the truth is ultimately,
but she mayn't demand it of me here in this courtroom
as of right.

ADAM.   She may not, no, I'll take an oath
on that. The young woman knows her way in the law,
I see. If she will swear to the truth of what
she's said, her mother's complaint is rendered null.
There is no objection I can see to that.

WALTER. And what have you got to say to all
of this, Frau Martha?

FRAU MARTHA.   If I am slow, Your Worship,
to respond to what you ask, blame it on
the stroke I've just now suffered which has paralyzed
my tongue. There are more than enough examples of wretches
who, to save their honor in the world, have perjured
themselves before the bar of justice. But to kneel
before the altar and swear falsely so as
to have yourself put in the stocks—this
is something new under the sun. If it
was proved someone other than Ruprecht slipped
into her room last night, if it was at all
possible to prove that, Your Worship, believe me—
I wouldn't have wasted another minute here
in court. I would have stood a chair outside

the door for her dowry, so she could start housekeeping
under the sky, and said: Go, my child,
the world is wide, and for the open spaces
no one charges rent, and long hair,
too, you have inherited, to hang yourself
with when the time arrives!

WALTER.   Frau Martha,
gently, gently.

FRAU MARTHA.   However, even though
she refuses to lift a finger for me in my case,
I have other ways to prove it, and seeing
I don't doubt that he and no one else
was the one to break my jug, the violence
of their denial makes me smell a rat.
The destruction of the jug was not the only crime
committed yesterday night! I have to tell
Your Worship that Ruprecht is called up;
in a matter of days in Utrecht he must swear
allegiance to the colors. But our young countrymen
don't like close-order drill. I can hear
him whispering: Evie, what do you think?
The world's a great big place. You've got the keys
to where the money's hid. But her heart
wasn't in it. And all that has followed afterward,
after I interrupted them—in which
his motive is revenge, hers love—becomes
understandable.

RUPRECHT.   Nasty buzzard! Crow! How dare
you talk like that! Steal money!

ADAM.   Silence in the court!

EVE. Him a deserter!

WALTER.   Stick to the jug. That's what
our subject is. Proof, proof, I want, that Ruprecht
broke it!

FRAU MARTHA. Very well, Your Worship. First
I'll prove, here in court, that Ruprecht broke the jug,
and then I'll search around for evidence I can find
at home.—I'm going to produce a witness who
will confirm my testimony about him, about
every word he said. I could have lined up

133

scores of them for you right off if I
had ever dreamt my own daughter would have failed
to support my word with hers. But if you summon
Frau Brigitta now, who is his aunt,
that's enough for me, because she will give
them the lie in everything they have said. For she,
at half past ten—do you hear, *before* the jug
was smashed—passed by and heard him talking to Eve
in the garden. And how a single tongue knocks
on its head this fairy tale of theirs, exalted sirs,
I'll leave it to you to judge.

RUPRECHT.   Who heard me—?

VEIT. Tante Brigge?

RUPRECHT.   Eve and me in the garden?

FRAU MARTHA.   Yes, him,
in the garden with Eve, at half past ten, before
he forced his way into her room at eleven, according
to his lying story—caressing her with his words
in one breath, pressing her hard in the next,
as if he was trying to persuade her to do something.

ADAM (*aside*).
Well, I'll be damned! The devil's doing his best
for me!

WALTER. Have the woman brought here, please.

RUPRECHT. Your Honors, hear me, there is not a single word
of truth in what she says!

ADAM.   Just wait, you rascal!
It's when criminals are on the run that jugs
get broken! Clerk Licht, go get Frau Brigitta!

VEIT. Boy, what have you been up to, good-for-nothing?
I'll wring your neck for you, I will!

RUPRECHT.   Why?
What for?

VEIT.   Why did you keep mum about fooling
with that Evie at half past ten in the garden?

RUPRECHT. Why? I'll tell you why—because it isn't
true! If Tante Brigge says it is,
then take me out and hang me. And while you're at
it, hoist her in the air, too, for my sake.

VEIT. If she says it's true—watch out! You
and that innocent Eve of yours, in spite of what
you tell the court, are hiding under the same
blanket, I'm convinced. There is some kind
of shameful secret here which she knows very
well, but which she will never breathe a word
about, for your sake.

RUPRECHT. Secret? What do you mean?

VEIT. Why did you pack your things last night? Now tell
me that!

RUPRECHT. My things?

VEIT. Yes, coat and pants and underwear;
the kind of bundle a traveler slings across
his shoulder.

RUPRECHT. I'll tell you why. Because I'm on
my way to Utrecht to join my regiment.
Thunder, do you think that I would—?

VEIT. Utrecht?
Oh indeed! In a great hurry to get to Utrecht,
are you? But only two days ago you couldn't
say if you would be leaving in five days' time
or six.

WALTER. Father Veit, do you know anything
with a bearing on this case?

VEIT. No, Your Worship,
nothing. When the jug broke I was home.
Nor, to tell the truth, when I consider
everything which might cause me to suspect
my son, have I seen any sign of something
else afoot. I came here fully convinced
of his innocence; my object, once the dispute
was settled, to see to it the engagement was dissolved
and the silver chain and token penny[7] he gave
the girl last fall returned. Fraud and flight
are as new to me and my gray hairs as to you.
But if it's true, the devil can have him, I
give up my interest.

---

7. *Token penny*: token of engagement.

WALTER.   Where's Frau Brigitta,
    Judge Adam, please!
ADAM.   Your Worship surely
    is fatigued. The damned case has no end.
    And there are still my accounts and files.
    —What time is it?
LICHT.   The clock just struck the half.
ADAM. Of eleven?
LICHT.   No, of twelve.
WALTER.   It doesn't matter.
ADAM. Either you or the time is mad. (*Looks at his watch.*)
                            Well, I'll be damned.
    So what's your wish, sir?
WALTER.   My opinion is—
ADAM. To stop now? Fine!
WALTER.   Just a minute. My
    opinion is to continue.
ADAM.   That's your opinion?
    Also fine! However, I could wind
    the case up to your satisfaction by nine o'clock
    tomorrow.
WALTER.   You know what my wish is.
ADAM. Just as you say. Clerk Licht, dispatch the bailiff
    to bring Frau Brigitta here without delay.
WALTER. Do please show—so as to save
    the time that is so precious to me—a more serious
    interest in the case, Judge Adam.
                            (*Exit Licht.*)

SCENE 10

ADAM (*standing up*).
    Meanwhile, sir, with your approval, might
    we take a little breather?
WALTER.   Well—. All right.
    There's something I have meant to ask you—
ADAM.   And the others, too,
    until Frau Brigitta appears—?
WALTER.   The parties, too?
ADAM. They'll be just outside the door, sir.

WALTER (*under his breath*).
Delays, delays! (*Aloud.*) Judge Adam, I do believe
I'd like a glass of wine while we are waiting.
ADAM. Oh certainly! Hey, Margaret! Why, I'm delighted,
Your Worship.—Maggie!
(*Enter the Maid.*)
MAID. Yes.
ADAM. What would you like?—
Leave, you people, leave.—Red from France?—
In the passageway outside.—Or Rhenish?
WALTER. A little
of our Rhenish.
ADAM. Good.—Until you are summoned back.
Now march!
WALTER. March? March where?
ADAM. From the sealed stock, Margaret.
Here's the key.
WALTER. Perhaps they should remain.
ADAM. Move, will you, march!—And Maggie, some fresh butter,
too, some Limburger, and the smoked goose that's so good.
WALTER. Judge Adam, just a minute! It's too much,
please.
ADAM. —Get out of here, do you hear me?
WALTER. Do you send the people away, sir?
ADAM. Your Worship?
WALTER. I ask if—
ADAM. Just for a little while, sir, till
Frau Brigitta appears—with your permission.
Or you don't think it's—
WALTER. Oh well. Do what you
think best. But is it worth the trouble? How
much time does it take to hunt the woman up?
ADAM. Today's the day for collecting firewood.
Most of the women are gone off to the woods.
It might be quite—
RUPRECHT. My aunt's at home.
WALTER. She is?
Oh well.
RUPRECHT. She'll be here right away.

WALTER.   Good, right
  away. And now we'll have some wine.
ADAM (*aside.*)
                                                   Damnation!
WALTER. But we must make haste, sir! And all I care for is
  a slice of dry bread with some salt.
ADAM (*aside*).
                                       Two minutes with the girl
  alone and—. (*Aloud.*) Dry bread! Salt! But that's
  no lunch!
WALTER.   It's what I want.
ADAM.   Some Limburger, at least—cheese makes
  the palate fit for wine.
WALTER.   All right—a piece of cheese,
  but nothing else.
ADAM [*to Maggie*].
                        Do you hear? And a white tablecloth,
  please—damask. Everything quite simple, but first class.
                              (*Exit Maid.*)
  We bachelor people, in spite of our bad reputation,
  have this advantage over the others, that
  while they must measure things out sparingly,
  for there are wife and children needing to be fed
  each day, we are able, without stinting, to enjoy
  ourselves with a good friend whenever that's our wish.
WALTER. Judge Adam, what I wanted to ask you, was—
  how did you hurt yourself? That's a nasty looking
  wound I see there on your head.
ADAM.   I fell.
WALTER.   You fell,
  did you? Ah so! And when? Last night?
ADAM.   This morning,
  half past five, as I was getting
  out of bed.
WALTER.   Fell over what?
ADAM.   To tell
  the truth, Your Worship—myself. I toppled and struck
  my head against the stove, but how it happened,
  I can't say.
WALTER.   Toppled backwards?

138

ADAM.   Backwards,
   why?

WALTER.   Or forwards. For there are bruises front and back.

ADAM. Yes, front and back.—Maggie!

            (*Enter the two Maids with wine, etc. They spread
                  a cloth and exeunt.*)

WALTER.   How did it happen?

ADAM. First one and then the other. First the edge of the stove,
   which knocked a hole in my forehead, here, then backwards
   to the floor, striking the back of my head.

                  (*He pours the wine.*)
                           If

   you please.

WALTER (*takes the glass*).

           If you possessed a wife, Judge, I'd be
   thinking other things.

ADAM.   You would?

WALTER.   Indeed
   I would. Because your face is scratched and scored
   all over.

ADAM (*laughing*).

        No, thank God, it wasn't female
   nails at work.

WALTER.   I'm sure. Still another
   bachelor's benefit.

ADAM (*laughing still*).

           Twigs for silkworms
   drying on the stove.—Your health!

              (*They drink.*)

WALTER.   And to have
   to lose your wig today of all days,
   just when you needed it to conceal your wounds!

ADAM. How right you are. But troubles always come
   in tandem. Here's a real ripe piece.

WALTER. Not too much. From Limburg?

ADAM.   Straight from Limburg,
   sir.

WALTER. But how the devil did it happen?

ADAM. What?

WALTER.   Losing your wig?
                            Well, you see,
  I was poring over a case last evening. Because
  I'd mislaid my glasses, I bent so low to the page
  my wig caught fire from the candle. Instantly
  I think: fire and brimstone poured on my sinner's
  head by the just heavens, and try to snatch
  it off my head; but before I'm able to untie
  the ribbons, up it goes in flames like Sodom
  and Gomorrah and I just manage to preserve my three
  remaining hairs.

WALTER.   Tut, tut. And your other
  one is in town?

ADAM.   At the wigmaker's.—But we musn't
  neglect our duties.

WALTER.   Please, no need to spoil
  our glass, Judge.

ADAM.   Well, I know, but time is passing.
  More, sir, do you care for? Here. (*Pours wine.*)

WALTER.   That Lebrecht—
  if what the yokel says is true, *he*
  had a bad fall, too.

ADAM.   I guess so. (*He drinks.*)

WALTER.   And if
  there's no getting to the bottom of things here in court,
  which I almost think will be the case, it shouldn't
  be hard for you, in your small village,
  to recognize the guilty party by his wounds. (*He drinks.*)
  Niersteiner?

ADAM.   What?

WALTER.   Or a good Oppenheimer?

ADAM. Niersteiner. Well, my word, I see you know
  your wine. Direct from Nierstein—as if I fetched
  it straight from there myself.

WALTER.   I tasted it three years
  ago at the winery.
                    (*Adam pours more wine in Walter's glass.*)
                        —How high up is your window?
  You, Frau Martha!

FRAU MARTHA.   My window?

140

WALTER.   Your daughter's bedroom
  window.
FRAU MARTHA. The room is on the ground floor, actually,
  but there's a cellar underneath—the window
  can't be more than nine feet from the ground.
  However, the whole thing's laid out in a way that doesn't
  encourage jumping. Two feet from the wall
  there is a grapevine whose gnarled branches climb
  along a trellis running the length of the wall;
  the window is itself entirely enclosed
  by the vine. A boar with his sharp tusks would
  have a hard time of it breaking through
  that vine.
ADAM.   It wasn't a boar got caught in it. (*Fills his own glass.*)
WALTER. How's that?
ADAM.   Oh, nothing. (*Drinks.*)
WALTER (*to Ruprecht.*)
                         Where did you hit the culprit?
  On the head?
ADAM [*to Walter*].
                Here, have some more.   No,
WALTER.
  never mind.
ADAM.   Oh, come on.
WALTER.   It's still half full.
ADAM. I'll fill it.
WALTER.   I said no.
ADAM.   To make it a good
  number.
WALTER.   Please.
ADAM.   You know—according to the Pythagorean
  system. (*Fills his glass.*)
WALTER (*again to Ruprecht.*)
        How many times did you beat the culprit
  on the head?
ADAM.   Once is the Lord our God;
  twice the chaos dark and void; thrice
  the starry cosmos. So here's to glasses three
  whose every drop's a sun, and with every glass
  thereafter, we down firmaments.

WALTER. How many times
did you hit the culprit on the head? You there,
Ruprecht, I am asking you.

ADAM. Come on,
we want to know! How many times did you lay
it on that scapegoat? Lightning and thunder, see,
he doesn't know how many times! Have you forgotten?

RUPRECHT. With the latch?

ADAM. Yes, whatever with—
who the devil knows?

WALTER. When you leaned out
of the window and struck at him.

RUPRECHT. Twice, Your Honors.

ADAM.
Good-for-nothing!
He remembered. (*Drinks.*)

WALTER. Twice! With two such blows you could
have killed him, do you realize?

RUPRECHT. Well, if
I had, I would have had him, which is just
the thing I wanted. If he was lying dead
in front of us, I could say: Judges,
there he is, you see, I didn't lie
to you.

ADAM. About that you're dead right! However—(*Fills his glass.*)

WALTER. But you couldn't recognize him in the dark?

RUPRECHT. No, sir, no! How could I?

ADAM. Why don't you keep
your damned eyes open? Clink glasses!

RUPRECHT. Keep them open! I kept them open and Satan
pitched sand into them.

ADAM (*muttering*).
Sand! Why don't you keep
your damned eyes shut, then? Here, Your Worship, a toast
to what we love the best. Clink glasses!

WALTER. To all
that's just and good and faithful, Justice Adam!
(*They drink.*)

ADAM. And once again, sir, and the last. (*He fills the glasses.*)

WALTER.   Surely you
  drop in from time to time to visit at Frau Martha's,
  Judge? Tell me, would you, who goes in
  and out of there, apart from Ruprecht?
ADAM.   No,
  not often. I'm sorry, sir, but I can't say
  who goes in and out of there.
WALTER.   You can't?
  You don't occasionally visit the wife of your
  old friend?
ADAM.   In fact, no. Only
  very seldom.
WALTER.   Frau Martha! Have you had
  a falling out with our Judge Adam? He says
  he doesn't often call on you.
FRAU MARTHA.   A falling
  out, Your Worship? Hm, let's see. I wouldn't
  say a falling out. I'm sure he thinks
  he's still a friend of mine. But I can't boast
  my old friend is often to be seen inside
  my house. The last time was nine weeks ago,
  and just in passing.
WALTER.   You say nine weeks?
FRAU MARTHA.   Yes, nine.
  This Thursday makes it ten. He came to get
  some seeds—of pinks and bears'-ears.
WALTER.   But Sundays,
  when he strolls out to his farm?
FRAU MARTHA.   Oh then. He might
  look in the window and say good day to my daughter
  and myself, but without stopping off to visit.
WALTER (*aside*).
                                        Hm?
  I wonder if I've done the man—. (*Drinks.*) I thought,
  since you ask the girl's assistance from time to time,
  perhaps you show your appreciation by calling
  on the mother now and then.
ADAM.   I don't know what
  you mean.

WALTER.   You don't? You said the girl was a help
   to you with the sick hens on your farm.
   Just today she gave you some advice,
   I think.
FRAU MARTHA.   She did, that's right, Your Worship. Yesterday
   he sent over a sick guinea hen that was perishing
   for sure. She had cured one for him with the pip
   a year ago, by cramming it, and she'll do
   the same with this one too. But as for his coming
   to say thank you—there's been no sign of him.
WALTER (*baffled*).
   —Another, Judge, if you will be so kind. Let's have
   ourselves another.
ADAM.   Oh, my pleasure! There. (*Fills the glasses.*)
WALTER. Your health!—But sooner or later, I am sure,
   you will hear Judge Adam knocking at your door.
FRAU MARTHA.   Do you
   think so? I doubt it. If I had Niersteiner to set
   before His Honor like the kind you are drinking there,
   like the kind my man, of blessed memory,
   who kept the gate, used to lay down in our cellar
   now and then, it would be a different story.
   But I, poor widow that I am, have nothing in
   my house to tempt a man like him.
WALTER.   And better so!

SCENE 11
Enter Licht, Frau Brigitta with a wig in her hands, and Maids.

LICHT. Please come in, Frau Brigitta.
WALTER.   Is she
   the woman, Clerk?
LICHT.   Frau Brigitta, Your Worship.
WALTER. Now I trust we shall be able to conclude
   this case. Girls, remove these things.
ADAM (*while the maids are clearing the table*).
                              Now Evie,
   pay attention. You do a good job with our pill
   and we will celebrate tonight at your place
   over a carp. That beast has got to swallow

the thing whole, right down. But if
it's too big, then he'll choke on it.
(*Exeunt Maids.*)
WALTER (*catching sight of the wig*).
What wig
is that Frau Brigitta has in her hands?
LICHT. Your Worship?
WALTER. That wig, I wonder?
LICHT. Well, sir—.
WALTER. Well?
LICHT. I'm sorry—.
WALTER. No one will tell me?
LICHT. Please, Your Worship—if
you will have His Honor interrogate the witness,
the ownership of the wig will be revealed, as
well as other things, I have no doubt.
WALTER. I don't
want to know who owns it, but how it came
into the woman's hands. Where did she find it?
LICHT. She found
it in Frau Martha's trellis. Hanging there
like a bird's nest in the meshes of the grapevine, just
below the window where the young woman sleeps.
FRAU MARTHA. At my house? Hanging in the trellis?
WALTER (*whispering to Adam*).
Judge Adam, if you
have anything you would like to impart to me
in confidence, I beg you, do so now,
for the sake of our court's good name.
ADAM. Have I
anything—? [*Pause.*]
WALTER. Nothing to say? Nothing at all?
ADAM. I swear—. (*Snatches the wig.*)
WALTER. This wig's not yours, then?
ADAM. This wig, by God,
is mine, sirs! The very one I gave the boy
a week ago to take to Master Mehl
in Utrecht.
WALTER. You gave who—?
LICHT. Gave Ruprecht?

145

RUPRECHT. Me?

ADAM. Placed in his hands a week ago, when he
was going off to Utrecht, to take and have
the barber clean—didn't I, you scoundrel, didn't I?

RUPRECHT. Didn't you? Well, yes, that's right, you gave me—.

ADAM. Then why did you fail to do it, failed, you thieving
rascal, to deliver it, as ordered, to the Master
in his shop?

RUPRECHT. Why? Why? I'll tell you why! Because I did—
I delivered it to the shop, into the Master's hands!

ADAM. You did? And that accounts for its dangling from
Frau Martha's trellis? Just wait, you gallows bird,
you don't get out of it like that. There's something
going on here that doesn't meet the eye,
rebellion is afoot, who knows what's afoot?
Sir, let me question the woman instantly.

WALTER. You gave
the wig—.

ADAM. Your Worship, last Tuesday when that fellow
went to Utrecht with his father's ox team,
he came into my office and said: Judge Adam,
do you need an errand done in Utrecht? My son,
I said, would you be good enough to go
and get this wig of mine repaired? I didn't
say: Go and hide it in your house,
wear it as a disguise and leave it hanging
on Frau Martha's trellis.

FRAU BRIGITTA. It wasn't, please,
Your Honors, I believe, that Ruprecht. Last night
when I went up to the farm to visit with my cousin,
who's ill in bed with child, going past the garden
I heard Evie really giving it to someone,
she was mad, she was, but keeping down her voice
because she was afraid of being overheard.
For shame, for shame! Oh, but you're vile! How
dare you? Go away! I'll call my mother!
I thought the Spaniards had come back.—So I call
to her through the fence: Evie, what's the matter?
Is there something wrong?—Dead silence.
Why don't you answer, Evie dear?—Auntie, yes,

what is it?—What are you up to there, I'd like
to know?—What do you think I'm up to?—Ruprecht,
is it, that's in there?—Ruprecht? Yes,
it's Ruprecht. Now let us be.—All right. But go
to bed. I think: Well, it's a lovers' quarrel—
which they do.

FRAU MARTHA.　　And then?

RUPRECHT.　　　　　　And then?

WALTER.　　　　　　　　　Quiet!
Let the woman finish.

FRAU BRIGITTA.　　　　　And then coming back
from the farm, about midnight it was, just
as I'm passing through the linden alley that's
near Martha's garden, past me gallops a bald-headed
fellow, clumping with a cloven hoof
and leaving in his wake a stink like burning pitch
and hair and brimstone. I say a God-preserve-us
and turn around in terror to see that bald head,
glowing palely just like wood decaying,
disappearing down the lane.

RUPRECHT.　　　　　　　God in Heaven!

FRAU MARTHA. Are you mad, Frau Brigge?

RUPRECHT.　　　　　　　　Do you think
it was the devil?

LICHT.　　Quiet, please!

FRAU BRIGITTA.　　　　　My stars,
I guess I know the thing I saw and smelled.

WALTER (*impatiently*).
Woman, denunciations of the devil don't fall within
the jurisdiction of this court. If there is someone else
you're able to inform about, please do, but spare
us one more charge against the old offender.

LICHT. If Your Judgeships would let the woman finish!

WALTER. Imbeciles!

FRAU BRIGITTA.　　　Please yourself. But Clerk Licht
there—he is my witness.

WALTER.　　　　　　What do you mean, your witness?

LICHT. I am, sir, yes—up to a point, I am.

WALTER. Really, it's too much—.

LICHT.   Sir, may I ask
  you most respectfully to let the woman
  tell her story to the end? I don't maintain
  it was the devil; but what she says about
  a bald head and a clubfoot and a dreadful
  smell, unless I'm much mistaken, is
  the truth.—So please continue.

FRAU BRIGITTA.   When I learned
  today to my surprise what had happened at
  Frau Martha's, I went back to the trellis where I
  had met the jug destroyer yesterday to see
  what I could find, and underneath the window
  he jumped out of I find footprints in the snow.
  What kind of footprints, do you ask, Your Honors?
  The right foot's neatly outlined in the snow,
  a human foot, just as a foot should be,
  the left's a great big lump, a stump, a monstrous
  cloven hoof.

WALTER (*exasperated*).
                  Silly maunderings! Pure nonsense!

VEIT. Can't be, woman!

FRAU BRIGITTA.   Yes, it is, I swear!
  First, a roundish patch of trampled snow,
  as if a sow had had herself a roll, there
  where he landed when he jumped; then issuing out
  of it a human foot, a cloven hoof, a human
  foot, a cloven hoof, straight out of the garden
  and abroad into the world.

ADAM.   I think the rascal
  didn't hesitate to dress up as the devil,
  damn his eyes!

RUPRECHT.   Do you mean me!

LICHT.   Be quiet, please!

FRAU BRIGITTA. The hunter who's found out the badger's track
  exults less than I did. Clerk Licht, sir,
  I call out, for sent by you, just then
  he's found me there—Clerk Licht, sir, call your sitting
  off, no need to sit in judgment on
  the jug destroyer, for he sits in Hell

148

already, and no worse place exists: here's the way
he went.
WALTER.   So you are convinced it was the devil?
LICHT. Your Worship, she's right about the tracks.
WALTER.   A cloven
   hoof?
LICHT.   A human foot, but like a cloven hoof.
ADAM. Good Lord, this thing is looking serious.
   How acute the arguments which men have tried
   to bring, in essay after essay, against
   the idea that a God exists; but as far as I
   am aware no atheist has ever proved
   the devil doesn't. The case before us seems
   to me especially worthy of examination.
   Before we arrive at a decision, I propose
   to put it to the Synod in the Hague as an interrogatory,
   if this court is competent to find
   it was Beëlzebub who broke the jug.
WALTER. Just the kind of proposal I would expect
   from you. And what do you think, Clerk Licht, sir?
LICHT. Your Worship doesn't need the Synod to reach
   a verdict. With your permission—if Frau Brigitta
   may complete her testimony, all
   the connections of the case will become quite clear.
FRAU BRIGITTA. So I said: Clerk Licht, let's follow these tracks
   in the snow a ways and find out
   where the devil has got off to. A good idea,
   Frau Brigitta, says he. Perhaps it isn't going
   very far out of the way if we head straight for
   Judge Adam's house.
WALTER.   Yes, go on—and you
   found what?
FRAU BRIGITTA.   Well, first, just past the garden, in
   the linden alley where the devil, bumping
   into me, shot out his evil-smelling
   brimstone cloud, we find a circle in the snow,
   such as a timid dog will make when it slinks
   away from before a cat who arches up
   its back at him and spits.
WALTER.   What next?

FRAU BRIGITTA. Not far
from there, beside a tree, he placed a monument,
a thing, good Lord, I shrank back from dismayed.
WALTER. A monument? What monument?
FRAU BRIGITTA. What monument?
Well, if you go—.
ADAM (*aside*).
My bowels, oh my bowels!
LICHT. Frau Brigitta,
you may skip that part, please, ma'am.
WALTER. What I'd like
to know, please, is: Where did those tracks lead to?
FRAU BRIGITTA. Where they led? To you, straight here to you,
just as Clerk Licht said.
WALTER. Here to us?
FRAU BRIGITTA. From the linden alley, across the village
common, along the carp pond, over
the bridge, then through the cemetery and straight
here to Judge Adam's house.
ADAM. To me?
FRAU BRIGITTA. To you.
RUPRECHT. But the devil doesn't live in the courthouse, surely!
FRAU BRIGITTA. How should I know where he lives, I'm
no honest woman if he didn't stop off
here. The tracks go right up to the door
in back.
ADAM. Maybe he was passing through—?
FRAU BRIGITTA. Maybe. Passed right through. It's possible.
The tracks in front—.
WALTER. There were tracks in front?
LICHT. No sign of any tracks in front, Your Worship.
FRAU BRIGITTA. Yes, all trodden down the snow was,
out in front.
ADAM. Came right through the house. Tracks
all lost. Well, I'm a scoundrel if that fellow
hasn't put one over on the law.
I'm no honest man, I'm not, if you
don't find the records in a state. If my accounts
don't tally any more, as I am sure

they don't, I won't be held responsible,
no sir!

WALTER [*dryly*].
      Nor will I. (*Aside.*) I can't remember
if it is his left foot or his right.
But it's one of them!—Your Honor, sir,
please pass your snuffbox over, if you would.

ADAM. Snuffbox?

WALTER.   Yes, your snuffbox. Would you bring
it here?

ADAM (*to Licht*).
      Give it to the magistrate.

WALTER. No need for ceremony, Judge. A step
will do it.

ADAM.   Done, sir, never worry. Give
it to His Worship.

WALTER.   I wanted to say something
to you privately.

ADAM.   Later, sir,
I'm sure—.

WALTER.   It's just as well.
            (*After Licht sits down again.*)
          Gentlemen,
I'd like to know—Is there anybody in the village
with misshapen feet?

LICHT.   Let's see. Well, yes, there is.

WALTER. There is? Who?

LICHT.   If you please, Your Worship,
that's a question for His Honor.

WALTER.   For Judge Adam?

ADAM. Don't ask me. I've been justice here for a mere
ten years. As far as I know, everybody's
feet are as they should be.

WALTER (*to Licht*).
      Who, I wonder,
did you mean?

FRAU MARTHA. Come, stick your feet out!
You're hiding them so nervously below
the table, a body almost thinks you made
the tracks.

WALTER.   Who made the tracks? Judge Adam?

ADAM.   Mine
   the tracks? Am I the devil. Is that a cloven hoof?
                    (*Exhibits his left foot.*[8])

WALTER. Upon my honor, that foot's fine. (*Speaking privily.*)
   Wind the session up at once!

ADAM.   If the devil
   had a foot like that, he could go to all
   the balls and dance till dawn.

FRAU MARTHA.   Yes, yes, Your Honor,
   but there's still—

ADAM.   Frau Martha, please!

WALTER.   Wind
   it up!

FRAU BRIGITTA. The only thing I have a little
   bit of doubt about is this imposing
   piece of finery.

ADAM.   What piece of finery?

FRAU BRIGITTA. This wig. Whoever saw the devil wearing one?
   The Dean when he is preaching from the cathedral pulpit
   doesn't wear a taller one, one thicker
   with tallow.

ADAM.   Frau Brigitta, our knowledge
   in this country of the infernal fashions
   is severely limited. Ordinarily, you hear
   it said, his own hair is enough for him.
   But I'm convinced that when he visits us,
   because he moves among the great ones
   of this earth, he dresses with some care.

WALTER.   You disgraceful
   man! Deserving to be driven from this court of law
   before the eyes of all the people. The only thing
   that saves you is my concern for the honor of the court.
   End the sitting!

ADAM.   I hope, sir—

WALTER.   Hope for nothing!
   Stand down from the bench!

---

   8. *Left foot.* His clubfoot. An error on Kleist's part? But it is better to think of it as
impudence.

ADAM.   How can you
  believe that I, the judge, was the one to lose
  his wig in the vine?
WALTER.   God forbid! Yours
  was destroyed by fire, like Sodom and Gomorrah.
LICHT.   Or rather,
  if I may, sir—his was the one the cat
  had kittens in.
ADAM.   Gentlemen, although
  appearances are against me, I beg you, don't
  act hastily. My honor is at stake.
  I fail to see you have a right to accuse
  me of anything, as long as the girl is silent. Here
  I sit, the judge, in Huisum; this wig
  I lay upon the table; whoever dares
  to assert it's mine, I summon him to say
  as much before the bench of Utrecht.
LICHT (*setting the wig on Adam's head*).
                                    As good
  a fit as if it was your own hair
  on your head.
ADAM.   That's defamation, sir!
LICHT. You disagree?
ADAM (*looking at himself in a mirror*).
                  It's too big for a cloak
  to put around my shoulders, let alone
  a cover for my head.
RUPRECHT.   He looks so fine, he does,
  damn him!
WALTER   Quiet, you!
FRAU MARTHA.   Oh, that's a judge,
  that one, damn him!
WALTER.   Once again: you end
  the sitting or I will!
ADAM.   Yes, yes, just as
  you say, sir!
RUPRECHT (*to Eve*).
             Eve, was he the one?
WALTER.   How dare
  you, you young lout!

VEIT.   That's enough, boy.

ADAM. Just you wait, you brute, we'll see!

RUPRECHT. Damned cloven hoof!

WALTER.   Bailiff! Bailiff!

VEIT.   I told you
    to shut up.

RUPRECHT.   Just *you* wait. I will give you something
    you can think about, today. Today
    you don't go throwing sand into my eyes.

WALTER.   Have you
    so little sense, Judge—?

ADAM.   Yes, yes, Your Worship—with your
    permission I'll pronounce the sentence.

WALTER.   Good.
    Do it.

ADAM.   The facts in this case have been determined, and Ruprecht
    there, that rascal, is the guilty one.

WALTER. Fine, fine. What else?

ADAM.   Our judgment is,
    that he must wear the iron collar—and by reason
    of his contempt of court I'm sticking him behind
    bars, too. How long his term shall run, we will
    determine later.

EVE.   Ruprecht?

RUPRECHT.   Prison?

EVE.   Iron collar?

WALTER. You needn't worry, children.—Done?

ADAM.   He
    can replace the jug or not, as far as I'm
    concerned.

WALTER.   Excellent. The sitting's over.
    And Ruprecht may appeal the verdict at
    the Superior Court in Utrecht.

EVE.   Go to Utrecht
    to appeal the verdict?

RUPRECHT.   I must appeal?

WALTER.   Damnation,
    yes! And till then—

EVE.   Till then—?

RUPRECHT.   To jail?

EVE.   An iron
   collar? And you, too, call yourself
   a judge? That shameless criminal who's sitting there,
   he was the one—
WALTER.   I order you to hold your tongue!
   Damnation! And till then, let no one harm
   a single hair of his.
EVE.   Ruprecht, arise!
   Judge Adam broke the jug!
RUPRECHT.   Oh, just you wait!
FRAU MARTHA. He did?
FRAU BRIGITTA.   The Judge?
EVE.   The Judge, yes! Ruprecht, up!
   He was the one last night, with your dear Eve!
   Catch him now and smash his face with both
   your fists!
WALTER (*standing up*).
      Stop! Whoever acts so as to cause—
EVE. It doesn't matter! You've got the collar anyway!
   Go and knock him off the bench!
ADAM.   Pardon me,
   good people. (*Makes off*).
EVE.   After him!
RUPRECHT.   He's going—grab him!
EVE. Quick, oh quick!
ADAM.   Dear me. [*Exit Adam.*]
RUPRECHT.   Damned limping devil!
EVE. You caught him?
RUPRECHT.   No, damn! It's his robe, his empty
   robe!
WALTER.   Go and call the bailiff!
RUPRECHT (*punching the robe*).
      Here's one for you!
   And here's another! And another! I wish it still
   was on your back!
WALTER.   Ruffian! I'll have order in this court!
   If you don't behave yourself, I'll see that you put
   the collar on today.
VEIT.   Mind your manners, scamp!

SCENE 12

All advance to front of stage.

RUPRECHT. Oh, Evie, I've treated you so shamefully
today! Good heavens! And yesterday as well!
My heart's treasure, do you think you ever can
forgive me?

EVE (*kneeling at Judge Walter's feet*).

If you won't help us, we are lost!

WALTER. Lost? Why?

RUPRECHT. Good God, what now?

EVE. Save Ruprecht
from the call-up. This next draft—for so
Judge Adam told me very privately—
is picked for the East Indies. And from there, as you
know very well, one out of three, no more,
comes back!

WALTER. To the East Indies? Have you lost
your wits?

EVE. To Bantam, sir, I know—oh, don't
deny it. Here's the secret letter of instructions
the government issued a short time ago
concerning the militia. You see how much I know.

WALTER (*taking the letter and reading it*).
Oh, this beats everything for cunning wickedness!
The letter's forged!

EVE. Forged?

WALTER. Forged! As sure
as I'm alive. Clerk Licht, now tell us: Are these
the orders sent you recently from Utrecht?

LICHT. These! That reprobate! A scrap of paper
he wrote out with his own hand! This present
call-up's meant for service here at home.
No one means to ship them to the East Indies.

EVE. No? Never, sir?

WALTER. I swear to you. And as
a further guarantee, I promise to buy
him out of going as a soldier if what you say
should happen.

EVE (*standing up*).

Good heavens, the lies that villain told
me, the fears with which he deliberately tortured me!
He came at night and pressed me to accept a trumped up
medical certificate that would exempt my Ruprecht
from all military service. And while his mouth
was busy saying this and promising that,
he sidled toward my room to fill the paper
out, and there demanded, sirs, from me
a thing so shameful, no decent girl would dare
repeat his words.

FRAU BRIGITTA.   Oh, he was wicked, the deceiver!

RUPRECHT. Never waste a thought on him, old Cloven Hoof,
dear girl! Why, if a horse had smashed the jug,
I would have felt as jealous as I did! (*They kiss.*)

VEIT. My idea exactly! Kiss as lovers
should, all discord banished; and if it's Whitsun
you would like, be married then!

LICHT (*at the window*).

Look,
oh look, how our Judge Adam, as if in mad flight
from the wheel and gallows, goes stamping across the furrows
of that field!

WALTER.   Judge Adam, is it?

LICHT.   .   Yes, it is!

A CHORUS. And now he's reached the road, see there! Oh how
his wig, that's jumping up and down upon
his back, whips him on!

WALTER.   Clerk Licht, sir, fetch
him back as quick as you are able! Lest he
by running from his troubles, should make them worse.
Of course I must suspend him from his judgeship,
and I appoint yourself to perform his duties
here in Huisum till further notice; but if
the accounts are in good order, as I trust
they are, I have no wish to compel him to desert
this place. So be so good as to go and bring
him back to us.

(*Exit Licht.*)

Finale

FRAU MARTHA.   Please, Your Worship, tell
me where the government is in Utrecht.
WALTER.   Why,
Frau Martha?
FRAU MARTHA (*testily*).
              Why? How should I know why—
but can't I get justice done my jug there?
WALTER. Excuse me, ma'am! You're right, you're right.
In the marketplace. The Superior Court
meets there on Tuesdays and on Fridays.
FRAU MARTHA. Very good. You'll see me there next week.

Penthesilea
A Tragedy

Cast of Characters

Penthesilea, Queen of the Amazons
Prothoe ⎫
Meroe ⎬ Amazon Princesses
Asteria ⎭
High Priestess of Diana
Achilles ⎫
Odysseus ⎪
⎬ Kings of the Greeks
Diomedes ⎪
Antilochus ⎭
Greeks and Amazons

Scene: A Battlefield near Troy

SCENE I

Enter Odysseus and Diomedes from one side, Antilochus from the other,
with soldiers.

ANTILOCHUS. Kings! Hello! What news since we met last
    at Troy?
ODYSSEUS. Bad news, Antilochus. Look there:
    the Greek and Amazonian armies fighting
    like two wolves—and can't say why, by god!
    If angry Mars or Delian Apollo
    doesn't lift his staff, or Zeus Cloudshaker
    pitch his crooked bolts between them, down dead
    the stubborn enemies will surely sink
    today, their teeth clamped shut in one another's
    throats.—Water in a helmet, quick!
ANTILOCHUS.   You Powers!
    Whatever do these murderous women want?
ODYSSEUS. Achilles and myself, with all the troop of Myrmidons,
    as the sons of Atreus advised,
    marched out into the field—for it had reached
    our ears that Penthesilea, rallying
    her snakeskin-skirted soldiers in the Scythian woods,
    and mad to fight, was winding through the mountain
    passes down to Troy to raise the city's
    siege. When we arrived at the Scamander River
    we heard more. Deiphobus, we heard, old Priam's
    son, marching out of Ilium at the head
    of a brigade, was on his way to meet
    his rescuer Queen in love and friendship. We
    ate up the miles to plant ourselves between
    our foes and block their union; all night long
    we forced our march along the winding track.
    But with first light, imagine our astonishment,
    Antilochus, to see strung out before
    us all along a broad valley, the Trojans
    in pitched battle with—the Amazons!
    Penthesilea, as a hurricane
    the ragged clouds, scatters the Trojan ranks
    in front of her as if she meant to blow

them clear across the Hellespont, right off
the face of earth!

ANTILOCHUS.   How strange, by all the gods!

ODYSSEUS. We close up ranks against their mad stampede,
which thunders down on us like an attack,
and make a wall of all our bristling spears.
This stops the son of Priam in his tracks;
and after a quick huddle we agree,
we Greeks, to offer welcome to the Queen,
who's also pulled her victory rush up short.
Who could have thought up anything simpler, better?
If I had prayed Athene for advice,
could she have whispered wiser policy?
She must, by Hades—this armed virgin
dropping from the skies into the middle
of our strife *must* fight on one side or
the other; and we will think her our friend
since she so clearly is the Teucrians' foe.

ANTILOCHUS. Of course! What else could you conclude?

ODYSSEUS. The two of us, Achilles and myself,
discovered her, the Scythian hero girl,
stationed at the head of all her troops of fighting
virgins, in the full pomp of war—her tunic
girded up, her helmet feather floating,
her horse's gold and purple tassels dancing
as it stamps the earth with restless hooves.
She looks a moment, thoughtful, at us Greeks,
her face a blank, as if we stood before
her carved in stone: this palm of mine, I swear,
is more expressive than her face was then—
until she sees Pelides. All at once
a hot flush burns her face, down to the throat,
as if the whole world had gone up in flames
around her. With a convulsive start, she jumps
down from her horse's back while shooting him
a frowning look and hands a girl the reins;
then asks what brings us to her in such high
and mighty state. My answer is, how glad
we Argives are to find new enemies
of the Dardanian race; how much we Greeks

have hated them and for so long; how much
it would help both, herself and us, to be
allies, and such and more as it occurred
to me. But in the midst of running on
like this, I notice with astonishment
she doesn't hear a word. Abruptly turning
to a friend beside her, wonderingly,
just like a girl of sixteen who's run home
from watching the Olympic games, she cries:
Oh Prothoe, such a man! I'm sure Otrere,
my dear mother, never laid her eyes
on such a man! Her friend is quite nonplussed
and can't think what to say, Achilles and myself
exchange a smile, but she herself stares
drunkenly again at the Aeginian's shining
shape—until the other one, sidling
shyly up to her, reminds her that
she hasn't answered me. At which, with flaming
cheeks—I don't know if from rage or shame—
that tinged her polished armor to the waist,
all at once distrait and proud and fierce:
She'd have me know (turning her face at last
toward me) that she was Penthesilea, Queen
of Amazons, and the answer that she had
for us lay ready in her soldiers' quivers!
ANTILOCHUS. That was the message, word for word, you sent;
but no one in the entire camp was able
to make head or tail of it.
ODYSSEUS.   At a loss, not knowing
what to think, ashamed and angry, back
we go to our own lines. We see our foes—
who've guessed across the distance our chagrin
and grin and hoot in mockery—run together
as if in triumph. What they think is,
they are the favored ones, in their delusion
judging she attacked them only through some
error which they'd soon clear up—back they'll
send the herald, offering her once more
the hand of friendship she had scorned. But before
their man can knock the dust from off his armor,

with loosed reins, roaring down, the centauress
rolls all before her like a mountain torrent,
them and us too, Greeks and Trojans both.
ANTILOCHUS. Incredible, Danaans!
ODYSSEUS.   Now begins
a fight the like of which was never fought
on earth since Furies were. As far as I
can see, in Nature there is force and counter-
force and no third thing. What puts the fire
out will not make water boil up into
steam, and vice versa. But now a fierce
foe of them both appears and when she does,
Fire's unsure if it shouldn't stream with Wet,
and Wet if it shouldn't soar with Fire skywards.
Hard-pressed by Amazons, the Trojan dives
behind his Greek opponent's shield, the Greek
protects him from the virgin crowding close
on his heels, and Greek and Trojan now
are almost forced, in spite of Helen's rape,
to stand together side by side against
the common foe.
                    (*A soldier brings him water.*)
                    Oh thanks! My throat is parched.
DIOMEDES. And ever since that day the battle's thundered
up and down this field with never flagging
fury, like a storm trapped in between
two tree-crowned cliff tops. Yesterday, when I
had brought the Aetolians up to reinforce
our lines, right then she hit us, with a thunder
crack, as if she meant, that crazy girl,
to split the whole Greek tree down to the root.
The finest blossoms of our race lie scattered
by the storm upon the battlefield,
Ariston, Astyanax, Menandros,
their smooth young bodies just piled dung for Mars's
audacious daughter's laurels. She has led
away, victoriously, more captured men
than she has left us eyes to count their loss,
or arms with which to set them free again.
ANTILOCHUS. And what she wants from us no one can fathom?

164

DIOMEDES. No, no one. That's the way it is—in spite
   of how we've plumbed our minds to find
   an explanation. Often, judging by
   her fierce pursuit of Thetis' son
   in the thick of battle, we have thought it must
   be personal hatred for him chokes her breast.
   The hollow-sided she-wolf, ranging woods
   deep-blanketed in snow, does not pursue
   with such hot hungriness the prey her hard
   eye's marked out for herself as she Achilles—
   up and down and in and out of our files.
   Yet yesterday, when for a moment only
   his life lay in her hands, back she gave
   it to him with a laugh, her gift—down he'd gone
   to Orcus, that's for sure, except for her.
ANTILOCHUS. What! Except for her? The Queen?
DIOMEDES.   Yes, her!
   For when those two, Achilles and herself, came face
   to face on the field at sundown yesterday,
   up storms the Trojan Deiphobus
   and stands beside her, shoulder touching shoulder,
   at the same time dealing Pelides a blow
   so shrewd it makes his armor ring so that
   the sound reechoes in the elm tree tops.
   The Queen goes white and down her weapons sink,
   two minutes long; then shaking wrathfully
   her locks around her flaming cheeks, she rears
   up high above her horse's back and brings
   her sword, as if fetched from the sky,
   a thunderstone, staight down on his neck,
   which sends the meddler rolling underneath
   the feet of Thetis' godlike son. He wants,
   the Peleid, by serving her the same,
   to say his thanks. But she, close hugging the neck
   and streaming mane of her pied mount, who champs
   his golden bit and veers away—she cheats
   Achilles' murder stroke, gives free rein
   to her horse, looks back, laughs out, and disappears.
ANTILOCHUS. How strange!
ODYSSEUS.   Now *your* news—how are things at Troy?

ANTILOCHUS. I'm sent by Agamemnon, and his question
  is: Would it be wiser, seeing how
  the situation's changed, to draw back?
  Our business is to break through Ilium's walls,
  not interfere between the army of
  an independent Princess and some goal
  of hers that's no concern of ours.
  If you are sure it isn't to relieve
  Dardanusburg the Amazon's marched here,
  he wishes you at once, cost what it may,
  to fall back with your men behind the Argive
  breastworks. If she follows after, he
  himself, Atrides, standing at the head of all
  the host, will study this enigma
  of a Sphinx, to see which way, in front
  of Troy itself, she'll jump.
ODYSSEUS.   By Jupiter,
  that's just what I think too! Do you suppose
  the son of Laertes likes to find himself
  mixed up in such a brainless business? Get
  Pelides out of here, will you, right now!
  For as the unleashed mastiff, baying loud,
  leaps pell-mell at the antlers of the hart,
  whom then the huntsman whistles back in fear,
  but the bitch has got her teeth locked fast
  in the great beast's neck and dances at his flank,
  through stream and over mountain, deep into the forest
  night—so he runs raving since he's glimpsed
  this rarest game between the boughs
  of war's wild wood. Shoot an arrow
  through his thighs so as to hobble him—
  for otherwise, he swears, he won't give up
  the chase till he has dragged her by her silky
  curls from off her tiger-spotted horse's
  back. Just try, Antilochus, why don't
  you, and see if your persuasive tongue has any
  effect on him when he's foaming at the mouth.
DIOMEDES. Kings, let us act together once again
  and calmly set our reason, like a wedge,
  against his mad determination. You

166

will soon know where, resourceful Laertides,
to find the crack in it. And if you don't,
if he keeps on, well then, I'll get two men,
we'll hoist him on our backs and dump him like
a log—since he's become an absolutely
senseless thing—inside the Argive camp.
ODYSSEUS. Let's go.
ANTILOCHUS. But look! Who's that racing toward us?
DIOMEDES. Adrastes. And how pale and scared he looks!

SCENE 2

Enter a Captain.

ODYSSEUS. What is it, Captain?
DIOMEDES.   News for us?
CAPTAIN.   The dismallest
    your ears have ever heard.
DIOMEDES.   What is it?
ODYSSEUS.   Speak!
CAPTAIN. Achilles—captured by the Amazons!
    And now Troy's walls are sure to stand for ever.
DIOMEDES. O you Olympians!
ODYSSEUS.   To bring such news!
ANTILOCHUS. When and where did this disaster happen?
CAPTAIN. A new attack by these infuriated
    daughters of the God of War, as hot as lightning,
    melted and dissolved the brave Aetolian ranks
    on our perimeter and sent them pouring,
    like a flash flood, back on us,
    the never beaten Myrmidons. We stiffen
    all along our line to hold against
    the helterskelter rush, but all in vain—
    it swamps us quite and tumbles us along,
    so far along that when we find our feet
    again and plant them fast, Peleus's son
    is nowhere to be seen. But then at last,
    out of the battle murk, beset all around
    by spears, he struggles into view, driving
    down a steep slope, warily, his chariot's
    course by good luck shaped toward us. Our rescue

167

cry's already bursting from our throats,
exultingly, when the sound dies on our lips—
for suddenly his team of four stop short
before a precipice and, rearing back,
look down from clouds into the yawning gulf.
Now all his mastery of the Isthmians' skills's
no good at all—the terror-stricken horses,
stamping back with twisting necks against
the falling lash, upset the car and themselves
with it, tumbling him, our son of the gods,
into the tangled harness of the wreck,
where he lies caught as if in a snare.

ANTILOCHUS.   He's mad!
    Wherever did he think—?

CAPTAIN.   Automedon,
    the nimble driver of his car, jumps down
    among the thrashing beasts and helps all four
    to stagger up again. But even as
    he's loosing all the traces wound around
    their legs, the Queen and her victorious troop
    come around at a hard gallop to the gorge
    below and block Achilles' road to safety.

ANTILOCHUS. Oh gods!

CAPTAIN.   Up short, in a great cloud of dust,
    she pulls her running mount; and lifting up
    her face, all glowing, to the height, measures
    with a glance the wall of rock—her helmet feather
    dipping rearwards as if frightened and trying,
    so it seemed, to pull her back. Then all
    at once she lets go of the reins: we see
    her, as if dizzied, press her slim hands to
    her forehead, tumbled over by her locks
    of hair. The Amazons, dismayed, crowd around
    her with importunate gesticulations,
    all imploringly. The one who seems
    her most devoted comrade throws her arm
    around her, while another, more determined,
    grabs her horse's reins—they mean to stop
    her going up by force. But she—

DIOMEDES. Oh no!
    She didn't dare!
ANTILOCHUS.   Let's hear it.
CAPTAIN.   Listen now.
    It's no use their attempts to hold her back,
    to either side she gently thrusts the women
    and clatters, at a restless trot, all up
    and down the stony canyon floor, searching
    for some narrow track to give her wish,
    though lacking wings, its way. Then all at once
    you see her, like a person gone berserk,
    scrambling up the sides of rock, in one
    place then another, burning with desire,
    full of senseless hope that that's the way
    to bag the quarry lying trapped above.
    But after she's attempted every rift
    and cleft the rains have worn into the cliff,
    she sees there is no climbing it; and yet,
    as if bereft of judgment, back she goes
    at it all over again, as if it were
    the first time. And indeed, upspringing traces where
    no traveler would ever dare set foot,
    the indefatigable huntress gains
    on the summit by an elm tree's height;
    and now she stands there, on a granite block,
    with no more footing than the chamois has;
    appalled on every side by towering rocks,
    unable to go forward or go back;
    the women's yell of terror cuts the air;
    down all at once she plunges, horse and rider,
    amid a rattling rain of loosened rocks,
    as if hellbent for Orcus, crashing down
    right to the bottom of the steep, and neither
    breaks her neck nor learns a grain of sense:
    only pulls herself together for
    another try.
ANTILOCHUS.   Hyena blind with rage!
ODYSSEUS. And what about Automedon?
CAPTAIN.   At last
    he jumps—the chariot and horses straightened

out now; in that same time Hephaestus could
have forged a whole new car of bronze, almost—
Automedon jumps on his seat and grasps
the reins: a stone is lifted from our Argive
breasts. Yet even as he turns the horses,
the Amazons spy out a path that slopes
up gently to the crest and send a great
shout up to call their Queen, the crazy one,
still riding madly at the sheer cliff side—
the valley's filled with cries of jubilation.
Hearing this, she pulls back on her horse's
reins; a lightning look finds out the path;
and like a bounding panther herself follows
her look's lead. Pelides, to be sure,
backwards struggling with his horses, managed
to make off; but he was soon lost sight
of among the glens, and what's become of him
I've no idea.

ANTILOCHUS.   He's captured, I am sure!

DIOMEDES. Up, my friends, think what to do.

ODYSSEUS.   What our own hearts
command us, Kings! Up, and from the Queen we'll
snatch him back again! And if this means
we have to fight an all-out war for him,
I'll fight *that* fight out with the two Atrides.

               (*Exeunt Odysseus, Diomedes, Antilochus.*)

SCENE 3
Enter a party of Greeks, on a hill above.

A MYRMIDON (*looking into the distance*).
Look! Isn't that a head, an armored one,
appearing just above that ridge, a helmet
shadowed by its crest? The puissant neck
that carries it? And now the shoulders and the arms,
shining in their steel? The mighty frame
of chest, and see, friends, don't you, strapped
around his waist the belt of gold?

CAPTAIN.   Whose waist?

MYRMIDON. Whose waist! You Argives, am I dreaming now?
　The blazed heads of his chariot horses, look
　at them! It's just their legs, their hooves, the ridge
　still hides! Now on the skyline car and horses
　show entire! Just so the glorious sun car
　climbs the sky on a bright day in spring!
GREEKS. Hurrah! Achilles! Son of the gods! It's him!
　And whipping on the quadriga himself!
　He's saved!
CAPTAIN.　　　Olympians! Glory ever-
　lasting's yours for this!—Odysseus!—
　One of you run and find the Argive chiefs!
　　　　　　(Exit a Greek on the double.)
　Danaans, do you see him coming?
MYRMIDON.　　　　　　　　Look!
CAPTAIN. What is it?
MYRMIDON.　　　　Sir, it takes my breath away!
CAPTAIN. Speak up!
MYRMIDON.　　　　His left hand, how far out it's stretched
　above his horses' backs, how he swings the whip
　above the four of them! How, goaded
　on by the sound of it alone, they beat
　the earth, the more than earthly beasts! In the streamers
　of their smoking breaths, by god, they draw the chariot
　on! You never saw the hunted stag
　race faster! The whirling wheels, spun solid
　rounds, fling back and break one's look!
AN AETOLIAN. But see, behind him—
CAPTAIN.　　　　　　　　　What?
MYRMIDON.　　　　　　　　The ridge line, see?
AETOLIAN. Dust—
MYRMIDON.　　　Dust billowing up like thunderclouds
　and rolling forward with the speed of lightning—
AETOLIAN.　　　　　　　　　God!
MYRMIDON. Penthesilea.
CAPTAIN.　　　Who?
AETOLIAN.　　　　　The Queen—hard on the heels
　of Peleus' son, with her whole gang of women
　tagging after.
CAPTAIN.　　Raving Fury!

GREEKS (*shouting*).
                              This way,
  here! Turn this way to us, son of the gods!
AETOLIAN. See how between her thighs she hotly hugs
  her tiger horse's trunk! How, leaning forward
  all along his mane, she drinks the opposing
  wind with thirsty gulps! She flies as if
  a bowstring shot her, Numidian arrows don't
  fly quicker! In the rear her panting army
  trails along like winded mongrels when
  the mastiff goes all out! Her helmet plume
  has trouble keeping up with her!
CAPTAIN.   Then is
  she catching up with him?
A DOLOPIAN.   Oh yes!
MYRMIDON.   Not yet!
DOLOPIAN. Danaans, yes she is! With every hoofbeat,
  monster-hungry, she eats up another
  piece of the ground between herself and him!
MYRMIDON. By all the gods that shield us from
  above, she's come along so fast she looks
  as big now as he looks! The wind's already
  blowing back into her face the dust
  his lagging run stirs up! The clods of earth
  his horses' hooves send flying back, her horse
  kicks up again into his chariot cab ahead!
AETOLIAN. And now—oh, but his bravado is
  too much, too mad!—he's veered off in a curve,
  he's playing games! Watch out—the Amazon
  will draw a chord to intersect his arc!
  You see? She's cut him off!
MYRMIDON.   Oh help us, Zeus!
  Already she is racing alongside him!
  Her shadow, like a giant's in the morning sun,
  is striking murder at him now!
AETOLIAN.   Not yet!
  He swings, all of a sudden—
DOLOPIAN.   Swings his horses'
  heads around!
AETOLIAN.   Again he's heading our way!

MYRMIDON. The tricky fellow's fooled her, oh, he has!
DOLOPIAN. See there, how she can't stop herself and over-
  shoots his car—
MYRMIDON.   Hits a stone so that
  she tosses in the saddle, stumbles—
DOLOPIAN.   Falls!
CAPTAIN. What?
MYRMIDON.   Falls! The Queen! She falls! And riding blindly
  over her into the ground a warrior
  girl—
DOLOPIAN. Another—
MYRMIDON.   And another—
DOLOPIAN.   And
  one more.
CAPTAIN.   They fall, friends, do they?
DOLOPIAN.   Yes, they fall—
MYRMIDON. Fall, Captain, as if melted down together
  in a furnace, horse and rider, making
  one big heap.
CAPTAIN.   I only wish they *were*
  a heap of ashes!
DOLOPIAN.   Dust, a murky cloud
  through which the gleam of arms and armor flashes—
  that's all you can make out, however hard
  you squint. A tangled knot of girls and horses:
  first Chaos out of which the world began
  was clearer.
AETOLIAN.   But look, a wind's sprung up, they're seeing
  daylight now and one girl's on her feet.
DOLOPIAN. How lively all of them are looking now,
  jumping after spears and helmets scattered
  around the field.
MYRMIDON.   Three horses and one
  rider still are lying there like dead—
CAPTAIN. The Queen, is it?
AETOLIAN.   Penthesilea?
MYRMIDON. The Queen?—Oh, no, don't show me what you see, eyes!
  There she stands!
DOLOPIAN.   Where?
CAPTAIN.   Tell us, tell us!

MYRMIDON. By the Son of Cronos, there, where she
    went down—in the shadow of that oak tree!
    Clinging to her horse's neck, bare-
    headed—don't you see her helmet on
    the ground? Her right hand weakly pushes back
    her hair and wipes the dust or blood—I don't
    know which—from her forehead.
DOLOPIAN.   God, it's her!
CAPTAIN. She's indestructible, the cat!
AETOLIAN.   A cat
    that takes a spill like that is done for—but
    not she!
CAPTAIN. And Pelides?
DOLOPIAN.   The gods are on
    his side! He's raced on past her three long
    bowshots till her eyes can barely make
    him out—the very *thought* of catching him,
    whipping her on always, is stopped dead
    now inside her panting breast!
MYRMIDON.   Hurrah!
    I see Odysseus there! And our army,
    all our Greeks—out into the sunlight,
    see, from the forest night, they're marching
    now!
CAPTAIN. Odysseus, is it? And also
    Diomedes? How far off is Achilles
    from them on the field?
DOLOPIAN.   Just a stone's
    throw, Captain, if that much. Already I
    can see his war car racing on the height
    above Scamander, at the edge of which the troops
    are quickly forming up. He's thundering
    along the ranks right now—
VOICES (*in the distance*).
                            Achilles, hail!
DOLOPIAN. They're calling out to him, the Argives—
VOICES.   Hail,
    Achilles! Son of Peleus, hail! Goddess-born
    Achilles, hail! All hail!

DOLOPIAN. He pulls his horses
up—before the assembled Argive princes
he pulls up! Odysseus is walking
up to him! Down from the seat he jumps, all masked
in dust! He gives the reins away! He turns
around! He lifts the heavy helmet off
his head! And all the kings of Greece surround
him! Loud huzzahing, crowding around his knees,
the soldiers carry him along with them!
Meanwhile Automedon keeps step beside
him with the steaming horses! The victory
parade is streaming this way, here they come
already! Hail to you, oh godlike man!
Look, oh look! It's him, Achilles' self!

SCENE 4

*Enter Achilles, followed by Odysseus, Diomedes, Antilochus,
Automedon and the quadriga, Greek soldiers.*

ODYSSEUS. I welcome you, Aegina's hero-prince,
with swelling heart! Winner just as much
in running from as to! By Jupiter,
if you behind your back, by your superior
wits, can make the enemy go sprawling
in the dust, think what will happen when
you make her meet you, man-god, face to face!
ACHILLES (*holding his helmet in his hand and wiping the sweat from
his brow. Two soldiers, without his noticing, take hold of
his wounded arm and begin to bandage it.*)
What's wrong? What is it?
ANTILOCHUS. You have won a race,
great son of the Nereid, with such
a show of speed as thunderstorms that whirl
across the champaign of the heavens, before the staring
world, can't match. By the hot-footed Furies!
I think I could outrun Remorse, as I
go jolting down the rough road of our
life, if I had a team of flyers like
your own—even though I had to lug
along, here inside my breast, the heavy

load of all the sins of high-walled
Ilium as well.
ACHILLES (*to the two soldiers, whose efforts seem to irritate him*).
          Fools!
A GREEK PRINCE.   Who?
ACHILLES. Stop bothering me, I say—
FIRST SOLDIER (*wrapping his arm*).
                       Will you hold still!
You're bleeding.
ACHILLES.   Well, all right.
SECOND SOLDIER.   Hold still, then, please!
FIRST SOLDIER. We have to bandage it.
SECOND SOLDIER.   No sooner said
than done.
DIOMEDES.   According to our first report,
my people's pulling back precipitated
you into your flight. I wasn't here;
Ulysses and myself were busy with
Antilochus, who's brought a message from
the sons of Atreus. But everything
I've seen convinces me your masterly
escape was part of a design that you
had worked out in advance. At daybreak,
when all of us were arming for the fight,
I do believe, unless I'm much mistaken,
that you had figured out already, in
your head, which stone you'd have the Queen go tripping
over—so sure each step seemed, by the deathless
gods, by which you led her around to it.
ODYSSEUS. But now, great hero of the Dolops race,
be so good, unless a better plan
occurs to you, to fall back at once
with us on the Argive camp. Atreus'
sons are calling on us to withdraw. By shamming
a retreat we'll seek to tempt her down
into the valley of the Scamander, where Lord
Agamemnon lurks in ambush, waiting
to go out to meet her in pitched battle.
By the Thunderer, there or nowhere
you will cool the heat that drives you without

letup, hounding you before it like
a buck! And my best blessing go with you.
For this Megaera ranging up and down
the battlefield and spiting all our efforts,
is an abomination to me too.
I hate the woman to distraction, yes,
and I would gladly see, let me confess it,
your footprint stamped upon her blooming cheek.

ACHILLES (*noticing his horses*).
They're sweating.

ANTILOCHUS.   What?

AUTOMEDON (*feeling their necks*).
                    Like lead.

ACHILLES.   Good, walk them up
and down. And when the air has cooled them off,
wash their chests and haunches down with wine.

AUTOMEDON. Here are the wineskins now.

DIOMEDES.   Dear man, you see
how we are fighting at a disadvantage
here. Women swarm all over every
hill, as far as our sharpest eyes
can reach; locusts settling on a ripened
cornfield don't swarm thicker. Whoever
wins the way he wanted to? Except yourself,
is there a man here who can say he's even
seen the centauress? It does no good
for us to march out with our golden armor
on and blaring out to her with trumpets
our princely rank—she hangs back
in the rear and will not budge. And if it's nothing
more than just the silver of her voice you'd like
to hear, ringing down the wind from far
away, you have a fight upon your hands first,
doubtful and inglorious, with running packs
of rabble soldiery who guard her close
like dogs of hell.

ACHILLES (*staring into the distance*).
            Is she still there?

DIOMEDES.   Excuse me?

ANTILOCHUS. She, the Queen?

CAPTAIN.   It's hard to see—out
  of the way there! Duck those crests!

FIRST SOLDIER (*still bandaging the arm*).

                                Another minute,
  please.

GREEK PRINCE. Oh yes, there, yes!

DIOMEDES.   Where?

GREEK PRINCE.   There, at that
  same oak tree where she fell. Her crest
  is swaying once again above her head
  and she seems recovered from her fall.

FIRST SOLDIER.   At last!

SECOND SOLDIER. Now you can use your arm just as you please.

FIRST SOLDIER. You're discharged now.

          (*They tie a last knot and let go of his arm.*)

ODYSSEUS.   Pelides, did you hear
  a word of what we said?

ACHILLES.   You said? No, not
  a word. What was it? What is it you want?

ODYSSEUS. What we want? Bizarre!—We were telling you
  about the orders sent us by the sons
  of Atreus! Agamemnon wants
  us all back in the Greek camp again,
  and right away. He sent Antilochus—
  look, will you [*pointing*], here he is—to notify
  us what the chiefs together have decided.
  Here's the plan: to tempt the Amazon
  to venture down to the Dardanusburg, where
  she will find herself between the Trojans
  and ourselves. Then there is no way out for her:
  the situation forces her to say
  whose friend she is; no matter whom she chooses,
  at least we'll know then what we have to do.
  I'm confident your good sense, Pelides,
  appreciates the wisdom of this move.
  For we'd be mad, by all the Olympians,
  when victory over Troy is our great aim,
  to get ourselves embroiled here with these women
  without an inkling what they want from us—
  if indeed there's anything they want.

ACHILLES (*putting his helmet on again*).
  Fight like eunuchs, if that suits you—myself, I am
  a man and mean to stand up to these women
  even if I have to do it single-handed!
  Continue if you like to skirt
  around them, hanging back inside the shady
  pine woods, full of impotent desire,
  keeping a safe distance from the heaving bed
  of battle—or not! It's all the same
  to me! You have, by Hades, my consent—
  go back to Troy! But what that Diana wants
  from *me*, I know it very well. She woos
  me through the air with feathered messengers,
  so many, that whisper her desires in
  my ear, with deathly hiss. I've never played
  the coy one with a beauty. Since my beard
  first sprouted, as you know, good friends,
  I've gladly done what all the ladies wished.
  And if it hasn't been the case so far
  with this one, by the God of Thunder here
  is why, because I've still not found the spot
  that's right, a clump of bushes where,
  without disturbance, just as she desires,
  I'll draw her down on a blazing couch
  of bronze and there embrace her. Well, you've heard
  me—leave, I'll follow soon enough. My hour
  to sport with Amaryllis isn't far off.
  But even if it takes me months and months
  to court her—years!—I'll never turn my chariot
  back to camp and friends, or even look at
  Pergamon again, till she's my bride
  and with her forehead wreathed in deadly wounds
  parades beside me through the streets of Troy,
  feet first! Now follow me!
                    (*Enter a soldier.*)
SOLDIER.   Achilles, she
  is looking for you—Penthesilea!
ACHILLES. As I for her. Is she back up on her Persian
  once again?

SOLDIER. Not yet. She's heading here
  on foot, but the horse is pacing at her side.
ACHILLES. Then comrades, fetch a horse for me as well!
  And follow me, my gallant Myrmidons!
           (Exit Achilles and his men.)
ANTILOCHUS. He's raving mad!
ODYSSEUS.   Quick, try and see what all
  your skill in speech can do, Antilochus!
ANTILOCHUS. Use force on him, that's what—!
DIOMEDES.   Too late, he's gone!
ODYSSEUS. The devil take this war with Amazons!
              (Exeunt.)

SCENE 5
Enter Penthesilea, Prothoe, Meroe, Asteria, Amazons.

AMAZONS. All hail, great victor, conqueror, all hail!
  Triumphant Queen of the great Feast of Roses!
PENTHESILEA. Triumphs—rose feasts—please don't talk to me
  about all that! Again I'm called to battle.
  The insolent young war god, I will tame
  him, comrades dear—ten thousand burning suns
  all melted into one huge fireball
  don't blaze so gloriously for me
  as beating him.
PROTHOE.   Let me beseech you—
PENTHESILEA.   No!
  My mind's made up. Sooner stop the waters
  shooting from the cliff than the cataracting
  torrent of my soul. I'll see him dust
  I kick through, high and mighty Greek, who on
  this glorious battle day confuses and
  distracts, as never was the case with me
  before, the martial exultation of my blood.
  Is that the conqueror, the all-feared
  she, the proud Queen of the Amazons,
  whom I see mirrored there in his bronze breastplate when we meet face to face? Oh,
  how the gods all hate me! Don't I feel—
  even as the Greek troops break and run

on every side before me—*crippled* at the sight
of this one hero, pierced within
my inmost being, I myself the beaten
and defeated one? I have no bosom—
then tell me where this feeling's lodged in me
by which I'm beaten down? I'll fling myself
into the thick of battle where he's waiting
for me with his scornful smile and prove
myself his conqueror—or die!

PROTHOE. If you would only lay your head, dear Queen,
on this faithful breast of mine. Your fall, which bruised
you in the bosom, has inflamed your blood, perturbed your mind—
you're trembling in every limb! Make no decision
now, we beg you, please, till you
have recovered your serener frame of mind.
Come, dear, and rest awhile beside me here.

PENTHESILEA. Why? What has happened? Tell me what
I've said. Whatever did—?

PROTHOE.   So as to win
a contest that excites your maiden ardor for the moment,
will you plunge us back into the touch-and-go
of battle? In your heart there lives a secret
wish, I don't know what exactly, that's
unsatisfied—will you, for its sake,
like a spoiled child, throw away the great
good fortune which has crowned your people's prayers?

PENTHESILEA. Hear her, do!—I curse my luck today!
My own soul's dearest friends team
together with the malignant fates to vex and injure
me! When Fame comes flying past me, if
I only stretch a longing hand out to try
and catch him by his golden locks of hair,
a spiteful power always steps into my way—
and my blood boils with pure defiance!—Leave!

PROTHOE (*aside*).
Protect her, will you, all you Heavenly Ones!

PENTHESILEA. Am I just thinking of *myself*, do just
my own desires call me back into
the field? Am I not thinking of our race,
of the destruction bearing down on us

with wingbeats you can hear above the loud
delirium of victory? Tell
me what has happened, that we can think of supper
and our beds as if our work were done. The harvest's
reaped, it's true, tied up in sheaves and all
our plenty piled in barns that loom up
in the sky—and yet a black cloud's hanging
over it which threatens to send ruin down
in one electric flash. The crowd of youngsters—
captives—never will you lead them, crowned
with wreaths, with trumpets' blare and cymbals' clang,
back home to our flower-scented glens.
At every crooked turning of the way
I see the son of Peleus leap out
on your cavorting, singing columns, harry
you and all your prisoners right up
to Themiscyra's ramparts, yes, in the sacred
shrine of Artemis rip the festive
rose chains off their limbs and load
our own with ponderous ones of bronze. Am I
supposed to drop out now from the hot
chase, now after five long sweat-filled days
of tossing in the saddle after him to bring
him down?—just now when the wind alone
my sword stroke makes must make him fall, like ripe
Italian fruit, beneath my horse's hooves?
Oh no! Before I leave unfinished what
I have so gloriously begun, before
I fail to seize with my two hands the wreath
whose rustle I can hear already on
my brow, before I fail to lead Mars's daughters,
as I swore, loud hurrahing to
the top of fortune—let Mars's pyramid
come crashing down on my head and on theirs:
I curse a heart unable to restrain itself!
PROTHOE. Your eyes, great Queen, are glittering quite strangely,
quite incomprehensibly, and I
begin to feel my bosom agitated
by such dark and dreadful thoughts they seem
engendered out of the eternal night.

The Greeks you dread so unaccountably,
they scattered every which way under your attack,
like straws before the wind; you have to search hard
just to see a spear point. Achilles,
thanks to where you've placed our people, is cut off
from the river. So don't you stir him up again,
keep out of sight—his next move, I can promise
you, will be to march his men back
to the Danaan lines. I myself will cover
our rear for you. By all the gods
of Mount Olympus, you will see, he won't
take back *one* prisoner from you! There'll be
no glint of weapons, even from miles off,
I swear, to scare the troops, no distant hoof
beat that will interrupt the laughter of
one girl—my own head is your guarantee!

PENTHESILEA (*abruptly turning to Asteria*).
Is what she's saying possible, Asteria?

ASTERIA. Your Highness, please—

PENTHESILEA.   Can I, as Prothoe
insists, lead the army home again
to Themiscyra?

ASTERIA.   Please excuse me, Princess,
but—

PENTHESILEA. Speak up, will you, now?

PROTHOE (*timidly*).
                              If you
would have the Princesses come forward here
and ask them their advice, I'm sure—

PENTHESILEA.   It's *her*
advice I want!—In just a few short hours,
what's become of me!—
                    (*Pause, to collect herself.*)
                              The army—tell
me, Asteria, might I now—
it's quite all right for me to lead it home?

ASTERIA. Well, since you wish it, Queen of Amazons—
let me confess how I have been *astounded*
by the spectacle presented here
before my unbelieving eyes. I left

the Caucasus with my own people a day
behind yourself and found I couldn't catch
up with you because your army raced before
me like a torrent, at a furious pace.
I only overtook you here, you know,
at dawn today, and ready to do battle.
Then from a thousand throats, exultingly,
the news was shouted out to me: Hurrah,
the victory is ours, everything
we wanted's won, the whole war's finished, done.
Delighted, I assure you, that your people's
prayers had been so promptly heard without
the need of any help from me, I issued
orders for our going back. But I
was curious to see the prisoners
that everybody boasted of as being
such great prizes—slaves, a handful, white
and shaking, met my eye, Argive trash
swept up on their own shields, which they'd thrown down,
by cooks and carriers of your baggage train. Before
the proud-walled Fortress Troy the whole
host of the Greeks still stands: Agamemnon,
Menelaus, Palamedes, Odysseus, Ajax,
Antilochus, and Diomedes too, they dare
to taunt you to your face. Yes, that young son
of Nereus' daughter, whom your own hand
should garland with red roses, he's full of such
effrontery, such impudence; he says,
out loud to all he says it, that he will plant
his foot on your royal neck. And my
great daughter of the God of War asks me
if she may lead a march of triumph home?
PROTHOE (*passionately*).
The heroes, lying creature, all who fell
before the Queen, in station, daring, beauty—
PENTHESILEA. Silence, hateful girl! Asteria feels
the way I do, there's only one man here
who is a fit prize for my sword—and that
one still stands in the field full of defiance!
PROTHOE. The Queen will not allow her violent passion—

PENTHESILEA. Viper, tie your tongue up!—you don't want
 to dare the anger of your Queen! Off, go!
PROTHOE. I do, I'll dare her anger! Let me never
 see your face again if I stand here,
 a coward, at your side, and play you false
 by speaking flatteries. The fire burning
 hotly in you now, undermines
 your fitness to conduct a war of virgins—no fitter
 than the poisoned lion is, after gulping down
 the hunter's treacherous bait, to match himself
 against his spear. By the immortal gods,
 in your present state of mind you'll never beat
 the son of Peleus; much rather, I'm
 convinced, by your madness you will lose
 us all the young men our arms have conquered,
 the prize of so much hard campaigning here.
PENTHESILEA. How odd, it's hard to understand!
 What's made a coward of you overnight?
PROTHOE. A coward, me?—
PENTHESILEA.   Yes, whom did *you* beat, I
 would like to know?
PROTHOE.   Lycaon, the young Prince
 of Arcady. You saw him, I am sure.
PENTHESILEA. Oh yes, of course. That was the one who stood
 there quaking, with his draggled helmet plume, when I paid
 the prisoners a visit yesterday—
PROTHOE.   Quaking,
 him! He stood up as boldly as your
 Pelides ever did! Hit hard
 by the arrows I let fly at him, he tumbled
 at my feet—and in the Festival of Roses
 I will be so proud, as proud as any
 one, to lead him to our holy shrine.
PENTHESILEA. Really? Goodness, what a fever she
 is in. All right—he's yours to keep, no one
 will snatch him from you now!—Fetch Lycaon
 from among the prisoners and bring him here!—
 Poor unwarlike creature, have him since
 you must, and run, for fear that you should lose
 him, far away from all the noise of battle,

hide yourself in the remotest mountain
valley, among sweet-smelling lilac groves,
where nightingales will pipe you sensual songs
and you can celebrate at once, you greedy
girl, the rite you're too impatient to postpone.
But never let me see your face again,
I banish you from our capital, go find
your consolation in your lover's kisses
when all else, fame, your country, close
affection, and your Queen and friend are dead to you.
Go, will you—no, I will not hear you speak
another word—and take your hateful presence
from my sight!

MEROE.   My Queen!

ANOTHER PRINCESS.   What have you said!

PENTHESILEA. Keep still! Whoever dares to plead for her
will learn what my revenge is like!

(Enter an Amazon.)

AMAZON.   Achilles,
Sovereign—on his way here!

PENTHESILEA.   He's coming, good.
Dear virgins, arm, now we are called to battle!
Pass up to me the spear that throws the truest,
the sword that flashes out most lightninglike!
Gods, grant me now, you must, the bliss
of stretching in the dust, beneath my foot, this
so hotly wished-for youth of mine. All
other happiness weighed out to me
as my life's share, I cede it back to you.
Asteria, I put you in command!
Keep the Greek troops busy, see to it
the violence of the fighting doesn't interfere
with me. No one here, whoever, is allowed
to strike a blow at him herself! An arrow,
death-edged, is reserved for her who dares
to lay a hand—what am I saying—
finger, on him! I, I only am
the one to bring him down. This steel I have
here, comrades, with the softest hug (since our
hugging must be done with steel), this steel

must draw him down onto my bosom, with
no pain. And flowers of the springtime, bear
him up as he sinks down so that no limb
of his will suffer hurt. Sooner would I
spare the blood out of my own heart. I'll never
rest till I have brought him down, out
of the sky like some bright-colored bird, here
to me; and when he lies with folded wings
before my feet, with not the least drop
of his royal purple lost, then let all
the Blessed Ones descend the sky to us
to celebrate our victory, then let
our march of jubilation homeward wind,
then am I your dear Queen of our Feast
of Roses! Now follow me!
> (*Sees Prothoe weeping and, distressed, turns back; suddenly
> throws her arms around her neck.*)
>   Prothoe! Dearest

sister! Will you follow me?
PROTHOE (*with breaking voice*).
>   All

the way to Orcus! The Blessed Isles, could I
go there without yourself?
PENTHESILEA.   Best of all
the world! You will? Good, then we'll fight and win
together, both or neither, and our watch-
word is: Roses to adorn the brows of our heroes,
or cypresses to plant above our own!
> (*Exeunt all.*)

SCENE 6

*Enter the High Priestess of Diana and priestesses, followed
by girls with baskets of roses on their heads, and prisoners
of war under an armed guard of Amazons.*

HIGH PRIESTESS. My darling little rose girls, let me see
what kind of harvest you have made in all
your wanderings around. Here where this lonely spring
comes gushing from the cliffside, in the pine tree's shade,

we can feel entirely safe. Pour all
your lovely roses out before me here.
FIRST GIRL (*tipping her basket*).
Oh, see what roses I have picked, our Mother!
SECOND GIRL (*doing the same*).
This lapful here is mine!
THIRD GIRL.   And these are mine!
FOURTH GIRL. And this entire springtime here, *I* picked!
                    (*All the girls empty their baskets.*)
HIGH PRIESTESS. We are as deep in flowers here as if
we stood on top of high Hymetta.
Never dawned a day so full of blessings,
O Diana, for your people! The mothers
bring me gifts, so do the daughters; dazzled
by the double radiance, I don't
know who is owed the greater thanks. But girls,
is this as much as you have got for me?
FIRST GIRL. What you see here is all that we could find.
HIGH PRIESTESS. The mothers were the harder workers then.
SECOND GIRL. In *these* fields, Holy Mother, plucking prisoners
is lighter work than roses. On all the hills
around us, as dense as are the rows of young
Greeks waiting there, like standing corn, for reaping
by the singing sickle-maids—as dense as
they, so sparse the roses of the valleys all
about here are, and so well fortified,
let me assure you, you would rather cut
your way through lances and thick-falling arrows
than through their tanglework of thorns. Just
look here, I beg you, at these fingers.
THIRD GIRL.   I dared
to crawl out on a cliffside ledge so as
to pick a single rose for you, though it
shone wanly through its dark green sepals,
for it was just a bud and not yet ripened
red for love. Yet I reached for it—
and without warning, slipped and fell down
an abyss, my god, so deep I thought I'd disappear into the womb of death. But I

had luck, for there below a rosebush stood
in brilliant flower, flowers enough
to celebrate ten Amazonian triumphs with.
FOURTH GIRL. I plucked a rose for you, our Priestess
of Diana, one rose only, only one;
but what a rose it looks, look, here
it is, a rose that's made to crown a king!
Penthesilea wouldn't want a finer
when she brings down the son of gods, Achilles.
HIGH PRIESTESS. Good, good. When Penthesilea brings him down,
hand that royal rose to her. But take
good care of it till she arrives.
FIRST GIRL. Next time our army of brave Amazons goes marching
out, with clash of cymbals, into the field,
we'll march along beside them, too, I know,
but you must promise me it will no longer
be to celebrate the victories our mothers
win, by picking roses to wind garlands.
Look here, this arm of mine's already heaving
javelins, and the shots that I send whizzing
from my sling hit the mark. Then pray,
why not? The roses for the wreath of *my*
young man already are blooming. May
he prove a brave opponent in the brawl,
he for whom this bowstring's stretched!
HIGH PRIESTESS.   You mean
that? Well, I'm sure that you're the one to know.
Already you've looked out your young man's roses?
Next spring, then, when they bloom again, go hunt
him up and down the battle lines, your youth.
But now your mothers' happy hearts demand
our haste: tie up these roses into wreaths!
THE GIRLS (*all together*).
To work! How do we start?
FIRST GIRL (*to Second*).
                          Glaucothoe, here!
THIRD GIRL (*to Fourth*).
Charmion, come!
                    (*They sit down in pairs.*)

FIRST GIRL.   It's for Ornythia,
   the wreath that we are twisting, who overcame
   Alcestes of the towering crest.
THIRD GIRL.   And ours
   for dear Parthenion, sisters, to wind around
   her Athenaeus, he who has Medusa
   on his shield.
HIGH PRIESTESS (*to the Amazon guard*).
                 Why don't you cheer your guests up,
   girls? Don't stand there in such utter helplessness,
   as if it's up to me to teach you what
   love's all about. Why don't you try to say
   a friendly word to them, hear what
   they'd like, the battle-weary fellows, what
   their wishes are, their wants?
FIRST AMAZON.   They say that they
   want nothing, Reverence.
SECOND AMAZON.   They're not very
   nice to us.
THIRD AMAZON. They're sullen, turn their backs
   on us insultingly when we come near them.
HIGH PRIESTESS. Good god, if they're not very nice to you,
   then make them so! Whatever do you think
   your purpose was when you drove at
   them with such hot impetuosity
   in the thick of battle? Tell them what's in store
   for them, to comfort them: then they won't be
   such unrelenting fellows.
FIRST AMAZON (*to one of the Greek prisoners*).
                 Would you care,
   young sir, to have me spread some soft rugs here
   for you to rest your limbs on? Or shall
   I heap you up a bed of springtime blossoms
   (for, oh, you seem quite dropping with exhaustion)
   in the shade of yonder laurel tree?
SECOND AMAZON. Shall I mix you sweetest smelling Persian oils
   with fresh drawn water from the spring,
   to make your dusty feet feel strong again?
THIRD AMAZON. Surely you will not refuse the orange
   nectar I bring you lovingly
   in my own hands?

ALL THREE.   Say something, speak! What can
we serve you with?
ONE OF THE GREEKS.   With nothing!
FIRST AMAZON.   You peculiar
foreign fellows! All your fretting, what's
the reason for it? Now that our bolts
are back inside their quivers, why should you be
so frightened at the sight of us? Can it be
the lion skins that scare you so?—You,
with the belt there, tell me what you are afraid of.
THE GREEK (*after giving her a long look*).
Those wreaths they're making there, I'd like to know—who for?
FIRST AMAZON. Who for? For you! Who else?
THE GREEK.   For us! And you
can say that to my face, you monster! Will you
hang our necks with flowers and march us off,
like beasts of sacrifice, to the slaughterers?
FIRST AMAZON. To the shrine of Artemis! What did you think?
To her shady oak grove, where raptures not to be
believed, past all conception, wait for you!
THE GREEK (*astonished, in an undertone to the other prisoners*).
Was ever there a dream as mad as what's the truth here?

SCENE 7

Enter an Amazon captain.

CAPTAIN. You here, Your Reverence! I'm surprised—a stone's
throw off our army's strapping weapons on
for the murderous finale.
HIGH PRIESTESS.   Our army! It's
impossible! Where, do you say?
CAPTAIN. On those flats there, licked level by Scamander's
stream. Listen to the wind that's blowing from
the hills and you can hear our Queen's voice
thundering, the clash of naked arms,
horses neighing, clarions, bugles, trumpets,
cymbals, all war's metal voices.
A PRIESTESS. Quick, who will climb that hill there?
THE GIRLS.   Me! Oh me!

(*They climb the hill.*)

191

HIGH PRIESTESS. The Queen's voice—but I can't believe it! Tell
    me why, if the fighting isn't over
    yet, she gave the order for the Festival
    of Roses?
CAPTAIN. The festival—she gave whom the order?
HIGH PRIESTESS. Me! To me!
CAPTAIN.   Where? When?
HIGH PRIESTESS.   Some minutes past,
    when I was standing in the shadow of that
    obelisk, Peleus' son, and she
    hard on his heels, roared past me like the wind.
    I cried, "How is it going?" to her racing
    by. "How is it going?—it's *going* to
    the Festival of Roses," she replied,
    "as you can see!" And riding hard, she shouted
    back: "See that there's lots of flowers, our
    Mother!"
FIRST PRIESTESS (*to the girls*).
            Can you see her, girls?
FIRST GIRL (*on the hilltop*).
                     No, we
    can't see a thing. You can't tell one crest from
    the next. The shadow of a storm cloud's over
    the whole field and all we can make out
    are crowds of soldiers surging back and forth
    in wild confusion, going for one another
    on the field of death.
SECOND PRIESTESS.   I think she means
    to cover our retreat.
FIRST PRIESTESS.   I think so too.
CAPTAIN. She's armed for *battle,* do you hear, against
    Achilles—and she's as fresh as the Persian horse
    that paws the sky beneath her, her glances burning
    brighter than they ever have from underneath
    her lashes, her young soldier's bosom breathing
    deep-drawn breaths of exultation, just
    as if she snuffed the air of battles now
    for the first time.
HIGH PRIESTESS.   What is she after, by
    the Olympians, when all the woods around

are stuffed with prisoners by the thousands—tell
me what's still left for her to conquer?
CAPTAIN.   What's still
    left for her to conquer?
THE GIRLS (*on the hilltop*).
                        You gods!
FIRST PRIESTESS. What is it? Has the shadow passed?
FIRST GIRL.   Holy
    ladies, come up here!
SECOND PRIESTESS.   No, tell us what
    you see.
CAPTAIN.   What there is left for her to conquer?
FIRST GIRL. Look, look, how through a rift in the dark clouds
    the sun streams out, cascading down
    on the head of Peleus' son.
HIGH PRIESTESS.   Whose head?
FIRST GIRL.   *His* head,
    of course! Whose else? He's standing on a hilltop
    all aglitter, his horse and he both uniformed
    in steel, the sapphire, chrysolite don't shoot
    such rays! The landscape all around,
    so bright and blooming, is shrouded now in the blackest
    night of storm—a background only, a sooty
    foil to make the sparkling solitaire
    blaze brighter!
HIGH PRIESTESS.   What business of our nation's is
    Achilles! Is it fitting for a child
    of Mars, a queen, to pay, when she's in battle,
    particular attention to one man?
                        (*To one of the Amazons.*)
    Arsinoe, present yourself before
    her, quick as you are able—tell her in
    the name of her whose priest I am, Mars has
    shown himself to all his brides; and by
    the goddess's stern anger, I call on her
    to lead the god home crowned and forthwith, in
    the Temple of Diana, inaugurate
    for him the holy Festival of Roses!
                        (*Exit the Amazon.*)
    Whoever heard of anything so mad!

FIRST PRIESTESS. Children, can you see the Queen yet?
FIRST GIRL (*on the hilltop*).

                                      Yes,
   we can! All the field is bright now, there
   she is!
FIRST PRIESTESS. *Where* is she?
FIRST GIRL.   Out in front
   of all our Amazons! Look how, her golden
   war dress gleaming, curvetting toward him, full
   of fight, she goes! You'd think what spurs her on
   is jealousy to overtake the hero-
   kissing sun in flight!—why, if she meant
   to soar up to the sky and make herself
   her high-placed rival's equal, the Persian mount,
   who does her every wish, could not, even
   with winged hooves, swing her higher!
HIGH PRIESTESS (*to the Captain*).
   Among all her comrades wasn't there a single
   one to sound the warning, hold her back?
CAPTAIN. Her princely retinue all tried to block
   her way. Where you are standing now, Prothoe
   did everything she could, exhausted all
   her arts of speech, in trying to persuade her to return
   to Themiscyra. She had stopped her ears
   to every voice of reason: by the Love God's
   most envenomed dart, they say, her virgin
   heart's been nicked.
HIGH PRIESTESS.   What are you telling me!
FIRST GIRL (*on the hilltop*).
   Oh, now they're coming up to each other!
   You gods up there, keep a tight grip on
   your earth! Now, even now, as I am speaking,
   like two stars, see, how they collide!
HIGH PRIESTESS (*to the Captain*).
                       The Queen,
   you say? But that's impossible, my friend!
   By the Love God's arrow—when? And where?
   She who wears the diamond girdle? Mars's
   daughter's self, who's lacking just that thing

which is the target of the poison-feathered darts,
a bosom?

CAPTAIN.   So at least the people say,
and Meroe just told me the same thing.

HIGH PRIESTESS. Oh dreadful!

(Reenter the messenger.)

FIRST PRIESTESS.   What answer did she give?

HIGH PRIESTESS. You got through with the message to the Queen?

AMAZON. I was too late, Your Holiness, forgive me.
There was such a crowd of women milling around
that even though I glimpsed her here and there,
I never managed to catch up with her.
But I came across Prothoe and in the minute's
time we had to speak, I told her what
your will was; her answer was—but the
confusion was so great I don't know if I heard
correctly what she said.

HIGH PRIESTESS.   And she said what?

AMAZON. She sat her horse and looked across, with moist
eyes as I thought, to where the Queen was. You,
I said, were very much incensed and asked
if our general had taken leave
of all her senses, to want to keep the battle
going for the sake of one man's head
alone. She said: Go back to your High Priestess
and tell her she should fall down on her knees
and pray this one man's head may fall to her,
for otherwise we're lost, both she and we.

HIGH PRIESTESS. She's racing headlong down the road to Orcus!
And it's not the foeman, when they meet,
who'll make her stoop, but the enemy that lives
in her own breast. She's carrying all of us
along with her into the abyss. In my mind I
can see the ship that bears us, tied and trussed,
to Hellas, pennants streaming from its peak
insultingly, already splitting with its prow
the foam of Hellespont.

FIRST PRIESTESS.   What does it matter
now? The bad news, here it is already.

SCENE 8

Enter a Colonel.

COLONEL. Run, run! But save the prisoners, priest!
   The whole Greek army's pouring down on us!
HIGH PRIESTESS. You gods of high Olympus—what has happened?
FIRST PRIESTESS. Where's the Queen?
COLONEL.   Fell fighting—all
   our Amazon army's scattered.
HIGH PRIESTESS.   You're insane!
   What do you think you're saying?
FIRST PRIESTESS (*to the guard of Amazons*).
                        Get the prisoners
   out of here!
               (*Prisoners are led off.*)
HIGH PRIESTESS. Now tell me: How
   did all this happen?
COLONEL.   It's an appalling tale—
  but very briefly, then. Achilles
  and the Queen, with leveled lances, encountered each
  other like two thunderbolts colliding
  out of clouds; their lances, frailer than
  their own sides, split. He, Pelides, stood
  the shock—she, unhorsed, seemed sinking down
  into death's dimming light. She floundered in
  the dust before him, helplessly exposed
  to all his rage, and so we thought he'd finish
  with her then and there and send her hurtling
  down to Orcus, all the way. But pale
  himself, he stands there like a shade of death,
  incomprehensibly. You gods! he cries,
  that dying look, how it transfixes me!
  Off his horse he leaps at once; and while
  our women, gripped by horror, stand there rooted,
  remembering the Queen's command, and don't
  dare raise their swords, he's at her side, bends boldly
  over the pale-visaged form, calls
  out Penthesilea! lifts her in his arms,
  and inveighing loudly against what he himself

has done, with his repeated cries of grief
woos her back to life!

HIGH PRIESTESS.   Achilles—what,
himself?

COLONEL. Away from her, abominable man
the Army roars! If he won't leave her side,
Prothoe shouts, kill him on the spot by way
of thanks; the straightest flying arrow is
the one for him! And making him jump back
from under her war horse's lashing hooves,
from his arms she wrests the Queen. Meanwhile
the wretched Penthesilea has come to,
and breathing brokenly, with torn breast
and disheveled, streaming hair, is carried to
the rear, where she is able to recover.
But he, the inexplicable Dolopian—
a God of Love, out of the blue, must
have melted down the heart within his breast
of thunder-hammered bronze—crying, Wait,
my friends, Achilles greets you in the name of peace,
he throws his sword away, his shield away,
rips his breastplate off—we could have beat
him down with clubs, or with our hands alone,
if our orders had allowed—and follows
after our Queen quite unafraid,
as if the reckless madman somehow knew
a ban preserved his life from our shafts.

HIGH PRIESTESS. And which one was it gave that insane order?

COLONEL. The Queen! Who else?

HIGH PRIESTESS.   But what a shocking thing!

FIRST PRIESTESS. Look, look, oh do, for here she comes herself
a living picture of despair, limping
painfully along beside Prothoe!

SECOND PRIESTESS. Gods in Heaven, what a sight she is!

SCENE 9
Enter Penthesilea, supported by Prothoe and Meroe,
with retinue of princesses.

PENTHESILEA (*in a feeble voice*).
Set the dogs on him! Stampede the elephants
with burning branches and trample him to death!

Run him down with chariots and mow
his ripe limbs with their scythes!
PROTHOE.   Dear Mistress, please,
we beg you—
MEROE.   Listen, do!
PROTHOE.   He's right behind
you—run, if you have any care for your
own life!
PENTHESILEA. To smash me in the breast the way
he did, Prothoe!—Isn't it as if
I stamped upon a lyre, in a rage
because the night wind stirred its strings
so that it whispered my name to itself?
If a bear came toward me feeling as I do
for him, I'd crouch down at its feet, oh I
would stroke a panther's fur.
MEROE.   Please, won't you run
away from here?
PROTHOE.   Escape while you are able?
MEROE. Try to save yourself?
PROTHOE.   A thing
unnameable, is that what we are going
to see done here on this spot?
PENTHESILEA.   Am I to blame
because I have to woo his feelings fighting
in the field? What is it that I want,
when I draw my sword on him? To send him flying
headfirst down to Orcus? No—the thing
I want so much, eternal gods above,
the only thing, is to draw him down
on this breast of mine!
PROTHOE.   She's raving—
HIGH PRIESTESS.   The poor
wretched girl!
PROTHOE.   She's not in her right mind!
HIGH PRIESTESS. Her mind's on him and him alone.
PROTHOE.   The fall
has driven her into complete distraction.

PENTHESILEA (*with forced composure*).
  All right. So be it. As you wish. I will
  control myself. It can't be otherwise:
  I promise to subdue my heart and do
  with good grace what necessity requires.
  And you are right, too. Why should I, like
  a child, because I couldn't please a passing
  fancy that I had, break with all my gods?
  We'll go then, come. I won't deny it would
  have made me happy. However—if happiness
  won't fall down from the clouds to me,
  I won't because of that storm heaven for it.
  Only help me to get started on our way—
  bring me up a horse and I will lead
  us home again, to our native land.
PROTHOE. A triple blessing on your words,
  my Sovereign, which so become a queen.
  Come, everything is ready for our flight.
PENTHESILEA (*seeing the wreaths of roses in the children's hands
  and her face turning red*).
                              What have you got there?
  Who ordered you to gather in the roses?
FIRST GIRL. Oh, but you're forgetful, asking that!
  Who else but—
PENTHESILEA.   Who? But who?
HIGH PRIESTESS.   —Now let your virgins
  celebrate the hotly longed-for feast
  of victory! Your own lips gave
  that order, am I right?
PENTHESILEA.   I execrate
  this vile impatience! Execrate this thinking
  about orgies in the middle of the bloody rage
  of mortal combat! Execrate desires
  which, in the chaste breasts of Mars's daughters,
  like dogs uncoupled, bay so loud they quite
  drown out the trumpets' brazen lungs and yelled
  commands of captains!—Victory, is it mine
  already, that you, with diabolical
  derision, already are parading up

to me in triumph?—I don't want to see
them! (*Pulls the wreaths to pieces.*)
FIRST GIRL. Queen, what are you doing?
SECOND GIRL (*picking up the roses*).
                                    For miles around,
  the spring has nothing more to offer for
  our festival.
PENTHESILEA. I wish the spring would wither!
  I wish the star on which we stand and breathe,
  lay snapped and broken like one of these roses!
  I wish that I could pull apart and scatter,
  like these flowers here, the whole celestial
  wreath of worlds!—Oh Aphrodite!
HIGH PRIESTESS.   The poor
  wretched soul!
FIRST PRIESTESS. She's lost and done for!
SECOND PRIESTESS.   The Furies
  have got hold of her!
A PRIESTESS (*on the hilltop*).
                    Virgins, I
  entreat you, Pelides is closing in, he's
  no farther off than a bowshot!
PROTHOE.   I beg
  you on my knees, then—save yourself!
PENTHESILEA.   My soul's
  worn out and sick to death! (*Sits down.*)
PROTHOE.   Oh horrible!
  Do you know what you are doing?
PENTHESILEA.   Run, if that's
  your wish.
PROTHOE.   And you—?
MEROE.   You'll stay
PROTHOE.   You mean—?
PENTHESILEA. I mean to stay right here.
PROTHOE.   What, you're mad!
PENTHESILEA. You heard me. I can't stand. Am I supposed
  to cripple all my limbs? Leave me alone.
PROTHOE. You poor lost woman, you! Did you hear,
  the Peleid is closing fast, a bowshot—

PENTHESILEA. Let him come. Let him plant his steel foot
  on my neck, as I deserve. Tell me why
  these blooming cheeks of mine should still remain
  divided from the mire out of which they came?
  Let him drag me home headfirst behind his horses,
  fling this woman's body here, so full
  of life, ignominiously into the open
  field to be a breakfast for his dogs,
  for abominable birds. Be dust, rather than
  a woman who lacks all interest for a man.
PROTHOE. My Queen!
PENTHESILEA (*tearing off her necklace*).
                   Away with this damned stuff!
PROTHOE. Eternal gods, is this that calm composure
  you were praising to me just before?
PENTHESILEA. And that thing too that's nodding from my head,
  what's there to nod about? Damned feather,
  even of less use to me than arrows
  and bright cheeks! Damned hand, that dressed me up
  so fine to fight today—and surely win,
  as they all promised me, damn those
  betrayers too! Oh, how they stood around
  me with their mirrors, left and right, the flatterers,
  praising to the skies the godlike lines
  of my suave, bronze-dressed limbs—a plague
  on them and their infernal tricks!
GREEKS (*offstage*).
  Keep it up, Pelides, don't lose heart!
  Press on a few more steps and she is yours.
PRIESTESS (*on the hilltop*).
  Diana of the Groves! My Queen, you're lost for sure
  if you don't run!
PROTHOE.   Dear sister heart of mine,
  won't anything I say persuade you to escape?
     (*Penthesilea, bursting into tears, leans against a tree;*
      Prothoe is suddenly moved to sympathy and sits down beside her.)
  But as you wish. If you can't move, won't move,
  well—then you won't! Stop crying, I'll stay here
  beside you. The impossible's impossible,
  what exceeds the limits of your powers,

you *can't* do: the gods forbid that I
should ask it of you! Girls, leave, please leave—
go find your way back to your native fields.
The Queen and I are staying here.

HIGH PRIESTESS. Wretched
woman, to support her as you do!

MEROE. Impossible, you say, for her to flee?

HIGH PRIESTESS. Impossible? When there is no external
force to hold her here, no hand of fate,
but only her own foolish heart—

PROTHOE. But *that's*
her fate! You think iron bands can't
be ripped apart, am I right? But still, it's not
outside the realm of possibility
that she should break such bands—yet not the feeling
you deride. What power rules in her,
she only knows—a riddle every bosom
is that feels. She strove to reach life's
summum bonum, brushed it, even had
it in her hand: now her hand refuses to reach out
and find another.—[*To Penthesilea.*] Come, let the whole
thing finish for you here upon my breast.
What's the matter, why these tears?

PENTHESILEA. The pain,
the pain—

PROTHOE. Where?

PENTHESILEA. Here.

PROTHOE. I'll have them bring
you—

PENTHESILEA. Nothing, nothing, nothing.

PROTHOE. Then try and get
a grip on yourself; very soon
it will be over with.

HIGH PRIESTESS (*under her breath*).
They're mad, the two
of them—!

PROTHOE (*also under her breath*).
Please, not a word.

PENTHESILEA. Suppose I still
   should do it, flee—then tell me what I need
   to do.
PROTHOE. You go to Pharsos. There you find
   your troops, which now are scattered all around,
   regrouping—those are their orders. You rest awhile
   and lick your wounds, and when the next day dawns,
   if that's your wish, you start the war of virgins
   up again.
PENTHESILEA. If only I were able—!
   If I only could—! The utmost human strength
   can do I've done—tried doing *more* than human
   strength can do—I staked my all on the throw:
   and now the dice are thrown and all's decided,
   that's what I must understand—I've lost.
PROTHOE. No, no, sweet heart, don't think that for a minute!
   Don't rate your strength so low. Don't place so mean
   an estimate on the prize you're playing
   for as to suppose that you've exerted
   every effort it deserves to win it.
   The string of pink and white pearls you yanked
   off your neck just now, is that the utmost
   treasure your soul has to muster? How many
   things you still can do in Pharsos so as
   to reach your goal, all sorts of things you haven't
   thought of! But now indeed it is
   almost too late.
PENTHESILEA (*stirring uneasily*).
                If I moved very fast—
   god, I am driven mad!—Tell me where
   the sun is.
PROTHOE. Right above your head, you'd
   make it there before nightfall. Unbeknownst
   to the Hellenes, we'd seal a pact with Troy,
   steal down on the bay where all their ships
   are beached, up these go in flames at a signal
   sounded in the night, their camp
   is stormed, their army squeezed between us front
   and rear, broken and disorganized
   and scattered to the winds, and every head

that's to our liking chased and overtaken,
caught and garlanded. What bliss I'd feel
if this might only happen! I'd wish no rest
but only to fight hard beside you, never
fearing the day's heat nor growing weary,
consuming all the strength my limbs possess
till my dear sister's wish was quite fulfilled
and Peleus' son, after so much effort,
sank prostrate at her feet, a beaten man.

PENTHESILEA (*who has been staring at the sun while Prothoe speaks*).
If only I were able, with broad extended,
beating wings, to split the air—

PROTHOE.   What's that?

MEROE. Whatever did she say?

PROTHOE.   What, Princess, do you see?

MEROE. What is she staring at?

PROTHOE.   Speak, my love!

PENTHESILEA.   Too high,
I know, too high—in fiery circles, astro-
nomically remote, he wheels lightheartedly
around me yearning upward toward him from
below.

PROTHOE. Who wheels, dear Queen?

PENTHESILEA.   Oh, never mind.—
How do we go? (*Pulling herself together, stands up*).

MEROE.   Then you've made up your mind?

PROTHOE. Then you're going to get up?—Well, do it, Princess,
like a giant! Never stagger even
if you have all Hades hanging from
your neck! Stand steady, steady as the arch stands
just because each block composing it
wants to fall! And as the keystone does,
expose your head to all the lightnings of the gods
and tell them, Strike me flat! Let yourself
be split down to the very ground, but never
waver in yourself again as long
as there is breath in your young breast to hold,
like mortar, all your frame of stone together.
Come, your hand.

PENTHESILEA.   Up there, or this way here?

PROTHOE. The cliff route's safer, but the going through
the valley's not so hard—which one do
you choose?
PENTHESILEA.　The cliff route! That way I am nearer
to him. Follow me.
PROTHOE.　　　　　Nearer whom,
my Queen?
PENTHESILEA. Your arm, dear girls.
PROTHOE.　　　　　　　As soon as you
have climbed that hill there, you are safe.
MEROE.　　　　　　　　Do come.
PENTHESILEA (*suddenly stopping while crossing a bridge*).
But listen: there is one thing still for me
to do, before withdrawing.
PROTHOE.　　　　　　Still to do?
MEROE. Which is?
PROTHOE.　　　You poor unhappy soul!
PENTHESILEA.　　　　　　　One
more thing, dear friends—and I'd be mad, you must
confess yourselves, to leave untried any
thing that still remains within the realm
of possibility.
PROTHOE (*angrily*).
　　　　　If that's the case,
I wish the earth would swallow us at once,
for rescue's out of the question now.
PENTHESILEA.　　　　　　What's wrong?
What have I done to her, you virgins, tell
me, please!
HIGH PRIESTESS. It's your idea—?
MEROE.　　　　　Here, still, you'd like
to try to—?
PENTHESILEA. Nothing, no! Oh, nothing what-
soever that might make her angry!—Only
pile Ida on Ossa and place myself,
quite quietly, on top.
HIGH PRIESTESS.　　Pile Ida—?
MEROE.　　　　　On Ossa—?
PROTHOE (*turning away*).
Oh, defend her, all you gods!

HIGH PRIESTESS. Oh, she is lost!

MEROE (*timidly*).
A feat like that's for Titans, don't you think?

PENTHESILEA. Indeed it is, it is—but how am I
a lesser one than they?

MEROE. How less than they!

PROTHOE. Good heavens!

HIGH PRIESTESS. But supposing—?

MEROE. Supposing you
were able to bring it off, a feat like that—?

PROTHOE. Supposing
that, what would you do?

PENTHESILEA. Oh imbeciles!
I'd reach into the sky and by his golden
locks of fire drag him down to me
below!

PROTHOE. Drag who?

PENTHESILEA. Him, Helios, when he
flies past me overhead!
(*The princesses, dismayed, stare at one another speechlessly.*)

HIGH PRIESTESS. Catch hold of her
and take her off!

PENTHESILEA (*looking down into the river*).
I must be mad! And all
the while he's lying at my feet! Oh take me—
(*Tries to jump into the river, Prothoe and Meroe restrain her.*)

PROTHOE. Poor unhappy thing!

MEROE. She's fallen lifeless,
like a rag of clothing, in our arms.

PRIESTESS (*on the hilltop*).
Achilles comes, you princesses! And all
our force of Amazons can't hold him off!

AN AMAZON. Oh save her, gods, and from his insolence
protect the Queen of Virgins!

HIGH PRIESTESS (*to the priestesses*).
Come, let's go!
The thick of battle is no place for us.
(*Exeunt High Priestesses, priestesses, and rose girls.*)

SCENE 10

Enter Amazons carrying bows.

FIRST AMAZON *(shouting into the wings).*
  Back, foolhardy man!
SECOND AMAZON.   He doesn't care.
THIRD AMAZON. Princesses, if we are not allowed
  to shoot at him, there is no stopping his
  mad rush!
SECOND AMAZON. We don't know what to do, Prothoe,
  tell us!
PROTHOE *(bent over the Queen).*
      Shower him with arrows, thousands
  of them!—
MEROE *(to the retinue of Princesses).*
          Water, quick!
PROTHOE.   But make sure not
  to shoot him dead!—
MEROE.   A helmet full of water,
  do you hear!
A PRINCESS *(filling a helmet with water and bringing it).*
          Here's the water!
THIRD AMAZON *(to Prothoe).*
                Don't
  you worry, we'll make sure!
FIRST AMAZON.   Take up positions
  here! And women, with your arrows graze
  his cheeks and singe his locks and let him taste,
  if for a second only, the kiss of death!
          (They bring their bows up to the ready.)

SCENE 11

*Enter Achilles, without helmet, armor, or weapons, followed
by Greek soldiers.*

ACHILLES. Young ladies, what? Whom do you mean these arrows
  for? Surely not for me, my unprotected
  breast? Shall I tear open my silk
  vest to let you see the inoffensive beating
  of my heart?

FIRST AMAZON. Yes, tear it open,
  if you like!
SECOND AMAZON. Please, there's no need of that!
THIRD AMAZON. Where he has got his hand now, let him have
  the shaft right there!
FIRST AMAZON.   So that his heart is ripped
  out of his breast and, spitted like a leaf, sent flying
  through the air!
AMAZONS IN CHORUS. Hit him! Shoot!
                (*They shoot over his head.*)
ACHILLES.   Please, please!
  Your eyes are better shots, believe me. By
  the gods of Mount Olympus, I don't joke,
  I feel myself pierced to my innermost
  and humbly kneel down at your pretty feet,
  a disarmed man in every sense.
FIFTH AMAZON (*struck by a spear from offstage*).
  The good gods! (*Falls.*)
SIXTH AMAZON (*also struck*).
                I'm hurt! (*Falls.*)
SEVENTH AMAZON (*also struck*).
                O Artemis! (*Falls.*)
FIRST AMAZON. The mad fellow! ⎫
MEROE (*bent over the Queen*). ⎬ (*together*)
                The poor wretch! ⎭
SECOND AMAZON.   Unarmed, he says! ⎫
PROTHOE (*also bent over the Queen*). ⎬ (*together*)
                Unsouled, I fear. ⎭
THIRD AMAZON.   While his men strike us down! ⎫
MEROE.   While our women fall! ⎬ (*together*)
  What can we do?
FIRST AMAZON. Bring up the war car with scythed wheels!
SECOND AMAZON.   Set the
  dogs on him!
THIRD AMAZON. Pitch rocks down from the battle
  towers of our elephants and bury him!
A PRINCESS (*suddenly leaving the Queen*).
  All right, I'll try a shot at him.
                (*Unslings her bow and strings it.*)

208

ACHILLES (*appealing to each Amazon in turn*).
         I'll never
think it! Sweet and silver-sounding as they
are, your voices give your words the lie.
Oh, you with your blue eyes, you're not the one
to set ferocious mastiffs on me, nor you
neither, you whose silky tresses look
so fine. Come, if you were too quick to give
the signal to let loose your howling dogs, I'm sure
you'd throw yourselves between their jaws and me
to shield my man's heart here, so warm
with love for you.
FIRST AMAZON.   The insolence of him!
SECOND AMAZON. The strutting popinjay!
FIRST AMAZON.   He thinks flattery—
THIRD AMAZON (*calling secretly to her*).
 Oterpe!
FIRST AMAZON (*turning around*).
    Oh, look there! Our best expert
with the bow! Open up your circle,
women, quietly!
FIFTH AMAZON. What's up?
FOURTH AMAZON.   No questions,
 you'll soon see.
EIGHTH AMAZON. And here's an arrow for you!
THE PRINCESS (*fitting the arrow to her bow*).
 I'll pin his thighs together with my shot.
ACHILLES (*to a Greek at his side with bow already drawn*).
 Shoot her!
THE PRINCESS. Heavenly Ones! (*Falls.*)
FIRST AMAZON.   The dreadful man!
SECOND AMAZON. Herself's the one who's hit and falls!
THIRD AMAZON.   Gods ever-
 lasting! Here's another troop of Greeks!

SCENE 12

Enter Diomedes and Aetolians from stage side opposite Achilles;
later, from Achilles' side, Odysseus and the army.

DIOMEDES. This way forward, my brave fellows, follow
 me! (*Leads them over the bridge.*)

PROTHOE. O Artemis the blessed, come save
    us now or it's all up with us!
    (With the help of Amazons, she carries the Queen to center stage.)
THE AMAZONS *(in disorder).*   We've been
    surrounded! We're cut off! We're prisoners!
    Run, women, run, it's each one for herself!
DIOMEDES *(to Prothoe).*
    Surrender!
MEROE *(to the fleeing Amazons).*
               Stop this panic! Stand and fight!
    Prothoe, see what's happening!
PROTHOE *(still crouched beside the Queen).*
                    Run
    yourself, do, follow them and if you can,
    return to set us free.
            (The Amazons disperse, Meroe following.)
ACHILLES.   Up and see
    if her head's showing!
A GREEK.   There!
ACHILLES.   You've won
    yourself ten crowns, my boy!
DIOMEDES.   Again—give up!
PROTHOE. To him who conquered her I'll give her up,
    not you! Whatever do you think? Pelides
    is the one!
DIOMEDES.   Then knock her down!
AN AETOLIAN.   Right, sir!
ACHILLES *(shoving the Aetolian back).*
    Whoever lays a finger on the Queen
    will leave this place a ghost! She's mine!
    Move, will you, you've no business here.
DIOMEDES. Oh, so she's yours! Well, look here, man,
    by Zeus the Thunderer's beard, on what grounds,
    by what right—?
ACHILLES.   On two grounds, first, this right,
    and secondly, this left. *(To Prothoe.)* Let's have her.
PROTHOE.   Here.
    Your magnanimity, I know, leaves nothing
    to be feared.

ACHILLES (*taking the Queen in his arms*).

        No, nothing. (*To Diomedes.*) Go on now and give
the women chase, keep after them—I'd like
to stay behind here for a minute. Go!
A favor to me. Don't object. I'd fight
all Hades for her, how much more yourself!
     (*Lays her down with her head propped against an oak tree root.*)
DIOMEDES. So be it! Follow me!
ODYSSEUS (*passing across the stage at the head of his troops*).

                    Hurrah for you,
Achilles, and again hurrah! The quadriga—
shall I send it on to you?
ACHILLES (*bent over the Queen*).

              No, there's no need.
Not yet.
ODYSSEUS. Fine. As you wish.—Now follow me!
Before the women have a chance to rally!
     (*Exeunt Odysseus and Diomedes from the side by which
           the Amazons have fled.*)

SCENE 13

ACHILLES (*opening the Queen's cuirass*).
  I fear she's not alive.
PROTHOE.   I hope her eyes
are closed forever to this desolate light!
The thing *I* fear is, she should wake.
ACHILLES. I hit her where?
PROTHOE.   Your blow tore her breast—
but she came around and, making a great effort, pulled
herself together; limping feebly, she let
us lead her here, where we were just about
to climb the cliff. But for whatever reason,
the throbbing of her wounded limbs or of
her wounded soul, she found it more than she
could bear you should have beaten her in battle—
her legs gave way, refusing her their service,
her wan lips babbled senseless things, and she
collapsed again into my arms.

ACHILLES.   There was
  a tremor, did you see?
PROTHOE.   Oh Heavenly Powers!
  Hasn't she drunk all the cup down yet?
  Look at her, poor creature—
ACHILLES.   See, she's breathing.
PROTHOE. Peleus' son, if pity's not an alien
  thing to you, if there is any feeling
  whatsoever in your breast, if her
  destruction's not what you desire, or seeing
  her susceptible and nervous nature
  fall into the toils of utter madness,
  then grant me a request.
ACHILLES.   Come on, come on!
PROTHOE. Remove yourself! She mustn't catch sight
  of you when she wakes. Go, admirable Prince,
  at once and take your men away with you;
  see to it that till the sun renews
  his light again, rising through the distant
  mountain mists, none comes near her to salute
  her with those words of death: You are
  Achilles' prisoner of war!
ACHILLES.   Because
  she hates me so?
PROTHOE.   Oh, never ask me why,
  great-hearted Prince! When she's escorted back
  to life again, so happily, upon
  the hand of hope, her conqueror should never
  be the first, unhappy, sight she sees.
  How many feelings stir inside a woman's
  breast that never were intended for
  the light of day. If, as her destiny
  demands, she must acknowledge, painfully,
  at last, that she is now your prisoner,
  don't ask it of her, I beseech you, please,
  until her spirit is prepared for it.
ACHILLES. My will, I have to tell you, is, to do
  with her just as I did with Priam's haughty
  son.
PROTHOE. You monster, no!

212

ACHILLES.   Is she afraid
  of that?
PROTHOE. You mean to do an unspeakable thing
  to her? This body here, atrocious man,
  as fresh and charming as a child with an armful
  of bright flowers—you mean to drag it, like
  a corpse—to desecrate it—?
ACHILLES.   Tell
  her that I love her.
PROTHOE.   What! But how—
ACHILLES. How, do you ask? I'll tell you *how*! Like men
  love women: respectfully, but full of longing
  too—in innocence, and yet desiring
  to take hers from her. I want the Queen to be
  my Queen.
PROTHOE.   Gods everlasting, say
  those words again. You want—?
ACHILLES.   Now may I stay?
PROTHOE. Man-god, let me kiss your feet! My feelings
  now are such that if you were not here
  in front of me, I'd go in search of you
  myself, as far as Hercules' Pillars
  if need be. But look, she's opening
  her eyes—
ACHILLES.   She moved—
PROTHOE.   It's time. You men there, go
  away! And you, quick, hide yourself behind
  this oak.
ACHILLES. Go, friends, withdraw.
                     (*Exeunt Achilles' men.*)
PROTHOE (*to Achilles, as he retreats behind the oak*).
                     Still farther off!
  And don't appear, I beg you, please, until
  you hear me call. Is that a promise? There's
  no telling what her state of mind will be.
ACHILLES. Just as you say, my dear.
PROTHOE.   And now let's see!

SCENE 14

PROTHOE. What a dreamer, Penthesilea,
  you are! Where, I wonder, has your restless

spirit wandered off to, strayed away into
what far-off fields of glory as if it hated
its own home? And meanwhile young
Prince Fortune, entering your bosom,
finds to his surprise the lovely lodging's
empty, turns impatiently on his heel
and is already heading back to Heaven.
Won't you, foolish darling, grapple your guest
to you? Come, sit up and lean against my breast.

PENTHESILEA. Where am I?

PROTHOE.   Don't you know your sister's voice?
The cliffside here, the bridge path, all the flowering
landscape—don't they recall you to yourself?
—And see these girls around you in a circle:
they stand as if before the entrance to
a better world and call out "Welcome!" to you.
—But you sighed. What is it?

PENTHESILEA.   Oh Prothoe!
I dreamt a dream so terrible! How sweet
it is, I want to cry, to wake and feel
this heart of mine, worn out by too much pain,
beat languidly against its sister one.
—It seemed that in the violence of war Pelides
struck me with his lance. In a great clatter of bronze
arms and armor, I crash to earth; the ground
reechoes to my fall. And while the army falls
back in dismay and I am lying there with all
my limbs entangled, in a flash he's off
his horse and coming toward me with a triumphant
step, to pick me, prostrate, up in his
strong arms, and all my tugging at this dagger
handle here is quite in vain, I'm
his prisoner and with a mocking laugh
he carries me off to his tents.

PROTHOE.   Not so,
my Queen! His spirit's too magnanimous
for mockery. If it were truth not dream,
believe me, what a moment of pure bliss
that would have been for you—one in which

214

the son of the gods might very well have knelt
down in the dust and done you reverence.
PENTHESILEA. A curse on me if ever I endure
such shame! A curse on me if ever I
accept a man I haven't won in worthy
fashion, with my sword!
PROTHOE.   Queen, calm yourself.
PENTHESILEA. Calm myself!
PROTHOE.   Your head is lying on my loyal
bosom, isn't it? Whatever fate's
impending over you, we'll bear it both
together—compose yourself.
PENTHESILEA.   I was as calm
just now, Prothoe, as the sea inside the cliff-
surrounded bay, no ripple of emotion wrinkling
my repose. But hearing "calm yourself"
uncalms me quite and whips me up, as the wind
the waters of great Ocean, into an instant
agitation. *Why* should I be calm?
You all stand around me very oddly,
so uneasily—as if a monster, frightful-
faced, hung at my back.—I told you, it
was just a dream, it's not—Or is it! Did I—?
Was it true? Speak, will you?—Meroe,
where is she? Megaris?
                    (*Looks behind her and sees Achilles.*)
                    Oh horrible!
The dreadful man is standing right behind
me now! With my free hand—(*Draws her dagger.*)
PROTHOE.   Unhappy girl!
PENTHESILEA. The vile woman, she's preventing me—
PROTHOE. Achilles, save her!
PENTHESILEA.   Oh, you're mad, you're mad!
He swore he'd plant his foot on my neck!
PROTHOE. His foot? You're raving—
PENTHESILEA.   Get out of my way!
PROTHOE. But look at him, you poor lost thing! Do you
see any weapons in his hands?
PENTHESILEA.   What's that you say?

PROTHOE. See, see, it's true! All ready, if you wish,
   to offer himself up to you to wear
   the flower chain.
PENTHESILEA.   No, it can't be.
PROTHOE.   Achilles,
   she says it can't be. *You* tell her!
PENTHESILEA.   I
   took *him* a prisoner?
PROTHOE.   Of course. Look there.
ACHILLES (*coming forward*).
   In every higher sense of that word, so
   you did, exalted Queen! And I should wish
   to pass my whole life, from now on, a fluttering
   captive in the net of your bright eyes.
          (*Penthesilea covers her face with her hands.*)
PROTHOE. Well, now you've heard it out of his own mouth.
   He fell, like you, when you two struck each other,
   in the dust; and while you lay unconscious
   on the ground, he was disarmed—is that correct?
ACHILLES. I was disarmed; they brought me here to kneel
   down at your feet.
         (*Drops on one knee before her.*)
PENTHESILEA (*after a short pause*).
        Indeed!—Then I cry welcome
   to you, charm of life, you red-cheeked god
   of youth! And oh my heart, let flow the blood
   that's lain piled up in both the chambers
   of this breast as if awaiting him. You bright-winged
   signaler of joy, you ichor of my youth,
   up, and course through all my veins, exulting,
   fly your crimson ensign in the two kingdoms
   of these cheeks—the young son of the Nereid
   is mine! (*Stands up.*)
PROTHOE. More temperately, please, my Queen.
PENTHESILEA (*coming forward*).
   Here to me, you virgins crowned with victory,
   Mars's daughters smeared with grime of war
   from head to foot, and lead the Argive youths whom you
   have conquered, each one, by the hand! You girls
   there, bring me all your baskets piled with roses—

but for so many heads we need more wreaths!
Out into the meadows, quick, and by
the exhalation of your own breaths force
the buds the springtime grudges! Priestesses
who serve Diana, to your duty in the Temple:
set the torches blazing, incense burning,
throw the great doors, jarring, open
to me, like the gates of Paradise! First
the fatted bull, the short-horned, to the altar—
let the shining iron fell him at one blow,
without a sound, so that the building shakes.
Our stout-limbed Temple servants, you hard-working
women—blood, the blood!—where are you? quick,
and wash the fretted wainscot clean with Persian
oils brought hissing from the coals. And the loose-
flying skirts and chitons, let them all
be tucked in place, fill up with wine, you golden
beakers, bugles shrill and trumpets thunder,
and let our loud harmonious rejoicing
cause the firmament to tremble all
the way down to its base!—Prothoe, help
me to rejoice, exult in triumph! Think,
dear friend, how I may make a feast more godlike,
more exuberant than Mount Olympus
ever celebrated, the marriage feast
of brides who woo their men in bloody battle,
of Mars's daughters and the sons of King Inachus!—
Meroe, oh, where are you? Megaris?

PROTHOE (*hiding her feelings*).
    Joy's just as bad as grief for you, I see,
you're driven raving mad by both of them.
You dream you are already home in Themiscyra;
and when you soar beyond all limits in this way,
I want to say the very thing to puncture
your delirium and bring you down
to earth. Just look around you, you deluded
girl, and tell me where you think you are?
Where are our people? Our priestesses?
Asteria, Meroe, and Megaris, where are they?

PENTHESILEA (*leaning on her breast*).
Allow me it, Prothoe! I'm a little
grubby child that's dived into this stream
of pure delight, for two seconds only;
with every wave that washes over me
a black spot on my heart is rinsed away.
The furious Eumenides retreat,
the air's astir around me, as if with godly
presences, how I would like to mingle
with that throng, I've never been so ripe
for death as now. But now what's most important
is, do you forgive me?
PROTHOE.   Oh, my Sovereign!
PENTHESILEA. I know, I know—well, my blood's better part
is your share in it.—Suffering, they say,
refines and elevates the soul, but that's
not been the case with me, dear heart; it has
exacerbated me and worked me up
into an unimaginable rage
against both gods and men. Queer, how I hated
any trace of joy in every face
I saw; the child that played in its mother's
lap seemed part of a conspiracy
to mock my pain. And now—how glad I'd be
if everything around me breathed only
happiness and pure content! Ah, friend!
How great-souled man can be, a hero, when
he suffers, but when he's happy, how divine!
—But now to business. Let the army make
its preparations to retire, quick
as possible. Troops and animals,
as soon as they are rested lead them out
in columns, with the prisoners, and point
your course toward home.—Where is Lycaon?
PROTHOE.   Who?
PENTHESILEA (*with gentle remonstration*).
Who, you ask me who! Am I hearing right?
That blooming hero of Arcadia
whom your sword won you—shouldn't he be here?

218

PROTHOE (*embarrassed*).
    He's in the woods, my Queen, where they are holding
    him with all the other prisoners.
    He's not allowed, according to the law,
    to come to me till in our homeland.
PENTHESILEA.   Bring
    him here! In the woods still, is he! At
    the feet of my Prothoe is his place!
    —Really, you are like a May frost here
    beside me, freezing up the newborn life
    of joy.
PROTHOE (*aside*).
        Ah, poor thing!—Yes, go and do
    just as the Queen commands.
              (*Signals an Amazon, who exits.*)
PENTHESILEA.   Now who will fetch
    the rose girls for me?
              (*Sees the roses on the ground.*)
        Look, these rosebuds here,
and so sweet smelling—!
        (*Passes her hand across her forehead.*)
        Such a bad dream, mine!
(*To Prothoe.*)
The Priestess of Diana, was she here?
PROTHOE. Not that I know, our Queen—
PENTHESILEA.   Then why
    these roses on the ground?
PROTHOE (*quickly*).
            Look over there!
    The girls who ransacked all the fields left
    a basketful of them behind. Now I
    call that a piece of luck indeed. I'll gather
    up the blossoms if you like, and twist
    a wreath for you to crown Pelides with.
            (*Sits down beside the oak tree.*)
PENTHESILEA. You darling, just the thing! How touched I am—
    all right! And these here, with their hundred petals,
    them I'll wind for your Lycaon. Come.
        (*Picks up roses too and sits beside Prothoe.*)

Music, women, music! I need soothing.
Let me hear a song to quiet me.
A YOUNG GIRL. What would you like?
ANOTHER.   The victory song?
PENTHESILEA.   —The hymn.
YOUNG GIRL. The hymn, then.—Poor deluded creature!—Sing!
CHORUS OF VIRGINS (*with music*).
    Great Ares is fled!
    See how his white horses,
    Afar off, breath fuming, go racing below, down to Orcus!
    The Eumenides, terrible, open the portals,
    And close them behind him again.
SOLO. *Hymen, where are you? Appear!*
    Kindle the torches and brighten all, brighten all!
    Hymen, where are you? Appear!
CHORUS. *Great Ares is fled!* etc.
ACHILLES (*sidling quietly up to Prothoe during the singing*).
    What am I getting into here, I'd like
    to know!
PROTHOE.   I ask your patience, generous-hearted
    man, one moment longer—you will see.
            (*When the wreaths are made, Penthesilea and Prothoe*
            exchange them, and regarding them together, embrace.
            The music ends. The Amazon reenters.)
PENTHESILEA. You've done as I commanded?
AMAZON.   Young Lycaon,
    Prince of Arcady, is on his way.

SCENE 15

PENTHESILEA. Come here to me, you sweet son of the Nereid,
    come here and lie down at my feet. Still closer!
    Boldly does it! You're not afraid
    of me, are you? Hate me horribly
    for beating you? Do say! The girl who knocked
    you down into the dust, does she frighten
    you?
ACHILLES. Like sunshine frightens flowers.
PENTHESILEA.   That's
    so very nicely said! Then see me as

your sun.—Lady Artemis, the fellow's
wounded!

ACHILLES.　　Just a scratch on the arm,
　no more.

PENTHESILEA. Pelides, please don't think I ever
　for a moment sought your life. True, I
　was glad with this right arm to have at you;
　but as you swayed and fell, I felt such envy
　of the dust that billowed up around you!

ACHILLES.　　　　　　　　　　　　　If
　you love me, not another word about
　it. Look, it's almost healed already.

PENTHESILEA.　　　　　　　　　I'm
　forgiven then?

ACHILLES.　　　With all my heart.

PENTHESILEA.　　　　　　　　Now—can
　you tell me what the boy with wings, the God
　of Love, must do to chain the ramping lion
　up?

ACHILLES. What he must do, I think, is stroke
　his bristly cheeks, then he'll sit still.

PENTHESILEA.　　　　　　　　Good, good!
　So you won't flutter more than the mild dove
　does, when a young girl loops the string around
　its neck. For feelings such as mine, they are
　so many hands and long to stroke your cheeks.
　　　　　　　　(*She winds garlands around him.*)

ACHILLES. Extraordinary woman, who are you?

PENTHESILEA. Come now—I said still! You'll soon find out.
　A garland, only, of these roses, which
　weigh nothing, around your head and neck—
　and now your arms and hands—down to the feet—
　and back up to your head again—it's done!
　Why do you breathe like that?

ACHILLES.　　　　　　　　　　The sweet scent
　of your lips.

PENTHESILEA (*bending backward*).
　　　　　　Oh, it's the roses scattering
　their scent.—No, no!

ACHILLES.   I thought I'd try them at
the stem.

PENTHESILEA. As soon as they are ripe, my love,
they're yours to pluck.
             (*Crowns his head with her last wreath and lets him go.*)
                         And now it's done—Oh look,
Prothoe, please, how well it suits him, the mist
of rosiness in which he's bathed! How
his face, as dun as thunder, glimmers through
it! The stripling day, when he's conducted
down the mountains by the hours and treads
the sparkling diamonds underfoot, hasn't
got so soft and mild a glance, I swear,
as he.—Speak, won't you? Don't you think there was
a kind of glisten, even, in his eye?
Really, when he looks like that you'd almost
doubt he's who he is.

PROTHOE.   And *who* is he?

PENTHESILEA.   Achilles!
(*To Achilles.*)
The man who slew the greatest one of all
the sons of Priam underneath the walls
of Troy—tell me, was that you? Really
you who nailed his racing feet together
with these hands and trailed his corpse around
the city from your axletree? Speak! You
seemed moved! Is anything the matter?

ACHILLES.   It
was me.

PENTHESILEA (*studying him closely*).
        Was he, he says.

PROTHOE.   It was, my Queen.
You can tell it by his panoply.

PENTHESILEA.   His what?

PROTHOE. His armor, see here, which his goddess
mother Thetis flattered out of Vulcan,
God of Fire, for him.

PENTHESILEA.   Very well—
then with this kiss I greet you, the most
unbridled of all men, now mine! Young

222

god of war, it's me whom you belong
to; and when people ask you, say *my* name.

ACHILLES. You dazzling apparition, descended here
below to me as if the sphere of ether
opened, mystery I'll never fathom,
who are *you?* Say your name?—How can
I, when my own soul, dazed with joy,
keeps asking me who its new owner is.

PENTHESILEA. When it does, tell these features over you
see here and that is name enough. But let
me give you this gold ring whose every marking
guarantees your safety; show it and
the way is clear for you to me. A ring
gets lost, though, names are easily forgotten—
if you forgot my name, misplaced the ring,
would you still be able to find my picture
in yourself? Your eyes shut, do
you see it still?

ACHILLES.   It's fixed as ineffaceably
in me as if in diamond.

PENTHESILEA.   I am Queen
of the Amazons, my race claims Mars as father,
great Otrere was my mother, and me,
the people call me Penthesilea.

ACHILLES. Penthesilea.

PENTHESILEA.   Yes, so I said.

ACHILLES. My swan song when I die is: Penthesilea.

PENTHESILEA. You're now at liberty and free to go
wherever you may wish among our troops
of women. It's another kind of chain,
now, I am thinking of, as light as wreaths
yet more unbreakable than bronze, to wind
around your heart and bind you to me with.
But till its links, each one, are hammered out
and shaped, with finest art, in the fire
of feeling, proof against the injuries
of time and chance, back to me you must
return as you are duty bound—to me,
you understand, my friend, who is

the one who will provide for every need
of yours or wish. You'll come back, will you?
ACHILLES.   Like
young horses to the sweet reek of the manger,
by which their life is fed.
PENTHESILEA.   Good, I'll rely
on that. We're setting out now on the ride
back home to Themiscyra; till we're there,
my entire stable's yours to choose from.
There are tents of purple here for you, and no
lack of slaves to serve your royal will.
But since I have so much to look to, on
the march, as I am sure you understand,
your place will have to be among the other
prisoners. Till Themiscyra, then,
oh goddess-born, when I'll be free at last
to dedicate myself completely, heart
and soul, to you.
ACHILLES.   Just as you say.
PENTHESILEA (*to Prothoe*).
                                        But what's
become of your Arcadian, I'd like
to know?
PROTHOE.   My Princess—
PENTHESILEA.   Dear Prothoe, it
would please me so to see you place the wreath
on his head.
PROTHOE.   He'll soon arrive. There is
no danger he won't have his wreath to wear.
PENTHESILEA. (*starting to rise*).
Well, then—I've many things to do, so please
allow me—
ACHILLES.   What?
PENTHESILEA.   Allow me to stand up.
ACHILLES. You're off, you're going, leaving me behind?
Without the explanation of these wonders
I'm on tenterhooks to hear?
PENTHESILEA.   Wait till
Themiscyra, friend.
ACHILLES.   No, here, my Queen!

PENTHESILEA. In Themiscyra, friend, not here—now let
  me go!
PROTHOE (*nervously restraining her*).
        Why, where is it you're off to, Queen?
PENTHESILEA (*surprised*).
  What kind of question's that? To fall the troops
  in, that is where. I have to speak to Meroe,
  Megaris too. Do I have nothing else
  to do now, by the Styx, than stand around
  and talk?
PROTHOE.   The army's still in hot pursuit
  of all the running Greeks. Let Meroe,
  who's captain of the van, take care of that—
  you still need to rest. As soon as all
  the enemy are driven back across
  Scamander, we'll parade the troops in triumph
  for you.
PENTHESILEA (*thinking it over*).
        Here on this field? You are absolutely
  sure?
PROTHOE. Absolutely sure, rely
  on it.
PENTHESILEA. All right. (*Turning to Achilles.*)
        Now ask away, but briefly, please.
ACHILLES. Why is it, extraordinary woman,
  at the head of a whole army, without
  provocation, like Athene from
  the clouds, you suddenly precipitate
  yourself into our strife with Troy? What goads
  you on against us Greeks, armed as you are
  from head to foot in bronze and spitting anger
  like a Fury, inexplicably—
  you who only need to quietly show
  yourself in all your charming loveliness
  for every man alive to grovel in
  the dust to you?
PENTHESILEA.   Ah me, son of the sea-born
  Nereid! The gentler way, the art
  of women—life has not allowed me that.
  I may not, like your country's daughters, choose

my lover from among the brilliant youth
who crowd together at the festivals to race
and wrestle one another in the games—may not
pin a bunch of flowers this or that
way on my breast, or dart a shy glance
to attract his notice—may not, in the night-
ingale-enchanted pomegranate grove,
when dawn begins to glow, bosom against
bosom, declare he's mine. On the blood-stained
battlefield I have to hunt him, the young
man my heart has picked out for itself,
with bronze arms savagely manhandle just
the one my soft breast is impatient to receive.

ACHILLES. Out of where did your law come, and how,
a law—if you'll forgive my saying so—
unwomanly, unnatural, and quite
unknown to all the rest of humankind?

PENTHESILEA. Out of the remotest urns of the most holy,
down slopes of time from summits Heaven hides
in perpetual mists, it came to us,
a mystery. Our first mothers' words
decreed it, son of Thetis, and dumbly we
receive them, as you do your first fathers' words.

ACHILLES. Can't you say more than that?

PENTHESILEA.   Very well.
Then listen.—Where the race of Amazons rules now,
a race of Scythians once lived, god-fearing,
free, and warlike, the equal of any
other people here on earth. Century
on century they called the fruit-tree-growing
Caucasus their own. Then Vexoris,
the Ethiopian king, appeared among
the foothills, quickly routed all the men
who stood against him, poured through all the valleys
killing all the old men and young boys
his naked sword could find—all that noble
breed of menfolk perished from the earth.
Like barbarians, the victors rudely
settled in our huts, gorged themselves on all
the plenty of our fields and, filling up

the measure of our shame, took our love
from us by force—they dragged the women from
their husbands' graves to their disgusting beds.
ACHILLES. Fate worked through death and ruin, Queen, to bring
your women's state to birth.
PENTHESILEA.   What's more than can
be borne, man struggles every way to shake
off from his shoulders; his lesser tribulations
only he puts up with, Prince Achilles.
Long nights through, in silence, secretly,
prostrated on the steps of Mars's shrine,
the women wore away the stones with tears
and prayers to be saved. Their violated beds
were caches for blades whetted to a brightness,
hammered in the fireplaces' flames out
of their own ornaments, their necklaces
and rings and brooches—they were only waiting
till the wedding day of King Vexoris and
Tanaïs, our Queen, to give each one
of them a dagger's kiss upon the breast.
And when the wedding day came around,
the Queen took hers and stuck it in his heart;
not that vile beast but Mars stood groom
to our Queen, and all that brood of murderers
were loved to death in one night, with our knives.
ACHILLES. Such an action carried out by women,
just imagine!
PENTHESILEA.   And then they held a council
where it was decreed as follows: Women
capable of acting so heroically
needs must be unfettered as the wind
that blows across the open steppes and shall submit
to men no longer. Let a state, a women's one,
complete in all respects, be instituted
where men's boastful, overbearing voices
shall never be allowed to clamor noisily
again, a state which gives itself its own
laws, worthily, obeys itself, defends
itself, and Tanaïs shall be its Queen.
The man who once claps eyes on our land

227

of women, he claps them shut forever. If
it happens that a boy should be the issue
of the tyrants' hug, down to Orcus
instantly he goes, right after his own
savage father.—Ares' temple filled up
at once with crowds of people, to crown Tanaïs
the Protectress of our new society.
At the most solemn moment, just as she climbed
the altar's steps to take the great gold bow
of Scythia, which only kings had wielded
heretofore, out of the hands of the ornately
robed High Priestess, a voice was heard to say:
"Men must feel only derision for
a state like this and it will surely crumble
under the first onslaught of a warlike neighbor.
For we are weak, we women; impossible
for us to pull the bow full stretch
with the ease men do, our swelling bosom
hampers us. The Queen did nothing
for a moment, waiting silently to see
what fate these words would have. But when she felt
a craven ripple spreading all around
her, her own right breast she ripped away and named
us archer women Amazons, or the Breastless
Ones, collapsing in a dead faint even
as these words were uttered! Whereupon
the crown was placed upon her head.

ACHILLES.   By Jupiter,
she needed no breasts, that one! She could have ruled
a race of men; I bow to her with all
my heart and soul.

PENTHESILEA.   Dead silence greeted what
she'd done, Pelides, broken only by
the bowstring's twanging as the corpse-white, stiffened
hands of the High Priestess let the weapon
fall. Down it went, the great gold bow
of our people, clanging three times like
a bell on the marble steps, and came
to rest, as still as death, before her feet.

ACHILLES. I do hope you are not inclined, in
   this state of yours, to follow her example?
PENTHESILEA. Not follow her example? Of course we do!
   Though we are not as quick as she about it.
ACHILLES (*shocked*).
                                    What!
   It's a fact, then, that—? Impossible!
PENTHESILEA.   No, why?
ACHILLES. This monstrous myth that you've been telling me,
   it's true, then. All these brightly blooming figures
   that surround you, the perfection of the sex,
   altars, each one, lavishly adorned
   for love to kneel adoringly before,
   they've been deprived, sacrilegiously,
   inhumanly—?
PENTHESILEA.   You didn't know?
ACHILLES (*pressing his face to her bosom*).
                             Oh Queen,
   this seat of youth and all its feelings of delight,
   for a mad idea's sake, barbarically—
PENTHESILEA. No need for you to take on so. These feelings
   all escaped from right to left and there
   they live the nearer to my heart. You won't,
   I trust, find I am lacking any.
ACHILLES.   Please!
   A dream dreamed in the morning hours seems
   much more real to me than now. But do
   continue.
PENTHESILEA. What?
ACHILLES.   The ending of your story's
   still to tell. This very independent
   women's state of yours, which got itself
   set up without the help of men, how does
   it propagate itself without the help
   of men? Does old Deucalion every now
   and then pitch you down one of his lumps
   of clay headfirst?
PENTHESILEA.   We make a yearly count;
   whenever our Queen decides it's time
   to make good what we've lost by death,

she summons our brightest blooming youth—
(*Stops and looks at him.*)
Why are you smiling?
ACHILLES.   Smiling? I?
PENTHESILEA.   It seemed
to me you smiled, dear boy.
ACHILLES.   Your beauty's fault,
which quite distracted me. Forgive me, please.
I was thinking, Did you come down to
me from the moon?
PENTHESILEA (*after a moment*).
                    We make a yearly count;
whenever our Queen decides the numbers
we have lost by death need making good,
she summons our brightest blooming youth
to her, from every corner of the land, and in
the Temple of the goddess Artemis calls down
the blessing on them, that Mars may plant their maiden
wombs with fruitfulness. This Festival
of Maids in Bloom, for so it's called, a solemn
and a quiet one—we wait till spring has breathed
away the winter's snowy coat and kissed
the breast of Nature, to observe it. Following
the Queen's petition of the god, the holy
Priestess of Diana enters Mars's
shrine and prostrate at the altar, conveys
to him the wish of our people's mother.
If the god gives ear—for often he
refuses, our snowy mountains grudge
us enough nourishment—through his priestess
he marks out for us some chaste and noble
stock, and they must take his place with us
and do his office. When we learn their name
and dwelling place, at once a jubilation
runs through town and country. Brides of Mars
is how we hail the virgins, their mothers' hands
press weapons on them, swords and arrows, other
hands which fly rejoicing around them dress
their limbs in the bronze wedding dress of war.
The glad day of our expedition's fixed,

the muted trumpets sound, the squadron, voices
hushed, swings into the saddle, and stealthily,
as if our mounts were shod in wool, through shining
nights, through woods and across valleys, we ride
the long trail to our chosen ones. Arrived
before their gates, women and horses take
a two days' rest: and like the fire-whipping
windstorm we burst into the forest where
their men are camped and blow the ripest ones,
who fall, like seeds, when tops of trees are wildly
pitching to and fro, back home to our
fields. And there we wait upon them, in Diana's
Temple, through many a holy ritual
that's called by us the Festival of Roses.
I know no more about it than its name,
for, except the brides, nobody is
allowed, on pain of death, to witness it.
And when at last the seed comes up and blossoms,
we load them down with gifts, each one, like kings,
and at the Feast of Fertile Mothers send
them home again in shining cars. This feast,
let me assure you, son of Thetis, it's not
our jolliest one—for tears aplenty flow
and many a heart that now heaves dismally
can't see why we should praise great Tanaïs
in every other breath. But you are dreaming,
I can see—of what?

ACHILLES.   I am?

PENTHESILEA.   You are.

ACHILLES (*abstracted*).
Impossible for me to put it into
words, love. So you will send me home too, do
you think?

PENTHESILEA. I cannot say, my darling. Do
not ask me.

ACHILLES.   It's so strange! (*Falls into thought.*)
                    But there is one
thing more I'd like you to explain.

PENTHESILEA.   With all
my heart, don't be afraid to ask.

ACHILLES.   I'd like
  to understand why *I* was just the one
  you gave such hot chase to—as if you knew
  the man you were pursuing.
PENTHESILEA.   And so I did.
ACHILLES.   But how?
PENTHESILEA. You won't smile at the silly girl I am?
ACHILLES (*smiling*).
  Repeating your own words—I cannot say.
PENTHESILEA. All right. I'll tell you how. I had, you see,
  already witnessed our Festival
  of Roses twenty-three times over, but
  always from far off, the noise of merry-
  making coming to me from the oak grove
  out of which the Temple rises, when
  Ares, at my mother's—Otrere's—death,
  chose me for his bride. For we Princesses
  of the royal house never take part
  of our own accord in the Feast of Maids in Bloom,
  the god, if he desires us, calls
  us to him ceremoniously by the mouth
  of the High Priestess. Even as I hugged
  my pale and dying mother in my arms,
  Mars's word was brought me in the palace,
  solemnly, commanding me to leave
  for Troy so as to bring him home from there
  victoriously wreathed. No substitute
  he ever named so pleased his brides as the race
  of Hellenes fighting in that place. At every
  corner you heard exclamations of delight,
  the marketplaces rang with epic songs
  rehearsing deeds done in the war of heroes:
  Paris' apple, Helen's rape, the squadron-
  marshaling Atrides, the quarrel over
  Briseïs, the setting fire to the ships, and Patroclus'
  death and with what pomp of triumph of
  revenge you did the last rites for him;
  and all the episodes of that great time.
  But I in my distress, I swam in tears
  and only half heard, as Otrere lay dying,

the message of the god. "Mother,
let me stay with you," I cried; "make use,
this last time, of the respect that's yours and send
these women back." But she, so much the Queen,
who long had wished to see me in the field—
lest her death should leave the throne without
an heir, a mark for some ambitious neighbor
race—she said: "Dear child, Mars summons you,
now go! You'll catch and crown Pelides, I
am sure. Become a mother, proud and happy
like myself—" And squeezing my hand gently,
died.

PROTHOE. Otrere named him to you, then?

PENTHESILEA. She named him, yes she did, Prothoe, as
a mother may, I'm sure, when it is just
between her daughter and herself.

ACHILLES.   What's this?
Am I to understand your law forbids it?

PENTHESILEA. It isn't right for Mars's daughters to go searching
out opponents of their own. Their duty is
to take the one the God of Battle puts
into their way. However—if an ambitious
spirit shows herself before the princeliest
of the foe, why, well and good! Prothoe, is
that right?

PROTHOE.   It is.

ACHILLES.   And then?

PENTHESILEA.   I cried a whole
month through, grief-stricken, on my mother's grave,
not touching once the crown that lay unclaimed
alongside it, till the clamor of the people, camped
impatiently around the palace, ready
to ride out, bore me up by force
and set me on the throne. With sad and dragging
steps I came to Mars's Temple, the ringing
bow of our Amazonian state
was handed me, it was as if my mother's
presence hovered in the air, and when
I took it nothing seemed as sacred as
fulfilling her last wish. I scattered her

sarcophagus with sweetest smelling flowers,
then led the army out toward Troy—less
to please the great god Mars who called
me, than poor Otrere's shade.

ACHILLES.   Your sorrow for
the dead crippled for a while that strength
which otherwise so graces your young self.

PENTHESILEA. I loved her.

ACHILLES.   Yes. And then—?

PENTHESILEA.   The nearer I
advanced to the Scamander, the louder all
the valleys we raced through reechoed
with the fighting over Troy, the less pain I
experienced and my soul, expanding wide, embraced
the great world of high-spirited war.
My one thought was: if each most glorious
moment history remembers were reenacted
here before me now, if all the company
of heroes sung in epic song descended
to me from the stars, I'd find no better
one to crown with roses than him my mother
chose—that dear, that savage, charming, dreadful
one by whom brave Hector fell! Pelides!
My one thought waking, one dream sleeping, was
of you! The whole world lay spread out before
me like some piece of woven stuff into
whose every giant square a deed of yours
was worked, and I, I burnt each one into
my heart, so white and pure, like silk, with fire
dyes. I saw how you struck down hard-running
Priam's son in front of Ilium; how
all afire in the ecstasy of triumph
you held your face averted while his bleeding
head was dragged along the naked ground;
how Priam came begging to your tent—and I
wept hot tears at the thought that though
you are so merciless, your marble bosom's
not unpierceable by feeling.

ACHILLES.   My
dear Queen!

PENTHESILEA.   But just imagine, if you can,
my state when I saw you yourself!—when I
caught sight of you in the Scamander Valley, among
the heroes of your nation, a sun among
the dim nocturnal stars! If War God
Mars, whipping his white horses, thundered
straight down from Olympus to greet his bride
in person, I would have felt the same! I stood
there blinded by the apparition after you
had vanished—just like a nighttime traveler
a bolt of lightning plummets down before,
like a soul who sees the gates jar open on
the glory of Elysium and then jar shut.
That moment told me what the feeling
was, Pelides, making such an uproar
in my breast—the God of Love had overtaken
me. But right off I made up my mind
to one of two things, win you for myself,
or die: and see, the nicer one I've managed.
—You're staring, why?
    (*Clash of weapons in the distance.*)
PROTHOE (*aside to Achilles*).
       Son of the gods, I beg
you, tell her what the truth is right away,
you must.
PENTHESILEA (*starting up*).
     Argives coming, women! Stand to!
ACHILLES (*holding her back*).
Easy! They are prisoners, my Queen.
PENTHESILEA. Prisoners?
PROTHOE (*aside to Achilles*).
       Ulysses, by the Styx!
Meroe's pushing back your Greeks!
ACHILLES (*muttering to himself*).
       I wish
they'd turn to stone, all!
PENTHESILEA.   What is happening?
ACHILLES (*with forced heartiness*).
You'll mother me the new god of our
Earth! Prometheus, he'll rise up from

his seat and make a proclamation to
the human race: here is a man as I
have wished for man to be! But I won't follow
you to Themiscyra, you rather me
to blooming Phthia: I rejoice, when
the war my people wage is done, to be
your escort there and set you, with what bliss
I can't express, on my father's throne.
                    (*Noise of clashing weapons continues.*)
PENTHESILEA. Whatever are you saying? Not one word—
THE WOMEN (*full of disquiet*).
    You gods above!
PROTHOE.   Nerides' son, please, will
    you—?
PENTHESILEA. What is wrong? What's going on here?
ACHILLES.   Nothing,
    not a thing, don't be alarmed, my Queen,
    the time is short, you see, if you're to hear
    what the gods together have decreed
    for you. It's true that by love's power I
    am yours, his fetters bind me to you for
    eternity; but by war's fortune you
    belong to me. For when we met in battle,
    divine girl, you fell at *my* feet,
    not I at yours.
PENTHESILEA (*drawing herself up*).
            Oh no, oh dreadful!
ACHILLES.   Love,
    let me implore you! Cronos' son himself
    can't change what's done. Control yourself, and when
    that messenger who's heading here delivers
    his report to me, a quite unpleasant
    one unless I miss my guess, listen
    just as if you were made of stone. For he's
    got nothing, you must understand, for you.
    Your destiny's complete, all's over;
    now you're my prisoner, a dog of hell
    would not keep so ferocious guard as I.
PENTHESILEA. Your prisoner?
PROTHOE.   It's so, dear Queen!

PENTHESILEA (*her hands uplifted*).
You deathless Powers of Heaven, hear, oh hear!

SCENE 16
Enter a Captain, and Achilles' men carrying his armor.

ACHILLES. What have you got to report?

CAPTAIN.   Fall back, Pelides!
The luck of battle, changeable as weather,
is luring on the Amazons again
to win—they're driving hard at our position
here, their war cry: Penthesilea!

ACHILLES (*standing up and ripping off the garlands*).
Quick, my weapons! Bring my horses up!
I'll cut them all to pieces underneath
my wheels!

PENTHESILEA (*her lip quivering*).
                    No, see how terrible the man
is! Can he be the same—?

ACHILLES (*savagely*).
                                    How far away
are they?

CAPTAIN.   You can see the Golden Crescent
in the valley now.

ACHILLES (*putting on his armor*).
                    Get her out of here!

A GREEK. But where to?

ACHILLES.   The Greek camp. I'll be coming after
you in a few minutes.

GREEK (*to Penthesilea*).
                              Up.

PROTHOE.   Oh Queen!

PENTHESILEA (*beside herself*).
Zeus, not a thunderbolt, not one, for me!

SCENE 17
Enter Odysseus and Diomedes, with the army.

DIOMEDES (*passing across the stage*).
Run, run for it, great hero of the Dolops tribe!

The women are about to cut the one
escape route open to you still!
(Exeunt.)

ODYSSEUS. Greeks, take away the Queen.

ACHILLES (to the Captain).

A favor, please,

Alexis: help her, would you?

GREEK (to the Captain).

She won't move.

ACHILLES (to the Greeks attending him).
The shield! The spear, too!
(Calling out, when he sees the Queen resisting.)
Penthesilea!

PENTHESILEA. Son of the Nereid! Then you won't follow
me to Themiscyra? Won't follow me
into that Temple jutting up from among
the oak-tree tops? Please come with me,
I've still not told you everything—

ACHILLES (now fully armed, going up to her and giving her his hand).
To Phthia,

Queen!

PENTHESILEA. No, Themiscyra, friend! I'll say
it for you once again, to Themiscyra,
where Diana's Temple juts up from
among the oaks. And even if Phthia
was the dwelling place of all the blessed,
still, oh still, my friend, to Themiscyra,
where Diana's Temple juts up high
among the treetops.

ACHILLES (lifting her up).
No, you must forgive
me, dearest girl. But I myself will build
you such a temple, so I will.

SCENE 18
Enter Meroe and Asteria, with the Amazon army.

MEROE. Cut him down!

ACHILLES (letting go the Queen and whirling around).
Do they ride the storm?

238

AMAZONS (*pushing in between Penthesilea and Achilles*).
    Free the Queen!
ACHILLES. In spite of this right arm you will!
        (*He tries to drag her off with him.*)
PENTHESILEA (*pulling him toward her*).
    Oh, you won't follow me? You won't?
        (*The Amazons stretch their bows.*)
ODYSSEUS. Run,
    you lunatic, run! It's no time now
    for getting obstinate.
        (*He drags Achilles off. Exeunt Greeks.*)

SCENE 19
Enter High Priestess of Diana and priestesses.

AMAZONS. We've won! We've won! We've won! The Queen is saved!
PENTHESILEA (*after a pause*).
    I curse your winning, it dishonors me!
    I curse each tongue exulting over it,
    the air that bears the noise of it abroad,
    I curse that too! By every law of chivalry
    wasn't I fairly his, thanks to the luck
    of battle? When men war, not with wolves and tigers,
    but one another, does martial custom ever
    countenance the setting free again,
    from the captor's bonds, the captive who
    surrendered in the field?—Oh son of Thetis!
AMAZONS. Gods almighty, are we hearing right?
MEROE. Come over here, High Priestess of Diana,
    please—
ASTERIA. Because we liberated her
    from shameful servitude, she's in a rage!
HIGH PRIESTESS (*detaching herself from the others and coming forward*).
    Well then, our Queen, with these outrageous words,
    I must confess, you've capped your deeds today
    in proper style. It's not enough you paid
    no heed to custom and went in search of your
    own man to fight; it's not enough, instead
    of making your opponent bite the dust,
    you did; it's not enough that his reward

for that should be your smothering him in roses;
no, on top of that you fly into
a passion and abuse your loyal people, those
who broke your chains, you turn away from us
and call your conqueror back. All right, you daughter
of great Tanaïs, I ask your pardon for the rash
way that we acted, a mistake, no more. I'm sorry
now for all the blood it cost us, for all
the prisoners we had to forfeit for your sake,
with all my heart I wish we had them back.
In the name of our people, I pronounce you free;
turn your feet whichever way you please,
go running, with your skirts aflutter, after
him who hung the chains on you and point
him out the breach we made in them, oh do!—
for your sacred rules of warfare, they demand it!
But as for us, you will allow it, Queen,
if we abandon the campaign and go our ways
back home to Themiscyra; we, at least,
we find it more than we can stomach to *beg*
those Greeks there, running hard to save their skins,
to stand and wait for us, to *plead* them down,
like you, into the dust before our feet
so as to crown them with our victory wreaths.
                              (*Pause.*)
PENTHESILEA (*swaying*).
  Prothoe!
PROTHOE. Sister heart!
PENTHESILEA.   Stand by me, please!
PROTHOE. Till death, you may be sure—but Mistress, you
  are trembling, why?
PENTHESILEA.   It's nothing, never mind.
  I'll pull myself together in a moment.
PROTHOE. You suffered a great sorrow. Bear it greatly.
PENTHESILEA. They're lost, are they?
PROTHOE.   My Queen?
PENTHESILEA.   That lovely lot
  of young men we brought down—and I'm to blame?
PROTHOE. Don't be upset. You'll make it up to us
  for them the next war.

PENTHESILEA (*her head against Prothoe's bosom*).
                    Never!
PROTHOE.   Queen?
PENTHESILEA.   No, never!
In everlasting darkness I'll go hide myself!

SCENE 20
Enter a Herald.

MEROE. A herald's here, my Queen!
ASTERIA.   And what's your wish?
PENTHESILEA (*with a quaver of joy*).
He's from Pelides!—What am I about to hear?
Prothoe, tell him, please, to go away!
PROTHOE. What message have you got for us?
HERALD.   Queen, I am sent
here by Achilles, the reed-crowned goddess
Thetis' son, to speak for him as follows:
Your longing is to carry him home captive
to your native slopes, his longing, on
the other hand, to carry you a captive
home to his: so he proposes that
the two of you shall meet upon the field
in mortal combat once again and let
the sword, the brazen tongue of fate, proclaim,
before the face of all the justice-dealing
gods, which one of you, the he or she,
according to the sacred verdict, deserves
to lick the dust up from before
the other's feet. Are you pleased to make such a trial?
PENTHESILEA (*paling for a second*).
May it take a bolt of lightning to untie your tongue
before you're able to start wagging it
again, damned speechifier! I am just
as pleased to hear a block of sandstone rumble
down from precipices fathoms high,
crashing into one wall then another,
an endless clatter. (*To Prothoe.*)
                    You will have to say
it over for me word for word.

PROTHOE (*trembling*).

> He's sent
> here by Achilles to call you out into the field.
> Refuse him right off and say no.

PENTHESILEA.   I can't
> do that.

PROTHOE. My Queen?

PENTHESILEA.   I'm challenged by the son
> of Peleus?

PROTHOE.   I'll tell him no, shall I,
> and send him back?

PENTHESILEA.   I'm challenged by the son
> of Peleus?

PROTHOE.   To battle, yes, my Sovereign,
> as I said.

PENTHESILEA. A man who knows I am
> too weak to match my strength with his, Prothoe,
> *he* calls me out into the field to fight?
> This heart of mine, it doesn't touch him till
> his sharp spear's torn a hole in it?
> Did all the things I whispered only strike
> his ear as pretty sounds, not sense?
> He has no thought now for the temple jutting up
> from among the treetops? Was the figure that my hand
> adorned with roses made of stone?

PROTHOE. Forget the unfeeling man.

PENTHESILEA (*fervently*).

> All right! Now I
> have got the strength I need to stand up
> to him: in the dust he'll find himself,
> though Lapiths, giants, all, come to his aid!

PROTHOE. Dear Queen—

MEROE.   But have you thought—?

PENTHESILEA (*interrupting them*).

> You'll have back *all*
> the prisoners again!

HERALD.   Then your will is—?

PENTHESILEA. To stand against him in the field. Before the face
> of all the gods—the Furies too, I call

them down as well—let him come out to meet me!
(*A peal of thunder.*)

HIGH PRIESTESS. Penthesilea, if you feel stung
by what I said, don't then make me suffer
further—

PENTHESILEA (*fighting back her tears*).
        Holy Mother, stop! Oh, you
will see, you didn't speak to me in vain!

MEROE. Reverend priest, use your authority
with her.

HIGH PRIESTESS. Queen, do you hear his anger?

PENTHESILEA.   Him
and all his thunder, I call them down on me!

FIRST COLONEL (*in alarm*).
    Princesses—!

SECOND COLONEL. It's impossible!

THIRD COLONEL.   We *can't*!

PENTHESILEA (*trembling with ferocity*).
    Come here, Ananke, with the dogs!

FIRST COLONEL.   Our troops
are scattered, down in strength—

SECOND COLONEL.   We're battle-weary!

PENTHESILEA. You, Tyrrhöe, with your elephants!

PROTHOE.   With dogs
and elephants you'll hunt him, Queen!

PENTHESILEA.   Come up,
you sickle-spinning chariots, and make
a harvest home of slaughtered Greeks, come on
in your grim files and reap the field! And you
who thresh this human crop so as to crush
it, stalk and seed, forever, my troops
of horse, here at my side in columns . . . form!
On all the horror-striking pomp of war,
the devastating, terrible, I call!
    (*Seizes the great bow from an Amazon. Enter Amazons with dog
      packs on the leash; later others with elephants, firebrands,
                scythed chariots, etc.*)

PROTHOE. Listen to me, my soul's love, please listen!

PENTHESILEA (*turning to the dogs*).
    Tigris, up, I need you now! Leaene,

up! And you, Melampus, shaggy-coated,
up! Up, Alke, you swift foxhound, Sphinx
up too! Alector, who can overhaul
the doe, Oxus, who pulls down the boar,
Hyrcaon, whom the lion never scares—
all up!

(*Great peals of thunder.*)

PROTHOE. She's gone out of her mind!

FIRST COLONEL. She's raving!

PENTHESILEA (*falls on her knees, showing every sign of madness, while the dogs set up a savage howling*).

O Mars the terrible, great founder of
my house, on you I call! Your brazen war
car, send it down, destroying god, to me,
here below to me where you beat down
the walls of towns and trample underfoot
the ranks of people wedged in streets—here
to me where I will mount inside, seize the reins,
race through the fields and out of storm clouds like
the thunderstone descend on that Greek's head!

(*Stands up.*)

FIRST COLONEL. Princesses!

SECOND COLONEL. Up, restrain her, she's gone mad!

PROTHOE. Oh listen, my great Queen, to me!

PENTHESILEA (*stretching the bow*).

What fun!

Can I still make my arrow hit the mark?

(*Aims at Prothoe.*)

PROTHOE (*diving to the ground*).

Good god!

A PRIESTESS (*darting behind the Queen*).

He's calling you, Achilles is!

SECOND PRIESTESS (*doing the same*).

He is!

THIRD PRIESTESS. Look there, behind you, look!

PENTHESILEA (*turning*).

Where?

FIRST PRIESTESS. I could swear I saw him.

PENTHESILEA. No, the Furies
haven't met together down here yet.
Ananke, follow me—you others too!

244

(*Exit Penthesilea with the troops, amid violent
thunder and lightning.*)

MEROE (*helping up Prothoe*).

How dreadful!

ASTERIA.　　　　After her, you women, fast!

HIGH PRIESTESS (*deathly pale*).

Deathless ones, what judgment have you passed on us?

(*Exeunt.*)

SCENE 21

Enter Achilles and Diomedes.

ACHILLES. Diomedes, listen, do—but not a word,
　I beg you as a favor, to that sour-faced
　old puritan Odysseus of what I am
　about to say to you—it makes me sick,
　I find it quite unbearable, I do,
　to see the way he clenches up his jaws.

DIOMEDES. You sent the herald to her, did you, really?

ACHILLES. I'll tell you, friend, but please, no comments from
　you, not a word, you understand?—This
　woman who's so wonderful, half Grace,
　half Fury, she's in *love* with me,
　and I, by Styx—by *all* of Hell—in spite
　of all the girls of Greece I love her too!

DIOMEDES. You do!

　　　　　Indeed I do. But a freakish notion
　that she's got, which for her is a religious
　thing, says I must fall to her sword fighting:
　not till then is she allowed to wind
　her arms around me as a lover. So
　I sent—

DIOMEDES. You're mad!

ACHILLES.　　　　The fellow doesn't listen!
　If he has not seen something with his own
　blue eyes, the thought of it, however long
　he lives, can never penetrate his skull.

DIOMEDES. You mean to say—? You really will—?

ACHILLES.　　　　　　　　　　　　　　Will

　I what, for Heaven's sake? What frightful thing
　is it that I'm about to do?

DIOMEDES.   Then you only
  called her out into the lists so as to—
ACHILLES. By cloud-shaking Cronos' son, there's
  nothing she will *do* to me, I tell you!
  Her arm would sooner launch a mad attack
  against her own self, her own bosom,
  hurrahing wildly when it saw the heart's-
  blood streaming from it, than strike me! I'll suit
  her wishes for a month, that's all, a month
  or two, no more—surely that won't cause
  your old peninsula the sea's been gnawing
  at since time began, to founder
  on the spot! Then I am free once more,
  she told me so herself, as free as a buck
  on the heath; and if she comes along with me
  and I can set her on my father's throne:
  by Jupiter, the bliss that will be mine!
                    (*Enter Odysseus.*)
DIOMEDES. Come here, Ulysses, please.
ODYSSEUS.   Achilles! You
  have sent the Queen a challenge to come out and fight!
  The troops are dropping with exhaustion—do
  you mean, man, still another time to venture
  what has been so many times a misadventure?
DIOMEDES. No, my friend, no ventures and no misadventures now.
  He's going to surrender to her, that is all.
ODYSSEUS. What!
ACHILLES (*his face turning a bright pink*).
                    Let me ask you not to shove
  your face in mine!
ODYSSEUS.   He's going to do what?
DIOMEDES. You heard me. Knock her helmet off; look fierce
  like a gladiator, rant and roar;
  thunder on her shield so that the sparks
  fly—then: dumbly fall down at her pretty
  feet acknowledging he's beaten.
ODYSSEUS.   Son
  of Peleus, is he in his right mind?
  Did you hear what he—?

ACHILLES (*holding himself in check*).
                              Let me beg you not
to clench your jaws like that, Ulysses. It
is catching, don't you know, and I start clenching
too—my fists!

ODYSSEUS (*furious*).
                         By Cocytus and its fiery waters,
I must know if I heard right or not!
Tydeus' son, I ask you to confirm by oath,
so I am absolutely clear about it,
if what I ask is so. He's going to surrender
to the Queen?

DIOMEDES.   That's right!

ODYSSEUS.   And go with her to Themiscyra?

DIOMEDES. Yes, that's so.

ODYSSEUS.   And our war for Helen
at Dardanusburg, the madman thinks he'll drop
it just like that, like a child a toy
because another bright thing's caught its eye?

DIOMEDES. By Lord Jupiter, I swear it's so.

ODYSSEUS (*folding his arms*).
    Unbelievable!

ACHILLES.   I heard him mention
the Dardanusburg.

ODYSSEUS.   What?

ACHILLES.   What?

ODYSSEUS.   I thought you spoke
to me.

ACHILLES. I?

ODYSSEUS. You.

ACHILLES.   I said: I heard you mention
the Dardanusburg.

ODYSSEUS.   Indeed I did!
Driven half-distracted, I asked if all
our fighting at Dardanusburg for Helen's
sake has been forgotten, like an early morning's
dream?

ACHILLES (*going up to him*).
          If Dardanusburg, Laertides,
sank from sight, in its place the waters,
blue-hued, of a lake; if in the night

247

moon-gray fishermen tied their skiffs up
to the weathercocks of Troy; if a pikefish ruled
in Priam's palace, rats or otters hugged
in Helen's bed—I'd care no more than I
do now.

ODYSSEUS. By the Styx's stream he's serious,
Tydides!

ACHILLES. By the Styx, by the Lernaean
bog, by Hades! By the world above, the world
below and any other place—I'm serious
indeed. I mean to see Diana's Temple!

ODYSSEUS (*in Diomedes' ear*).
Be a good fellow, Diomedes, please,
and don't allow him to depart from here.

DIOMEDES. Good fellow—yes, indeed! If you are good
enough to lend me your two arms, I will.
(*Enter the Herald.*)

ACHILLES. Oh, is she coming out to fight? Let's hear!

HERALD. Yes, she is coming out, Nerides, she is
on her way right now—but bringing dogs
and elephants and howling cavalry.
What they all have to do with single combat,
I don't know.

ACHILLES.   That's what they do, she had
to do it. Come!—Oh, she's a cunning one,
by the immortal gods! With dogs, you say?

HERALD. That's right.

ACHILLES.   And elephants.

HERALD.   So that you shake
to see them, Pelides! If she meant
to go against the two Atrides camped
in front of Fortress Troy, she could not come
in more menacing force.

ACHILLES (*to himself*).
                    I'll have them eating out
of my hand, I'm sure.—Now follow me!—They're all
tame creatures, really, like their Queen!
(*Exit with his men.*)

DIOMEDES.   He's mad!

ODYSSEUS. Grab hold of him and tie him up, you Greeks!

DIOMEDES. Here come the Amazons right now—men, run!
    (*Exeunt.*)

SCENE 22

Enter the High Priestess, white-faced, Priestesses, and Amazons.

HIGH PRIESTESS. Quick, some rope here, women!
FIRST PRIESTESS.   Reverence!
HIGH PRIESTESS. Knock her down and tie her up!
AN AMAZON.   You mean
 the Queen!
HIGH PRIESTESS. I mean that mad dog! Human
 hands can't hold her any more.
AMAZONS.   Holy
 Mother, you seem quite beside yourself!
HIGH PRIESTESS. The three girls detailed by us to restrain
 her, down into the dust she kicked them, in
 a rage; when Meroe fell down in her path,
 on her knees, and pleaded with her in the name
 of love and friendship, she loosed the dogs at her.
 When I took just one step toward
 her from the distance, the insane creature shot
 me such a baleful look, and stooping down
 without a moment's hesitation grubbed a rock
 out of the ground with both her hands—it would
 have been the end of me if I hadn't beat
 a quick retreat into the crowd.
FIRST PRIESTESS.   How terrible!
SECOND PRIESTESS. Oh dreadful!
HIGH PRIESTESS.   Now she's raving up and down
 among the howling dogs, foaming at
 the mouth and calling them her sisters,
 and like a Maenad dancing wildly through the fields,
 she brandishes the bow and urges on
 the murder-breathing pack around her knees
 to catch the finest beast, she claims, that ever
 coursed this earth.
THE AMAZONS.   Gods of Orcus, how
 you punish her!

HIGH PRIESTESS.   So lay a rope snare,
  Ares's daughters, where the paths cross, covered
  with some brush, to catch her when she comes.
  And when you've snared her foot, jerk her down
  as if you had a rabid dog to deal
  with; we'll truss her up and take her home and see
  if there's still any hope of saving her.
AMAZON ARMY (*offstage*).
  We've won! Hurrah! We've won! The Greek is down!
  The hero's hers! Now our victorious Queen
  will crown his head with roses!
                    (*Pause.*)
HIGH PRIESTESS (*her voice choked with joy*).
                    Am I hearing
    right?
PRIESTESSES AND AMAZONS. The gods be praised!
HIGH PRIESTESS.   It was a cry
  of joy and exultation, wasn't it?
FIRST PRIESTESS. The victory cry, and never did it strike
  my ear more blessedly!
HIGH PRIESTESS.   Who'll go and find
  out for me what has happened, girls?
SECOND PRIESTESS.   Quick, Terpi,
  up that hill and tell us what you see!
AN AMAZON (*having climbed the hill, aghast*).
  You horror-striking gods of Hell, come witness here
  for me—I can't believe my eyes!
HIGH PRIESTESS.   Good god,
  you'd think she's seeing the Medusa!
PRIESTESSES.   Speak up, will
  you, tell us what you see!
AMAZON.   Penthesilea—
  stretched out flank to flank with her ferocious
  brutes, a woman born out of a woman's womb
  and tearing—tearing limb from limb the young Achilles!
HIGH PRIESTESS. Horror, horror!
ALL.   Oh, what monstrousness!
AMAZON. Here comes Meroe, leaden colored as a corpse,
  to report this gruesome mystery to us.
                    (*Descends from the hilltop.*)

SCENE 23
Enter Meroe.

MEROE. Diana's holy priestesses, and you
  chaste daughters of the War God, listen to
  me, do! The Gorgon out of Africa I am,
  to turn you into granite where you stand.
HIGH PRIESTESS. Go on, you fearful messenger, and speak!
MEROE. You know how she went out to meet the young
  man that she loves, she whose name from now
  on's unpronounceable—in the confusion
  of her young girl's senses, arming her
  hot wish to have him with all war's frightful
  instruments. She pressed along amid
  her yelping dogs and elephants, the longbow
  in her hand—the ghastly shape of civil strife,
  when he comes striding on with giant steps
  of terror, trailing blood and whirling his
  red torch above the heads of thriving cities,
  doesn't look so hideous. Achilles
  who, our soldiers swear, had only called
  her out into the field so as to *let*
  her triumph over him in battle, the young
  fool—for he too on his side (the gods
  are great!), he loved her, his youth moved by hers,
  and wished to follow her to where she wished
  to lead him, to Diana's Temple—he,
  Achilles, marches out to meet her, full
  of blissful expectations, and leaves his comrades
  in the rear. But when he hears her bearing
  down on him so horridly, who's only
  brought a spear along (suspecting nothing)
  for appearance' sake, he stops dead in his tracks
  and turns his slender neck to listen, bolts
  away aghast, and stops, and bolts again:
  like a young deer high in a ravine whose ears
  pick up off in the distance the grim lion's roar.
  He cries "Odysseus!" so anxiously,
  looks timidly around and cries "Tydides!"

too, and turns to run back where his comrades
are; and stops, the line of his retreat
already cut, lifts up his hands dismayed
and ducks and looks for cover, the unlucky man,
beneath a pine tree's dark and drooping boughs.
Meanwhile the Queen comes up, her mastiffs at
her heels, spying far across the woods
and rises like a hunter; and when he puts
the boughs aside so as to fall down at
her feet, "Aha, his horns betray the stag!"
she shouts, and bends the bow back so the two
ends kiss, and raises it, and aims, and shoots,
and drives her arrow through his throat; he falls;
a hoarse hurrah goes up among our warrior
women. He is still alive, however,
the poor man, the arrow sticking far out
of his neck; he struggles up off the ground
with rattling breath, and topples over, and
gets up again, and tries his best to run;
but "Sick him, Tigris, sick him, Sphinx," she screams,
"Leana, Hyrcaon, Melampus, Dirke, sick him!"
and throws herself—with the whole pack, Diana!
throws herself on him and drags him, drags
him by his helmet crest—a she-dog flank
to flank with hes, one beast hanging
from his breast, another from his neck—crashing
down to earth so that it shakes! He,
weltering in the purple of his blood, touches
her soft cheek and cries, "Whatever
are you doing, Penthesilea,
my bride? Is this the Feast of Roses
that you promised me?" The hungry lioness
that ranges snow wastes howling for her prey
would have heard his cry. But *she*—she rips
away his body armor with a jerk
and sinks her teeth in his white breast, dogs
and woman struggling to outdo each other: Sphinx
and Oxus with their fangs in his right side,

hers in his left. When I came up, the blood
was dripping from her mouth and hands.
                    (*Horror-stricken pause.*)
Did you hear me, women? Say so, if you did,
and show you're still alive.

FIRST PRIESTESS (*weeping on the Second's breast*).
                              A girl so good,
so well behaved, Hermia, so clever with
her hands at making things! So charming
when she danced and sang! So full of dignity,
intelligence and grace!

HIGH PRIESTESS.   That's no child
Otrere ever bore! The Gorgon must
have hatched her in the palace!

FIRST PRIESTESS (*continuing*).
                              You thought
the nightingale that haunts Diana's Temple
bore her in her nest. The oak tree
rocked her in its top, she piped and sang
and sang and piped through the silent night
so that the traveler, arrested, felt,
far off, his heart swell with emotion. She
would never bring her heel down on the spotted
snake that writhed beneath her foot; no sooner
did she plant an arrow in the wild boar's
breast than she would wish it back again,
its dimming eye could draw her down upon
her knees before it, melting with remorse.
                    (*Pause.*)

MEROE. She's standing there beside his corpse now,
absolutely mute, a sight to shudder at,
the dog pack snuffling around her knees, the bow
cocked on her shoulder triumphantly—staring
off into infinity as if
it was an empty page. Our hair on end,
we ask her what she's done. Dead silence.
Did she know us? Silence. Would she like
to come along with us? Still silence. Horror
seized me and I ran straight here to you.

SCENE 24

*Enter Penthesilea, Prothoe, and others, with the body
of Achilles under a red carpet.*

FIRST AMAZON. Look, look, you women, here she comes—not laurel
   around her brow but nettles twisted up
   with withered hawthorn, following the grisly
   corpse and shouldering the bow exultantly,
   as if she's killed a deadly enemy!
SECOND PRIESTESS. Those hands, dear gods!
FIRST PRIESTESS.   Women, never look!
PROTHOE (*sinking on the High Priestess's breast*).
   Dear Mother!
HIGH PRIESTESS (*in horror*).
             Goddess, hear me: I am not
   to blame for this atrocity!
FIRST AMAZON.   She's stopping
   right in front of the High Priestess.
SECOND AMAZON.   Look,
   she's pointing!
HIGH PRIESTESS. Get away from me, you monster,
   get away, you creature out of Hell! Here, take
   this veil and hide her from our sight.
       (*Pulls off her veil and throws it in the Queen's face.*)
FIRST AMAZON.   A walking
   corpse, she doesn't blink an eye—
SECOND AMAZON.   She keeps
   on pointing—
THIRD AMAZON. Points again—
FIRST AMAZON.   She keeps on pointing
   down at the High Priestess' feet—
SECOND AMAZON.   Oh look!
HIGH PRIESTESS. What do you want from me? Away, I tell
   you! Join the ravens, specter! Go and rot!
   A look from you and all my serenity of life
   is struck dead.
FIRST AMAZON. See there, we've understood her—
SECOND AMAZON.   Now
   she's quiet.

FIRST AMAZON. What she wanted was for us
 to lay Pelides down before the Priestess
 of Diana's feet.
THIRD AMAZON.   Why just before
 the Priestess of Diana's feet?
FOURTH AMAZON.   What is
 she thinking of?
HIGH PRIESTESS.   What business has this *corpse*
 got here in front of me? Bury it under
 mountains, out of reach, and along with it
 all memory of your deed! You—you—I don't
 know what to call you, a member of the human race
 no longer—did *I* require this of you,
 this horror? If a tender reproach from the mouth
 of love can lead to such abominations,
 then let the Furies come to teach us
 gentleness.
FIRST AMAZON. She keeps staring at the Priestess.
SECOND AMAZON. Straight into her face.
THIRD AMAZON.   Without flinching,
 steadily, as if she meant to look
 right through her.
HIGH PRIESTESS.   Go, Prothoe, go, I beg
 you, I can't stand the sight of her, and take
 her off somewhere, away!
PROTHOE (*in tears*).
        What misery!
HIGH PRIESTESS. Some resolution, please!
PROTHOE.   The thing she did's
 too awful; no, I can't.
HIGH PRIESTESS.   Compose yourself.—
 The mother that she had, she was so lovely.—
 Go on, will you, offer her your help
 and lead her off.
PROTHOE.   I never want to lay
 my eyes on her again!
SECOND AMAZON.   Look how she's staring
 at the narrow-shafted arrow!
FIRST AMAZON.   How
 she turns it every way.

THIRD AMAZON. Studies it!

FIRST PRIESTESS. The arrow, isn't it, she killed him with?

FIRST AMAZON. Right, ladies, that's the one!

SECOND AMAZON. Look how she wipes
the blood off—doesn't miss a spot!

THIRD AMAZON. I wonder what she's thinking now?

SECOND AMAZON. The feathers,
too, the way she dries them, draws them out
into their curl! So nicely! Everything
just as it should be! Look!

THIRD AMAZON. Is that a thing
she always did?

FIRST AMAZON. Did herself?

FIRST PRIESTESS. Her bow
and arrows, she has always cared for them
with her own hands.

SECOND PRIESTESS. The bow's a holy
thing for her, no doubt of that!

SECOND AMAZON. She's slipped
the quiver off her shoulder and dropped the arrow
back into its place.

THIRD AMAZON. All done.

SECOND AMAZON. That's it.

FIRST PRIESTESS. And now she looks around her at the world again—!

SEVERAL WOMEN. A look of woe, dear gods, as desolate
as empty wastes without a blade of grass!
Gardens devastated by the lava spilling
from the burning bowels of the earth and spewed out
over all the flowers on its breast, look sweeter
than her face.

PENTHESILEA (*shudders violently and lets go of the bow*).

HIGH PRIESTESS. The dreadful girl!

PROTHOE (*frightened*).
Now what,
now what?

FIRST AMAZON. The bow, the bow, it's falling from her hand!

SECOND AMAZON. Look how it teeters—

FOURTH AMAZON. Sounds aloud, and sways,
and falls—!

SECOND AMAZON. And shudders one more time
  on the ground—
THIRD AMAZON.   And dies—even as it was born
  to Tanaïs.
(Pause.)
HIGH PRIESTESS (turning suddenly to Penthesilea).
      Great Sovereign, forgive
  me, do! Diana is content with you
  again, the anger of the goddess put
  to rest. The great founder of our women's state,
  Tanaïs, let me say it now, never
  drew the bow more worthily than you.
FIRST AMAZON. She doesn't speak—
SECOND AMAZON.   Her eyes are filling up—
THIRD AMAZON. She lifts a bloody finger—why? What does
  she mean to—look!
SECOND AMAZON.   A sight to rend the heart
  far worse than knives!
FIRST AMAZON.   She wipes a tear away.
HIGH PRIESTESS (falling back on Prothoe's bosom).
  Diana, such a tear!
FIRST PRIESTESS.   Such a tear
  that slips inside the human breast, sets all
  the fire bells of feeling ringing, cries
  Misery! so loud its fellows, quick to wake
  in every eye, rush out of doors and gathered
  to a sea, bewail the blackened ruins of her soul!
HIGH PRIESTESS (bitterly).
  Yes, yes—but if Prothoe refuses her
  her help, she'll die here in her misery,
  for sure.
PROTHOE (her face expressing the violent struggle going on inside her, going up
  to Penthesilea and speaking in a voice still convulsed by sobs).
      Won't you please sit down, my Queen?
  Rest awhile here on my faithful breast?
  You have fought so much on this dreadful day,
  suffered so much too—won't you find
  relief from so much suffering on
  my loyal breast?
(Penthesilea looks around as if to sit down.)

257

A seat here! See, she wants
one.
> (*Amazons roll a stone up; Prothoe eases Penthesilea down
> on it and then sits down herself.*)
Sister heart, you know me, don't you?
> (*Penthesilea looks at her and her face brightens a little.*)
I'm
Prothoe, the one who loves you so.
> (*Penthesilea caresses her cheek.*)
How much
you touch me, how my heart goes down upon
its knees to you!
> (*Kisses the Queen's hand.*)
You must be quite worn out,
I'm sure. How plain to see the kind of work
you do, love! Oh well—our victories
don't come so clean and every dyer's hand
tells what his trade is. All the same—what
do you say to washing up now, hands and face?
> (*Penthesilea looks down at herself and nods.*)
She'd like it, good.
> (*Signals the Amazons, who go for water.*)
You'll feel the better for
it, feel refreshed, and stretched out at your ease
on cool carpets, recruit the strength you've spent
today.

FIRST PRIESTESS. But take care when you sprinkle her
with water—she'll remember everything.

HIGH PRIESTESS. I hope she will indeed.

PROTHOE.   You do?—*I* fear
it.

HIGH PRIESTESS. Why? Why do you? (*Seeming to consider.*) But that's too
risky, surely,
for then Achilles' corpse would have to be—

PENTHESILEA (*shoots a blazing look at the High Priestess.*)

PROTHOE. Enough, enough!

HIGH PRIESTESS.   No, no, my Queen, it's nothing,
all shall stay just as it is.

PROTHOE.   That victory
  wreath of yours—of thorns!—come, take it off,
  we all know how you triumphed. Let me undo
  your collar too—that's better, isn't it?
  Look there! A cut, and deep enough! Poor soul,
  you really had hard work of it! That makes
  your triumph all the more!—O Artemis!
      (*Two Amazons bring a marble basin, broad and shallow, filled*
                     with water.)
  Set it down here, will you?—Shall I bathe
  your young head now? And it won't frighten you?
  What's that you're doing?
      (*Penthesilea slides down from her seat onto her knees in front*
        of the basin and pours water over her head.)
                  Look at her! And if
  that wasn't very bravely done, my Queen!
  Do you feel better now?
PENTHESILEA (*looks around.*)
               Oh Prothoe!
      (*Pours water over herself again.*)
MEROE (*elated*).
  She spoke!
HIGH PRIESTESS. Praise Heaven for it!
PROTHOE.   Fine, that's fine!
MEROE. She's back to life, and us!
PROTHOE.   Oh, wonderful!
  All the way under with your head, love! Right!
  And once again! That's right, that's right! Like a young
  swan!
MEROE. How lovely!
FIRST PRIESTESS.   How she stoops her head!
MEROE. And lets the water trickle down!
PROTHOE.   Enough,
  now?
PENTHESILEA. Oh, how wonderful!
PROTHOE.   Now we must set
  you back on the stone.—Quick, priestesses, your veils,
  so I can dry her streaming locks! Yours, Phania!
  Terpi, too! I need your help, my sisters!

We'll wrap her head and neck completely up!
Good, good!—And now up on the seat again!
> (*She wraps the Queen up and lifts her back on the seat, holding
> her in a tight embrace.*)

PENTHESILEA. How I feel!

PROTHOE.   Well, don't you?

PENTHESILEA (*murmuring*).

            Yes, pure bliss!

PROTHOE. My own heart's sister, my dear friend, my life!

PENTHESILEA. Oh, tell me—am I in Elysium?
And you one of those nymphs, forever young,
who serve our glorious Queen when she descends,
amid the oak grove's quiet whispering,
into her crystal grotto? Do you wear,
for my delight alone, just her features, dear
Prothoe's face!

PROTHOE.   Oh no, oh no, my Queen.
It's me, Prothoe, no one else, who holds
you in her arms, and what you see around
you here is still the world, the infirm world,
which the gods look down on only from far off.

PENTHESILEA. Oh well, But that's good too, that's fine.
It doesn't matter.

PROTHOE.   What, my Sovereign?

PENTHESILEA. I'm quite content.

PROTHOE.   If you'd explain—it's hard
to understand—

PENTHESILEA.   That I still am, contents
me. Now let me rest.

> (*Pause.*)

MEROE.   Surprising words!

HIGH PRIESTESS.   How wonderful
a change!

MEROE.   If we managed to elicit from her,
cleverly—?

PROTHOE.   What made you think you had gone down,
already, to the shadow realm?

PENTHESILEA (*after a pause, in a kind of rapture*).
                                        I feel
  such bliss, my sister! More than bliss! How ripe
  for death, Diana, do I feel! I've no
  idea what happened to me here, it's true,
  yet I could gladly die right now believing,
  as I do, I conquered him.
PROTHOE (*behind her hand to the High Priestess*).
                                        Remove
  the body instantly!
PENTHESILEA (*sitting up energetically*).
                                        Who is it that
  you're talking to, Prothoe?
PROTHOE (*as the bearers hesitate*).
                                        Move, will you?
PENTHESILEA. Great Diana, then it's true?
PROTHOE.   What's true,
  my love?—Crowd close together here!
          (*Motions to the priestesses to shield the corpse with their
                  own bodies as it is being lifted up.*)
PENTHESILEA (*covering her face with her hands, in delight.*)
                                        Sacred
  gods, I am not brave enough to turn
  and look!
PROTHOE.   What is it, Queen? What idea
  do you have?
PENTHESILEA (*turning to look*).
                  Oh love, you're joking with me.
PROTHOE. Never, by immortal Zeus!
PENTHESILEA (*becoming impatient*).
                                        Holy ladies,
  step aside, please!
HIGH PRIESTESS (*crowding close to the others*).
                  Dear, dear Queen!
PENTHESILEA (*jumping up*).
                                Why shouldn't
  I, by Artemis? It's not the first
  time that he's hid behind my back!

MEROE. Look, look,
the dread that's stealing over her!
PENTHESILEA (*to the Amazons carrying the body.*)
Stop
right there! What's that you've got? I want
to know. Now stop!
(*Pushes through the women and discovers the corpse.*)
PROTHOE. My Queen, I beg you, don't
look further, don't!
PENTHESILEA. That's him there, women, is
it him?
ONE OF THE BEARERS (*as the corpse is set down*).
That's who?
PENTHESILEA. It's not impossible,
I know it very well: to hit
a swallow on the wing and then to make
that wing whole, it is nothing for
me, really, or coax the stag with arrows to the park.
But the bowman's skill—don't you rely on it!
For when it is a case of getting off
a master shot plump into the heart
of happiness, the spiteful gods direct
our hand. Did I hit too close? Speak, is
it him?
PROTHOE. By all Olympus' grim gods,
don't ask me that—
PENTHESILEA. Out of my way! Even
if his wound gapes open at me like
the jaws of Hell, I'll look at him!
(*Lifts the carpet.*)
Who did
this, tell me—*monsters!*
PROTHOE. Must *you* ask that?
PENTHESILEA. Sacred Artemis, your daughter's done
for, finished, now!
HIGH PRIESTESS. She's falling!
PROTHOE. By the deathless
gods, you women should have followed my
advice! Unlucky girl, how much better
off you would have been, stumbling around

in darkness with a mind eclipsed eternally,
than wake to see this dreadful day again!
—Hear me, dearest, do!
HIGH PRIESTESS.   Our Queen!
MEROE.   Ten thousand
   hearts are ready to divide your pain!
HIGH PRIESTESS.   You must
   get up!
PENTHESILEA (*raising herself part way*).
        What bloody roses these are! What
   a wreath of wounds around his head! And smell
   these buds which, scattering around their fresh
   scent of the grave, make a feast at last—
   for worms.
PROTHOE (*softly*).
        And yet in spite of all—Love twined
   these wreaths around him, didn't he?
MEROE.   Twined
   them around too tight!
PROTHOE.   With all their thorns unstripped,
   in his rush to bind him for eternity!
HIGH PRIESTESS.   Don't stand
   there, go away!
PENTHESILEA.   But there is one thing I must know:
   who was it took my place, sacrilegiously,
   and paramoured with him? I don't want to know
   who slew the living man; she's free as birds
   to go which way she wants. Who killed the man
   already killed, is what I ask—now tell
   me who it was.
PROTHOE.   What, my Sovereign?
PENTHESILEA. Please understand me. I don't want to know
   who stole the Promethean spark out of his breast.
   I don't because I don't. For so I feel:
   she is forgiven, let her go. But the thief
   who wickedly slunk past the open gate
   so as to smash her way through snowwhite
   alabaster walls into the temple; who
   mangled the young man who was the very image
   of the gods, so horribly, that life and rot

263

will not dispute possession of him; who
hewed and hacked him so that pity has
no tears for him, and love, undying love,
like a whore must turn away now he
is dead—I'll be revenged on her! Now speak!

PROTHOE (*to the High Priestess*).
    What I am to tell the poor distracted creature?

PENTHESILEA. I am waiting for your answer.

MEROE.   Our Queen,
    if it helps to ease the pain you feel, then choose
    whichever one of us you please to be
    revenged on. All of us stand ready here,
    offering ourselves.

PENTHESILEA.   Watch out—or next
    I'll hear you say I was the one.

HIGH PRIESTESS (*muttering*).
                          Who else,
    poor wretch, but you—?

PENTHESILEA.   Damned princess of the dark not light,
    how dare you—?

HIGH PRIESTESS.   Bright Diana, be my witness!
    All our people gathered around you here
    will back up what I say! Your arrow was
    the one that struck him down—and would to god
    that it had been no more than that, your arrow!
    But as he fell you threw yourself on him,
    you and all your dogs, in the confusion
    of your maddened senses sank—but my lips, for trembling,
    can't shape the words to say it. Never ask me!
    Come, let's go.

PENTHESILEA.   First I must hear what happened
    from Prothoe.

PROTHOE.   Please don't ask me that,
    my Queen!

PENTHESILEA. You mean that I—? You claim I—him—
    My dogs and I together—? You say hands as small
    as these—? And a mouth like this, with love-swelled
    lips—? Shaped for such a different service
    than to—! Helping each other to go at

it, avidly, the mouth and then the hand,
the hand and then the mouth—?
PROTHOE.   Oh Queen!
HIGH PRIESTESS.   Alas
for you!
PENTHESILEA. No, hear me, I will never be
persuaded by you, no! If it was spelled
in lightning on the night and the thunder told
me it, still I would tell it back: you lie!
MEROE. This faith that she's so stubborn in upholding,
let her, do, it isn't we will try
to shake her in it, ever.
PENTHESILEA.   Then how was it
that he did nothing to defend himself?
HIGH PRIESTESS. He *loved* you, poor unhappy wretch! He wanted
you to take him prisoner, and that
was why he came to meet you, why he challenged
you! With a heart that overflowed with peace
and sweetness he came on, so as to follow
you to Artemis's shrine. But you—
PENTHESILEA. But I—
HIGH PRIESTESS.   You shot him—
PENTHESILEA [*tonelessly*].
                              Tore his flesh to shreds.
PROTHOE.   Poor Queen!
PENTHESILEA. Or did it happen otherwise?
MEROE.   Horrors!
PENTHESILEA. *Kissed* him dead, did I?
FIRST PRIESTESS.   Good heavens!
PENTHESILEA.   Didn't
kiss him, no? Really tore his flesh
to shreds? Please say!
HIGH PRIESTESS.   Alas, alas, for you!
Hide yourself away! Be swallowed up
in everlasting night!
PENTHESILEA.   —An error, then,
I see. A kiss, a bite—how cheek by jowl
they are, and when you love straight from the heart
the greedy mouth so easily mistakes
one for the other.

MEROE.   Gods eternal, help
  her!
PROTHOE (*seizing hold of her*).
  Come away!
PENTHESILEA.   No, stop!
    (*Wrenches herself free and kneels before the corpse.*)
                          Unhappiest
  of men, forgive me, please! It was a slip—
  I swear it, by Diana—of the tongue, no more,
  because I am remiss and fail to stand
  guard over my rash mouth the way
  I should. But now I say it to you as
  I meant it, unmistakably.
                     (*Kisses him.*)
                               Just so,
  beloved, that and nothing more.
HIGH PRIESTESS.   Remove
  her now, will you!
MEROE.   Why should she stay here any
  longer?
PENTHESILEA. Think how often it's the case,
  with her arms wound around her darling's neck, a woman
  says she loves him, oh, so much she's ready
  to *devour* him for love. But then when it
  comes down to it, the poor fool finds
  she's had a bellyful of him already.
  Well, my darling, that was not my way.
  You see: when I wound *my* arms around your neck
  I did exactly that, devour you.
  I wasn't such a mad one as might seem.
MEROE. Did you hear that? Oh, she's a monster!
HIGH PRIESTESS. Seize her, take her off!
PROTHOE.   Queen, come along!
PENTHESILEA (*letting herself be lifted up*).
  All right, all right, I'm ready.
HIGH PRIESTESS.   You agree
  to come along with us?
PENTHESILEA.   With you—oh no!—
  Go back to Themiscyra and be happy,
  if you can—

and you especially, dear Prothoe—
all of you—
And—something I will whisper to you privately,
the others must not hear: the ashes of
Queen Tanaïs, scatter them
to the winds!

PROTHOE.   And you, dear sister heart?

PENTHESILEA. And I?

PROTHOE.   Yes, you!

PENTHESILEA.   I'll tell you, then. I
abjure the law of our women, I
will follow the young man who's lying here.

PROTHOE. What's that, my Queen!

HIGH PRIESTESS.   Oh poor thing, poor thing!

PROTHOE. You mean—?

HIGH PRIESTESS.   Intend—?

PENTHESILEA.   What? Yes, I do,
oh yes!

MEROE.   Good heavens!

PROTHOE.   One thing, sister, only
let me say—(*Reaches for Penthesilea's dagger.*)

PENTHESILEA.   Very well, what is it?—You
are fumbling at my belt, whatever for?—
Oh, I see. Then just a minute, please. I didn't
understand.—Here, take the dagger.
          (*Pulls the dagger from her belt and gives it to Prothoe.*)
                    Do
you want the arrows too? (*Unslings her quiver.*)
                    I'll empty
the whole quiver for you—there!
          (*Dumps the arrows on the ground.*)
                    In one
way, though, it's tempting—
          (*Picks up several arrows.*)
                    For it was
this one, wasn't it—or not? Or this one here—?
Yes, this one, right!—What difference does it make!
Here, take them, they are yours, take all of them!
     (*Sweeps them all together in a bundle and hands them to Prothoe.*)

PROTHOE. Give them here.

PENTHESILEA.   For now I will descend
   into myself, as if into a mine,
   to dig a killing feeling out as cold
   as iron ore. This ore, I will refine it, in the burning
   fire of my misery, into hard
   steel; then in the hot corrosive poison
   of remorse, steep it through and through; to hope's
   eternal anvil next I'll carry it,
   to hone and point it dagger sharp; and to
   this dagger now I offer up my breast:
   like so! and so! and so! And once
   again!—And now all's well.
                         (*Topples and dies.*)
PROTHOE (*catching the Queen*).
                              She's dead!
MEROE.   She's followed
   him in fact!
PROTHOE.   And better so. For there
   was no more going on here for her any
   more.
                    (*Lays her on the ground.*)
HIGH PRIESTESS. Oh how infirm man is, you gods!
   The snapped and broken blossom lying here,
   how mightly she thundered, high upon
   the peaks of life, a little while ago!
PROTHOE. She fell because she bloomed too proud and strong!
   The dead oak stands, defying wind and weather,
   the gale pulls down the good wood with a crash,
   for with his fingers he can fasten in its crown.

Prince Frederick of Homburg
A Play

Cast of Characters

Frederick William, Elector of Brandenburg
The Electress
Princess Natalie of Orange, his niece, Commander of a Regiment of
   Dragoons
Field Marshal Dörfling
Prince Frederick Arthur of Homburg, General of the Cavalry
Colonel Kottwitz, of the Princess of Orange Regiment
Hennings ⎫
Truchss ⎬ Colonels of the Infantry
Count Hohenzollern, of the Elector's Suite
Golz ⎫
Count George von Sparren ⎪
Stranz ⎬ Captains of the Cavalry
Siegfried von Mörner ⎪
Count Reuss ⎭
A Sergeant-Major
Officers, Corporals, and Cavalrymen; Gentlemen and Ladies of the
Court; Pages, Footmen, Servants; Men and Women of all ages

[Time: June 9–12, 1675]

ACT I

Fehrbellin: a Garden in the Old French Style.
In the background a castle, with a ramp leading down from it.
It is night.

SCENE I

The Prince of Homburg, bareheaded and with his shirt open at the
throat, nodding half asleep, is seated underneath an oak tree twining a
wreath. The Elector, his wife, Princess Natalie, the Count of
Hohenzollern, Captain Golz, and others tiptoe silently out of the
castle and look down at him over the balustrade of the ramp.
Pages with torches.

THE COUNT OF HOHENZOLLERN. The Prince of Homburg, our gallant
    cousin,
  who's led the cavalry in a hot chase
  of the flying Swedes for three whole days and only
  now is back again, quite out of breath,
  here in headquarters at Fehrbellin—your orders were
  for him to pause no longer than three hours'
  time to feed his men and mounts and then
  immediately push on again to Hackelberg
  against Count Wrangel, who's been digging in
  as fast as he is able at the Rhyn?[1]
ELECTOR.   Just so!
HOHENZOLLERN. His squadron captains having all been duly
  ordered to ride out of town upon the stroke
  of ten tonight, as is the plan, down
  he throws himself on the straw, exhausted,
  panting like a hunting dog, to rest
  his weary limbs a little before the battle
  we must fight at dawn.
ELECTOR.   I know—so I've
  been told. And now?
HOHENZOLLERN.   And now the hour has struck,
  the cavalry mounted up and trampling
  the field outside the gate, who should it be

---

1. Not, of course, the Rhine, but a tributary of the Havel.

that's missing? The Prince no less, their own commanding
officer! With torches, lanterns, candles
the hero's sought—and found where do you think?
           (*Takes a torch out of the hands of a Page.*)
Look there, on that bench, our sonambulist,
where the moonlight drew him (though you won't believe
me) in his sleep—lost in dreams, he acts
posterity's part and himself weaves the glorious
crown of fame to set on his own head.

ELECTOR. Oh no!

HOHENZOLLERN. It's true! Look down in that direction;
  there he sits!
           (*Shines the torch down on him from the ramp.*)

ELECTOR.   He's fast asleep? But that's
  impossible!

HOHENZOLLERN. He's fast asleep! Call out
  his name to him and over he will go, you'll see.
                (*Pause.*)

ELECTOR. The young man's ill, I'm quite convinced.

PRINCESS NATALIE. He needs a doctor—!

ELECTRESS.   We should help him, so
  it seems to me, not spend our time in making
  fun of him!

HOHENZOLLERN (*handing back the torch*).
         How kind you ladies are,
  but he is in good health, by God
  my own's no better! And in the morning when
  we meet the Swede upon the field, *he*
  will learn how good! Oh, you may take my word
  for it, it's nothing more than a fit of mere
  distractedness.

ELECTOR.   Well, I must say, I thought
  it something you invented! Follow me,
  my friends, we will study him a little closer
  up.
              (*They descend the ramp.*)

A GENTLEMAN (*to the Pages*).
        Stand back there with the lights!

HOHENZOLLERN.   No, let them, friend,
  it doesn't matter! All the village could

go up in flames and he would pay it no
more mind than the diamond on his finger does.
> (*They form a circle around him, lit by the Pages' torches.*)

ELECTOR (*stooping toward him*).
What's that he's making there—a willow wreath?

HOHENZOLLERN. Willow wreath indeed, my Lord! A laurel
wreath is what it is, just like the ones
he's seen on the brows of heroes' portraits
hanging in the Berlin Arsenal.

ELECTOR.   And pray
tell me where he found laurel growing in my sandy
Brandenburger soil?

HOHENZOLLERN.   God only knows!

GENTLEMAN.   Perhaps
among the gardens in the back, where the gardener grows
all sorts of foreign plants.

ELECTOR.   Good heavens, but
it's strange! And yet I'll give you odds I know
what's causing all the agitation in this young fool's
breast.

HOHENZOLLERN. I'm sure you do! Tomorrow's battle,
Sir! Already in his mind, I'll bet,
he sees astronomers weaving suns into
a victor's crown for him.[2]
> (*The Prince holds up the wreath to look at it.*)

GENTLEMAN.   Now see,
he's finished it!

HOHENZOLLERN.   Oh, what a pity there's
no mirror here! For then he'd run to stand
in front of it and try the wreath on
this way then another, as vain as any
girl with her new bonnet.

ELECTOR.   Really—I
must see how far gone the fellow
is!
> (*He takes the wreath out of the Prince's hand, who blushes
> and looks up at him. The Elector winds his neck chain around
> the wreath and gives it to the Princess; the Prince jumps up.*)

---

2. I.e., by naming constellations after him.

The Elector and the Princess, who holds the wreath aloft, step
backward; the Prince follows after her with outstretched arms.)

HOMBURG. Natalie! Dear girl! My bride!

ELECTOR. Quick, vanish out of sight!

HOHENZOLLERN.   Whatever did
he say, the fool?

GENTLEMAN.   What's that he said?

> (*All retreat up the ramp.*)

HOMBURG.   Prince Frederick!
My own father!

HOHENZOLLERN.   What the hell!

ELECTOR (*backing away*).
                      For God's
sake, open up that door!

HOMBURG.   Oh, mother dear!

HOHENZOLLERN. He's raving! He's—

ELECTRESS.   Whom did he mean by that?

HOMBURG (*snatching at the wreath*).
My darling! Don't, please, run away from me!
Oh Natalie! (*Captures one of the Princess's gloves.*)

HOHENZOLLERN. Good heavens, what was that
he got?

GENTLEMAN. The wreath?

NATALIE.   No, no!

HOHENZOLLERN (*pushing open the door*).
                      In here, my Lord,
at once! So that it's all a blank again
for him!

ELECTOR.   Back into nullity and namelessness,
Sir Prince of Homburg, back! It's on the field
of battle, if you please, we'll see each other
next! Such things are never won in dreams!

> (*Exeunt all. The door slams shut in the Prince's face. A pause.*)

SCENE 2

The Prince stands amazed for a moment in front of the door; then,
wondering, descends the ramp, the hand holding the glove pressed
to his forehead; turns, when he reaches the bottom, to stare back
up at the door.

SCENE 3

*Enter the Count of Hohenzollern through a garden gate below,
followed by a Page.*

PAGE (*whispering*).
Sir Count, one moment, if you would!
HOHENZOLLERN (*impatiently*).
                              Sh-h-h, cricket,
please!—All right, what is it?
PAGE.   I am sent—
HOHENZOLLERN. Oh, you will wake him with your chirping—please!
PAGE. The Elector sent me here. You must not, when
    the Prince awakes, breathe a word to him
    about the little joke the Elector allowed
    himself to play on him just now.
HOHENZOLLERN. (*whispering*).
                              I mustn't,
    mustn't I? Well, curl up in the wheatfield
    and have yourself a nap. It didn't need
    a messenger to teach me that. Now jump!
                    (*Exit the Page.*)

SCENE 4

*Hohenzollern stands a short distance behind the Prince, who is
still looking up along the ramp.*

HOHENZOLLERN. Arthur!
                    (*The Prince collapses.*)
                    And down he goes! A bullet wouldn't
    have done a better job. (*Goes up to him.*)
                    But what I am
    most curious to hear from him is the story
    he'll make up to explain his lying down
    and dozing off in this place here.
                    (*Stoops over him.*)
    Now Arthur, hear me! What's possessed you? I
    would like to know what you are doing, here
    in this place, in the middle of the night?
HOMBURG. Goodness me, old fellow!

HOHENZOLLERN. Really, I must say!
You are our cavalry's commanding officer,
yet they are already an hour's march
before you—while you lie stretched out
in the garden fast asleep.
HOMBURG. What cavalry?
HOHENZOLLERN. The Sultan's Mamelukes!—As I live
and breathe, he's quite forgotten he is Colonel-
in-Chief of the cavalry of Brandenburg!
HOMBURG (*leaping up*).
My helmet, quick! And armor, too!
HOHENZOLLERN. Indeed,
indeed! And where might they be, please, I wonder?
HOMBURG. On your right, Heinz, on the stool.
HOHENZOLLERN. On
the stool—what stool?
HOMBURG. I laid them down there, I
am sure I did—!
HOHENZOLLERN (*looking hard at him*).
Then go and get them from
that stool yourself!
HOMBURG (*looking at the glove in his hand*).
What glove is this I've got?
HOHENZOLLERN. I've not the least idea. (*Aside.*) Oh damn! He must
have pulled it off the Princess's arm up there
and no one saw! (*Peremptorily.*) Come on now, jump! Why are
you standing here? Prince, move!
HOMBURG (*throwing the glove away*).
Yes, right away!
Hey, Franz! The rascal was supposed to wake me up!
HOHENZOLLERN (*watching him*).
He's raving mad!
HOMBURG. Dear Heinrich, let me swear
to you I've no conception where I am.
HOHENZOLLERN. In Fehrbellin, poor mixed-up dreaming fellow,
in one of the allées that winds along the garden
at the castle's back!
HOMBURG (*aside*).
Oh, how I wish the night
would swallow me from sight! I've done

276

it once again—gone stumbling around in moonlight
in my sleep! (*Recovering himself.*)
     Forgive me, do! I recollect
it now. It was so hot last night I found
it almost unendurable in bed,
so crept, half dropping with fatigue, outdoors
into the garden—and because the evening
wound me in its arms with smiling tenderness,
its bright blond tresses dripping with perfume,
oh, like the Persian to his bride I laid myself
in her lap here.—What time is it?
HOHENZOLLERN.   Half past
eleven.
HOMBURG. All the squadrons have moved out,
have they?
HOHENZOLLERN. Of course! At ten—as planned.
The Princess of Orange Regiment, riding
in the lead, has reached the heights of Hackelberg
already, I am sure, where the cavalry's mission
is to screen the army's silent march-up
in the morning to face Count Wrangel.
HOMBURG.   It doesn't matter,
really! Old Kottwitz is in charge;
he understands the maneuver's purpose perfectly.
And anyhow I should have had to come
back here at two this morning, all the way,
to learn the battle order; much better I
stayed put. And now let's go! The Elector's ignorant
of this?
HOHENZOLLERN. Oh, I should think! Long since
tucked up and fast asleep.
 (*They start to go; the Prince stops short, turns, and picks up the glove.*)
HOMBURG.   Oh what a strange
dream I have dreamt. It seemed
the castle of a Prince, glowing with gold and silver,
sprang open to me suddenly, and down its marble
ramp from high above all those who are
most dear to me descended: the Elector, our Princess
his good wife, and—there was still a third. . . .
Now what the devil was her name?

HOHENZOLLERN.   Whose name?

HOMBURG (*trying to remember*).

That one—the one I mean! A deafmute would be able
to pronounce her name for you!

HOHENZOLLERN.   The Lady Platen?

HOMBURG. Good God, no!

HOHENZOLLERN.   Do you mean Dame
Ramin?

HOMBURG. No, never, Heinrich!

HOHENZOLLERN.   Bork?

Or Winterfeld?

HOMBURG.   Oh no, oh no, for pity's
sake! You see the setting, miss the pearl
that it sets off.

HOHENZOLLERN. Well, damn it, who? How can
I guess it? Tell me who you mean?

HOMBURG.   Oh, never
mind! It doesn't matter in the least! Since I
awoke, the name has gone completely out of my head—
but you don't need to know it for what I am
about to tell you now.

HOHENZOLLERN.   Fine—good. Go on,
then!

HOMBURG. Yes—but you mustn't interrupt me any
more!—And the Elector, lofty-browed as Zeus,
bore in his hand a crown of laurel: standing
face to face with me, he wound the chain
he wears around his neck around the wreath,
so that my soul leapt up in flames, and handed
it, so she might place it on my brow,
to—Heinrich, oh!

HOHENZOLLERN.   To whom?

HOMBURG.   Oh Heinrich!

HOHENZOLLERN.   Tell me who!

HOMBURG. I'm sure it was the Lady Platen.

HOHENZOLLERN.   Lady
Platen who is off in Prussia now?

HOMBURG. Lady Platen. I'm quite sure. Or maybe
Dame Ramin.

HOHENZOLLERN. Oh, Dame Ramin was it?
With that red hair of hers! Or Lady Platen
with those impish violet eyes! We know how much
you like her.

HOMBURG.   Like her, yes.

HOHENZOLLERN.   So she, you say,
presented you the wreath?

HOMBURG.   Aloft, just like
the spirit of Glory, she lifted up the wreath,
the neck chain dangling from it, as if
her purpose was to set a crown
on a hero's head. My hands reach out—
with inexpressible emotion, I
reach out to accept the crown: my whole desire
is to sink down at her feet.
But like the haze that hovers in the valleys, which the wind,
arising, blows away with its fresh
breath, up the ramp the figures seem
to fly. Endlessly, right up to Heaven's
door, the ramp, when I step on it, seems
to reach, and right and left I blunder
anxiously with outstretched arms to try
and catch the one, of all those dear, most
dear. In vain! The castle door springs open,
lightning flashes out from deep within
and swallows her, the door swings to again
with a loud crash. In my pursuit, a glove
is all that I am able, with a pull, to strip
off the dear dream-figure's arm. And a glove,
almighty gods, when I awake, is what
I find I have here in my hand!

HOHENZOLLERN.   Well, I'll
be damned!—And now your thought is that the glove
is hers?

HOMBURG. Is whose?

HOHENZOLLERN.   Why, Lady Platen's!

HOMBURG.   Lady
Platen's, yes. Or Dame Ramin's.

HOHENZOLLERN (*laughing*).

Oh, what
a rascal, I must say, you are, you
and all your visions! Tell me, do,
what assignation you had here with flesh
and blood, not dreaming in the least but wide awake,
whose souvenir still sticks there in your hand!

HOMBURG. An assignation, me! By my dear love—!

HOHENZOLLERN. What the devil! Why should I care who
it was, the Lady Platen or maybe Dame
Ramin. On Sunday there's a post that goes
to Prussia, that's your quickest way for finding
out if your dear love is looking for a glove.
—Enough! It's twelve. Why are we chattering here?

HOMBURG (*staring dreamily in front of him*).
You're right. Let's go to bed. But Heinrich, what
I'd like to ask you is, the Electress and her niece,
the charming Princess Natalie, who arrived
in camp just recently: Are they still here?

HOHENZOLLERN [*sharply*].
What's that to you?—I wonder if the fool—?

HOMBURG. What's that to me? I was supposed to send
a troop of thirty men to escort them from
the fighting zone. So I had to detail Ramin
for the job.

HOHENZOLLERN. Oh please! They're long since gone!
Gone or just about to go! Ramin
was standing ready at the gate the entire evening,
if not longer. Come along! The clock's
struck twelve; I'd like to get a little rest
before the battle starts.

(*Exeunt.*)

SCENE 5

*The Castle Hall. [2 a.m.] In the distance, the sound of firing.
Enter the Electress and Princess Natalie, in traveling dress,
with Ladies-in-waiting, conducted by a Gentleman of the Court;
the two seat themselves at the side. Then the Elector, Field
Marshal Dörfling, the Prince of Homburg with a glove tucked in
his doublet, the Count of Hohenzollern, Count Truchss, Colonel*

*Hennings, Captain von der Golz and other Generals, Colonels and
Officers all enter.*

ELECTOR. Who is that firing? Götz?

FIELD MARSHAL DÖRFLING. That's Colonel Götz,
Your Lordship, yes, who departed with the vanguard yesterday—
he's dispatched an officer to us already
to let you know there's no cause for alarm.
The Swedes have pushed a thousand man as far
as the Hackelberg. But Colonel Götz says he
will have those heights for you—he promises.
You may proceed, he says, as if his vanguard's
taken them already.

ELECTOR (*to Officers*). Gentlemen,
the Marshal knows the plan of battle—be
so good as to take your pencils out and note
it down.
(*Officers gather around the Field Marshal on the opposite side
from the Elector and take their tablets out. The Elector turns
to speak to the Gentleman.*)
Ramin has brought the coach up, has
he?

GENTLEMAN. In a moment, Sire. They're harnessing
the horses now.

ELECTOR (*sitting down in a chair behind the Electress and Princess Natalie.*)
Ramin will be your escort,
Elisa dear, with thirty strapping troopers
at his back. You go to Chancellor Kalkhuhn's
castle that's near Havelberg, across
the river, where you needn't fear to see
a single Swede.

ELECTRESS. And the ferry's running, is it?

ELECTOR. At Havelberg? Oh yes, we've taken care
of everything. And anyhow it will be day
before you come to it. (*Pause.*) Dear Natalie,
how still you are! Whatever is the matter, my
sweet child?

NATALIE. I'm apprehensive, uncle dear.

ELECTOR. And yet my little daughter is as safe as she
  can be, as safe as when her mother held
  her in her arms.
  (*A moment of silence.*)
ELECTRESS. And when do you suppose we'll see
  each other again?
ELECTOR. When God gives me
  the victory, as I don't doubt he will—
  perhaps this very day.
  (*Pages appear and serve the Ladies breakfast. Meanwhile Field
    Marshal Dörfling is dictating to the Officers. The Prince of
  Homburg, holding pencil and tablet, stares sideways at the women.*)
FIELD MARSHAL. Now, gentlemen,
  His Majesty's plan of battle has for its objective
  to smash the fleeing Swedes completely to bits
  and cut them off from the bridgehead on the Rhyn by which
  their rear is presently secured. Colonel Hennings—
HENNINGS. Sir!—(*Begins to write.*)
FIELD MARSHAL. —who commands the army's right, as is
  His Lordship's wish, by stealthily advancing
  through the Hackelbüsche marshes, will seek
  to turn the enemy's left flank and boldly
  interpose his troops between it and the three
  bridges; then joining forces with Count Truchss—
  Count Truchss!—
TRUCHSS. Yes, sir! (*Begins to write.*)
FIELD MARSHAL. —then joining forces with Count Truchss
    (*pauses*),
  who's meanwhile placed his cannon in position on the heights—
TRUCHSS. —"*his cannon in position on the heights*"—
FIELD MARSHAL. You've got that down?
  (*Continues*)—will seek to drive the Swedes into the swamp that lies
  behind their right.
  (*Enter a footman.*)
FOOTMAN. The coach is here, my Lady.
  (*The Ladies rise.*)
FIELD MARSHAL. The Prince of Homburg—
ELECTOR (*also getting up*).
  Captain Ramin is ready?

FOOTMAN. In the saddle and waiting at the gate.
(*His Highness and their Ladyships make their adieux.*)
TRUCHSS (*writing*). —"that lies
behind their right."
FIELD MARSHAL. The Prince of Homburg—where's
the Prince of Homburg?
HOHENZOLLERN (*in a furtive whisper*).
Arthur!
HOMBURG (*starting*).
Sir!
HOHENZOLLERN. Stop dreaming,
man!
HOMBURG. What are the Marshal's orders?
(*Blushing, he looks down at his tablet with the pencil poised
in his hand.*)
FIELD MARSHAL. Just as he did at Rathenow, His Lordship
gives the glorious command of all the horse
of Brandenburg to the Prince of Homburg—(*pauses*)
—this, however, without the least reflection
on Colonel Kottwitz, who's expected to assist
him with his counsel—(*In an undertone to Captain Golz.*)
Isn't Kottwitz here?
GOLZ. No, General, he sent me in his place, as you
can see, to learn what our orders are.
(*Again the Prince steals a glance toward the Ladies.*)
FIELD MARSHAL (*continuing*).
—to the Prince of Homburg, who is ordered to take up
a position on the level ground close by the tiny
hamlet of Hackelwitz, opposite
the enemy's right wing, but out of range
of cannon shot.
GOLZ (*writing*). —"out of range of cannon shot."
(*The Electress ties a scarf around the Princess's neck. The Princess,
about to put her gloves on, looks about her as if missing something.*)
ELECTOR (*going over to her*).
What's wrong, my little girl?
ELECTRESS. Is there something you
have lost?
NATALIE. I don't know, Aunt, my glove—
(*They all look around them.*)

283

ELECTOR (*to the Ladies-in-waiting*).

                                                  Good ladies,

  if I might prevail on you to lend
  us your assistance?

ELECTRESS (*to the Princess*).

                           There it is, child, in

  your hand.

NATALIE.   The right one, yes—but not the left.

ELECTOR. Perhaps it's upstairs in your bedroom?

NATALIE (*to Lady Bork*).

  Gertrude dear—!

ELECTOR.   Do hurry, please!

NATALIE.   On

  the mantelpiece, I think!

                (*Exit Lady Bork.*)

HOMBURG (*aside*).

                   Good God, what's that

  she said? (*He pulls the glove out of his doublet.*)

FIELD MARSHAL (*looking at the sheet of paper in his hand*).

  —but out of range of cannon shot. (*Continues.*)
  His Excellency the Prince—

HOMBURG.   Why, it's the glove

  she's looking for!—(*Looks from glove to Princess, Princess to glove.*)

FIELD MARSHAL.   —by His Lordship's strict
  command—

GOLZ (*writing*).

      —*"by His Lordship's strict command"*—

FIELD MARSHAL.   —will not,

  no matter how the battle goes, budge
  from the position to which he's been assigned—

HOMBURG.   I must

  know now, this very instant, if it's hers!

    (*He drops glove and a handkerchief together on the floor, then stoops
      to retrieve the handkerchief, leaving the glove exposed for all to see.*)

FIELD MARSHAL (*astonished*).

  Your Excellency, what is it?

HOHENZOLLERN (*whispering*).

                   Arthur!

HOMBURG.   Sir!

HOHENZOLLERN.   I think
  you've lost your wits!
HOMBURG.   What are you orders, sir?
            (*Puts pencil to paper again. The Field Marshal looks
                at him inquiringly for a moment. Pause.*)
GOLZ (*having noted down the order, recites*).
  —"*not budge from the position to which he's been assigned*"—
FIELD MARSHAL (*continuing*)
  —until the enemy's left wing,
  under the combined attack of Hennings and Truchss—
HOMBURG (*whispering to Golz and peering over at his notes*).
  Who, Golz, who? Me, does he mean?
GOLZ.   Yes, you!
  Who else?
HOMBURG.   I'm not to budge from my position—?
GOLZ. Yes, that's right!
FIELD MARSHAL.   You've got that down?
HOMBURG (*aloud as he writes*).
                              "*—not budge
from the position to which I've been assigned"—
FIELD MARSHAL.   —until
  the enemy's left wing, under
  the combined attack of Hennings and of Truchss, is broken
  and thrown back upon his right, and all
  his forces, reeling now, are driven pell-
  mell backwards, straight into the swampy ground
  behind with all its dikes and ditches and canals,
  and there the plan of battle calls for us
  to annihilate them.
ELECTOR.   Lights here, pages,
  please! My dears, your arm!
            (*Moves toward the exit with the Electress and the Princess.*)
FIELD MARSHAL.   At this point,
  he will give the order for the trumpets to be sounded—
ELECTRESS (*to Officers, who bow to her*).
  Gentlemen, good-bye! We mustn't interrupt
  you.
            (*The Field Marshal also bows to her.*)

ELECTOR (*stopping short*).
  Look down there, I do believe it's Natalie's
glove! Please, would you?
GENTLEMAN.   Where?
ELECTOR.   At the Prince our cousin's
feet!
HOMBURG (*gallantly*).
  My feet, you say—? Does this belong
to you? (*Picks up the glove and brings it to the Princess.*)
NATALIE. Oh, thank you, my dear Prince.
HOMBURG (*in a state of complete confusion*).
           It's yours,
you say?
NATALIE. Yes, mine; the missing glove.
      (*She accepts it from him and draws it on.*)
ELECTRESS (*to the Prince, as she leaves*).
           Good-bye!
Good luck! My blessings all go with you! Make
it so we'll meet again soon—yes, meet happily!
    (*Exeunt Elector, Electress, and Princess, followed by Ladies,
       Gentlemen, and Pages.*)
HOMBURG (*stands thunderstruck; then turns and marches triumphantly
  back among the officers. He pretends to write.*).
 "At this point he will give the order
 for the trumpets to be sounded!"
FIELD MARSHAL (*looking down at his sheet of paper*).
        At this point he
will give the order for the trumpets to be sounded.
    (*Then looking up and considering the Prince.*)
         —But lest
there be the least misunderstanding and the blow should be
delivered prematurely—(*He pauses.*)
GOLZ (*writing*).
      —"least misunderstanding
 and the blow should be delivered prematurely"—
HOMBURG (*whispering to Hohenzollern, in a state of high excitement*).
 Oh Heinrich!
HOHENZOLLERN (*exasperated*).
     Now what's eating you? What is it now?
HOMBURG. Good God, you didn't see?

HOHENZOLLERN. No, nothing! Won't
you please shut up!
FIELD MARSHAL (*continuing*).
—the Prince will only
sound the attack (I emphasize the point)
when His Lordship sends an adjutant to him
to tell him so, and not before.
(*The Prince is staring dreamily at the ground.*)
—You've got that down correctly?
GOLZ (*writing*).
"—sound the attack
when His Lordship sends an adjutant to him
to tell him so, and not before."
FIELD MARSHAL (*raising his voice*).
And you have got it down too, Excellency?
HOMBURG. Marshal, sir?
FIELD MARSHAL. You have it written down?
HOMBURG. —sound the trumpets for the attack?
HOHENZOLLERN (*speaking in a whisper, with exasperated emphasis*).
Sound the trumpets!
Damn it, Arthur! *Not before His Lordship—*
GOLZ (*doing the same*).
Not till he himself—
HOMBURG (*interrupting them*).
*Not till he himself—*Yes, yes! I heard
you! Not before—I know! But then I give
the order for the trumpets to be sounded!
(*Scribbles in his notebook.—Pause.*)
FIELD MARSHAL. Baron Golz,
be good enough to note the following:
I also wish to speak to Colonel Kottwitz,
if that is at all possible, before
the engagement starts.
GOLZ (*with a significant nod of his head*).
I'll see he's told so, sir.
You may rely on it.
(*Reenter the Elector.*)
ELECTOR. Well, gentlemen,
it's turning gray outside. You have your orders
noted down, do you?

FIELD MARSHAL.　　　　They do, my Prince!
　All your officers know exactly what
　your plan of battle calls on them to do.
ELECTOR (*taking up his hat and gloves*).
　Good, good.—And you, Sir Prince of Homburg, you
　I recommend to get some rest. You've cost
　me, as you know, just recently, by your light-
　minded actions at the Rhine, two victories:
　conduct yourself today so that
　I'm not deprived of still another, and one
　on which no less than throne and kingdom, all
　that I possess, depend!
　　　　　　　　　(*To the Officers.*)
　　　　　　　　Now let's be off!
　—Where's Franz?
　　　　　　　　　(*Enter a groom.*)
GROOM.　　　　Here, Sir!
ELECTOR.　　　　　The white, Franz, right away,
　I'll ride the white! Before the sun is in
　the field today, *I* mean to be!
　　　(*Exit the Elector, followed by Generals, Colonels, and Officers.*)

SCENE 6

HOMBURG (*advancing to front of stage*).
　Now mounted on your rolling sphere, stupendous Fortune,
　the corner of whose veil a puff of wind has lifted
　for a moment, like a sail, today—
　keep rolling on! Already I have felt
　your light caress, already, Lady Luck,
　as you darted past me, you smiled and shook a pledge
　out of your overflowing Horn. Today,
　O skittish daughter of the gods, I chase you on
　the battlefield, I'll catch you up, dear runaway,
　and make you pour out all your blessings at my feet—
　though iron chains should bind you seven times over
　to Sweden's loud triumphal battle car!
　　　　　　　　　(*Exit.*)

ACT II

The Battlefield near Fehrbellin

SCENE I

Offstage Colonel Kottwitz, Count Hohenzollern, Captain von der Golz, and Officers, at the head of the cavalry.

VOICE OF COLONEL KOTTWITZ. Halt, cavalry—dis . . . *mount!*
HOHENZOLLERN AND GOLZ (*entering*).

                                              Halt, men,
and down!
VOICE OF KOTTWITZ. Who'll help me off my horse, friends?
HOHENZOLLERN AND GOLZ.   Here we
come, old man! (*They exit again.*)
VOICE OF KOTTWITZ. Thanks, thanks! How hard it gets, confound
it all! For what you've done for me, I wish
you each a faithful son who'll do the same
for you in your decline!
    (*Enter Kottwitz, followed by Hohenzollern, Golz, and others.*)
KOTTWITZ.   With a horse between
my knees I don't know age; but let me once
dismount, and such a strife begins you'd think
that body and soul had parted company
and gone to war, those two! (*Looks around him.*)
                        But where is our
commanding officer, His Excellency
the Prince of Homburg?
HOHENZOLLERN.   He'll soon be back.
KOTTWITZ. And where did he go off to?
HOHENZOLLERN.   To that village you
rode past and never noticed in the shrubbery.
AN OFFICER. He took a spill last night, I heard.
HOHENZOLLERN.   So I
heard too.
KOTTWITZ.   He fell, did he?
HOHENZOLLERN.   Oh, nothing serious!
The black he's riding shied in going past
the mill. But he slid nimbly down the off

side and didn't hurt himself at all.
It's not worth mentioning.

KOTTWITZ (*walking up a rise*).

As I live
and breathe, a glorious day! A day the Lord God
made for better things than killing one
another! See the sun touch all the clouds
to rose, and with the lark our feelings, loud
exulting, mount up into the haze of heaven!

GOLZ. Were you able, sir, to speak to Marshal
Dörfling?

KOTTWITZ (*coming down to front stage*).

Hang it, no! What does he think?
Am I supposed to be an arrow, a bird,
a thought, that he should have me fly about
the whole damned battlefield? I hunted
him on top of Hackelberg, where the vanguard
is, then down below at Hackel's foot,
among our rear—and the one I didn't find
was just himself, the Marshal! So back I came
to my own troopers here.

GOLZ.   He won't like that, I am sure.
It didn't seem an unimportant matter
he wished to talk to you about.

AN OFFICER.   Here comes
the Prince of Homburg, our Colonel!

SCENE 2

*Enter the Prince of Homburg with a black cloth wound
around his left hand.*

KOTTWITZ.   Greetings,
my young Prince! Look, will you, how, while you
were in the village, I've deployed our men along
the bottom road! I think you'll find you like
what I have done.

HOMBURG.   Good morning, Kottwitz, friends!
—You know there's nothing that you do that I
don't praise.

KOTTWITZ.   What took you to the village, Arthur? My,
but you look solemn!
HOMBURG.   I—I visited the chapel
I saw peeping out of the village's still shrubbery.
The bells rang just as we passed by
to call to prayer, and I felt a wish to kneel
down at the altar, too.
KOTTWITZ.   A pious young man
you are, I must say! Well, things commenced
in prayer are crowned in their conclusion with fame
and victory!
HOMBURG   There's something, Heinrich, I
have meant to ask you—
            (*Leads Count Hohenzollern a few steps forward.*)
            At the briefing yesterday,
remind me, what did Dörfling say I am
to do?
HOHENZOLLERN. Your mind was elsewhere, I could see.
HOMBURG. Elsewhere, yes—on other things. I don't
know what was wrong. I get mixed up when I
take down dictation.
HOHENZOLLERN.   Luckily, it isn't
much, this time, you need to keep
in mind. Truchss and Hennings, who command
the foot, will make the attack; your assignment
is to hold back here with all
your cavalry, prepared to charge, but only
when the order's given you.
HOMBURG (*after a pause, staring down before him dreamily*).
            How strange
it was!
HOHENZOLLERN. *What* was, old man?
            (*He studies the Prince.—Cannon fire erupts.*)
KOTTWITZ.   Hear that,
you fellows, do you! Mount, men—in your saddles!
That was Hennings and the battle has begun!
            (*All climb the rise.*)
HOMBURG. Who did you say it was? What—?
HOHENZOLLERN.   Colonel
Hennings, Arthur—he has sneaked around

old Wrangel's back. Come over here where you
can see it all.

GOLZ (*looking out*).

    Just see what a deployment he
is making toward the Rhyn!

HOMBURG (*shading his eyes*).

      That's Hennings over
there, on our right?

FIRST OFFICER.   Yes, Excellency.

HOMBURG. Well, damn it, how is that? He was positioned
yesterday on our left!

      (*Cannon fire in the distance.*)

KOTTWITZ.   Oh thunder,
look! Twelve cannon Wrangel's opening fire
with on Hennings there!

FIRST OFFICER.   They build redoubts,
those Swedes!

SECOND OFFICER. Go up, they do, by God, as high
as that church steeple in the village just behind
them!

      (*Firing nearby.*)

GOLZ. Truchss! It's him!

HOMBURG.   That's Truchss?

KOTTWITZ.   Yes, Truchss himself—
attacking straight ahead to come to Hennings'
aid.

HOMBURG. How come Truchss commands
the center today?

     (*Violent cannonading.*)

GOLZ.   Good God, look!
I think the village is on fire now!

THIRD OFFICER. It's burning—yes, it is!

FIRST OFFICER.   It's burning, yes!
Already flames are licking up the tower!
I see their couriers scattering right and left!

SECOND OFFICER. The Swedes are moving!

KOTTWITZ.   Where?

FIRST OFFICER.   On their right wing!

THIRD OFFICER. Oh yes, I see! Formed up in columns, three
    whole regiments! To reinforce their left,
    I think.
SECOND OFFICER. That's right, by God! And there's their cavalry,
    to shield the right wing's move.
HOHENZOLLERN (*chortling*).
                             Oh, they will turn
    tail fast enough again when they catch sight
    of us down in the bottom here!
                    (*Musket fire.*)
KOTTWITZ.   Look, brothers,
    look!
SECOND OFFICER. Hear that!
FIRST OFFICER.   The muskets firing!
THIRD OFFICER. They've come together at the redoubts!
GOLZ.   My God,
    I've never heard, in all my life, such cannonading!
HOHENZOLLERN. Shoot! Shoot all you like, and rip the womb
    of earth to dig your bodies' graves!
           (*Lull.—A shout of triumph in the distance.*)
FIRST OFFICER.   O God
    of battles, high above, who gives, alone,
    the victory: old Wrangel's on the run!
HOHENZOLLERN. No—look again!
GOLZ.   By God, man, yes! His left,
    look there! He's pulling out of the redoubt with all
    his pieces!
ALL.   Victory! Hurrah! Hurrah!
    We've won the victory!
HOMBURG (*running down the slope*).
              Come, Kottwitz, follow
    me!
KOTTWITZ. Oh, not so fast, my boys!
HOMBURG.   Come on,
    now! Sound the trumpets! Follow me!
KOTTWITZ.   Be calm,
    please!
HOMBURG (*wild*).
    Heaven, Hell, and earth as well!

KOTTWITZ.   According
  to His Lordship's orders yesterday, we mustn't
  move except upon command. Golz, read
  them out to him.
HOMBURG.   Except upon command? God, Kottwitz,
  you're content to amble at a pace as slow
  as that? Your heart, man: hasn't it commanded
  you already?
KOTTWITZ.   Commanded me?
HOHENZOLLERN.   I beg
  you, please!
KOTTWITZ.   My heart, you ask?
HOHENZOLLERN.   Oh listen,
  Arthur, do, to reason!
GOLZ.   Colonel, listen!
KOTTWITZ (*offended*).
  So! You speak to me like that, do you,
  young man?—Well, if I had to, I could tie
  that nag you prance around on to my horse's tail
  and haul him after me! March, march, sirs, on
  the double! Trumpeter—the attack! We charge
  the enemy! And Kottwitz at your side!
GOLZ (*to Kottwitz*).
  No, never, Colonel, never—stop!
SECOND OFFICER. But Hennings hasn't reached the Rhyn bank yet!
FIRST OFFICER. Relieve him of his sword!
HOMBURG.   Relieve me of my sword?
        (*Pushes the Officer back.*)
                                      Why,
  what impertinence! Did you forget the ten
  commandments of the March of Brandenburg?
  Your sword, and scabbard, too!
        (*Rips away the Officer's sword and sword belt.*)
FIRST OFFICER (*staggering back*).
                 By God, my Prince,
  what you have done—!
HOMBURG (*following after him*).
               Your tongue's still wagging—?
HOHENZOLLERN (*to the Officer*).
  Quiet! Are you mad?

HOMBURG. Orderlies!
(*Giving them the sword.*)
Conduct this officer to headquarters and place
him under arrest.
(*To Kottwitz and the other Officers.*)
Now, gentlemen, your orders:
The man who will not follow his commander into battle—
he's a villain! Who remains behind?
KOTTWITZ. You heard me once already. What's the fuss
about?
HOHENZOLLERN (*conciliatorily*).
It was advice, no more, we offered
you.
KOTTWITZ. The responsibility is yours.
You lead, and I will follow.
HOMBURG (*pacified*).
Mine the respons-
ibility. Now, brothers, after me!
(*Exeunt all.*)

SCENE 3
A Peasant's House in a Village
*Enter a Gentleman of the Court, wearing boots and spurs, to
a Peasant and his Wife, who are seated at a table working.*

GENTLEMAN. Good day to you, good people! Can you put up
some guests, I wonder, in your house?
PEASANT. We can,
we can—with pleasure!
WIFE. And who might they be, sir?
GENTLEMAN. Our Sovereign's wife, and country's gracious mother—
no less a one! Her carriage broke its axle
just outside the village gate. But as
we've heard the battle's won, there is no need
for us to continue on to Havelberg.
PEASANT AND WIFE (*springing up*).
The battle's won? Thank God!
GENTLEMAN. You didn't know?
The Swedish army's been defeated,
if not for ever for a year at least,

and the Marches spared their army's fire and sword!
—But here she is now, our royal Princess!

SCENE 4

Enter the Electress, pale and drawn, followed
by several Ladies.

ELECTRESS (*in the doorway*).
Dear Lady Bork, and Winterfeld—your arm,
I need your arm!
NATALIE (*hurrying to her side*).
               Oh mother dear!
LADIES.   Good God,
how pale she is—she'll fall!
              (*They support her.*)
ELECTRESS.   Bring up a chair
for me, I must sit down.—Did he say dead?
He's dead?
NATALIE.   My dearest!
ELECTRESS.   I must speak to him
myself, the man who brought the news.

SCENE 5

Enter Captain von Mörner, wounded, with two troopers
helping him.

ELECTRESS.   You've come
to tell me what, grim herald?
MÖRNER.   What
these eyes, alas, themselves have seen, dear Madam,
to my everlasting sorrow.
ELECTRESS.   Speak, then—do!
MORNER. The Elector is no more!
NATALIE.   O God above,
must we be dealt so terrible a blow?
         (*Buries her face in her hands.*)
ELECTRESS. Tell me how he fell! As lightning strikes
the traveler in the night, lighting up the world
for him in one last crimson flash, strike *me*
with your words; and after you have spoken—come
the thunder clap and impenetrable night!

296

MÖRNER (*advancing to stand before her, supported on either side by the two cavalrymen*).

No sooner did the Swedish enemy,
hard-pressed by Truchss, begin to waver
than the Prince of Homburg drove across the plain
at Wrangel. He had broken through two lines
of men, sabering them as they fled, when he found
himself confronting a redoubt which rained down
shot so murderous on him his troops
were beaten flat like wheat—he had to call
a halt between the hills and wood to collect
his scattered force.

NATALIE (*to the Electress*).
                              Dear, steel yourself!

ELECTRESS.   Please, darling—
Then?

MÖRNER. Then at this very moment, emerging
from the dust, we see His Highness advancing
on the enemy beside the color-bearers
of Colonel Truchss's corps. Upon a white horse,
gloriously, he sat, effulgent in the sun's rays,
lighting up for us the way to victory.
We gather, all of us, together on
a hillside, anxiously, to make
him out amid the enemy fire; when suddenly
the Elector, horse and rider both, goes down
into the dust before our eyes. Two color-bearers
stumble over him so that their falling
banners overspread his form.

NATALIE.   Dear mother!

FIRST LADY. Heavens!

ELECTRESS.   On, go on!

MÖRNER.   The Prince's pain,
on seeing this, is indescribable;
and goaded on by rage and mad revenge,
like a bear he bursts out of his covert
and charges, we with him, the enemy
position. The trench and earthworks guarding
it are overrun in the attack, the garrison
is put to flight, scattered all about

and cut down on the field, the Swedish cannon,
flags, drums, standards, all their baggage
captured and made ours. And if the bridgehead
on the Rhyn had not allowed them to escape
the slaughter, not a man of them would ever
have survived to sit by his ancestral
fireside and say: I saw him fall,
the hero, yes, I did, at Fehrbellin!

ELECTRESS. A victory that cost too dear! It doesn't
gratify me, no! Oh, give me back
the price you paid for it!

(Swoons.)

FIRST LADY.   Lord help us, she has fainted!

SCENE 6

Enter the Prince of Homburg.

HOMBURG. My dearest Natalie! (*Presses her hand to his heart with feeling.*)

NATALIE.   It's true, then, Prince?

HOMBURG. I wish my answer could be no! I wish
I could call back his heart to life with blood
from my heart here!

NATALIE (*drying her tears*).

                    And have they found his body
yet?

HOMBURG. Until this moment my entire occupation's
been revenge on Wrangel—where might I
have found the time for such a care till now?
But I have sent a squad out on the battlefield
to look for it; and I don't doubt its being
found before nightfall.

NATALIE.   In this awful war,
who'll curb the Swedes now, tell me? Who
protect us from the swarm of enemies his fame
and fortune drew down on us?

HOMBURG (*taking her hand*).

                 I, Princess, I—
your cause is mine. Like Michael with his flaming sword,
I'll stand astride your throne's deserted steps!
The Elector hoped, before the year was out,

to see the Marches, every corner, free.
Well, then—I'll be the executor of his
last will!

NATALIE.   My dear, dear cousin!
                    (*Withdraws her hand from him.*)

HOMBURG. Natalie! (*Hesitates a moment.*)
                    What will you do now, I
am wondering?

NATALIE.   Yes, what am I to do
now that this thunderbolt has churned up
all the ground on which I stood? My father,
mother, both sleep in their grave in Amsterdam;
my house's chief possession, Dordrecht, is
a heap of blackened ruins; my cousin, Prince Maurice
of Orange, is harried by the Spanish tyrant's
troops and is hard put to it to succor
his own children; and now the last prop
holding up the vine of my felicity
has been knocked out. Today has orphaned
me a second time!

HOMBURG (*putting his arm around her waist*).
                    My dearest friend! If this
were not a time entirely claimed by mourning,
I would speak as follows: let the tendrils
of your vine wind themselves around *my* heart,
which, growing, blooming all alone these years,
yearns for your sweet blossoms' scent!

NATALIE.   Dear, dear cousin!

HOMBURG. Yes, you will—you will?

NATALIE.   Yes, if I am
allowed to wind myself into its very pith
and substance. (*Leans upon his breast.*)

HOMBURG.   What? What's that you said?

NATALIE.   Go now!

HOMBURG (*still holding her*).
Into its very core, into my heart of heart's core!
Natalie! (*He kisses her. She breaks away.*)
                    Oh God, if only he
whom we weep for stood here now and could see

how we are one! If only we could stammer:
Father, bless us, please!
(*He buries his face in his hands; Natalie turns back to the Electress.*)

SCENE 7

Enter a Cavalry Sergeant, running.

SERGEANT.   By God, my Prince,
I hardly have the courage to tell you what
a rumor's going around! The Elector lives!
HOMBURG. He lives!
SERGEANT.   By God, he does! Count Sparren brought
the news just now.
NATALIE.   Good Lord! Dear mother, did
you hear? (*Falls on her knees in front of her embracing her around the waist.*)
HOMBURG.   I can't believe it—! Who, you say—?
SERGEANT. Count George von Sparren—he saw him with his own two
eyes at Hackelwitz, safe and sound
with Truchss's corps!
HOMBURG.   Old fellow, on the double!
Fetch him here to me!
(*Exit Sergeant.*)

SCENE 8

Enter Count George von Sparren and Sergeant.

ELECTRESS.   Don't plunge me for
a second time into the depths!
NATALIE.   No, mother dear!
ELECTRESS. Prince Frederick is alive?
NATALIE (*supporting her with both hands*).
                    You stand upon
the summit of existence once again!
SERGEANT (*coming forward*).
                    Here is
the officer.
HOMBURG.   Count Sparren, sir! You saw
His Majesty alive and well at Hackelwitz
with Truchss's corps?

SPARREN.   Your Highness, yes, I did,
   in the parson's yard, surrounded by his staff
   and giving orders for the dead of both sides to be buried!
LADIES. Lord God, in your lap—! (*All embrace.*)
ELECTRESS.   Daughter!
NATALIE.   No,
   it's hardly to be borne, such joy! (*Buries her face in her aunt's lap.*)
HOMBURG.   But from the distance,
   at my troopers' head, I thought I saw
   him struck by cannon shot and fall into the dust,
   him and his white charger.
SPARREN.   Yes, the horse
   went down, and horseman too. But the man riding
   him wasn't our Prince.
HOMBURG.   Not our Prince?
NATALIE. Oh, wonderful! (*Stands up beside the Electress.*)
HOMBURG.   Go on, then—speak! Every word
   you say sinks, like gold, into my heart!
SPARREN.   Now hear
   a story, a more moving one was never told!
   Our monarch who, deaf to every warning,
   was riding his white horse again, the pure white
   stallion Froben bought him a short time ago
   in England, was once again, as always, the target
   of the enemy's cannonades. The members of his suite
   could hardly come within a hundred yards
   of him; shells, bullets, grapeshot poured
   down on him in a swollen flood, and all
   who lived still in that deadly current made desperately
   for the shore; he, he only, the intrepid swimmer,
   never wavered, but beckoning his comrades on,
   stroked boldly upstream toward the source.
HOMBURG. Yes, yes, by God! It was a fearful sight.
SPARREN. Brave Froben, our Prince's Master of the Horse,
   who's closest on his heels of all the suite,
   calls across to me: "Oh, damn that horse,
   one great white blaze, for whom I paid
   out so much gold in London recently!
   Fifty ducats I would gladly give now
   to have him mouse gray from his muzzle to his hocks!"

And pulling alongside him, anxiously,
he says: "You've got a skittish beast there, Sir,
allow me, please, to put him back to school!"
Then off he jumps from his own bay and seizes
hold of our monarch's horse's reins.
The Prince, dismounting, with a quiet smile replies:
"The schooling it's your wish, old fellow, he
should have, it isn't something he will ever
learn by day. I beg you, take him far
away from here, behind those hills, and there
the enemy won't notice his shortcoming!"
Upon which, mounting Froben's bay, he turns
back to where his duty summons him. But hardly
was Froben mounted on the white
when a deadly charge of lead from the redoubt brings
horse and rider down into the dust, a sacrifice
to his fidelity—and after that
no sound was heard to come from him again.
                    (*Silence.*)
HOMBURG. He's been rewarded! If I had ten lives,
    I could not spend them better!
NATALIE.   Froben, you
    brave man!
ELECTRESS.   Oh, admirable soldier!
NATALIE.   Less than he
    would still deserve more, much more tears.
                    (*They weep.*)
HOMBURG.   Enough!
    To business. Where's the Elector? Is Hackelwitz
    headquarters now?
SPARREN.   Oh, sorry, sir! His Majesty's
    departed for Berlin, where all his generals
    are asked to follow him.
HOMBURG.   What? To Berlin!
    Is the campaign over then?
SPARREN.   But I'm astonished
    this is news to you! The Swedish general,
    Count Horn, arrived in camp; there promptly followed
    the proclamation of an armistice. And if

302

I've understood Field Marshal Dörfling right,
negotiations now are under way the result
of which may very well be peace.

ELECTRESS.   Praise God
that all concludes so gloriously! (*She rises.*)

HOMBURG.   Come, we
will follow him to Berlin instantly!
Could you find a place for me inside your coach,
I wonder, to speed my getting there? I've just
a line or two to write to Kottwitz, I
can join you in a moment. (*Sitting down to write.*)

ELECTRESS.   With all my heart!

HOMBURG (*folds the note and hands it to the Sergeant; then turns back to the
Electress, meanwhile quietly slipping an arm around Natalie's waist.*)
I have a request I am quite diffident
about putting into words, which I hope
I may confess to you on the way.

NATALIE (*disengaging herself from him hurriedly*).
Bork, my scarf, please, quick!

ELECTRESS.   A request?
Of me?

LADY.   Why, Princess, you are wearing it!

HOMBURG (*to the Electress*).
What, you have no idea?

ELECTRESS.   None whatsoever.

HOMBURG. Not an inkling—?

ELECTRESS (*breaking off*).
                    Never mind! I'd not
say no to anyone today, about
no matter what, and least of all to him
who won us the great victory! Now come along!

HOMBURG. Oh Mother, do you know what you've just said?
May I interpret it the way I wish?

ELECTRESS. Come, will you—more about it in the carriage!

HOMBURG. Come, your arm!—O *Caesar divus,* I
have stood my ladder up against your star!
                    (*He leads the Ladies off, followed by the others.*)

SCENE 9

Berlin. The pleasure garden of the old Electoral Palace. In the rear the Cathedral, brightly illuminated, with steps leading up to the portal. Ringing of bells. Froben's body is carried in and laid upon a splendid catafalque.

Enter the Elector, Field Marshal Dörfling, Colonel Hennings, Count Truchss, and other Colonels and Officers. Opposite them Officers with dispatches.—In the Cathedral as well as on the square, a crowd of people.

ELECTOR. Whichever officer it was who led
  the cavalry today and advanced against
  the enemy without permission, who would
  not wait until the order came from me
  so that the Swede was made to flee before
  Colonel Hennings could destroy his bridges—he
  is guilty of a capital offense and I order
  him to appear before a military court.
  —The Prince of Homburg wasn't leading them?
TRUCHSS. No, no, Your Majesty!
ELECTOR.   And how do I
  know that?
TRUCHSS.   His own men told me so
  before the battle started, they will swear
  to it. He took a tumble with his horse
  and badly hurt his head and legs. They saw
  him being bandaged up in the church.
ELECTOR.   All right.
  Our victory was brilliant; tomorrow I
  will thank God for it at the altar. But even
  were it ten times more a victory,
  it doesn't pardon him through whom chance gave
  it me. There's many another battle still
  to fight and I insist upon the law of strict
  obedience. Whoever led the charge
  today, let me repeat, has forfeited
  his head: a court-martial must call him to account.
  And now, friends, follow me—we go to church!

SCENE 10

Enter the Prince of Homburg carrying three Swedish flags; Colonel Kottwitz carrying two; Count von Hohenzollern, Captain Golz, and Count Reuss with a flag apiece; other Officers, Corporals, and Cavalrymen carrying flags, drums, and standards.

DÖRFLING (*catching sight of the Prince*).
The Prince of Homburg!—Truchss, what have you done!
ELECTOR (*taken aback*).
From where do you appear, Prince?
HOMBURG (*taking two steps forward*).

                  From Fehrbellin,
Your Highness—bringing you these trophies
of our victory. (*Lays the three flags at the Elector's feet,
followed by Officers, Corporals, and Men who do the same with
the trophies they are carrying.*)
ELECTOR (*disconcerted*).

          But I heard that you were hurt,
and badly too. Count Truchss!
HOMBURG (*gaily*)

                I'm sorry!
TRUCHSS.   Good
God, I'm dumbfounded!
HOMBURG.   Yes,
my bay fell just before the battle
started; but my hand here, which a surgeon wrapped
up for me, was hardly more than scratched.
ELECTOR. Then you're the one who led the cavalry?
HOMBURG (*looking at him in surprise*).
I? Yes, of course! But do I need to tell
you that? The proof lies there at your feet.
ELECTOR.   I'll have
his sword, please—lock him up!
DÖRFLING (*shocked*).

               What, him?
ELECTOR (*walking among the flags*).

             Why, Kottwitz,
greetings!

TRUCHSS (*under his breath*).
> Damn!

KOTTWITZ.   By God, I'm too—

ELECTOR (*looking at him steadily*).
>   What's that
> you say?—See what a crop of glory
> we have reaped! Unless I'm much mistaken, these, here,
> are the colors of the Swedish Royal Guards!
> > (*Picks up a flag, shakes out its folds, and looks at it.*)

KOTTWITZ.   Your Highness?

DÖRFLING. Sir?

ELECTOR.   I'm right! And go back all the way
> to King Gustav Adolphus' time! What does
> the motto say?

DÖRFLING.   *Per aspera ad astra.*[3]

ELECTOR. It didn't hold for them at Fehrbellin.
>   (*Pause.*)

KOTTWITZ (*hesitantly*).
> If I might have a word, Sir, with you—!

ELECTOR.   Yes,
> what is it?—Take the flags, drums, standards,
> everything, into the cathedral and hang
> them from the pillars; they'll do very well
> tomorrow in our victory service.
> > (*The Elector turns to the couriers, receives their dispatches,*
> >   *breaks the seals, and immerses himself in them.*)

KOTTWITZ (*under his breath*).
>   By God,
> that's pushing things too far, I think!
> > (*Hesitates, then picks up his two flags; the other officers and*
> > *men do the same. When the only flags remaining are the Prince's*
> > *three, Kottwitz picks these up as well so that he carries five.*)

AN OFFICER (*going up to the Prince*).
>   Your sword,
> sir, please.

HOHENZOLLERN (*with his flag in his hand, placing himself alongside the Prince*).
> Now gently, Arthur!

---

3. "By hard ways to the stars."

HOMBURG.   Am I dreaming
  or awake? Can this be real? It must be
  I am raving!

GOLZ.   Prince, give up your sword,
  I counsel you—and not a word!

HOMBURG.   I'm to be
  locked up?

HOHENZOLLERN. That's so!

GOLZ.   You heard it!

HOMBURG.   But I'd like
  to know the reason why.

HOHENZOLLERN (*emphatically*).
                Not now. You attacked
  too soon, we told you so, remember! Your orders
  were: not to budge from your position
  till commanded!

HOMBURG.   Help, friends, help, I'm going
  mad—!

GOLZ (*interrupting*).
      Do hold your tongue, you must!

HOMBURG.   The defeated
  army was the Brandenburger, I
  suppose!

HOHENZOLLERN (*stamping his foot*).
      That hasn't got a thing to do
  with it! *The law is: obedience!*

HOMBURG (*bitterly*).
  Ah yes!

HOHENZOLLERN (*leaving his side*).
      It doesn't mean your neck.

GOLZ (*also stepping away from him*).
            Tomorrow
  morning, I should think, you're out.
       (*The Elector folds up the dispatches and rejoins his officers*
                 standing in a group [to one side].)

HOMBURG (*unbuckling his sword*).
              My cousin
  Frederick has in mind to play the Brutus
  with me, as it seems, and sees the scene
  already sketched on canvas: himself erect

on the curule seat, before him on
the table the Articles of War of Brandenburg,
and in the foreground all the Swedish flags.
By God, though, I'm no son who looks up
in awed wonder from underneath the ax.
My heart is German, the old stamp of German,
and what it understands is magnanimity
and love; and if he acts the antique Roman
toward me now, inflexible as marble,
well, I pity him, I do indeed!

ELECTOR. Take him back to headquarters at Fehrbellin
and have a court-martial convened to try him.
(*He enters the Cathedral, followed by officers and men holding
the captured flags aloft. While the Elector and his suite
kneel at Froben's coffin and pray, the flags are hung from
the pillars. Dirge music.*)

ACT III
Fehrbellin

SCENE I

A Prison

The Prince of Homburg. In the background two cavalrymen standing
guard. Enter the Count of Hohenzollern.

HOMBURG. Now look who's there—friend Heinrich! Welcome!
Come to tell me I'm set free, I'm sure!

HOHENZOLLERN (*startled*).
God be praised for it!

HOMBURG.   For what?

HOHENZOLLERN.   You're free?
Your sword's returned?

HOMBURG.   To me? Oh no!

HOHENZOLLERN.   No?

HOMBURG.   No!

HOHENZOLLERN. Then why did you say free?

HOMBURG (*after a moment*).
        I thought you came
to tell me that. It doesn't matter, though!

HOHENZOLLERN. I'm sorry, but I don't know anything.

HOMBURG. It doesn't matter, do you hear? He'll send
    somebody else to tell me. (*Goes to bring up two chairs.*)
                   Do sit down.
    What's happening? The Elector's back now,
    is he, from Berlin?
HOHENZOLLERN (*preoccupied*).
              Came back last evening, yes.
HOMBURG. Did the victory service come off just as planned?
    But of course it did—I know! The Elector was
    there too?
HOHENZOLLERN. Yes, he, the Electress and Princess Natalie.
    The church blazed bright with candles for the occasion,
    and during the Te Deum you could hear the batteries
    on the palace square firing with solemn pomp.
    The Swedish flags and standards, suspended trophy
    fashion from the pillars, fluttered overhead
    and from the pulpit you were named, for so
    His Majesty commanded, the victor of the day.
HOMBURG. Yes, so I heard. And have you other news
    you've come to give me? My friend, your face is not
    I think, a very bright one! Speak!
HOHENZOLLERN.   Who was
    it you spoke with?
HOMBURG.   With Golz, just now, inside
    the castle where, as you know very well,
    my trial was held.
                 (*Pause.*)
HOHENZOLLERN (*looking at him thoughtfully*).
           I wonder, Arthur, what
    you think of your position, now it has changed
    so strangely?
HOMBURG.   What I think? I think the same
    as you and Golz—and as the judges, too!
    The Elector did what he must do, according
    to his duty. But now he'll heed his heart. "You've been
    at fault," he'll tell me very gravely, mention
    death, perhaps, imprisonment. "However,
    I've decided to give you back your freedom"
    —and around the sword that won him his great victory,
    to demonstrate his graciousness, perhaps

he'll wind a golden decoration. But if
he doesn't, that's fine, too—for I don't,
considering everything, deserve it!
HOHENZOLLERN.   Arthur,
   Arthur! (*Stops.*)
HOMBURG. Well?
HOHENZOLLERN. And that is what you think?
HOMBURG. I do indeed! I know he loves me, loves
  me like a son; I've had a thousand proofs
  of it since I was little. Why these misgivings?
  Didn't he take more delight in my growing
  fame, or so it seemed to me, than I did
  myself? For everything I am, don't I
  have him to thank? And yet it's your idea
  the plant he nursed with his own hands, with so
  much care, unfeelingly, because it bloomed
  a little hastily, a little too
  exuberantly, he'd stamp into the dust
  with bitter hate? Why, his worst enemy
  would never think that of him, how much less
  should you, who know and love him dearly.
HOHENZOLLERN (*with great deliberation*).
                            Arthur,
  you have just been tried by court-martial,
  and yet you still believe—
HOMBURG.   *Because* I've just
  been tried! Oh, merciful God! Nobody presses
  things so far unless he means to grant
  a pardon in the end. It was there, just there,
  before the bar of justice, my trust flowed back
  into my heart. Is death the fitting penalty
  for rolling in the dust, two minutes sooner
  than my orders called for, the whole Swedish
  army? What other crime have I
  on my conscience? No, I can't believe he ever
  would have had me called before that bench
  of heartless judges, owls hooting an incessant
  dirge whose single note was: execution
  by a firing squad, unless his aim
  is, godlike, to descend into their midst and with

his royal verdict cancel theirs. No, friend;
he makes these clouds to lower over me
only so as, ascending like the sun, to pierce
their mist and bathe me in his radiance.
If that's his pleasure, I can let him have it!
HOHENZOLLERN. That may be. But they say the court's announced
its verdict.
HOMBURG.   Yes, I know; it's death.
HOHENZOLLERN (*astonished*).

And how
do you know that?
HOMBURG.   Golz heard the court hand down
its sentence; he told me.
HOHENZOLLERN.   But good God,
man, it doesn't worry you?
HOMBURG.   Worry
me? No, not at all.
HOHENZOLLERN.   You're mad, quite mad!
On what, pray, do you base your confidence?
HOMBURG. On my own heart and what it has
to tell me! (*Jumps up.*) Leave me, please! I see no reason
why I should torment myself with futile
doubts! (*On second thought sits down again.—Pause.*)
The court had no choice but to find
for death; the law by which it acts requires
that. But sooner than allow so cruel
a sentence to be executed, sooner than
expose this heart of mine, that loves him so
devotedly, to bullets fired when a square
of linen drops, he'd open his own breast and let
his own blood dribble in the dust.
HOHENZOLLERN.   But Arthur,
listen to me—
HOMBURG (*his temper rising*).
Please, old fellow!
HOHENZOLLERN.   Marshal Dörfling—
HOMBURG. Heinrich, leave!
HOHENZOLLERN.   One more thing you must
know, yes! If you dismiss it too, I'll hold
my tongue.

HOMBURG (*turning back to him*).
          I've told you: I know everything.
But go ahead.

HOHENZOLLERN. Just now Field Marshal Dörfling
has, with his own hand—the procedure's most
unusual—delivered the death sentence
to the castle. But he, instead of pardoning you
forthwith, as the verdict of the court explicitly
permits, commanded it should be presented
him for signature.

HOMBURG.   That means nothing, I
repeat.

HOHENZOLLERN. Means nothing!

HOMBURG.   For his signature?

HOHENZOLLERN. I swear it; on my word of honor.

HOMBURG.   Not the sentence,
no! You mean the minutes of the proceedings.

HOHENZOLLERN.   I mean
the sentence that condemns you to be shot.

HOMBURG.   Who told
you so?

HOHENZOLLERN. Himself, Field Marshal Dörfling!

HOMBURG.   When?

HOHENZOLLERN. Just now.

HOMBURG   Returning from His Majesty?

HOHENZOLLERN. Returning from His Majesty—as he
came down the castle steps! He added,
seeing how dismayed I looked, it wasn't
over yet, tomorrow was another day
which still might see a pardon come to you;
but his lips, from which the blood had drained, contradicted
their own words, and said: Not so, I fear!

HOMBURG (*standing up*).
It can't be—no!—that he's revolving in his heart
such monstrous resolves! For a flaw so tiny in the diamond
just presented him that it can hardly
be detected with a lens, to tread the donor in the dust!
An action that would wash the Dey of Algiers white
as snow, plant silver wings on Sardanapalus'
shoulders and make him shine angelically,

translate the tyrant emperors of Rome,
the whole succession, innocent again
as suckling babes, to God's right hand!

HOHENZOLLERN (*also standing up*).
You must, dear fellow, see things as they are.

HOMBURG. And that was all the Marshal had to say?

HOHENZOLLERN. What else was there to say?

HOMBURG.   The hope I had,
the trust!

HOHENZOLLERN. I'd like to know if you remember
ever doing anything, knowingly
or otherwise, insulting to his pride
as our ruler?

HOMBURG.   Never!

HOHENZOLLERN.   Think.

HOMBURG.   No, never!
Even his shadow on the ground I worshiped!

HOHENZOLLERN.   Arthur,
please don't be offended with me if I doubt
your word. The Ambassador from Sweden has arrived
and his business, I am told, concerns the Princess
Natalie. But something the Electress said
provoked His Lordship mightily; the talk
is, the young lady's made her choice
already. You don't play a part in this,
do you?

HOMBURG.   Oh God above, what's this?

HOHENZOLLERN.   Do you
play any part in this, I ask?

HOMBURG.   I do, I do!
It's clear now, everything; the Swedish offer
is my ruination. I'm to blame
for her refusal; we're engaged, we two!

HOHENZOLLERN. You fool, you unthinking fool! What have you done?
I cautioned you, a loyal friend, I cautioned
you how many times!

HOMBURG.   Help me, Heinrich—
save me, or I'm lost!

HOHENZOLLERN.   I will, I will—
but how to find the way out from this trouble?
—Perhaps you ought to go and see the Electress.
HOMBURG (*whirling around*).
Guard!
SOLDIER (*at the rear*).
        Sir!
HOMBURG.   Call your commanding officer!
(*Snatches a cloak from its nail on the wall and claps a plumed hat,
· lying on the table, on his head.*)
HOHENZOLLERN (*helping him on with the cloak*).
Be shrewd in how you manage it and it
will save your skin, this interview. For if
the only way the Elector can make peace
is by paying Sweden the price we know, you'll see
how soon he will be reconciled with you—
how in a matter of hours you'll be free.

SCENE 2

Enter the Commanding Officer.

HOMBURG. Stranz, I am in your charge! I wish an hour's
leave, with your permission, to go upon
an urgent business.
OFFICER.   No, my Prince, I don't
have charge of you. My orders say that you
are free to come and go just as you wish.
HOMBURG. Extraordinary! So—I'm not a prisoner?
OFFICER. Excuse me, sir, you are—of your parole!
HOHENZOLLERN (*starting to leave*).
Good, fine! That's all that matters.
HOMBURG.   Yes, good-bye!
HOHENZOLLERN. Wherever the Prince goes, his chains go too!
HOMBURG. It's only the castle I am going to, to see
my aunt; two minutes and I'm back again.
(*Exeunt.*)

SCENE 3

*The Electress's apartment
Enter the Electress and Natalie.*

ELECTRESS. Come, daughter, come, it's time! Count Horn, the Swedish
envoy, and his people all have gone; I see

314

a candle burning in your uncle's closet. Wrap
your shawl around yourself and slip into his room
and see if you can save your friend.
(*They are about to leave.*)

SCENE 4
Enter a Lady-in-waiting.

LADY. Prince Homburg, Madam—waiting at the door! I hardly
could believe my eyes!
ELECTRESS (*taken aback*).
Oh God!
NATALIE. The Prince
himself?
ELECTRESS. But surely he's not been released?
LADY. He's outside in his cloak and hat, extremely
agitated and begging for a word with you.
ELECTRESS (*angrily*).
He doesn't think! To violate his word
like that!
NATALIE. Who knows what drove him to it?
ELECTRESS (*after a moment's thought*).
Show him in.
(*Sits down.*)

SCENE 5
Enter the Prince of Homburg.

HOMBURG. My mother! (*Falls on his knees before her.*)
ELECTRESS. Prince, whatever are you doing
here?
HOMBURG. Oh, let me hug your knees!
ELECTRESS (*suppressing her emotion*).
You are
a prisoner, Prince Frederick, and yet
I see you here! Why do you pile a new
offense on the old?
HOMBURG (*clamorously*).
Are you aware
of what is being done to me?
ELECTRESS. I am, I am—
but what can I, a helpless woman, do?

HOMBURG. Dear mother, you would never speak like that
  if you were shivering, as I am, in the cold of death!
  To me you seem possessed of Heaven's own
  powers, the power to save poor mortal lives—
  you, the Princess, all your ladies, everyone
  around me here! Why, I could throw my arms
  around the vilest fellow of the baggage train
  who tends your horses, and beg him: Rescue me!
  I, only I, in all God's wide wide
  world, am helpless, cast off, powerless.
ELECTRESS. You're not yourself at all! Now tell me what
  has happened!
HOMBURG.   Coming here, I saw my own
  grave, in the torchlight, being dug, which tomorrow
  morning will receive my bones. Look here
  at these eyes, Aunt, that look at you—
  their purpose is to drown them in everlasting
  night, drive bullets through this breast of mine.
  The windows giving on the marketplace where the desolate
  spectacle will be enacted, are
  already spoken for; and the man who,
  standing on the top of life today, sees forward
  still into the future as if into
  a fairyland, tomorrow lies between
  two narrow boards, a reeking corpse, and over
  him a stone to tell you once he was.
>   (*The Princess, till now standing at a distance and leaning
>   on the Lady's shoulder, is shocked by these words and sits
>   down at a table in tears.*)
ELECTRESS. My son, my son! If that is Heaven's will,
  then you must arm yourself with courage and composure!
HOMBURG. Mother, God's earth is so fair! I beg
  you, don't, before my hour comes, let
  me go down among the shadows! If he believes
  I'm guilty, let him punish me some other
  way, why must it be by bullets? Let
  him degrade me to the ranks, cashier me ignominiously
  and drive me from the army—God in Heaven,
  since I've seen my grave my only thought
  is, Let me live, I don't care how!

ELECTRESS. Stand up, my son—oh, do stand up! You're so
  unnerved you don't know what you're saying. Try
  to get a grip on yourself!
HOMBURG.   Aunt, no!
  Not until you swear you'll go to him
  and humbling yourself before that exalted countenance,
  win back my life from him! The dear friend
  of your girlhood, Hedvig, long ago in Homburg,
  as she lay dying, confided me to your
  care, saying: "Oh, be a mother to him when
  I'm gone." And kneeling at her bedside, most profoundly
  moved, you bent to kiss her hand and this
  was your reply: "He'll be my son as if
  I had begotten him myself." Now I
  remind you what you promised! Go to him
  as if you had begotten me yourself,
  say, "I beg for mercy, mercy! *Let him go!*"
  and then come back to me and say, "He has!"
ELECTRESS (*in tears*).
  My dear, dear son! I've done it all already,
  what you ask! But all my pleading was in vain!
HOMBURG. My every claim to happiness I here
  renounce. No longer have I any wish
  for Princess Natalie's hand, don't fail to tell
  him that—the tenderness I felt for her
  is now extinguished, utterly. She
  is free as the doe upon the heath again,
  free to give her hand, her lips to whom
  she pleases, as if I never were, and if
  it is the King of Sweden, Karl Gustav,
  she chooses, why, good luck to her! Back
  I'll go to my estates along the Rhine
  and there I'll build up, pull down, till I drip
  with sweat, sow and reap for my own use
  as if for wife and child, and when I've reaped
  I'll sow again, and so pursue the round
  of days till evening comes and life declines
  and dies.
ELECTRESS. All right! But back you go to prison
  now, that is my favor's first requirement
  of you!

HOMBURG (*standing up and turning to the Princess*).
     Poor girl, such tears! The sun goes up
today upon the death of all your hopes!
Your feelings chose me first, and a look as pure
as gold assures me they will never choose another.
What is there that I, so comfortless myself,
may find to give you comfort? Go
and join your cousin Thurn in the nunnery on the Main.
Search in the mountains for a baby, blond-haired
like myself, to buy with gold and silver,
press him to your breast and teach his lips to stammer
mother—and when he's grown a man, show
him how the lids of dead men's eyes
are closed: for that is all the happiness you may
expect!
NATALIE (*smiling bravely as she rises and gives him her hand*).
    Go, my hero, back into your cell!
And on your way back, look again, composed
and calm, at the grave they've dug for you. It's not
the least bit darker, deeper than those
that yawned beneath your feet a thousand times
on the battlefield! I am true
to you come life, come death. And meanwhile I
myself will try with our uncle to see
if I can find the words to touch his heart
and rescue you from all this misery.
                  (*Pause.*)
HOMBURG (*clasping his hands together prayerfully and gazing at her in rapture*).
If two wings waved, dear Princess, on your shoulders,
I'd think you were an angel, literally!
Oh God, I heard correctly, didn't I—
you will plead for me? Where have you
kept hidden up till now your arrows of persuasion
that you dare to assail His Majesty in such a business?
Oh, light of hope that reinspirits me!
NATALIE. God will send me the shafts to hit the mark!—
But if the Elector finds it out of the question,
quite impossible that he should change
the verdict of the court—so be it! Brave man
that you are, bravely you'll submit to it,

and the one who proved triumphant a thousand times
in life, in death will prove triumphant too!

ELECTRESS. But go now! We are letting slip the favorable
time!

HOMBURG. May all the saints above protect
you! So farewell! Do send me, please, some sign
of your success, of whatever you achieve!

(Exeunt.)

ACT IV

SCENE 1

The Elector's Chamber

He is standing at a desk with candles on it, papers in his hand.
Natalie enters at center door and kneels down at a distance.—
Pause.

NATALIE. Noble uncle, Prince of Brandenburg!

ELECTOR (putting down the papers).
Natalie! (Goes to raise her up.)

NATALIE.   No, please!

ELECTOR.   What is it that
you'd like?

NATALIE.   To plead for mercy, in the dust here
at your feet, as it is right and proper that I should,
for Cousin Homburg! I don't want to have
him for myself—though my heart is filled with longing
for him, I confess; oh, I don't want him for
myself—let him marry whom he pleases;
all I wish, dear uncle, is that he
should go on living as he is, a free
and self-sufficient being who gives me pleasure
simply by existing, like a flower.
And now you've heard my plea, dear Majesty
and friend, I know you'll never shut your ears
to it.

ELECTOR (raising her up).
My darling girl, to ask me such
a thing! Our Cousin Homburg's guilty of a grave
offense!

NATALIE.   But uncle dear!

319

ELECTOR.   Well, isn't he
a man convicted of a grave offense?
NATALIE.   Oh, surely
   it was innocent, the error, a blond
   and blue-eyed little thing which forgiveness should
   have raised up from its knees before it had
   the time to ask: forgive me! Surely you
   won't spurn it from you with a kick,
   but rather press it to your heart for the sake of him
   who mothered it into the world, and say: Come, come,
   don't cry, you're just as dear to me as unwavering
   obedience! What seduced him in the shock of battle
   to overstep the law was zeal for your
   own fame. And having overstepped it in the fire
   of his youth, then what did he do?—in the fire
   of his manhood trod the fiery dragon in the dust!
   To crown his head because he conquered, then
   cut off his head—oh, surely that's not something
   history demands you do. Dear uncle,
   that would be an action *so* sublime
   one would almost have to call it cruel, inhuman:
   yet God has made no milder man than you.
ELECTOR. Dear child, see here! If I were simply a tyrant,
   what you say, I feel this very strongly,
   would already have made my heart melt
   in its iron cage. But *I* ask you:
   May I suppress the verdict of the court? What consequences
   would that have?
NATALIE.   For whom? For you?
ELECTOR.   For me?
   No, not for me! Good God, young woman,
   is there nothing higher in your scale of things
   than me? Are you completely ignorant
   of that sacred object soldiers worship
   called the Fatherland?
NATALIE.   Oh, Sir, why should
   you be so very fearful? The Fatherland
   indeed! It won't collapse on the spot
   because your heart is moved to mercy! You
   grew up in camps. To overrule the court

and tear up its decree for you is rank
disorder; for me it is the very consummation
of good order. Yes, I know, I know:
the rules of war must never be allowed
to fall into contempt—nor must our tender
feelings, equally! The Fatherland
we owe to you, good uncle, is a mighty
fortress; it will weather heavier storms
by far than a victory that didn't come
exactly as was called for in the battle plan;
the future years will see its walls extend
on every side, the citadel enlarging
still as heir succeeds to heir and battlement
crowds battlement as if sprung up by magic,
to our friends' delight and enemies'
dismay! But for its stones to hold together
and endure beyond my uncle's autumn years
of quiet glory, it doesn't need the cold
and lifeless mortar of a dear friend's blood.

ELECTOR. Does Cousin Homburg think the same as you?

NATALIE. The same as me?

ELECTOR.   Does he believe it doesn't
   matter one way or the other, for
   the Fatherland, which holds sway, law
   or arbitrariness?

NATALIE.   The poor, unhappy
   youth!

ELECTOR. But does he?

NATALIE.   Uncle dear, the only
   answer I can give your question is,
   a flood of tears.

ELECTOR (*surprised*).
                But I don't understand,
   dear girl? Has something happened?

NATALIE (*in a quavering voice*).
                      All he thinks
   of now, the only thing, is being saved!
   The gun barrels leveled at him by your firing
   squad have stared him out of countenance,
   oh dreadfully, and reeling back in shocked

surprise he knows no wish but one, to live:
all the March of Brandenburg might sink before his eyes
in lightning and thunder and he would never think
to ask, What's happening?—Oh, what a hero's
spirit you have broken!
(Turns away weeping.)

ELECTOR (utterly shocked).
No, impossible,
dear Natalie! He begs for mercy, actually?

NATALIE. If only you had not condemned him, ever!

ELECTOR. No, answer me—he's begging for his life?
Good God, what's happened, child? You're crying so!
You spoke to him? Please tell me everything!
You spoke to him?

NATALIE (leaning on his breast).
Just now I did, in Aunt's
apartment. He came slinking up to us,
imagine, in the dark, enveloped in a cloak,
a broad-brimmed hat on his head: a fearful,
frightened, utterly ignoble figure,
a pitiful, a shameful sight! I never
would have dreamt a man whom history
has singled out as one of her own heroes
could have sunk so far. It's true I am
a woman and shrink back from a worm that comes
too near my heel. But so unmanned, so crushed,
so little like a hero, death, although
it wore a hideous lion's shape, should never
find me, no!—Oh, what do human greatness,
human glory amount to!

ELECTOR (in a state of confusion).
Very well, take heart,
then, my dear child: by God who rules the earth
and heavens, he is free!

NATALIE.
He's what, Your Highness?

ELECTOR. Pardoned! I'll have the order sent
at once for his release.

NATALIE.
Dear uncle, is
this really true?

ELECTOR.
You've heard what I just said!

NATALIE. He's pardoned, is he? He won't die?

ELECTOR.   I swear
it! On my word of honor! How should I
oppose what such a soldier thinks? You know
the high regard in which I hold the Prince's
feelings in all things. If he can find
it in himself to say the sentence is unjust,
I cancel it: he's free!
              (*He brings up a chair for her.*)
           Do sit down
a moment, please.
           (*Seats himself at the desk and writes.*)

NATALIE (*murmuring to herself*).
            Heart, heart, why do?
you beat so in your cage?

ELECTOR (*as he writes*).
              The Prince is still
here in the castle?

NATALIE.   Sire, no. He has
returned to his confinement.

ELECTOR (*finishes writing, seals the letter, and comes back to the Princess*).
              Weeping so,
she was, my darling daughter, little niece!
And I, whose duty is to make her happy,
am the one who caused the clouds to gather
in the bright blue weather of her eyes! (*Puts his arm around her.*)
             This letter here—
perhaps you'd like to bring him it yourself?

NATALIE. To the Town Hall jail? I may?

ELECTOR (*pressing the letter into her hands*).
              Why not?—
Guards, here!
            (*Enter Guards.*)
      The coach, please, right away! The Princess
has important business with the Prince of Homburg!
            (*Exeunt Guards.*)
Then he can thank you on the spot for what you've done.
            (*Embraces her.*)
My dear, dear child! Am I in your good graces
once again?

NATALIE (*after a pause*).
        I've no idea, and shan't
inquire, what it was that moved you to be merciful
so suddenly. But I am sure, Sir, in
my heart I'm sure you never would descend
to playing jokes on me. Let the letter say
whatever it may say, my faith is, he
is saved—and for that I have yourself to thank!
                (*Kisses his hand.*)
ELECTOR. For sure he is, dear girl! As surely as
the Prince himself desires to be saved!
                (*Exeunt.*)

SCENE 2

The Princess's Apartment
Enter Princess Natalie, followed by two Ladies-in-waiting
and Captain of the Cavalry Count Reuss.

NATALIE (*hurrying*).
  What's that you have there, Count Reuss? Regimental
business? How important is it? Can't
it wait till morning?
REUSS (*holding out a letter to her*).
                Madam, it's from Colonel
Kottwitz!
NATALIE.   Quick, then, give it here! What's
in it?
REUSS. A petition, quite outspoken as
you'll see, but most respectful too, addressing
His Grace on behalf of our General,
the Prince of Homburg.
NATALIE (*reading*).
              "Most Obedient Entreaty
of the Princess of Orange Regiment."—(*Pause.*) And whose
hand was it wrote this?
REUSS.   Colonel Kottwitz's—the Colonel
wrote it out himself, as the shaky scrawl
proclaims. And his own noble name leads off
the list.
NATALIE. The thirty signatures that follow?

REUSS. Yes, our officers'—they follow one
  another according to their bearer's rank.
NATALIE.   And now
  you forward it to me—pray, why?
REUSS.   My Lady—
  humbly to entreat you, as our chief,
  to add your name to it as well, there
  at the head of all, in the space left blank for you.
                    (*Pause.*)
NATALIE. But His Highness, as I hear, is pardoning
  the Prince, my cousin, of his own accord,
  so there's no need for such a step.
REUSS (*delighted*).
                             Is that
  so? Really?
NATALIE.   All the same, I'll not refuse
  to sign—this sheet of paper, if we use
  it the right way, could tip the scales of our
  Sovereign's judgment; he would even welcome
  it, perhaps, as helping him to arrive
  at a decision. Here I set my name, then, and with
  it my own person, at the head of all.
                    (*Goes to sign the sheet.*)
REUSS. How much we are obliged to you indeed!
                    (*Pause.*)
NATALIE (*turning back to him again*).
  The only regiment that I see here,
  Count Reuss, is mine! Bomsdorf's cuirassiers,
  and the Götz and Anhalt-Pless dragoons—why shouldn't
  they be down here too?
REUSS.   Not, as you
  perhaps may fear, because their hearts beat fainter
  for him than our own! Unluckily
  for our petition, Colonel Kottwitz is quartered
  far away in Arnstein, which puts some miles
  between himself and all our other regiments
  encamped near here. So our sheet of paper,
  in the little time at our disposal, wants
  an opportunity to gather strength
  by enlisting the support it has in every quarter.

NATALIE. Wants, your sheet of paper, I imagine,
    for that reason, weight. Are you quite certain,
    Count, if you were stationed in this place and able
    to address the officers collected here, they'd join
    in your petition too?
REUSS.   Those here in town?
    Why every man jack of them! All the cavalry
    would put their names down on the spot; by God,
    I think we'd have no trouble getting *all*
    the Brandenburger army to subscribe an appeal!
NATALIE (*after a moment's silence*).
    Why don't you send out officers to push
    the matter here in camp?
REUSS.   Oh no—if you'll
    excuse me! That the Colonel says he'll never
    do! He has no wish, he says, for doing anything
    which might be misinterpreted.
NATALIE.   He's odd,
    he is, that gentleman! So bold, and then
    so careful!—But luckily, as I have just
    remembered, the Elector detailed me to order
    Kottwitz, since the stabling there is much
    too cramped, to move our squadrons here. I'll sit
    down right away and do so.
                    (*Sits down to write.*)
REUSS.   Wonderful,
    my Lady Natalie! A luckier thing
    for us could not have happened!
NATALIE (*as she writes*).
                      Use this, Count
    von Reuss, to best effect.
           (*Folds and seals the letter, and rises again.*)
                  But understand
    me! For the present, the letter must remain
    inside your wallet; you don't gallop off
    to Arnstein to give it Kottwitz till I tell
    you to! (*Gives him the letter.*)
A FOOTMAN (*entering*).
           The coach commanded for you by His Majesty
    stands harnessed, Madam, in the yard below.

NATALIE. Then bring it to the door. I'm coming down
at once! (*Pause in which she walks over thoughtfully to the table drawing on
her glove.*)
      I'm off, dear Count, to pay a visit
to the Prince of Homburg—would you care to come?
There is a seat for you inside my coach.
REUSS. I would indeed, my Lady—I am honored!
        (*Offers her his arm.*)
NATALIE (*to the Ladies*).
Follow us, my friends. (*To the Count.*)
        Perhaps I may
decide there you should go ahead!

SCENE 3

*The Prince of Homburg [who has just returned from the castle] hangs
his hat on the wall and drops down negligently on a cushion
on the floor.*

HOMBURG. Our life, the Dervish says, is but a journey,
and a short one—oh, how true! From eighteen
inches over ground we pass to eighteen
under—but I'd much prefer dismounting halfway there! Today you hold your head high
on your shoulders, tomorrow bow it trembling
on your breast, the third day, where is it?—
at your own feet! It's true, they say a sun
shines there as well as here, and shines upon
much fairer fields: I do believe it, I—
the only trouble is, the eye that is supposed
to witness all those glories is rotting in the grave!

SCENE 4

Enter an Orderly holding aloft a torch.

ORDERLY. Her Highness, Prince Natalie of Orange!
HOMBURG (*jumping up*).
  Natalie!
ORDERLY. And here she is—
  Her Ladyship!
(*Enter Princess Natalie and Count Reuss, with Ladies following.*)

NATALIE (*to the Count, with an inclination of her head.*)
    If you would give us leave to be
alone a moment, Count? (*Exeunt Count Reuss and Orderly.*)
HOMBURG.   Your Ladyship!
NATALIE. My good, my dearest cousin!
HOMBURG (*leading her forward*).
          Tell me why
you've come, oh do! Am I a dead man still?
NATALIE. No, no, all's well, just as I promised you.
 You're pardoned, free. And here's the letter, which
 he wrote himself, confirming it.
HOMBURG.   But it's
 not possible, I'm sure it is a dream!
NATALIE. Read it, won't you? Read it for yourself.
HOMBURG (*reading*).
 "Sir Prince of Homburg! When I ordered you
 to be confined for launching your attack
 too soon, I believed it was my duty: I
 was sure you felt the same. But if you think
 that you have been unjustly treated, tell
 me so in two words, please, and you
 shall have your sword back instantly."
   (*Natalie turns white. There is a pause. The Prince regards
    her not knowing what to think.*)
NATALIE (*with forced gaity*).
 And there it is! A line from you is all
 that's needed—! Dear, sweet friend! (*Squeezes his hand.*)
HOMBURG.   Your Ladyship!
NATALIE. Oh, what a blessed moment this is for
 me! Here's your pen. Now take it, please, and write!
HOMBURG. And this mark is his signature?
NATALIE.   An *F*;
 he signs his name so!—Bork, dear, please rejoice!
 His kindness, oh I knew it, is as boundless as the sea.—
 A chair here, he must sit down now and write.
HOMBURG. He asks if I think—?
NATALIE (*interrupting*).
      Yes, of course! Sit down!
 Now hurry, do—I'll dictate what you need to write.
   (*Pushes a chair up behind him.*)

HOMBURG. Please, I would like to read the letter over.

NATALIE (*snatching it out of his hand*).

Why? You saw your own grave in the churchyard
yawning up at you with open jaws.
There is no time to lose. Now write!

HOMBURG (*smiling*).

                             Oh really,
hearing you I'd think it was a panther
leaping at my throat.

        (*Sits down and picks up the pen; she turns
             away to hide her tears.*)

NATALIE.   Now write, if you
don't want to put me in a temper!

HOMBURG (*ringing for a servant, who enters*).

                           Pen
and paper, wax, and my seal, please.

       (*The servant brings him these and exits. The Prince begins to
      write. Stops. Then tears the sheet of paper in two and throws
               it under the table.*)

Oh, that's too stupid, much. (*Takes another sheet.*)

NATALIE (*picking up the torn sheet*).

                      But how can you
say that? My God, how good this is, it's perfect!

HOMBURG (*muttering*).

Pooh! It's how a scoundrel goes about
it, not a Prince.—Now let me think again.

     (*Pause. Reaches for the Elector's letter in the Princess's hand.*)

What was it that he said, exactly, in the letter?

NATALIE (*holding it away from him*).

Nothing, not a thing!

HOMBURG.   Please give it here.

NATALIE. You've read it once already!

HOMBURG.   That's no matter.
I only want to see how I should answer
him. (*Unfolds the letter and re-reads it.*)

NATALIE (*under her breath*).

     Good God, that's it, we've reached the end!

HOMBURG (*surprised*).

Look there! Extraordinary, on my life!
You must have missed this part.

NATALIE. I didn't! Which?

HOMBURG. He leaves it up to me—*I* must decide!

NATALIE. Of course!

HOMBURG [*ironically*].
Very noble-minded of him, oh indeed!
Just like great souls should behave!

NATALIE. Oh yes,
his magnanimity is limitless!—
Now do what you are called upon to do
and send him his two words. They are a mere
formality, the pretext which is needed—
give it to him and the quarrel's over instantly!

HOMBURG (*putting the letter aside*).
No, love! The matter needs some thinking on
until tomorrow.

NATALIE. Who can understand
you! Why this sudden change, I'd like to know?

HOMBURG (*passionately, rising out of his chair*).
Oh, please stop questioning me! You don't consider
what the letter says! His stipulation:
if I think I've been unjustly treated—
I can't meet, and if you press me, in
my present frame of mind, to answer him,
by God, I'll write: with perfect justice
yes, you've treated me! (*Sits down again, elbows bent upon
the table, and pores over the letter.*)

NATALIE (*white-faced*).
You've lost your mind!
What kind of thing is that to say? (*Bends over him, much moved.*)

HOMBURG (*gripping her hand*).
One moment,
please! It seems to me— (*Thinking hard.*)

NATALIE. What seems to you?

HOMBURG. It's becoming clear to me what I must write.

NATALIE (*anguished*).
Oh Homburg!

HOMBURG (*taking up the pen*).
Yes, I'm listening. What is
it?

NATALIE. Dearest friend! I honor it, the feeling
  that has taken such possession of you. But I tell
  you solemnly: the regiment that will conduct
  the final rites for you tomorrow, with carbines
  leveled from across a mound of new dug
  earth, is ordered up and reconciled
  to what its duty is. If your nobility
  of mind forbids you to oppose the sentence, to cancel
  it by doing as his letter asks,
  then I assure you he will act, as in
  this present juncture matters stand,
  sublimely, and full of pity, execute
  the sentence on you in the morning!
HOMBURG (*writing*).

                                        I don't care!
NATALIE. Don't care!
HOMBURG.   He can do just as he pleases, let
  him—I must do just as I should!
NATALIE (*horror-struck, going up to him*).

                          A more
unnatural man—! Is that what you are writing
there?
HOMBURG (*concluding*).
    "Signed Homburg, Fehrbellin, the twelfth
  day of the month." And that is that. Franz, here!
              (*Seals the letter in an envelope.*)
NATALIE. Great God above!
HOMBURG (*standing up [to the servant]*).
                    Would you take this letter to the castle,
  to His Majesty?
                (*Exit the servant.*)
        I shouldn't want to act
  a dishonorable part before a man
  who acts so honorably toward me. My offense,
  I see it now, is heavy, very heavy;
  if the price of his forgiveness is my arguing
  it out of him, then I don't want it, no!
NATALIE (*kissing him*).
  Here, I must kiss you, oh I must! Even if
  a dozen bullets bore you down into the dust right now,

I still could not, amid my tears, keep back
the exultation I should feel and I
would say: you please me, very much! But meanwhile,
seeing you may follow your own heart,
I allow myself to follow mine. Count Reuss!
   (*The orderly opens the door to the Count, who enters.*)
REUSS. Your Highness!
NATALIE.   Off to Arnstein, sir, to Colonel
 Kottwitz, with your letter! The Regiment is ordered
 here, the Elector wishes it, I'll expect
 to see them marching up before midnight!

ACT V

SCENE I
The Castle Hall
Enter the Elector, half-dressed, from his cabinet adjoining,
followed by Count Truchss, Count Hohenzollern, and Captain
von der Golz.—Pages holding candlesticks.

ELECTOR. Colonel Kottwitz? With the Princess's dragoons?
 Here in Fehrbellin?
TRUCHSS (*opening the window*).
     It's true, Your Highness!
 Marched them here, the Colonel has, and there
 they stand below.
ELECTOR.   Well, gentlemen—will you
 explain this mystery? Who ordered him
 to come?
HOHENZOLLERN. I don't know, Sir.
ELECTOR.   The place he was
 assigned by me is Arnstein! Downstairs,
 one of you, at once, and bring him here!
GOLZ. He'll be along, Sir, very soon, I'm sure!
ELECTOR. Where is he, then?
GOLZ.   The Town Hall, so
 I hear, where all the officers who serve
 your house are now assembled.
ELECTOR.   And why are they
 assembled there? What for?

HOHENZOLLERN.   I've no idea.

TRUCHSS. Sir, may we have permission to go there
   too, for a short while?

ELECTOR.   Go where? The Town Hall?

HOHENZOLLERN. Yes. We gave our word we would appear.

ELECTOR (*after some hesitation*).
   —Dismissed!

GOLZ.   Let's go then, my good gentlemen!
                    (*Exeunt officers.*)

                    SCENE 2

ELECTOR. Peculiar, very! If I were the Dey
   of Tunis, faced with something so ambiguous
   as this I'd sound the alarm at once. I'd lay
   the silk cord,[4] ready, on my desk,
   I'd barricade the gate and bring up
   howitzers and cannon. But since it's Hans Kottwitz
   out of Priegnitz comes upon me in this way,
   unauthorized and unallowed, I'll do
   it as we do such things in Brandenburg:
   take hold of him by one of his three silver
   hairs and lead him quietly, with his
   twelve squadrons, back to Arnstein, where old Hans
   belongs. Why wake the sleeping town?
          (*Steps over to the window again for a moment, then to the
                table and rings. Enter two Servants.*)
                    Jump down and ask,
   pretending it's yourself that wants to know,
   what's going on at the Town Hall.

FIRST SERVANT.   Right,
   my Lord! (*Exits.*)

ELECTOR (*to the Second Orderly*).
          But you please bring my clothes to me.
          (*Exit Second Servant, who returns with the clothes. The Elector
          puts them on, with all his princely jewels and chains of office.*)

4. For the traitor to hang himself with.

SCENE 3
Enter Field Marshal Dörfling.

FIELD MARSHAL. Rebellion, Sir!

ELECTOR (*still dressing*).

Please, Marshal, please! You know
how I detest it when people burst into my quarters
unannounced. Now what is on your mind?

FIELD MARSHAL. Forgive me, Sir, but it is something very
serious that brings me here. Colonel
Kottwitz has marched his troops to town without
authority; one hundred officers
or so are crowded around him in the Knights' Hall;
a petition's being circulated whose intention
is to challenge you in your prerogatives.

ELECTOR. I know, I know! I'm sure it has to do
with Homburg—an attempt to save his life.

FIELD MARSHAL.   It is!
How did you guess?

ELECTOR.   I did? Good!—Well, I share
their feelings.

FIELD MARSHAL. The rumor is the madmen mean
to hand up their petition to you, in
the castle here, today, and if your wrath
is still implacable and you insist
on the sentence—hardly do I dare
to use such words!—they have in mind to liberate
him from confinement forcibly!

ELECTOR (*grimly*).

Who told you that?

FIELD MARSHAL. Who told me it? The Lady Retzow, my
wife's cousin, very trustworthy
she is, I do assure you! Just this evening,
at her uncle's—he's von Retzow, don't
you know, the bailiff—officers from camp
were there who openly discussed the brazen
scheme.

ELECTOR. A man must tell me that before
I'll credit it! To protect him from such heroes,

all I need to do is stand my boot
outside his prison door!
FIELD MARSHAL. I beg you,
Sir, if you mean to grant a pardon to the Prince,
then do it now before some dreadful thing
occurs! An army, as you know full well—
it loves its heroes! Don't, however, let
this spark which warms its courage turn into
a conflagration devouring all around
it. Kottwitz and the men he has collected don't
know yet that you've been warned, most loyally,
by me; before they come, give back the Prince
his sword, which after all he quite deserves
to have returned to him. By your doing so,
the annals of the world will have one act
the more of greatness to record, and one unhappy
deed the less.
ELECTOR. Ah, but there, you see,
I must consult first with the Prince. It wasn't by
an arbitrary act he was imprisoned,
nor can he arbitrarily be freed.
—When the gentlemen arrive, I'll speak to them.
FIELD MARSHAL (aside).
Damnation! Every arrow I let fly
his armor turns aside.

SCENE 4

Enter two Footmen, one carrying a letter.

FIRST FOOTMAN. Sir, Colonels Kottwitz, Hennings,
Truchss, and others request an audience!
ELECTOR (*to the other Footman, as he accepts the letter*).
From the Prince of Homburg?
SECOND FOOTMAN. Yes, Your Highness.
ELECTOR. And whom did you receive it from?
SECOND FOOTMAN. The Swiss guard at the gate, who had it from the
Prince's orderly.
ELECTOR (*goes over to the table to read the letter; having done so, turns to call
a Page*).
Oh Prittwitz, let me have

the order for the Prince's execution. Also
bring me, if you would, the safe-conduct
for the Swedish envoy, Count von Horn.
                    (*Exit the Page; to the First Footman.*)
Show Colonel Kottwitz and his party in.

SCENE 5

Enter Colonel Kottwitz, Counts Truchss, Hohenzollern, Sparren,
Reuss, Captains von der Golz and Stranz, and other officers.

KOTTWITZ (*the petition in his hand*).
My Prince and Sovereign, allow me humbly,
in the name of the whole army, to present this plea
to you!
ELECTOR. Before I accept it, Kottwitz, tell
me who it was that called you here.
KOTTWITZ (*staring*).

                                With my

dragoons?
ELECTOR.   With all your regiment! I gave
you Arnstein for your billet.
KOTTWITZ.   Sir, *you* did,
your order called me here!
ELECTOR.   What? Show it to
me.
KOTTWITZ. Here it is, my Lord.
ELECTOR (*reading*).

                    "Signed Natalie,
at Fehrbellin, by order of my uncle, His Highness
Frederick William."
KOTTWITZ.   Good Lord, Prince,
I hope it comes as no surprise to you!
ELECTOR. No, no! What I mean is—tell me who
it was that handed you the order.
KOTTWITZ.   Why,
Count Reuss!
ELECTOR (*after a short pause*).

                No, on the contrary—I'm pleased
to welcome you!—You and your twelve squadrons
are appointed to conduct, at break of day tomorrow,

the final honors which we'll show to Colonel Homburg,
under sentence by the law.

KOTTWITZ (*dismayed*).
                                    Your Majesty!

ELECTOR (*giving him back the order*).
    Your regiment, I wonder, is it still
    drawn up below under cover, as the phrase goes,
    of the shades of night?

KOTTWITZ.   The shades of night, my Lord—?

ELECTOR [*sharply*].
    Why haven't you found billets for your men?

KOTTWITZ.   I have,
    Sir, they have all been billeted, here
    in Fehrbellin, according to your orders.

ELECTOR (*pivoting toward the window*).
                                    What?
    When I looked down two minutes past—? By God,
    sir, you have hunted stables up at top
    speed, I must say! Well, good, that's very good!
    I welcome you again! What business brings
    you here? What news have you?

KOTTWITZ.   I have, Sir, a petition
    for you from your faithful troops.

ELECTOR.   I'll take
    it now!

KOTTWITZ. But the words you spoke a moment ago
    have struck down all my hopes.

ELECTOR.   And other words
    may raise them up again. (*Reading.*)
                            "A Petition of His Majesty
    entreating Clemency for our General,
    Prince Frederick of Hesse-Homburg, charged
    with the commission of a Capital Offense."
                            (*To the Officers.*)
    A fine name, that, you gentlemen,
    not unworthy you should rally to him in such
    numbers. (*Looks down at the sheet of paper again.*)
                Tell me, who wrote this?

KOTTWITZ. Sir, I did.

ELECTOR.   Is the Prince acquainted with its contents?

KOTTWITZ. No, Sir, not at all! The idea was
our own, entirely, and ours alone what's written
there.

ELECTOR. Your patience for a moment, please. (*Goes over to the table
and reads the petition from beginning to end.—Long pause.*)
How strange! Old soldier that you are, and still
you don't hesitate to defend the Prince's
action? You justify his charging Wrangel
before I gave the order?

KOTTWITZ.   Your Majesty,
old Kottwitz does!

ELECTOR.   On the battlefield, you saw
things differently.

KOTTWITZ.   My judgment was at fault,
Sir, yes! The Prince knows war, he understands
it; I was wrong, I should have bowed at once
to his decision. The Swedish left
was giving way—they started marching over
reinforcements from their right to bolster
it. If he had waited for your order, time
would have been allowed them to reestablish their position
in the ravines—and then you might have kissed good-bye
forever, Sir, to all your hopes of victory.

ELECTOR. So that is how it pleases you to understand
the battle! Well, the mission I gave Colonel
Hennings was to seize the bridgehead covering
Wrangel's rear. If you had not ignored
my orders, Hennings would have gone ahead
and launched his blow. In two hours' time you would
have seen the bridges going up in flames
and his detachments firmly planted on the Rhyn.
Then all of Wrangel's forces would have been
annihilated, in the bogs and ditches, to a man.

KOTTWITZ. Sir, only hopeless amateurs, not soldiers like
yourself, imagine they'll reach out and seize,
at once, the greatest crown that Fortune has
to give; until today you always took
whatever she might offer. The dragon that
laid waste the March is reeling back with bleeding
head—what more should you expect from one

338

day's work? What difference does it make to you
if he lies panting in the sands and licks his wounds
for two more weeks? We've learned the trick of beating
him, and how we long, your soldiers, to repeat it!
Allow us one more bout with Wrangel, face
to face, and that will end the business, we
will chase the Swedes into the Baltic! Rome
wasn't built in a day.

ELECTOR.   How dare you hope
for that, you foolish man, if anyone who has
a mind to can seize the reins of our war car
for himself? Do you think luck will always smile
upon the disobedient? I've no
desire for a victory that's a bastard child
of the slut chance. I love the law and her
I will uphold, who is the mother of my crown
and begetter of my long lineage of victories.

KOTTWITZ. The highest law that should hold sway in our
commander's breast is not your own will,
its exact decrees, Sir—those are the letter
of the law. The loftiest law, the crown of all,
is our Fatherland—it is yourself
as your head wears that crown. Why, I ask,
should you be so concerned about the enemy's
being beaten exactly as the rule book calls
for, if only he is overthrown with all
his banners and rolling at your feet? The rule
that beats him is the only rule! The army
whose delight it is to serve you—would
you have it be a senseless instrument,
a dead thing, like the sword you've got tucked in
your golden belt? A little, meager spirit
that one was, a man who never raised
his head up to the stars, who first taught
such a thing! What bad, shortsighted policy,
because quick-acting instinct comes to grief
in one case, to rule it out thereafter
in instance after instance in which spontaneous
impulse, it alone, can save the day!
Do I, you think, pour out my blood upon

the battlefield for pay—for gold coin
or for honors? God forbid, my blood comes
at a dearer price than that! Oh no! My joy
and my delight, for which I am beholden to no
man, which I possess without the need
to speak a word, I have in your great
goodness, glory, the fame, continually
growing, of your great name! Sir, that's the wage
for which I sell my heart! Admit, shall we,
you doom the Prince for winning by a way not called
for in the battle plan; and one fine morning, I,
with all my squadrons, wandering like a shepherd
here and there, stumble, between wood and cliff,
on victory, by a way not called for in the battle plan:
by God, I'd be a precious rascal if
I failed to do exactly what the Prince
did—eagerly! And if you took the regulations
out and said: "Kottwitz, you've just forfeited
your head," I'd answer: Yes, I know, Sir, here
it is, it's yours. I bound myself to defend
your throne with all my heart and soul—my head
was not excepted. So I don't give
you more than what's your own!

ELECTOR.   An extraordinary fellow,
yes, you are—you're more than I can deal with!
I find my mind suborned by all your cunning
arts of rhetoric, who am too much
inclined already, as you know, to sympathize
with what you feel. So I will call an advocate
to plead my case and end the argument.
                    (*Rings, and a servant enters.*)
I'd like the Prince of Homburg brought here from the jail!
                    (*Exit the servant.*)
Believe me, he will teach you what obedience
and discipline should be! I've got a letter
here from him, at any rate, that has
a different ring indeed from all those sophistries
you've spun out, like a clever schoolboy, for
my benefit. (*Goes back to his desk and picks up a sheet of paper.*)

340

KOTTWITZ (*surprised*).
　　　　What's that—? Bring whom—?
HENNINGS.　　　　　　　　　　The Prince
　to speak for him?
TRUCHSS.　　　　Impossible!
　　　　(*The officers crowd together uneasily, whispering.*)
ELECTOR.　　　　　　　This second
　composition here, whose is it?
HOHENZOLLERN.　　　　　Mine,
　my Prince!
ELECTOR (*reading*).
　　　　"Proof that Elector Frederick,
　for the Prince of Homburg's deed, himself must
　bear—" I call that nervy, yes, I do,
　by God! The responsibility for the Prince's
　criminal offense you throw on me?
HOHENZOLLERN. I do, Sir, yes, on you; I, Hohenzollern!
ELECTOR. Now, by God, this beats the old Greek stories!
　One fellow proves that Homburg isn't guilty,
　another comes along to prove *I* am!
　Out with it—your grounds for saying so!
HOHENZOLLERN. Please recollect, Your Highness, the night we found
　the Prince asleep beneath the plane trees
　in the garden, dreaming, as I'm sure he was,
　of the next day's victory, and in his hand
　a laurel wreath. You wished, it seemed, to sound
　his heart; smiling quietly, you drew the crown
　away from him and wound the chain that hangs
　around your neck among its leaves, and then
　gave crown and gold chain, twined together, to her Ladyship,
　your noble niece. The extraordinary vision
　causes our Prince to jump up with a blush;
　his hand goes out to claim so sweet a prize,
　which so dear a hand now seems to proffer him.
　But you step backwards hastily and draw
　the Princess back with you; the door above
　swings open to receive you, Princess, chain and laurel
　wreath all disappear at once, and—clutching
　to him a glove snatched God knows from whose hand,

341

he doesn't—there he stands, a solitary
figure in the dreaming dark.
ELECTOR.   A glove? What glove?
HOHENZOLLERN. Sir, let me finish, please! The whole thing
  was a joke; yet what it meant to him I soon
  found out. For when I slipped back through
  the garden gate, coming on him as it might
  have seemed by chance, and woke him and he got his wits
  together, joy unspeakable suffused
  his being at the recollection, a thing more touching
  you cannot conceive! At once, down
  to the last detail, he told me all, as if
  it were a dream he'd dreamt: no dream, he thought,
  in all his life had seemed so vivid—. And an absolute
  belief took hold of him high Heaven had vouchsafed
  him a clear sign; everything his spirit
  had beheld, lady, laurel wreath,
  and chain of honor, God would grant him on the coming
  day.
ELECTOR. Dear me! How strange! About that glove—?
HOHENZOLLERN. Oh yes—. Now that part of his dream, materialized
  between his fingers unaccountably,
  both cast down and raised up his faith. At first
  he looks at it in wonder—white, the glove
  is, by its shape and fashion seems a woman's—
  but since he spoke to no one in the garden
  from whose arm it might have come,
  and since, too, I kept breaking in on his
  dazed wonderment to remind him of the briefing we
  must soon take part in at the castle, he tucks
  the glove inside his doublet and soon forgets
  what he can't understand.
ELECTOR.   And then?
HOHENZOLLERN.   And then
  he took his pencil and his tablet and reported
  to the castle, to listen very faithfully
  to the Marshal read the orders. Now the Electress and the Princess,
  as it happens, are present in the great hall, too,
  about to ride away. How conceive
  his immense astonishment when Princess Natalie

begins to search around her for a missing glove—
the very one he has tucked in his doublet!
Time and time again the Marshal calls
him to attention: "Sir Prince of Homburg!"—"At your orders,
sir!" he answers, trying mightily
to collect his wits. But he is wonderstruck,
completely: a bolt from Heaven falling on
him wouldn't have the least—!

                                  (Stops.)

ELECTOR.   And was it really
Princess Natalie's glove.

HOHENZOLLERN.   Indeed it was!

      (The Elector is made thoughtful.—Hohenzollern continues.)
He is a stone; standing there, the pencil
in his hand, he seems a living man, it's true,
but all sensation is extinguished
in him, as if by magic. Not until the cannon
fire is falling thunderously in our ranks
next morning does he come back to life again
and ask me: "Good old Heinrich, tell me, at
the briefing yesterday, what was it Dörfling
said I am to do?"

FIELD MARSHAL.   I'll back up every
word of that, Sir, yes! The Prince, I well
remember, never heard a word of what
I said; I've often seen him with his head among
the clouds, but so removed from everything
I never saw him till that day.

ELECTOR.   And so,
unless I quite mistake your words, what
must follow for me, with inexorable logic,
is: if I had not allowed myself
a dubious amusement with the young dreamer
in his helpless state, he never would
have proved delinquent in his duty: at the briefing,
his mind would not have been on other things;
in the fighting, he never would have failed
to follow orders. Right? Confess it! Isn't
that your meaning?

HOHENZOLLERN. Draw your own conclusions,
Sire.

ELECTOR. What a fool you are, an idiot!
If you had not said, Come down to the garden,
Sir, and see!—my curiosity
would not have been aroused and I shouldn't have played
that harmless joke of mine on the dreaming Prince.
And so, with equal justice I declare:
The one who is to blame for his mistake
was you!—The wisdom of my officers is truly Delphic!

HOHENZOLLERN. Sir, I've said enough. I'm sure my words
won't fail to make an impression on your heart!

SCENE 6

Enter an Officer.

OFFICER. The Prince, my Lord, is coming presently.

ELECTOR. Good. Show him in.

OFFICER. Please, one more minute, Sir.
As we were going past the churchyard gate,
he asked the sexton to admit him briefly.

ELECTOR. To
the churchyard?

OFFICER. Yes, Your Highness.

ELECTOR. Why?

OFFICER. To tell the truth, I don't really know. I think
he wished to see the grave you ordered dug
for him.
(*The Officers crowd together, talking.*)

ELECTOR. Oh well. When he appears, be sure
to let him in at once.
(*Goes back to the table and turns over papers.*)

TRUCHSS. Sir, here he is
now, with the guard.

SCENE 7

Enter the Prince of Homburg, Officer of the Guard, and Men.

ELECTOR. My dear young Prince, I've called
you here to ask your help! This petition I
am holding in my hand has been presented

me, on your behalf, by Colonel Kottwitz,
with a hundred noble names, look here, subscribed
below. The army craves your freedom, sir,
and does not look with favor on the sentence passed
upon you by the court. Pray, read it for yourself
and know what it contains.
                    (*Hands Homburg the sheet.*)
HOMBURG (*after glancing at it briefly, looks around the circle of officers.*)
                    Kottwitz, what
a faithful friend you are, I want to shake
your hand! You put yourself out for me more,
much more than my behavior toward you on
that day deserves. But now go back to Arnstein,
where you came from, please, at once, and never
stir from there; I've thought about it long and hard
and wish to suffer death, the death to which
I am condemned. (*Hands him back the petition.*)
KOTTWITZ (*confounded*).
                    Oh no, My Prince, don't say
that!
HOHENZOLLERN. Does he *want* to die—?
TRUCHSS.   He mustn't die,
he shan't!
OFFICERS (*together, crowding forward*).
                    Your Majesty! Great Prince! Elector!
Hear us, do!
HOMBURG.   Hush, friends! My mind's made up,
unalterably! I wish to glorify,
before the eyes of the whole army, the sacred
rule of war against which I offended,
by freely choosing death! How little worth,
my brothers, is the paltry victory which I
might wrest from Wrangel, compared with that supremest
triumph won tomorrow over the direst
enemy we know, the one inside
ourselves: insolent defiance, arrogance!
May he be humbled in the dust, the foreign Prince
who seeks to bend us to his yoke, and the Brandenburger
live a free man on his native ground;

for it is his, and his delight its golden
meadows, his alone!

KOTTWITZ (*much affected*).
                                My son! My dearest
friend! I don't know what to call you!

TRUCHSS.   God
in Heaven!

KOTTWITZ.   Let me kiss your hand!
                        (*All crowd around him.*)

HOMBURG (*turning to the Elector*).
                                But you,
my Prince, whom once I had the right to use
a dearer name in speaking to—alas,
now forfeited—I stoop before you, overcome
with feeling! Forgive me if, that fateful day,
my zeal to serve you was too headlong, heedless—
now death washes all my guilt away.
I accept with all my heart the judgment
passed on me and cheerfully submit to it;
but it will comfort me to know that you
on your side, too, have shed the rancor
that you felt; in sign of which I ask you, now
as I prepare to take my leave, to grant
me a request.

ELECTOR.   Young hero, speak your wish!
Whatever it may be, it shall be done,
on my honor as a chevalier!

HOMBURG.   Don't buy
a peace from Karl Gustav with your niece's hand,
Sir! Send his agent packing, him and his
insulting offer—write them your reply in chain shot!

ELECTOR (*kissing him on the brow*).
So be it; as you say! And with this kiss,
my son, I set the seal of my consent
on your last request. Why should there be another
sacrifice to add to all the others,
one moreover only wrung from me
by war's misfortunes? Every word you utter
is the promise of a victory whose flowering
will crush our enemy into the dust! She is

the Prince of Homburg's bride, I'll write so now
to Sweden; his, no other's, who forfeited
his life, for Fehrbellin, on the altar of the law;
the King must fight his ghost for her
on the battlefield, for his spirit marches on
in death before our army's streaming flags!
                 (*Kisses him again and raises him up.*)
HOMBURG. Oh see, now you restore me back to life!
I pray that every blessing may be yours
which seraphim, on their cloudy thrones,
pour down, with loud-exulting cries, on heroes'
heads! Go forth, great Sovereign, to fight
and, even if the whole world should defy
you, conquer—for you are worthy of no less!
ELECTOR. Officer of the Guard, conduct him back to prison!

SCENE 8

Natalie and the Electress appear in the doorway, behind them
Ladies-in-waiting.

NATALIE. Please, Mother, please! Don't talk to me about
propriety! The properest thing for me,
at such a time, is to show my love for him!
—My dear, my poor, unhappy friend!

HOMBURG (*making for the exit*).
                       Let's go!
TRUCHSS (*holding him back*).
  No, never, Prince!
               (*Officers bar his way.*)
HOMBURG.   Come, take me off!
HOHENZOLLERN.   Elector,
  can your heart—?
HOMBURG (*wrenching himself free*).
               Tyrants, do you want
to see me dragged in chains to execution?
Now let me go! The world and I are quits!
           (*Exit with the Guard.*)
NATALIE (*her head pressed against her aunt's bosom*).
  Earth, open up your arms to me! Why see sunlight any more?

SCENE 9

FIELD MARSHAL. Good God, it had to come to this, did it!
> (*The Elector whispers earnestly to an officer.*)

KOTTWITZ (*frigidly*).
And now, Sir, after all this, may we go?

ELECTOR. No, not at all! I'll tell you when you are dismissed!
> (*Looks him in the eye, very hard; then picks up from the
> table the papers which he asked the page to bring him
> and turns to the Field Marshal.*)

Here is Count Horn's safe-conduct! It is my Cousin
Homburg's wish, I know, which I have pledged
my word to carry out—in three days' time
we go to war again!
> (*Stops. Looks briefly at the death sentence again.*)

And pray, how would *you* judge
it, gentlemen? In this past year the Prince
of Homburg, thanks to his unruliness
and reckless indiscretion, has cost me two
great victories and marred a third. Well, it
has been an education for him—would
you risk a fourth time with him, men?

KOTTWITZ AND TRUCHSS (*together*).

What's that—?

Do you—? Oh, godlike Prince—!

ELECTOR.   Well, would you, would
you?

KOTTWITZ [*with some sarcasm*].
By the living God, if you were tottering
on the brink of ruin, about to plunge
into the abyss, he wouldn't even *think*
of drawing his sword to help you, rescue you,
unsummoned!

ELECTOR (*tearing up the death sentence*).
Then follow me, good friends, into the garden!
> (*Exeunt.*)

SCENE 10

*The Castle with its ramp leading down into the garden, as in
Act I. It is night again.*

348

*Enter the Prince of Homburg, blindfolded, with Captain Stranz
leading him, through the lower garden gate. Officers of the
Guard.—In the distance, drums beating the funeral march.*

HOMBURG. Now immortality, you're mine, entirely
  mine! Your light shines through my blindfold
  with the brilliance of a thousand suns! On either shoulder
  wings unfold, my soul mounts up into the silent
  upper spheres; and as a ship, borne
  forward by the wind, sees dropping fast behind
  the busy port, so all life sinks
  and fades for me into the haze—and now
  I still can make out shapes and colors,
  and now all's shrouded in a thickening mist.
     *(Drops down on a bench beneath the oak tree in the middle of the
       garden. Captain Stranz steps away to peer up the ramp.)*
  How sweet the night-violet's odor is!
  You smell it, don't you, too?
STRANZ *(coming back).*
                  Carnations, sir,
  they are, and gillyflowers.
HOMBURG.   Gillyflowers—
  how do they come here?
STRANZ.   I've no idea.
  Some young girl must have planted them.
  —Would you care for this carnation, sir?
HOMBURG.   How kind
  of you! When I go home I'll see it's put
  in water.

SCENE 11

*Enter on the ramp above the Elector carrying the laurel wreath,
with the gold chain wound around it, the Electress, Princess
Natalie, Field Marshal Dörfling, Colonel Kottwitz, Hohenzollern,
Golz, etc., Ladies, Officers, and torchbearers.—Hohenzollern
leans forward over the balustrade and signals with a handkerchief
to Stranz, who leaves the Prince's side and whispers to the guards.*

HOMBURG. Dear Stranz, how bright it has become!
STRANZ (*coming back to him*).
    Your Highness, please be good enough to rise.
HOMBURG. What is it!
STRANZ.   Nothing you need fear. I only
    mean to take the blindfold off.
HOMBURG.   Has my
    last hour of endurance struck?
STRANZ.   It has, it has
    indeed! (*Removes the blindfold.*)
          Now hail to you, good Prince, all blessings
    yours—for you are worthy of no less!
    (*The Elector hands the wreath, from which the gold chain dangles,*
    to the Princess and leads her by the hand down the ramp, followed
    by Gentlemen and Ladies. Princess Natalie, surrounded by
    torchbearers, advances to face the Prince, who rises dumb with wonder;
    she sets the wreath on his head, hangs the chain around his neck
    and presses his hand to her heart. The Prince falls in a faint.)
NATALIE. Heavens—killed with joy!
HOHENZOLLERN (*catching him as he falls*).
                   A hand here—help!
ELECTOR. Let the cannon's thunder wake the Prince!
    (*A salute is fired, a march sounds, the castle blazes into light.*)
KOTTWITZ.   Hail, hail
    to him, all hail the Prince of Homburg!
OFFICERS.   Hail!
    All hail!
ALL.   All hail to him who conquered gloriously
    at Fehrbellin!
                (*Momentary silence.*)
HOMBURG.   No, it's a dream! Do say—
    is it a dream?
KOTTWITZ.   A dream, what else?
OFFICERS.   To arms! To arms!
TRUCHSS. To arms and into battle!
FIELD MARSHAL.   Victory!
ALL. Down, enemies of Brandenburg, into the dust!

A Fragment of
the Tragedy of Robert Guiscard
Duke of the Normans

TRANSLATOR'S NOTE

The subject of Kleist's attempt to write a heroic tragedy is Robert de Hauteville (ca. 1015–1085), the Norman adventurer who, setting out from a village near Coutances, conquered southern Italy. Unlike his fellow countryman and conqueror, William, he is little remembered today; yet in the words of John Julius Norwich (*The Normans in the South, 1016–1130*), he shook Christendom to its "very foundations" and caused "the imperial thrones of East and West alike to tremble at his name." Early in his career of conquest he was nicknamed the Guiscard (the Cunning) and that remained his name ever after.

Robert was preceded as captain of the main Norman faction in Italy by his elder brothers, William the Iron Arm, Drogo, and Humphrey, each in turn. Count Humphrey made Guiscard protector of his son and heir, Abelard; but at his brother's death in 1057 Robert possessed his nephew's lands for himself and the Normans acclaimed him as Humphrey's successor. In 1059 Pope Nicholas II rewarded him, for services, with the Duchy of Apulia and Calabria and also threw in Sicily. The lordship of these lands was mostly prospective; Guiscard still had to fight Greeks, Lombards, and Arabs for their possession. In 1074, grown very powerful indeed, Duke Robert *consented,* on a third appeal by the Greek Emperor Michael VII, to have his daughter Helena betrothed to Michael's son. When Michael was deposed, Guiscard went to war against Byzantium. A first expedition conquered Illyria and pushed into Macedonia. Constantinople lay ahead. But meanwhile Duke Robert had been summoned back urgently to Italy by the Pope to repel the German Emperor. By the time Robert returned to the attack in 1084, Alexius Comnenus had driven the Norman force virtually into the Adriatic. The Duke, though an old man now, captured Corfu and then sailed to join his son on the island of Cephalonia. But the Norman troops had been devastated by an epidemic in the winter and Guiscard came down with the fever. The ship sought shelter in the nearest anchorage, and there in Cephalonia in 1085 Duke Robert Guiscard died.

Kleist departed from the historical facts by placing the action of his play before the gates of Constantinople. He makes Helena a widowed Empress; she never advanced so far. Guiscard had three sons; none of whom bore his name. Kleist calls the Duke's brother and Abelard's father Otto, not Humphrey. Abelard, cheated of his inheritance, rebelled against his uncle and then against his uncle's heir; he was not engaged to Helena, nor did he take part in the campaign against Byzantium. The Guiscard had two wives, the second called Sichelgaita. (The uncouth name is Lombardic.) Sichelgaita was not at all the fainting Duchess of the play, but a great burly woman who fought mightily in battle beside her husband—John Julius Norwich calls her "the closest approximation history has ever dared to produce of a Valkyrie."

Cast of Characters

Robert Guiscard, Duke of the Normans
Robert, his son
Abelard, his nephew
The Duchess Cecilia, Guiscard's wife
Helena, Guiscard's daughter and the widowed Empress of Greece,
  betrothed to Abelard
Old Man
Deputation of Warriors
Norman People

Scene: *A hill with cypresses in front and standing on it Guiscard's tent, in the Norman camp before Constantinople. Several fires are burning in the foreground, fed from time to time with frankincense and other strong-smelling herbs. In the background the fleet.*

SCENE I

Enter a deputation of Normans in full military dress, accompanied by a crowd of people of all ages.

PEOPLE (*in agitated movement*).
  Side by side we march with you, good fathers,
  praying fervently, to the Guiscard's tent! A cherub
  leads the way, from God's right hand, when you
  go out to shake the rock around which our
  whole army, mad with fear, boils
  and seethes in vain! Fall on him like a thunderbolt,
  that rock, and open up a way to lead
  us out of the horrors of this nightmare camp!
  Unless he acts at once to save us from the plague
  that Hell inflicts on us so cruelly,
  this point of land will rise up from the sea
  a burial mound for all his people's corpses!
  With giant steps of terror, she marches through
  the trembling ranks exhaling from her swollen lips
  her bosom's poisonous reek full
  in their faces! Wherever her foot turns,
  to ashes horse and rider fall behind
  her on the spot, and friends recoil in fear from friends,
  bridegrooms from their brides, mothers from their children.
  Abandoned on a hillside, their wailing carries
  to us from across the distant waste where ghastly
  birds of prey, with flapping wings, darken,
  like clouds, the day and plummet on the abject
  forms below! And him as well—never mind
  how unafraid, how stubborn the man is,
  the dragon's bound to overtake him too,
  and he'll discover, if he won't retreat,
  that what he's conquered for himself in that
  imperial city there is nothing but

355

a gaudy tomb! And instead of our children's blessing
our children's curse, a monster, will one day
settle on it howling maledictions from an iron
breast against the one who led their fathers
to destruction, and with horny claws, insultingly,
rake his silver bones out of the earth!

SCENE 2

Enter an Old Man.

A WARRIOR. Come here, Armin, will you?
SECOND WARRIOR.   They howl and roar,
   whipped up by storms of fear, they seethe and boil
   just like the open sea.
THIRD WARRIOR.   Some order there!
   That sea will soon swamp Guiscard's tent.
OLD MAN (*to the people*).
   All those who have no business here—clear out!
   These women, children, why should they be here?
   We want the men-at-arms, those twelve,
   and no one else.
A NORMAN (*calling out of the crowd*).
               We beg permission—
A WOMAN.   Beg,
   in our distress—
OLD MAN.   You heard me, out of here!
   I wonder if you mean to rebel against
   the Duke, for that is how it looks to me.
   You'd like it, would you, if I spoke to Guiscard?
THE NORMAN. Speak for us, you only, no one else,
   and your gray hairs! But if he will not listen,
   the unrelenting man, then like a trumpet
   of loud brass set the misery of all
   our people to your lips and thunder what his duty
   is into his ear—! We've suffered all a people can.
FIRST WARRIOR. Look there!
SECOND WARRIOR. The flap of Guiscard's tent—it's lifting!
THIRD WARRIOR See—the Empress of the Greeks!
FIRST WARRIOR.   Why, that is what
   I call a piece of luck, my friend! Now our petition's
   heard at once.

OLD MAN.   Be quiet, will you? Don't dare make
   a sound! I say it once again: I'll lend
   my voice to meek entreaty, not revolt.

SCENE 3
Enter Helena.

HELENA. Good people, the children of the best of fathers, pouring
   down from all the hills in noisy streams—
   tell me what has driven you, almost before
   the new day's given notice of its coming in the east,
   here to this tent among the cypresses?
   Have you forgotten it, the strict rule
   of war commanding silence in the night? Is the discipline
   that soldiers keep entering the circle where daring
   battle schemes are being plotted
   so unknown to you a woman must teach
   you it? By the Eternal Powers, is this
   the love you talk so much about: with rattling swords
   and shields and shouting out his name to startle
   up off the arm of sleep, where it has just
   now found a morning hour's rest, my
   old father's head? To rudely wake
   the good man who, as you know very well,
   has battled three whole sweating nights
   against the raging pest among us, striving
   to beat back the dreadful inroads it
   is making on all sides! However—it
   is surely something urgent brings you here,
   whatever it may be, and I can't choose
   but hear; for men like you, whatever they may do,
   there's always a good reason for it.
OLD MAN.   Guiscard's
   exalted daughter, your forgiveness, please!
   If our deputation, with the people at its side,
   came on the tent a trifle noisily,
   I censure it myself. But do consider
   that we thought Guiscard no longer asleep.
   Look: the sun is well up in the sky,
   and as long as we Normans can remember his head

357

was always lifted from the pillow hours before
it rose. Our suffering, supportable
no longer, brings us here, to hug his knees
and beg him for deliverance. But if,
as you say, he is sleeping still, whom his ceaseless
efforts have worn out and flung down
on his cot, why then we'll wait in silence
here, respectfully, till he salutes
the light, and occupy the time meanwhile
with praying he'll wake up in cheerful spirits.

HELENA. But shouldn't you prefer to come back later,
friends? So great a sea of people as we have
around us here, no matter how calm
it may be, is a sea still, with waves
that never stop their beating. Go back
to camp and stand beside your standards there,
just as you are, in your full dress: at the first
flutter of his eyelash, I'll send his own son
to report you it.

OLD MAN.   Dear Lady, let
us stay! Unless you have another reason,
unexpressed, for sending us away,
you needn't fear for your good father's rest.
See how your kindly smiling face has already
smoothed our turbulence. The sea out there,
though all the boisterous company of winds
has fled, though pennons droop on the mast
and ships drag on the towrope—the sea
sounds louder in the ear than we. Allow
us, do, to wait right here till Guiscard wakes.

HELENA. Oh, very well, friends—stay if you wish. And unless
I'm much mistaken, I hear his step inside
the tent already.

(Exit.)

SCENE 4

OLD MAN.   How strange!
FIRST WARRIOR.   She hears his step
inside the tent, yet he was fast asleep
a moment ago.

358

SECOND WARRIOR. It seems to me she wanted
  to get rid of us.
THIRD WARRIOR.   By God, I thought
  so too. She circled around her meaning, her words
  only grazing it. I was put in mind
  of the cat and the hot porridge in the proverb.
OLD MAN.   Yet in
  the past she seemed to like our coming here.

SCENE 5
Enter a Norman.

NORMAN (*pointing at the Old Man*).
  Armin!
OLD MAN. God save you, Francis! What's the news?

NORMAN (*pointing likewise at the First Warrior*).
  Marin!
FIRST WARRIOR. Have you some word for us?

NORMAN.   Yes, greetings
  from Calabria; a voyager from home
  has just arrived.
OLD MAN.   From Naples? Really!
FIRST WARRIOR.   Why
  do you look around you so uneasily?

NORMAN (*catching both men by the hand*).
  Look around uneasily? You must
  be mad. There's not a worry on my mind.
OLD MAN. Your lips are white, man! What's the matter? Speak!

NORMAN (*after looking around again*).
  Then hear. But what you hear—no comment on
  it even with a look, much less with words.
OLD MAN.   You frighten
  me. What's wrong?

NORMAN (*aloud to the crowd, who are staring at him*).
          How is it here, good friends?
  The Duke will soon appear, will he?
VOICE FROM THE CROWD.   We hope
  so, yes.

359

ANOTHER VOICE. The Empress's gone to summon him.

NORMAN (*drawing the two forward and speaking secretively*).
When I was standing guard at midnight, here
in front of Guiscard's tent door, suddenly
a pitiful groaning started up within,
a heavy panting like a sick lion gasping
out its soul. At once commenced a furious
running to and fro, the Duchess shook
awake a servant with her own hand, who rushed
around lighting candles, then plunged out of the tent.
Summoned by him, the family race past
me, all, in wild alarm: the Empress
in her nightdress, with the two Princes by the hand,
the nephew of the Duke in a cloak he's just snatched up,
his son with hardly more than a shirt on; last
of all the servant—with a thing all muffled up
beside him that at my challenge names itself
a knight. Well, if you rigged me out in petticoats
I'd be a woman quite as much as that one
was a knight; for everything, cloak, boots,
spiked helmet, hangs on the fellow
as if upon a nail. So I catch him by the sleeve,
already prey to a foreboding, turn
him with his face into the moonlight, and recognize—
guess who? The Duke's own doctor, Hieronymus.

OLD MAN. The doctor!

FIRST WARRIOR.   You Eternal Ones!

OLD MAN.   And so
you think he's feeling poorly, ill, perhaps—?

FIRST WARRIOR. Ill? Sick with plague!

OLD MAN (*clapping his hand over First Warrior's mouth*).
                    Keep still, will you?

NORMAN (*after a frightened pause*).
                              I never
said it, I. You've heard my story—judge
it for yourself.
          (*Robert and Abelard can be seen conversing in the
          entrance to the tent.*)

FIRST WARRIOR. The canvas parts and our
  two Princes come!

SCENE 6

Enter Robert and Abelard.

ROBERT (*coming forward to the brow of the hill*).
                Whoever is the spokesman
  for this crowd, let him step forward.
OLD MAN.   I am.
ROBERT.   You!
  Your judgment's younger than that thatch of yours
  and all your wisdom's only silver hairs.
  Granddad, thank your years for shielding you,
  for otherwise you'd not depart from before
  your Prince's face unchastised. What a green
  thing you have done, not at all the action
  of the brave friend of our family
  who once watched over Guiscard's crib, if it's true
  that you have made yourself the leader of this crowd—
  a mob that runs around the whole camp
  with weapons drawn like mutineers and, so
  my sister tells me, calls our General from his tent
  with curses roared out loud enough
  to wake him from the sleep of death. Now is it true?
  What should I think, draw what conclusion? Speak!
OLD MAN. We did so, yes: called out for the General
  to appear to us. But your sister, I am sure,
  never said we did so by screaming curses
  in the air, for she, as far back as I'm able
  to remember, was always well disposed toward us,
  and never less than truthful toward yourself.
  At my age you would still not know how one
  should show respect for our General;
  if I were your age, on the other hand,
  I'd understand, I'm sure, what is due
  a soldier. Go back inside and listen close
  to all your father's words, if you wish
  to know how I am spoken to; and I,
  if I forget, in speaking, what is owed

361

to you in dignity, I'll turn with a shamed
face to my great-grandbabes and ask
to be instructed: for I taught them those
things in their swaddling clothes. With all humility,
my Lord, we beseeched the Guiscard, as our ancient
Norman use and custom is, to appear
to us; and if he graciously consents,
it won't be, I can tell you, for the first time—
but by God, sir, if he, like you, refuses!

ROBERT. Your speech, old fool, confirms the very thing
it would deny. No swaggering young puppy
shows himself more pert than you in your
unbridled insolence. Oh, you still have
to learn, I see, the meaning of obedience.
Then listen closely, do, to me and I
will teach you it. What was your duty when
I reprimanded you? To save all
your objections and march this crowd away from here
without delay. That was the only answer
you were called upon to make. So when
I order you to leave this place at once,
do just, I hope, as you've been taught, and do
it instantly, without a murmur, now!

ABELARD. I see you scattering around your anger and your orders
far more prodigally than the good Duke your father
ever taught you to. I'm not surprised
such hot abusive words have been received
quite coolly; I compare them to the common noises
of the day, which no one hears because one hears
them all the time. I fail to see that anything
blameworthy's happened here. That this old man
spoke out with a bold spirit, spoke out proudly,
does him no discredit. Two generations
have given him their full respect,
and now he is a short step from the grave
let him be spared affronting by the third.
If they were mine, these unawed people
who displease you so, I shouldn't wish
them otherwise than as they are, unawed;
for his freedom's what the Norman's wedded to,

and I would hold in veneration the man
and wife who, in the bed of battle,
beget the fame that I enjoy. The Guiscard
understands this perfectly, it pleases him
his warriors should give his mane a tug;
the son's smooth hide, however, shudders
even if a soldier makes to take
a step toward him. Do you think the Norman crown
is yours beyond a doubt that you act with such
highhandedness? By love you have to win it, do you hear?
Right doesn't give it you, love can!
There's not a glimmer of the Guiscard in you, no,
that name, at least, you shan't inherit;
when you need them most, just then you slap
them smartly in the face, the very ones who now
might set you on the top of fame. But the Norman
fighting man has not been utterly
forsaken, as perhaps you think, deprived
of all his friends; if you're not one of them,
well, I am, and gladly too. To hear the supplicant's
entreaty, that's not hard to do—to give
it hearing, not give in to it; and if you
in your capacity as general
command this assembly to disperse, I in mine
command it to remain!—You've heard what I have said,
you men! I'll answer for it to the Duke.

ROBERT (*meaningfully, under his breath*).
  I know you now for what you are, my evil
  genius—thanks! But the game's not yours
  yet, by no means, as skillful as your play is. Shall
  I demonstrate to you why I am sure
  to win, let the cards lie as they may?

ABELARD.   And you
  mean what by that?

ROBERT.   Now mind my words; you'll understand
  me very soon. (*Facing toward the people.*)
                  Great Guiscard's sons, whom I
  would now dismiss and he hold here by flattery—
  I call on yourselves to judge! Between
  the two of us decide, and contradict

the one command or other. So—no more,
for more's fainthearted. By the grace of God
I am your Sovereign's son; and he—bred big
by accident to be a Prince. My only
purpose is to put his egregiousness to the test,
test whether, in the balance of your souls,
his words weigh more than mine!

ABELARD. Sovereign's son?—I'm that as much as you!
My father sat on the throne before
yours did! Did so with acclaim, and with more right.
My kinship with the people, as Otto's son and rightful
heir, is a closer one than yours. Who are
you, after all? The son of my protector merely,
whom the Duke my father put in charge to superintend
my realm! And now we'll do as you propose,
I'm quite agreeable.—Decide between
us, men! You're free to stay here at my bidding.
Speak, if you wish to, do, as if
I were Duke Otto, he himself.

OLD MAN. A man can see, sir, you're your father's son,
and I am sure your uncle, our great Prince,
when once his final hour comes, would die
rejoicing if he had a son like you.
To look at you, for me, is to grow young
again, miraculously; for just as you
stand here before us, our friend, so once
the Guiscard stood, when Otto died, like you
in shape and speech and manner, idol of the Norman
people, gloriously! May all those blessings
which, like clouds, hover over good
men's heads, rain down on you
and cause the tree of your good fortune to flourish
mightily! Your uncle's favor—that's your sun—
oh, let it shine on you always, as
it has till now; and as for what the earth
in which your fortune's tree is rooted may
contribute—never doubt us, sir! But there's
no need, if you'll forgive my saying so,
to force its growth by manuring it unwisely.
Keep, if possible, the field of your ambition clean.

You've bested him in many a contest heretofore,
in this one now consent to be defeated;
and since yours is simply leave, and his an order,
allow us, as I'm sure you will, to obey
the more peremptory one. (*To Robert, frigidly.*)
                              Sir, if you order
us to leave, we won't defy you. You
are Guiscard's son, what more is there to say!
Now tell us if we may return, and when,
and I'll lead these men away.

ROBERT (*hiding his discomfiture*).
                              Come back
tomorrow.—Or, my friends, if you wish, today,
at noon, if time permits.—So: very good.
The Guiscard's now engaged in weighty business,
but for an hour only; when he's done,
if he should wish to speak to you, I'll come
myself, I will, to fetch you here.

ABELARD.   But you treat
the army like a woman, yes, a pregnant
one, who mustn't be alarmed! You hide
the truth from them—now why? Are you afraid
of what might come to birth? (*Turning to the crowd.*)
                              The Duke's not feeling
well.

OLD MAN. O Lord of Heaven and Earth! Do you mean
he's caught the plague?

ABELARD.   No, I've no fear of that—
though his doctor did express misgivings, yes.

ROBERT. I hope lightning out of the clear sky,
traitor, blasts your tongue!
                              (*Exits into the tent.*)

SCENE 7

A VOICE FROM THE CROWD.   You flights of Heaven's
angels, save us now!

ANOTHER.   We're lost, all
our people lost!

365

A THIRD.   Lost, without the Guiscard,
 hopelessly!

A FOURTH. Hopelessly!

A FIFTH.   All hope
 of rescue gone for us, here in this sea-
 surrounded land of Greece!

OLD MAN (*to Abelard, with uplifted hands*).
          No—tell
 me, is it true?—You're a messenger of ruin!
 Is he infected with the plague?

ABELARD (*descending the slope*).
         I've told you, it's
 a thing by no means certain yet. The only
 sure sign of the plague is death itself,
 a speedy one, so he denies he has
 it. You know him, he would deny
 it even in his throes. Nonetheless
 his doctor, mother, daughter, his own son,
 as you have seen, are quite convinced of it.

OLD MAN. Does he feel feeble, sir? That is a symptom.

FIRST WARRIOR. Do his insides feel on fire?

SECOND WARRIOR.   Burning up
 with thirst?

OLD MAN. Does he feel feeble? Answer me
 that first.

ABELARD. A little while ago, when he lay
 stretched out on the carpet of his tent, I went up
 to him and said: How are you feeling, Guiscard?
 He replied, "Not bad, not bad—but I
 would like the Titans' help to shift this little
 hand!" He said, "It's Etna you are fanning,
 stop!" when the Duchess, standing off from him,
 fanned his breast with an egret plume;
 and when the Empress, moist-eyed, brought
 a cup to him and asked him if he cared
 to drink, he said, "The Dardanelles, dear child!"
 and drank.

OLD MAN. Oh terrible!

ABELARD.   But it doesn't stop
   him crouching like a tiger in his tent and staring
   at the Empire's battlements glittering over there.
   You still can see him at it—map in hand,
   revolving undertakings in his mind, tremendous ones,
   as if his life stood at the starting post.
   Today he sent an emissary to Loxias and Nessus,
   the Greek princes, who have been ready for
   a long time, as you know, to deliver him
   the city's keys in secret, on one condition,
   but one he has resisted with praiseworthy
   stubbornness—the message that he sent them now
   concedes the point.[1] In short, you men, if he
   is still alive at nightfall you will see
   him press on in his frenzy and issue
   orders for a main assault; the prospect so
   excites him, he has already asked his son
   for his opinion.
OLD MAN.   If he only would!
FIRST WARRIOR.   Oh, if
   we might march into battle at his back!
SECOND WARRIOR.   If he
   would only lead us, our hero whom
   we love, in war and victory and death,
   for many a year!
ABELARD.   Yes, yes, that's just what I say too!
   But Guiscard's boots will sooner march
   against Byzantium, his glove will sooner
   thunder on its iron gates, oh sooner
   will its arrogant battlements stoop
   before his empty shirt, than that this *son,*
   with Guiscard here no longer, should wrest the crown
   from Alexius the rebel there!

---

   1. The point Guiscard concedes the traitors in Constantinople (as the sequel would
have shown) is that he himself should seize the crown rather than that the Empress of
Greece, whom Alexius Comnenus had banished, should seize it in the name of her
children. [H.v.K.]

SCENE 8
Reenter Robert from the tent.

ROBERT.   Normans, hear!
  The Guiscard's business is completed, he is coming
  now.
ABELARD (*dismayed*).
      Coming now? Impossible!
ROBERT. You two-faced hypocrite, now I'll expose
  you for the miscreation that you are!
                    (*Exit again into the tent.*)

SCENE 9

OLD MAN. Oh Abelard, what kind of work is this?
ABELARD (*paling for a moment*).
  I spoke the truth, and I am not afraid
  to give my head in pawn to your revenge
  if I deceived you, ever! When I left
  the tent he lay sprawled out and lacked
  the strength, I thought, to lift a limb. But it's
  no news to you his spirit is absolute
  master of itself and its own fate!
A BOY (*who has climbed halfway up the hill*).
  Oh look! The tent flap's parting!
OLD MAN. Good boy! Do you see him? Speak!
BOY. Yes, father, I can see him plain! In the middle
  of the tent I see him, erect upon his own
  two legs! He fits the armor around his swelling
  chest, on his bulky shoulders the gold
  chain! He settles firmly on the high dome
  of his head the great helmet with its nodding plume!
  Oh, look there now, oh do—it's he himself!

SCENE 10
Enter Guiscard, with the Duchess, Helena, Robert, and retinue
following.

PEOPLE (*shouting with exultation*).
  Hurrah! It's him, it's Guiscard! Live forever!
                    (*Caps fly in the air.*)

368

OLD MAN (*amid the shouting*).

Oh Guiscard, welcome, welcome! Prince, have you
come down to us from Heaven, as I think? For that
is where we thought you'd gone already—among
the stars!

GUISCARD (*holding up his hand*).

The Prince my nephew—where is he?

(*All fall silent.*)

Come and stand behind me.

(*The Prince, who had mingled with the crowd, mounts the slope
under the Duke's steady gaze and stations himself behind him.*)

Stay right there—

and not a word, you understand? I'll speak
to you in private afterwards. (*Turns to the Old Man.*)
You're spokesman, Armin, for this crowd?

OLD MAN.   I am

indeed, my General!

GUISCARD (*to the deputation*).

Look here, you men,

when I heard what was going on, inside
my tent, I was very much surprised! For these
are not the worst men I see here
in front of me, and it is nothing trivial,
I know, you come to me about, and I
don't want to hear at second hand what urgent
matter makes you seek my presence. Quick,
old fellow, tell me what it is! A new trouble,
is it? Something you would like from me? Can I help
you in some way? Or offer comfort? Speak!

OLD MAN. Yes, something we should like to ask of you.

But it has no connection, as you may
suppose, with our uproariousness now, our hunger
for the sight of you. Your benevolence
would fill us all with shame if you should think
a thing like that. Our loud rejoicing, when you stepped
out of the tent, arose from something else
entirely, do believe me, Sir; not only
from the joy we feel at seeing you,
but from our feeling *overjoyed* because
we had falsely thought we should never

set eyes on your face again, O Captain
whom we worship!—because of the dumbfounding rumor,
which you will allow me to repeat to you,
that the breath of pestilence had touched
the Guiscard too—!

GUISCARD (*laughing*).
       The pestilence touched me!
You must be mad, I think! Do I look like
a man who's sick with plague? A man who stands
in front of you possessed of all his life
and vigor? In full command of all his limbs?
Whose clear-ringing voice peals freely from his breast
and fills, like steeple bells, the air around?
That's a man who's caught the plague? Oh please!
My state is blooming, do you want to haul
me off among the rotting corpses in the field?
What the blazes, no! I'm not about to let
myself be buried yet in this camp here—
I'll come to stop in Stambul, not before!

OLD MAN. Our Prince whom we adore! Those cheerful words give
us back a life we thought we'd lost! If only
there might never be a tomb to shut
you up in! Might you be immortal, Sire,
as your deeds!

GUISCARD.   Now as it happens, oddly,
just today I don't feel quite my usual
lively self: although I would not say
I am unwell, much less plague-sick! It's nothing
more, I'm sure, than fretting over
my poor men because of all the torments
of these recent days.

OLD MAN.   You mean, then—

GUISCARD (*interrupting him*).
        Never mind,
it's not worth our discussing, no! There's not
a hair of mine, as you know very well,
has ever caused this old head here
even to itch! My body's triumphed over
every illness up to now. And even
if it were the plague, I promise you:

she'd make *herself* sick gnawing on these bones
of mine!

OLD MAN. At least from now on if you would
allow the sick to be our care! Not one
among them, Guiscard, would not rather die
abandoned, helplessly exposed to every
ill, than that yourself, our one and only,
forever irreplaceable brave Prince
should succor him and he should tremble lest
he pay your mercy back with the ghastliest
of deaths.

GUISCARD. So many times already I
have told you people it—since when have my words
ceased to carry weight? It's not because
Guiscard is reckless he will not shun contact
with the sick, nor is it chance explains my coming
through unscathed. About that there's a story
to be told.[2] However, in conclusion:
Save your fears on my account! And now
to business. Why have you come here? Go on
and speak! And briefly, please—I've matters waiting
for me in the tent.

OLD MAN (*after a short pause*).
                    You know it, sir, you feel
it just as much as we—on whom does our
distress weigh heavier than you? When the moment of decision comes,
as it already—
        (*Guiscard looks around him and the Old Man stops.*)

DUCHESS (*in a low voice*).
                    Is there something
that you want—?

ROBERT.   Would like—?

ABELARD.   You need—?

2. According to Anna Comnena in her memoirs of the life of her father, the Emperor
Alexius, Guiscard placed his trust in a prophecy which said that he would meet his death
in Jerusalem and only there. Anna Comnena reported him as having died in Corfu
(actually it was Cephalonia) in a place where once a great city stood whose name was
Jerusalem.

DUCHESS.   God
 in heaven!
ABELARD.   What's the matter?
ROBERT.   What is it?
DUCHESS. Speak, Guiscard, do!
           (*The Empress pushes a large drum behind him.*)
GUISCARD (*easing himself down on the drum, under his breath.*)
                          Dear child!—Now tell
 me what is on your mind, Armin? Say what
 you have to say and let the words pour out—
 I don't like nervous stuttering!
           (*The Old Man, thinking, stares down at the ground.*)
A VOICE OUT OF THE CROWD.   Why
 does he delay?
ANOTHER VOICE. Old granddad, speak!
OLD MAN (*recollecting himself*).
                          You know
 why we are here—and who should know it better
 than yourself on whom the hand of fate
 rests heaviest? Just as, great bridegroom
 of the goddess Victory, you went to fling yourself
 into the bed of your dear bride, bosom all
 afire, your arms already reaching out
 to consummate the nuptials—directly in your way
 the horrid pestilence stepped! It's quite true,
 as you say, you're still untouched yourself,
 but not your people, they who are the pith
 and substance of your loins, now poisoned and incapable
 of further deeds; and every day, like firs
 before the storm, your faithful followers' heads
 bow in the dust. The struck down man's
 unable to stand up again, and where
 he sinks, there is his grave. He tries,
 again he tries, unspeakable
 his efforts to stand up: but it's no use!
 His plague-corrupted bones give way and back
 again he sinks into his grave! Yes, in
 the terrible confusion that overtakes
 his mind at last, you see him bare his teeth
 atrociously against both God and man,

howling savagely against his friend,
his brother, father, mother, children, his
own bride when she comes near him.
DUCHESS (*sinking on her daughter's breast*).

         God

in Heaven!
HELENA. Mother dear!
GUISCARD (*languidly turning his head*).

       What's wrong with her?
HELENA (*hesitating*).

I think—
GUISCARD. Take her into the tent!

     (*Helena leads the Duchess off.*)
OLD MAN.   Well, since

it's short speech you prefer: Oh, lead us from this swamp
of death! You savior of the people in their need,
already you have succored scores, don't
deny your army the only medicine
can make us well again, oh don't
deny us Italy's airy skies,
but lead us home, home to our own land!